The Great Vanishing Act

Blood Quantum and the Future of Native Nations

FULCRUM

Library of Congress Cataloging-in-Publication Data

Names: Hill, Norbert S., editor. | Ratteree, Kathleen, editor. | Oneida
    Nation, sponsoring body.
Title: The great vanishing act : blood quantum and the future of native
    nations / Norbert S. Hill, Jr. and Kathleen Ratteree
Description: Golden, CO : Fulcrum Publishing, 2017.
Identifiers: LCCN 2017013625 | ISBN 9781682750650 (paperback)
Subjects: LCSH: Blood quantum (United States law)--Social aspects. | Indians
    of North America--Tribal citizenship. | Indians of North America--Ethnic
    identity. | BISAC: SOCIAL SCIENCE / Ethnic Studies / Native American
    Studies. | HISTORY / Native American.
Classification: LCC KIE2145 .G74 2017 | DDC 342.7308/72--dc23
LC record available at https://lccn.loc.gov/2017013625

Fulcrum Publishing has made its best efforts to locate and credit original sources for the artwork used in this book. Please contact us if we have made any errors or omissions.

Image use: "Quantum Envy" Cherokee beaded bandolier bag/Martha Berry (front cover and page viii); "Blood Bling" CDIB card necklace/Kristen Dorsey Designs (p. xi); "The First Americans"/Sam English (p. 76); "Legacy of Disenrollment" political cartoon/Marty Two Bulls (back cover)

10 9 8 7 6 5 4 3 2

Fulcrum Publishing
4690 Table Mountain Dr., Ste. 100
Golden, CO 80403
800-992-2908 • 303-277-1623
www.fulcrum-books.com

THE GREAT VANISHING ACT

Blood Quantum and the Future of Native Nations

EDITED BY KATHLEEN RATTEREE
AND NORBERT HILL

CONTENTS

Part 2: Decolonizing History

Part 3: Decolonizing Biology and Demography

Part 4: Policy, Law, and Nation Building

Part 5: Where to Go from Here? Moving Forward

"Quantum Envy" Cherokee beaded bandolier bag, **Martha Berry**

FOREWORD

For as long as one can remember, the first peoples of this land have had strong identities, as well as remarkable knowledge of their bloodlines. Just as their histories held great significance, so did the family, which expanded outward to embrace the extended family and nation, reaching out even further into the cosmos. Each nation was autonomous and possessed a strength of its own, especially in its spiritual ways. For example, as but one of the many prayer women of my nation, I have been painted and painted others with the deep blood-red earth paint, which is the symbol of life. We call this paint *ma'etom*, which is a derivative of the word for blood, *ma'e*. *Ma'e*, blood, is essential for life.

Language is critical to culture. The first peoples have their own names for themselves, but are now known collectively in the English language as American Indians or Native Americans. Contemporary natives have ongoing responsibility as caretakers of the earth, which they maintain through their ceremonies. Furthermore, just as their grandfathers learned about tribal prophecies, they do as well. Today's generations live in the time of those prophecies. Sadly, the prophecies tell of native cultural disintegration, erosion of tribal languages, loss and continual destruction of the land, and severe earth changes thought to be brought about by the numerous strangers from the east and their descendants. The natives were warned to avoid them.

When the strangers arrived as predicted, they quickly assumed positions of power and dominance by establishing their government and organizations and instituting their laws. The seeds of colonialism were planted and took root on Turtle Island. At that time, our ancestors occupied an entire continent that stretched from ocean to ocean, and the strangers coveted the land that lay between. Initially, transfer of lands was effected through treaties between sovereign nations. Huge land cessions were exchanged for certain services and annuities. When treaty-making ended, devastating anti-Indian land policies such as the General Allotment Act of 1887 were enacted by the federal government. Through that piece of legislation alone, Native Americans lost 90 million acres of land. Land loss was and is particularly devastating, since most if not all natives have a strong, spiritual attachment to the land, which is like a mother or grandmother to them.

The Indian Reorganization Act of 1934 (IRA) was even more shattering to natives, because the legislation defined who "Indians" were. The more salient points: "Indians" were members of *federally recognized* tribes; they and their descendants must have resided on reservations on June 1, 1934; and "Indians" were also defined as *all other persons of one-half or more Indian blood.*

One-half or more Indian blood! Adding the issue of blood quantum to Indian policy 82 years ago was akin to opening Pandora's Box at a different time and place. I am about one month older than the IRA, and I am affected by it. My so-called Membership Identification Card (CDIB) states that my total blood is 4/4 in the Cheyenne-Arapaho Tribes. (I once heard an esteemed Montana spiritual leader in Rome, Italy, refer to his CDIB card as a "pedigree card.") Actually, I am Cheyenne. I do not need a card to tell me that.

I grew up in the westernmost part of the Cheyenne and Arapaho Territory. My Cheyenne grandfather constantly admonished me to marry a Cheyenne. Yet when I dated a Cheyenne, he would quickly point out that we were related. It seemed I was related to the entire tribe. Finally, I found the solution and married a Cheyenne and Arapaho man. Grandfather, however, chose to refer to him only as "the Arapaho." My husband was 7/8 Cheyenne and Arapaho, making our children 15/16. The mathematics gets a little complicated, but suffice it to say that unless my grandchildren marry an enrolled Cheyenne and Arapaho, the family line will become extinct with them.

Although the IRA began the fractionating of the blood of tribal members, John Collier, BIA Commissioner for FDR from 1933 to 1945, also gave tribal governments the power to establish their own membership requirements, including blood quantum measurements. So tribal nations hold a very fragile tomorrow in their hands. They can choose to either increase or decrease tribal blood quantum–fraction enrollment requirements. They can choose to institute lineal descent. Or they can combine a person's different tribal blood quantum to total enough for enrollment in one nation.

Furthermore, tribal leaders should also seek answers to pertinent questions: Is it important that a citizen of the nation speak the mother tongue? Is it important that a citizen of the nation participate in tribal ceremonies? Is it important that a citizen of the nation be involved in the life of the community? Is it important that a citizen of the nation integrates and lives its values? Tribal governments must look to wisdom from the past to formulate visions for the future, so that the peoples of the first nations will be alive as long as earth shall endure. Tribal leaders are the ones who will ensure that in future times our languages will still be spoken, our values will still be practiced, our ceremonies will still be observed, our families will still be strong, and tribal governments will still be self-reliant.

Tribal citizens must become informed of where we are and where we are going on the explosive issue of blood quantum. The chapters in this book are a tool for self-education and constitute possible road maps for the future. Arguably, using blood quantum as a measurement for tribal membership could continue to dilute our *ma'e*, our blood, until the tribes cease to exist. A matter of life or death.

– Dr. Henrietta Mann

"Blood Bling" CDIB card necklace, **Kristen Dorsey**
(Kristen Dorsey Designs)

Acknowledgments

A big *yaw^ko* to the Oneida Nation Trust Enrollment Committee members: Dylan Benton, Linda Dallas, Debra Danforth, Melinda Danforth, Norbert Hill Jr., Jennifer Hill-Kelley, Carole Liggins, Eric McLester, Loretta V. Metoxen, Tracy Metoxen, Debra Powless, Rita Reiter, Elaine Skenandore-Cornelius, Cheryl Skolaski,, Lois Strong, Susan White, and Brandon Yellowbird-Stevens. We would also like to thank the Sustain Oneida subcommittee for their continued support and dedication: John Breuninger, Brooke Doxtator, Heather Heuer, Norbert Hill Jr, Jennifer Hill-Kelley, Carrie A. Ninham, Melissa Nuthals, Kathleen Ratteree, Elaine Skenandore-Cornelius, Cheryl Skolaski, Tamara Van Schyndel, Rebecca Webster, and Susan White.

Thanks also to Dottie Krull, Megan Hill, and the Oneida Nation Business Committee. Finally, a big *yaw^ko* to Sam Scinta, Rebecca McEwen, Alison Auch, Melanie Roth and all the dedicated, brilliant staff at Fulcrum Publishing.

PREFACE

By Kathleen Ratteree and Norbert Hill

John Mohawk once wrote,

> Lightning strikes the earth hundreds of times every day but produces fire only rarely, and those fires seldom burn very far from the point of impact. Over centuries, however, some fires can be expected to be significant. When conditions are right, fires can burn huge areas and conceivably change the world they touch forever. Revitalization movements –movements to create conscious change in the culture inspired by visions, revelations, or challenging circumstances – have appeared among human populations in history in a manner resembling lightning fires.

Blood quantum, imposed from within and without, has shaped Native identity and has been the primary determinant of deciding *"Who is an Indian"* for more than a century. The conversation about Native identity – sometimes civil, sometimes violent – has been going on in Indian Country far longer than that. And it will continue whether blood quantum laws are changed or not. We are indeed living in challenging circumstances when it comes to navigating what it means to be Native: tribal disenrollment, DNA testing, egg and sperm banks, CDIB cards, online dating, ethnic student groups on college campuses, and debates over sports mascots all challenge our definitions of what being Native is. And what it is not. As you read these words, there are hundreds, thousands, millions of voices talking, writing, texting, Tweeting, Instagramming, Snapchatting, Facebooking, YouTubing and (insert newest app/technology here)-ing about blood quantum, identity, and belonging. There are many lightning strikes. And many fires. Now conditions are right. Like Malcom Gladwell's "tipping point," we have reached a moment of critical mass. A moment in history where significant cultural and intellectual change has begun. This collection captures a small segment of this spreading fire.

Why Write This Book?

Although the idea for this book began in Oneida, Wisconsin, the final product spans the globe. Authors and artists from Native nations across the continental United States, Canada, Hawaii, New Zealand, and Japan have contributed to this book. A colorful spectrum of men and women, enrolled Native citizens, "descendants," non-Natives, youth and elders, university professors, poets, playwrights, activists, artists, lawyers, historians, and policy makers. People who have been deeply and personally affected by blood quantum policies made during their parents,' grandparents', or great-grandparents' time. People who have devoted their lives and careers to studying and fighting for their convictions. People who have struggled within the paradigm of blood quantum in their lives and in their families.

This book was born out of the Oneida Trust and Enrollment Committee (OTEC), which is a group of elected, engaged Oneida citizens responsible for the management of Tribal trust funds, processing enrollment requests, maintaining membership records, and recording population changes. Decades ago, the community realized something alarming: the number of Oneida citizens who meet the 1/4 blood quantum requirement to enroll in the Oneida Nation was declining, but detailed discussions were not happening. In 2008, the committee took action to engage the Oneida Nation because unless blood quantum requirements were changed, there would be no eligible Oneida left to enroll. Taking action, OTEC began a tribal-wide campaign to educate Oneida citizens about their population realities, and this book is a natural outgrowth work of the past four years' work. It would not have been possible without OTEC's support, and all royalties and proceeds are being donated directly back to OTEC to continue their important work.

The Oneida are not unique in this respect; this scenario is occurring all across Indian Country. The title of this book plays on the myth of the "vanishing Indian," a concept that reached its height in the late 19th century when most Native peoples in North America had been "contained" on reservations or reserves. At the time, they were facing very physical threats of removal, genocide, forced assimilation, and boarding schools. In the 21st century, this myth has shape-shifted into more subtle and insidious forms. Blood quantum, the concept that being Native requires a quantifiable attribute – in other words, blood – has become the new "vanishing Indian." Drop below a certain arbitrary fraction and – poof! – the Indian has disappeared. Although the term "blood quantum" is in the title of this book, and is scrutinized from many different perspectives, this collection is really about belonging. It asks, and attempts to answer, *What does it mean to belong? And who gets to decide?*

The deeper we went down the rabbit hole of blood quantum, the more questions we found: *Where would we begin? What would the book look like?* We began a long series of conversations with Fulcrum Publishing to wrap our minds around the scope of this book. Once we hit upon the idea of an anthology, the question then became *Whose voices and opinions should be included?* Norbert and Megan Hill reached out to their vast professional and personal network to recruit potential writers and artists. Kathleen contacted the writers to pitch the book. She spent the next year having some incredible conversations with brilliant, passionate people all over the world. She asked them, "What excites you? What have you always wanted to write about? Okay. Do that here, in this book." People were excited, and that excitement spread quickly. Often, writers came to us after hearing about the project and asking to be a part of it. While the logistics of coordinating so many different personalities, styles, and time frames was often overwhelming; we hope the end result will speak for itself.

When we began this project, we were aware of the fact that, for the most part, writings on blood quantum, racial politics, and Native identity have taken place within the academy. Many fine books have been written on these subjects over the past several decades. Unfortunately, these books don't usually see the light of day outside the university. Our mission was to create a volume that would be accessible to primarily a Native audience – citizens, lawmakers, and tribal leaders – some knowledgeable and some who are approaching these issues for the first time.

What Is It All About?

This collection is unique because it has what Norbert calls "two-way vision:" one nearsighted and one farsighted. The former looks at the immediate challenges in Indian Country in the United States, and the latter looks out and beyond at belonging, identity, and struggles for long-term survival of indigenous peoples around the world.

To approach the complex concepts of blood quantum and identity, we came up with four broad categories: blood quantum as (1) cultural metaphor, (2) as decolonization of history, (3) as decolonization of biology and demography, and (4) as nation building. A fifth section ties everything together and challenges us to create solutions for the future. Like blood, the categories are fluid and authors and artists often move between them; however, their essays usually focus on one area specifically.

The book opens with more personal accounts of blood quantum and identity, with chapters by Richard Hill, Adrienne Keene, Leslie Logan, Olivia Hoeft, satirical fiction by Robert Chanate, and poetry and a play by Reed Bobroff. The book then moves toward the combination of personal and historical with chapters focused on the decolonization of history by Suzan Shown Harjo, Doug Kiel, Debra Harry and Leonie Pihama, and Julia Coates. In the next section, Kim TallBear, Russell Thornton, Jessica Kolopenuk, and Maile Taualii turn the decolonizing lens to more numerical and biological issues, such as the role of genes and DNA testing in determining who is "counted" as Native. The fourth section turns to lessons on the role of policy, law, and nation-building efforts in defining Native identity with chapters by Jill Doerfler; David E. Wilkins and Shelly Hulse Wilkins; Miriam Jorgenson, Adrian Smith, Terry Cross, and Sarah Kastelic; Richard Monette; Rebecca M. Webster; and Yuka Mizutani. The collection is capped by Stephen Cornell and Joseph P. Kalt; Gyasi Ross; and LaDonna Harris, Kathryn Harris Tijerina, and Laura Harris, tying together the book's themes and ideas while also looking ahead to the future. Interspersed throughout the text are original art pieces by talented Native artists that range from political cartoons (Marty Two Bulls) to traditional beadwork (Martha Berry) to metallurgy and jewelry (Kristen Dorsey) to acrylic on canvas (Sam English).

So What Now?

Clinical psychologist Mary Pipher wrote that "cultural change is a million subversive acts of resistance." Our world is in turmoil. Ethnic relations have taken on new, sometimes frightening, often complex dimensions. Indeed, as we write these words, the Standing Rock opposition to the Dakota Access Pipeline (DAPL) protestors are being bombarded with rubber bullets, dogs and mace. These acts of violence are a stark contrast to the talk of building trust. President Donald J. Trump has stepped into the White House as the 45th President of the United States. His stance on U.S federal policies with Indian Country is worrisome unknown.

In such a world we are often tempted to turn away. Disengage. Shut down. However, as the writers in this collection attest, conditions are ripe for change . We are at a point where we are ready to change the script on what it means to be Native. We are ready to more deeply engage with the most difficult questions we face as human beings: *"Who are we? and Who gets to decide?"* Whether readers are cheering, fuming, or apathetic when they read these chapters, it is our deepest hope that this book will fuel their excitement, frustration, questioning, and above all *engagement*. Engagement, meaning the courage to put yourself out there, constructively share your ideas, and, above all, to *listen* to others. Spread the fire.

Kathleen Ratteree and Norbert Hill
Oneida, Wisconsin
January, 2017

References

Gladwell, Malcom. *The Tipping Point: How Little Things Can Make a Big Difference*. Back Bay Books. 2002.

Mohawk, John, C. *Utopian Legacies: A History of Conquest and Oppression in the Western World*. Clear Light Publishing. 1999.

Pipher, Mary. *Reviving Ophelia: Saving the Selves of Adolescent Girls*. Riverhead Books. 2005.

"Identity is important. The colonists were very successful 'radicalizing' indigenous identities such that people talk about being 25 percent of this or 40 percent of that, but one does not belong to a nation based on one's blood quantum. Belonging to an indigenous nation is a way of being in the world. Holding a membership card is not a way of being and money can't buy it."

– John C. Mohawk
Seneca
(1945–2006)

Part 1

CULTURAL
METAPHOR

LOVE IN THE TIME OF BLOOD QUANTUM

by Adrienne Keene

"Every Native born into this world is a victory against colonialism and attempted genocide. You are the resistance. You are hope made flesh."

– Ruth Hopkins
Dakota/Lakota

Last year, I sat in the back of a lecture hall filled with Native students attending Ivy League institutions. We were gathered together for the annual All Ivy Native summit, where American Indian, Alaska Native, and Native Hawaiian students from each of the eight Ivy League schools (plus a handful of other local/elite schools) gather to socialize, commiserate, and discuss important issues in Indian Country. In this session, students were engaged in an activity comparing "Western success" to "Native success." As a PowerPoint slide reading "Western success" showed on a bright screen, students yelled out terms like "money!" "a good job!" "power!" "individual success!", and a student facilitator transcribed onto the chalkboard. As we transitioned to Native success, the tone shifted. "Taking care of family!" "Community connection!" "Giving back!" There were slight murmurs of agreement with each. "Marrying someone from your tribe!" The crowd erupted in laughter, but also claps, snaps, and sounds of agreement. "Having Indian babies!", and the noise grew louder, until the facilitator called the group back to order.

At the time, I laughed and whistled along with the crowd, and only later did I reflect on the moment and wonder what it meant that a group of highly successful, highly educated young Natives—in many ways poised to be the next leaders of Indian Country—reacted most strongly to "Native success" being defined as marrying a Native person and having Native babies.

In the 1700s when the colonizers introduced the concept of blood quantum, they could have never imagined a world of OK Cupid, Tinder, Native peoples with Ivy League PhDs, or tribal communities with multibillion dollar casinos. What does it mean to take a hundreds-year-old colonial concept and apply it to love and dating in the 21st century?

As a single 30-year-old Native woman, these conversations abound in my everyday life. In many ways, I have invited and welcomed these conversations through a series of posts on my blog, *Native Appropriations*, entitled "Love in the Time of Blood Quantum."[1] In these posts I laid out my own complicated feelings of dating-while-Native. The comments and conversations that ensued after my posts were sometimes hard to hear for their pain and heartbreak, but I am immensely grateful for the ways they affirmed, but also challenged and pushed my own thinking.

In this chapter I hope to just brush the surface of exploring the concepts of dating, love, and blood quantum through my own experiences and the blog. This is not meant to be an exhaustive conversation, nor is it meant to be representative of every facet of Indian Country. I can only speak from my experiences as a heterosexual, cis-gendered,[2] light-skinned, suburban/urban mixed Cherokee, as well as share the voices and stories that others have graciously shared with me.

In 2011, I wrote the first "Love in the Time of Blood Quantum" post that attempted to lay out some of the quandaries I faced in my desires to date Native men. Reading it now, much of it makes me cringe. However, I feel that the comments are some of the best on any post on the blog, and I am appreciative of the way they made me question my assumptions and privilege, and really forwarded my thinking. These two paragraphs sum up the bulk of my argument from that piece:

> So, I say all this as a Native woman in her mid-20's, who is thinking about (at some point) settling down, having a family, raising kids, etc. I think about these issues constantly. I am lucky that my children will be able to enroll in the Cherokee Nation no matter what, since we don't use blood quantum for membership, but I worry about how they will be perceived

if they want to be involved in Native community activities if they are even more mixed than me. I get crap constantly for the way I look and not being "Native enough"–even when the work I do is completely for Native communities and all about giving back. I think I've cried more tears in graduate school over identity politics than anything else, and I can't bear the thought of my future (albeit fictional at this point) children dealing with that pain. I know they will be culturally connected no matter what, but what does that mean for my future mate?

I would absolutely love to end up with a Native man. But you need to find me one first. My friends and I joke that educated, motivated Native men are like unicorns... magical, mystical creatures that you've heard of, and special enough that if someone gets one, they're holding on and not letting go. This is not to seem like I'm hating on the Native men of the world. I just don't come into contact with them that often in my whitewashed East Coast world. The draw of a Native guy is simple: I don't want to have to explain everything all the time. I want someone who "gets it." I want to make cultural references and jokes, I want someone who understands what it feels like to be invisible, marginalized, and silenced, I want someone who supports my activism and social justice work. Can I find that in a non-Native guy? Yes, and I have. Though they tend to be other people of color.

Reading this now, years later, makes me embarrassed (so young and naïve!), but time and maturity gave me space for reflection and growth. In the second iteration of the post ("Revisiting Love in the Time of Blood Quantum") in 2013, I laid out two of my largest oversights and ways my thinking matured.

First, the original piece was incredibly heteronormative. I never meant to generalize to all Native experiences with the post, but I realized that not even mentioning my blinding hetero/cis privilege in all of this was hurtful and harmful. In subsequent conversations with some of my queer Native friends, I listened to their stories, and realized that their experiences are in many ways similar, but are further complicated by a panoply of struggles that I can't even begin to imagine. By way of example, a reader shared her thoughts on how as a queer 20-year-old woman, she is already forced to think about her future children:

I'm only 20 years old, in my 3rd year of undergrad, and am already having anxiety about whether or not my future children will be "Native." My tribe has a 1/4th blood requirement and the only way my children would be enrolled is if my sperm donor (if that is the path my future partner and I decide to take) was at least a quarter Ojibwe.

Now queer people trying to start families is already complicated enough with strict adoption requirements, not to mention the huge costs of sperm donor and similar avenues. Throw Native and blood requirement on top of that, I am prematurely freaking out about my future family.

And the biggest stress for me is not that my children won't be enrolled (because they will be Anishinaabe no matter what), but that my parents and my family will not recognize my children as their grandchildren, because I am queer and I may or may not be the birth mother of my children. As Native people, we all know how important family is, and not just immediate family but aunties, cousins, uncles, grandparents, and so on. I'm worried about how my children will learn about their culture and where they come from if my entire family doesn't claim them or me and my future partner.

The queer Native struggle is real y'all.

Current hetero-patriarchal gender constructions in our communities are another result of colonialism, and LGBT relationships add layers of complication, since they don't fit the western established "norm" for nuclear families. The experiences of LGBT Natives deserve and warrant further discussion, and I hope that we can create spaces for those conversations.

The next way my thinking has, shall we say, *matured* since the first post: the term "Unicorn." I have come to deeply regret putting that out in the universe and letting it be absorbed into the Native lexicon. It completely reflected my experiences at the time – I put Native men on a pedestal like they deserved all our reverence and solemn respect. Admired for their rarity, like an endangered species at the zoo. And it has continued to haunt me. I've met women when I'm "on the road" who have introduced their partners to me as "this is my unicorn _____." A friend called a fancy dress she wore at a conference her "unicorn slayer" dress. Another friend referred to a beau as "Dr. Unicorn." When I started dating a particular guy a couple years back, I got a text from a friend excitedly proclaiming, "AK, you found your unicorn!" I had even started using it with a qualifier to describe *any* man of color I was dating. "He's a Black unicorn!"

I now think this is a problem. One that was pointed out in the comments of the first post, and something I dismissed at the time. Exalting Native men like they're the be-all-end-all discounts the rarity and specialness of educated, motivated Native women. I've started to feel that it creates a situation where Native men know they're special and rare, and don't treat Native women with the respect they deserve – because there's always another eager, intelligent Native woman when you're through with that one. Or maybe that's just been my experience?

Here is the original comment, so you don't have to take my word for it:

> But, no matter where I look, in what circles I move, I have been, without exception, disappointed in the Indian men I've met and dated. In my experience, they know we think of them like magical unicorns and they take full advantage of that fact. I can't name even one faithful, monogamous indian man in my history. And I wonder about their perspective: Indian women are just as rare. Why aren't they looking just as hard for me? Is that some sort of inherent difference between men and women, or do our societies teach indian men to value indian women differently? What gives?

Disclaimer: I know lots of great Native men. Lots of respectful, kind, wonderful Native men. I see many positive examples of Native relationships in my life, in my family, and in my close friends. I encounter them often. I want to make generalizations in order to talk about something that I think many of us see, but don't always acknowledge. I am not saying *every* Native man is disrespectful or a philanderer.

The other piece I've watched in myself and my friends is turning Indian men into a series of checkboxes, seeing how many "requirements" they fulfill, and leaving themselves in unhappy, unfulfilling, or even dangerous relationships because their man clicks so many of the boxes. Again, I'll return to the comments from the first post, this one from my classmate in undergrad. "M" is one of our mutual friends:

> I wonder how many babies are born in situations where BQ was the agenda, rather than love...

I also wonder how many native women feel like they can't leave a bad situation because it feels like a betrayal of their tribe... or their partners make it appear that way?
I like what M. posts from time to time from Toni Morrison, because it reminds me of all this...
"Love is or it ain't. Thin love ain't love at all."
I am thinking love by fractions can be pretty thin love..."

Love by fractions *is* pretty thin love. I think that's the biggest way my thinking has changed. In my original post I was so focused on the appeals of a Native partner that I forgot about the most important thing of all – this is supposed to be about love. I don't want to just date so I can have an Indian baby, I want to fall in love. I want to find someone who loves all of me – the Indian parts and the non-Indian parts. My highly critical lens on the world, my passion for my community, my height, my light eyes, my light skin, my "low blood quantum" – I want someone who loves *all* of that. If you look back at my original post, all I really said is I wanted someone who "gets it." Someone who can laugh at inside Indian jokes, feel comfortable in and around Native communities, who understands oppression and marginalization, and supports social justice. Who said that person has to be Native? (I know, I did. That was me.)

For me, many of my checkboxes stemmed from my own deep insecurities about my identity, something that is readily apparent in the original post. I worried that my children wouldn't "pass" as Indian if they were more mixed than me, and I worried that they wouldn't be accepted in Native circles if they were a low-blood-quantum Cherokee. Those fears are still real, but I also have come to realize that I was also afraid that I wasn't "Indian enough" to be the sole carrier of culture in my future-fictional-family, that I didn't know enough about being Cherokee, about traditional culture, language, whatever, to pass it along to my children. I wanted someone who knew *more* than me who could take on that role. I now see how shortsighted that was, because in the subsequent years I've also come more and more to value the culture of my own Cherokee community, and I know no matter what, I want my kids to be not just Indian, but *Cherokee*. Unless I end up with a Cherokee partner, that's all on me no matter what – and I am completely capable of handling that on my own.

I often have long conversations about these very issues with friends, and they have made me realize that I am actually in a privileged position. Being a citizen of the Cherokee Nation, we don't have a blood quantum requirement for tribal citizenship. So no matter how things shake out, as long as my child comes out of me (that's a whole other issue), he or she can be enrolled Cherokee. We also are matrilineal, so my kids will have a clan too.

But for some of my friends from other communities, their tribes *do* have blood quantum requirements. For some of them who are already mixed, either with other tribes or other races, if they don't have kids with someone from their community, their offspring won't be able to be enrolled. When your tribe has less than 1,000 members, that becomes an issue – the pool is quite small. There are also issues brought by casinos, and money has brought a whole new level of complication to the issue of relationships and children – only enrolled children have access to tribal resources. So even while my friends can espouse about how blood isn't what makes you Indian, about community connection, culture, and family being more important – they're still stuck in a situation where their values aren't matched by others in the community, and it has real implications for them and their children. Another commenter (and a close friend) tied it up succinctly:

> Becoming (or creating) a citizen of a tribal nation is a way of protecting our sovereignty and passing on our culture. Do we have a duty to make more Indians? Do we have to do it with other Indians? What defines an Indian and who decides?

Colonialism leaves quite a legacy, doesn't it? That to me is the saddest and most frustrating part of all this. Notions of "blood fractions" are colonial constructions, designed to "breed out" Indians, and now they are being used by our own communities to further restrict not only the futures of our tribes, but our right to love. So is reclaiming your right to love whomever you want an act of decolonization? Or is it weakening modern tribal sovereignty? I'm still not sure.

A new development and complication that I can't imagine any of our ancestors could have pictured is the addition of scientific technology and language of genetics[3] to the creation of Native children. In honor of turning 30 I started a new savings account – for freezing my eggs. I'm not the first of my Native friends to think about or undertake preemptive egg preservation, and in many ways I still can't wrap my head around the fact that this is something I'm considering and feel is necessary. That we as Native women are willing to undergo what is by no means a simple, inexpensive, or easy procedure to ensure the future progeny points to how deeply the desires, and perhaps sense of responsibility run.

When I think about egg freezing and donation, I start to think in hypotheticals that complicate the whole way we think about enrollment, blood, and belonging. What if I were to use a donor (non-Native) egg to have a baby? I would be listed on the birth certificate as the mother, though technically I share no genetic material with the child, and if the father (or sperm donor) were non-Native, the child would have no "Indian blood" – yet could still be enrolled in the tribe, because the enrollment office doesn't ask whose egg was used to have the child on the enrollment application.

The inverse is that I've heard rumors that I can't, as a Native woman, donate my eggs if I choose not to use them, because there are potential complications with the Indian Child Welfare Act, which prioritizes and protects the right to place Native children put up for adoption in Native homes. Presumably the Cherokee Nation could "claim" a child made with my egg as a tribal descendant and therefore would be subject to Indian Child Welfare Act policies (in what world that would make practical sense, I don't know). Then I think about sperm donation – do sperm banks keep a list of tribal affiliations with donors? Does that matter? Where do I find a Native donor? Does that matter? Wouldn't the same theoretical rules around ICWA apply to sperm donations?

My close friend who underwent egg extraction and preservation did it largely to appease her family, who were worried her nomadic, creative lifestyle would never lend itself to settling down and having children. She told me about her procedure in a casual manner, like it was just something we all might have to do at some point. But at the end of our conversation she mentioned, with a laugh, that she had the eggs stored at a facility near her homelands, though it was more expensive, because she "wants them to hear the songs." Despite her relaxed approach, each of those frozen cells, to her, are still a part of her and her culture, and still represent the future of her people.

To me, what it comes down to is this: Where does Native identity live? In single reproductive cells? In "genetic memory"? In "blood"? Or in family, in culture, in connection, and community? Or in all of the above?

Beyond thinking about my future-fictional-children, I am also faced with the daily reality that a non-Native partner also often means deep ignorance of Native identity, experiences, and issues. In today's world of online dating and smartphone dating applications, I can now filter results by race/ethnicity, so I can literally search for a Native potential partner with a few clicks. By and large though, the searches in my predominantly white communities turn up with zero results, or those who have clicked the box have limited ties or no tribal affiliation. As a light-skinned person, I can choose to disclose about my identity in these virtual interactions, and have oscillated back and forth between saying upfront in my short bio that I am a Native person, or waiting until the first conversation or even first meeting in person. Oftentimes when the bio does say Cherokee or Indigenous, or I have a photo of myself wearing regalia, the conversations that follow are full of stereotypical, hurtful, and ignorant comments from other users. Jessica Deer, a Mohawk woman from Kahnawake, has chronicled her online dating experiences on Twitter using the hashtag #sh**whiteguystellme (without the asterisks). She uses her Mohawk name as her user name, and like me, doesn't "look" like the stereotypes of Native people. Some of the (more tame) statements she's compiled include:

> *"Oh, you're part Mohawk? You've got blonde hair. Not normally a trait you'd expect from Mohawk nationalities."* #**Sh**WhiteGuysTellMe**

> *"Nice. So no taxes for you right?"* #**Sh**WhiteGuysTellMe**

> *"Awesome I have a thing for Pocahontas." (When finding out I'm Mohawk.)* #**Sh**WhiteGuysTellMe**

> *"I'm Mohawk."*
> *"That's awesome. But you have white as well?"* #**Sh**WhiteGuysTellMe**

In a CBC interview,[4] she said, "For the most part, it's really hard to find a Native person on Tinder,[5] and when you do, it's like you found the jackpot." But her interactions with non-Native men largely turn to ignorance quickly. She reflects, "When they find out I'm Mohawk, 90% of the time it goes into questioning my identity." Like me, these interactions have caused her to reflect on what she desires in dating, and made her take the application less seriously. "I still use Tinder, but it really made me think about what I want in a relationship, and I don't want ignorance towards Indigenous people. I mean, I'm open obviously to dating different people, but it made me take it less seriously."

Right now, I'm in the process of challenging myself to think about my own love in a decolonial frame – because my sheer existence as a Native woman is an act of resistance. My ancestors were killed, forcibly assimilated, and sterilized to prevent my existence, yet here I am. I can't escape the weight of that reality. I push myself to remember that love is not about creating future tribal citizens, and that finding support, fulfillment, and care is a revolutionary act as well. As Audre Lorde put it, "Caring for myself is not self-indulgence, it is self-preservation, and that is an act of political warfare." I also know that no matter what, my future children, regardless of their heritage or genetic makeup, will continue that legacy of resistance and will be strong, beautiful *ani yunwiya*. They will be, in the words of Ruth Hopkins, "hope made flesh."

Opening myself up to these reflections and collecting these stories and thoughts from friends and community members has raised more questions than answers for me. I feel simultaneously deeply troubled and uplifted by the conversations, and can't offer any concrete conclusions, other than an acknowledgment of how prominent, yet hushed, these concerns, beliefs, and feelings of responsibility are in Indian Country.

Having the blog posts as markers of my own growth and thought process has led to a very public process of reflection, but one I've been grateful to have. By putting my personal struggles and insecurities out in the open, I hope that we can begin to deconstruct the problematic nature of some of our deeply held beliefs as a community, and search for alternatives and answers that are more inclusive and reflect the vibrant, modern, complicated lives we lead as Native peoples in the 21st century. I do know now that the conversation is much bigger than I once thought. The layers of identity, love, and yes, blood quantum, can't be unpacked in two blog posts and a book chapter. But what it boils down to for me, right now, is the perhaps trite idea that "Love in the Time of Blood Quantum" shouldn't have to look any different than love at any other time. Love is or it ain't. Thin love ain't love at all.

Notes

1. "Love in the Time of Blood Quantum," http://nativeappropriations.com/2011/04/love-in-the-time-of-blood-quantum.html; "Revisiting Love in the Time of Blood Quantum," http://nativeappropriations.com/2013/09/revisiting-love-in-the-time-of-blood-quantum.html.

2. A person whose self-identity matches with the biological sex assigned at birth; not transgender.

3. For an in-depth exploration of the role of genetics and DNA in con-

versations about Native identity, belonging, and ancestry, Kimberly Tallbear's *Native DNA* (University of Minnesota, 2013) is an incredible resource.

4. "How One Woman Called Out Racist Guys on Tinder" (July 21, 2015), http://linkis.com/www.cbc.ca/radio/new/RneLA.

5. Tinder is a smartphone-based dating (or hook-up) application, in which users swipe left or right (no or yes) on other users in their geographic location. Decisions are made based on photographs and a short bio, and if two users "match" (both swipe right), they are able to chat using the application.

IT'S IN THE BLOOD, AND IN THE EARTH – HAUDENOSAUNEE DESCENT AND IDENTITY

by Richard Hill

Most wizards these days are half-blood anyway.
If we hadn't married Muggles we'd've died out.

Ron Weasley, discussing blood purity

Perhaps the most famous 21st-century half-breed or "half-blood" is Harry Potter. In his case, the term "half-blood" was given to humans with at least one non-human parent. The term "mudblood" was also used – a derogatory term for someone not of pure-blood wizard heritage. In the world of Potter, there is a great deal of prejudice toward his kind.

Seneca leader Gaiänt'wakê, or Cornplanter (1750–1836), was another famous "half-blood." He reported that he was the half-breed son of John Abeel of Fort Plain, New York. Since the Seneca, and all Haudenosaunee or, more commonly, Six Nations (Seneca, Cayuga, Onondaga, Oneida, Mohawk, and Tuscarora), follow the mother's bloodlines to determine identity and nationality, Cornplanter was considered a Seneca, even though he was known by the names John Abeel or O'Bail or O'Bailes. Cornplanter once complained about the increasing number of children born to white fathers. This was somewhat disingenuous because he himself had a white father. Because the Seneca are matrilineal, the biological father does not play a role in the determination of who is Seneca. Cornplanter argued that half-breeds did not fit into Seneca society and should be taken care of by the American government.

In the 1880's, fifty years after Cornplanter's death, the United States Republican Party broke into two factions: the Stalwarts and the Half-Breeds. Their internal feud over political patronage got so intense, it resulted in the assassination of James Garfield (Half-Breed) in 1881 so that Chester A. Arthur (Stalwart) could take office. The internal dispute over the degree of blood needed to remain Haudenosaunee never went so far as the Republicans took it; however, issues of identity and what constitutes a Haudenosaunee citizen have become increasingly significant in light of the U.S. Department of Homeland Security's demand for "verifiable proof of citizenship" for all U.S. citizens over the past decade. The instances of Harry Potter, Cornplanter, and the 19th-century Republication Party demonstrate how the concept of the "half-breed" was formed in the American consciousness and how this idea has changed over time.

Being Haudenosaunee

In the oral recitation of the Gayanashagowa (Great Law of Peace), the Peacemaker came among the Seneca, Cayuga, Onondaga, Oneida, and Mohawk Nations (who call themselves collectively *Haudenosaunee*, meaning "People Building a Long House"), who were warring among themselves at that time. Although they derived from a common core and spoke the same language, these relatives began killing each other, and the Peacemaker was sent by the Creator to restore the Good Mind and peaceful relations.

At one point, as he was building a consensus-based decision-making model, the Peacemaker encountered a group of Oneidas. He explained how the new system would work, allowing for individual voices to be gathered at the family clan level, and how consensus on matters would work its way up through the clans, through the nations, and finally to a Grand Council of the United Native Nations.

There was one big problem. The Oneidas, having fallen into generations of blood feuds, had forgotten their clan identities. However, the Peacemaker resolved this quickly by saying, "OK, you will be Bears, you will be Turtles, and you will be Wolves," pointing to each subgroup that had gathered. Problem solved. By this the Peacemaker meant that in order for peace to prevail, everyone mattered and everyone had to have a clan identity so their voice could be heard at some level of governance.

The family clan has always been(?) the basic social, cultural, political, and spiritual unity of Haudenosaunee society. The Peacemaker ended up defining forty-nine clan groupings among the original Five Nations. There are fifty leaders, but the Chief Tododaho is considered to belong to all the people, so he does not have a clan identity. At the same time, the Peacemaker stated that humans are all part of *one family*, thinking with *one mind*, and speaking with *one voice*. This indicates that his key underlying message was that *all* humans had to be treated fairly and equally if peace is to prevail. Humans had to sense that justice was fairly applied to all, and not to just a few. All humans were sacred and deserving of respect.

Among the Haudenosaunee, women have a unique social, cultural and political status. Women, and their children, are bound to each other by ties of blood, and form into family clans, which are inherited through the mother's bloodline. This forms a series of sisterhoods, with forty-nine clans identified around nine different animals and birds.

Representing the earth dwellers are the Bear, Wolf, and White-Tail Deer Clans; representing the water dwellers are the Eel, Turtle, and Beaver Clans; and representing those that fly in the sky are the Hawk, Heron, and Snipe Clans. However, there are variants within each of those clans – such as Big Bear, Suckling Bear, or Mud Turtle, Painted Turtle, Big Turtle – that make forty-nine distinct families. Or rather used to. Today, some of these clan families have been collapsed into one, like the Snipe Clan, which used to be Common Snipe, Plover, and Killdeer Clans.

The most important thing about clan identity is that it creates unity across political boundaries, and connects humans to the earth. Being a member of a clan has privileges and obligations. There are particular rules about whom one can marry or have children with, as there is a prohibition against doing so within the clan, no matter what the national identity of the father. In other words, someone of the Bear Clan of the Mohawk Nation is considered a direct relative of everyone else in all the other Bear Clans of the other Six Nations. They are considered to have common female ancestry.

The old villages of bark-covered longhouses were clan-defined spaces. Inside each of these longhouses were several families, all related through common blood from the female lineage. When a couple decided to live together, the man moved into the longhouse of his wife. Their subsequent children would belong to the clan of the mother. Her relatives formed the extended family of that child. Kinship relations became paramount in building a stable, productive Haudenosaunee society.

Tuscarora scholar J.N.B. Hewitt (1859–1937) noted that the *Ohwachira* (Haudenosaunee term for "family") is the bloodline within a clan that established the mother as primary. The term "mother" was applied to the birth mother as well as her sisters and all the women of her generation "in the collateral lines of descent" – meaning the mother's cousins. The second significant family member was the mother's brother, and the term "uncle" was also applied to all collateral males. Your birth father, of a different clan, is called "father," but so too are any of his brothers, whereas the primary male in the clan is the "uncle," or mother's brother.

Haudenosaunee kinship terms create unique relationships based upon age distinction and subsequent duties and obligations. Haudenosaunee identity is tied to where one sits within the larger family framework. This creates a system of honor and respect for where you are within the clan family.

There is a cultural concept of the two sides of the house, meaning that family clans are divided into two sides, each having customary obligations within their side of the house, and to those on the other side. To reinforce the idea of identity, each side of the house sends participants to conduct the ceremonies. The opposite side of the house conducts funerals for the grieving side. In this way, interdependence is developed between the sides. This interdependence is a cornerstone of Haudenosaunee society. One has to know where one sits in order to know his/her obligations.

Additions to the Clans

According to the *Jesuit Relations* of 1645,[1] most of the Oneida men at that time were killed by the Huron, so the Mohawks sent "some men to be married to the girls and women who had remained without husbands, that the nations should not perish." Since marriage or making children within a clan was prohibited, the husband/father had to come from the other clans. Both the Oneida and Mohawk have only three clans – Turtle, Wolf, and Bear. It is unclear how the Mohawk men were matched up with Oneida women.

One or more *ohwachira* comprised what is called a clan. Hewitt writes, "An *ohwachira* as an organized body of persons tracing descent of blood from a common mother ... forming an exogamic[2] incest group by a rigid prohibition of sexual relations among its members formerly under penalty of death to the guilty couple; the *ohwachira*, however, did on occasion exercise the right of adopting a person or persons of alien blood, the blood tie being then a fiction of law of adoption." Contemporary oral tradition does not speak of execution; however, such relations are certainly shunned, and any children from a same-clan union would not be able to hold any titles within Haudenosaunee society.

While blood descent is important to the Haudenosaunee, history has shown us that people can be "added" to those bloodlines under the cultural protocol of the society. Normally called adoption, there is a tradition by which a person's identity can be transformed. They can be given a new identity, one linked to a new family lineage. Women were responsible for adoption. They would certainly consult with the men, but it was within their authority to decide on adoption.

Adoption of Mary Jemison

Mary Jemison, called Deh-he-wä-mis (1743–1833), was captured by the Shawnee and given to two Seneca sisters, who took her to their village of She-nan-jee (Geneseo). In her memoir she recalled her adoption. They first removed her tattered clothes, washed her down, and redressed her in new Seneca clothing.

Then they took her to their lodge and sat her in the center, where she was soon surrounded by all of the women from the village. These women began to mourn the loss of a deceased relative with the "most dismal howling, crying bitterly, and wringing their hands in all the agonies of grief." Then one of the women stepped forward and intoned the following speech:

> Oh, our brother! alas! he is dead – he has gone; he will never return! Friendless he died on the field of the slain, where his bones are yet lying unburied! Oh! who will not mourn his sad fate? No tears dropped around him: oh, no! No tears of his sisters were there! He fell in his prime, when his arm was most needed to keep us from danger! Alas! he has gone, and left us in sorrow, his loss to bewail! Oh, where is his spirit? His spirit went naked, and hungry it wanders, and thirsty and wounded, it groans to return! Oh, helpless and wretched, our brother has gone! No blanket nor food to nourish and warm him; nor candles to light him, nor weapons of war! Oh, none of those

comforts had he! But well we remember his deeds! The deer he could take on the chase! The panther shrunk back at the sight of his strength! His enemies fell at his feet! He was brave and courageous in war! As the fawn, he was harmless; his friendship was ardent; his temper was gentle; his pity was great! Oh! our friend, our companion, is dead! Our brother, our brother! alas, he is gone! But why do we grieve for his loss? In the strength of a warrior, undaunted he left us, to fight by the side of the chiefs! His warwhoop was shrill! His rifle well aimed laid his enemies low: his tomahawk drank of their blood: and his knife flayed their scalps while yet covered with gore! And why do we mourn? Though he fell on the field of the slain, with glory he fell; and his spirit went up to the land of his fathers in war! Then why do we mourn? With transports of joy, they received him, and fed him, and clothed him, and welcomed him there! Oh, friends, he is happy; then dry up your tears! His spirit has seen our distress, and sent us a helper whom with pleasure we greet. Deh-he-wa-mis has come: then let us receive her with joy! – she is handsome and pleasant! Oh! she is our sister, and gladly we welcome her here. In the place of our brother she stands in our tribe. With care we will guard her from trouble; and may she be happy till her spirit shall leave us.

The women treated her like a long-lost relative who has returned. In fact, the two sisters had lost a brother in the French and Indian War, and they went to Fort Duquesne to receive either a prisoner, or an enemy's scalp, to compensate them for their loss. Jemison explained that when warriors returned from battle they often had scalps of the enemy, or prisoners which were offered to the families that lost a warrior in that engagement. She noted that the family could either seek vengeance by executing the prisoner, or, as more the case, they would adopt them, and treat them kindly.

"My sisters were very diligent in teaching me their language; and to their great satisfaction, I soon learned so that I could understand it readily, and speak it fluently. I was very fortunate in falling into their hands; for they were kind, good-natured women; peaceable and mild in their dispositions; temperate and decent in their habits, and very tender and gentle toward me. I have great reason to respect them," recalled Jemison.

There a few other accounts of adoption of prisoners by the Haudenosaunee that affirm this situation. Basically, an adoptee is given a new identity, tied to the woman of a certain clan, given a clan name, and for all intents and purposes looked at as a blood relative. From that day forward, their old identity was not to be mentioned. The children born of an adopted female would also be members of the same clan family as the mother. There are also many accounts of white men being adopted as part of the treaty-making process. In the Haudenosaunee mind, in order to create peace, all treaty partners had to be considered relatives. It is unclear if the treaty-making adoptions made the treaty partner a Haudenosaunee citizen in the same way that the Jemison style of adoption did.

Changing Kahnawake Clans

Research conducted by anthropologist Gerald Reid and published on the Kahnawake Longhouse website enlightens us about the changing nature of clan identity in that community. Kahnawake is a Mohawk community near Montreal, which began as a community of Catholic converts. In 1667, a group of Oneida and Mohawk moved from the aboriginal lands home near Albany, New York, and settled at La Prairie, a French Jesuit retreat south of Montreal. Most had been converted to Catholicism by Jesuit missionaries who wanted to remove them from the influence of their Longhouse relatives. In 1676, the inhabitants at Kentá:ke ("on the prairie," the name given to La Prairie by the Mohawks) relocated to Kahnawake ("by the rapids"), further up the St. Lawrence River. Kahnawake became part of the Seven Nations of Canada, maintaining a political, cultural, and religious network with other converted communities of Nippissing, Algonquian, Abenaki, and Huron communities, as well as fellow Mohawk converts at Akwesasne and Kanesatake.

Since 1840, a governing council of seven chiefs represented the seven different clans residing at Kahnawake: Ratiniáhten ("Turtle"), Rotikwáho ("Wolf"), Rotiskerewakaká:ion ("Old Bear"), Rotiskerewakekó:wa ("Great Bear"), Rotinehsí:io ("Snipe" or "Plover"), Rotineniothró:non ("Rock" or "Stone"), and Rotihsennakéhte ("Deer"). The Snipe, Rock, and Deer Clans assimilated into the Mohawk community, likely from other Haudenosaunee communities or the affiliated Seven Nations of Canada. They appear to have stayed in power until at least 1923, but there is evidence that in 1898, the people of Kahnawake identified their traditional chiefs as representing only four clans Old Bear Clan, Wolf Clan, Turtle Clan, and Snipe Clan.

In an 1888 petition advocating for an elected system, 210 Kahnawa'kehró:non ("People of Kahnawake") submitted seven petitions, one from each of the seven clans: Rotinesiioh ("Snipe Band"), Rotisenakete ("Deer Band"), Ratiniaten ("Turtle Band"), Rotiskerewakekowa ("Big Bear Band"), Rotikwaho ("Wolf Band"), Onkwaskerewake ("Small Bear Band"), and Rotineniotronon ("Stone Band").

However, in 1927 a Longhouse group, trying to reconnect to their older Mohawk Identity, organized itself around the three original clans (Turtle, Black Bear, and Wolf), each with a chief and clan mother. Historical documents show that a Deer Clan persisted outside of this group at that time. In the 1930s, internal dissensions led to the Longhouse group breaking into two, and later three factions, each with their own longhouse, but they all retained the three-clan system.

The lesson from this case is that the need for Mohawk identity persisted, and in order to show unity with the other Haudenosaunee communities, the Longhouse movement restored the three family clans associated with the Great Law of Peace. Yet, if that law is based upon individual freedom and respecting the rights of the individual, you have to wonder why only three clans are allowed. What happened to the Indigenous right of defining oneself for those whose ancestry ties them to other clans?

Tuscarora White Bear Clan

Tuscarora leader Clinton Rickard (1882–1971) married Beulah Mt. Pleasant, whom he said was of the "White Bear family line in the Bear Clan." In his biography, he stated that this clan originated in Pennsylvania after a young Tuscarora girl was kidnapped by the whites. This was likely when the Tuscarora had relocated there, seeking refuge from a series of wars in the early 18th century. To avoid a retaliatory war, the white settlers gave the Tuscarora one of their girls, who was a twin that was adopted into the Bear Clan ("tihre-cha'?k"). The descendants of this adopted twin became known as the White Bear Clan ("tihrehtsyaks" or "tihréčha?ks"), according to Rickard. However, he also noted that marriage between the White Bear people and the Black Clan people was prohibited, as "they are both of the same family."

J.N.B. Hewitt also married a White Bear clan woman named Eliza Mt. Pleasant, sister to Chief John Mt. Pleasant, who is listed as a Bear Clan chief. The White Bear Clan has become a source of controversy recently, but historical records show that this clan was selecting leaders in the 19th century. Those who identified as White Bears are being denied a voice within a system that is predicated upon respecting the voice of all people, as established by the Peacemaker under the Great Law of Peace, by those that argue only the clans defined in the Great Law of Peace will have a voice under that system. What are the human rights of people who don't have such a clan identity under that law?

A similar story can be told of the Seneca Nation that today has eight clans. However, when the Haudenosaunee Confederacy was first established, the Beaver, Heron, and Deer Clans were not part of those original eight. These new clans resulted from the adoption of Huron and other Natives into the Seneca Nation, as seen in the Mary Jemison example. They were allowed to keep their family identity, and meet within their original clans. However, they would be governed by the original Seneca clans on land and jurisdictional matters.

Genetic Realities

The community at Grand River, near Brantford, Ontario, is the largest Haudenosaunee community in North America, and the largest "reserve" in Canada. Today, membership in that community totals nearly 28,000 individuals. When the community was founded, fewer than 2,000 Haudenosaunee, Creek, Cherokee, Tutelo, and a few other Nations relocated there after 1784. The dramatic increase did not result from a strict following of clans and kinship rules.

There was a shift from the old clan-defined longhouse, operated under the authority of the women, to the single-family log cabin, which was generally operated by men. Colonization had introduced new social influences, and as men took over farming, which used to be a woman's responsibility, and women adopted the domestic chores of their neighbouring white settlers, something changed within.

In addition, many of the British, Scottish, and Irish officers associated with the British Indian Department, which was the main agency by which the Crown of Great Britain had maintained its treaty relationship with the Haudenosaunee since the 1740s, took on Haudenosaunee women as their spouses. Normally, their children would have been considered Haudenosaunee, following traditional lines of descent. However, English society was paternal in descent, and these children were given English names and took on English identity, which meant a different perception of status and privilege.

A community of 2,000 cannot grow to 28,000 in 200 years without new blood being added to the cultural mix. The same is true for other Haudenosaunee communities. Currently, some nations have only 1,500 to 2,000 citizens. Can they maintain a culturally pure identification? Can their nations survive with a strict adherence to former bloodlines and clan identities? More and more are suggesting that the only way to survive is to adopt our relatives whose mother did not have one of the nine clans. Like Mary Jemison, they can become Haudenosaunee, and their children can be proud to be citizens of the oldest-continuing political system in North American that was predicated on equality and justice. The time has arrived when we need to heed the words of the Peacemaker that we are to treat each other as if we are of one family.

Notes

1. Reports written by Jesuit missionaries in the field during the seventeenth century.

2. Marriage outside of a specific group.

GOOD GUIDANCE

by Leslie Logan

I had the good fortune of spending a significant chunk of my developmental years being raised by my grandparents. My parents split when I was four; they were young, ill-equipped, and fitfully disengaged from the rather large task of raising three young children. So my older brother and I went to live with my grandparents. This was the best thing that could have happened to us.

My grandparents lived in a small, three-bedroom house on the Tonawanda Indian Reservation in Western New York. My grandfather was a chief for the snipe clan in the traditional Longhouse, and one of the last surviving medicine men of his time. My grandmother was the clanmother for the bear clan.

My grandfather was involved with other Native leaders throughout the Iroquois Confederacy, but also traveled throughout Indian Country to conduct ceremonies and support other Native efforts at the time. He was very much involved in the protection of Native land rights, land claims, fishing rights, sovereignty, and the cultural preservation efforts of other tribes. In the summer, my grandparents would load up the station wagon, pack in with my aunt, and we would road-trip across the country to meet with the Native people of Third Mesa, Mojave, Mt. Shasta, Neah Bay, the Black Hills, Pine Ridge, and places closer to home.

My grandfather also held encampments with groups of urban Indians and I remember sleeping in a tent in the field for weeks at a time. He was on a mission to properly instruct and impart all that we should know about our traditions, stories, plant life, song, dance, cultural lifeways, values, and beliefs. My brother and I were exposed to a culturally rich and diverse Native world, and learned directly and indirectly not only about ourselves, but about other Native people, their communities, their foods, their songs, environs, and issues.

I learned that all the brown people we met on our travels were different; they had their own languages; their own Creation stories; their own customs; and different dress, songs, dances, and reasons for those. Yet of course, I realized we share certain similarities and worldviews, including a respect for the environment, historical struggles, a tenacity to protect land and water rights, and a commitment to strong spiritual and cultural survival, but also that we as Native people share the need and desire to ensure a lasting and sustainable future for our particular tribe. We all still have a driving need to maintain our Nations as separate and distinct; to preserve those characteristics and qualities that set us apart and make us unique, Native people.

My grandparents opened up my world beyond the small confines of the Tonawanda Indian Reservation and showed me the value of being part of a richly diverse Native universe. Along the way I came to understand and identify with the special qualities that come with being Seneca. In our culture, one of the primary duties of women is to procreate, to massage the earth, and to bring forth future generations of Seneca people.

In both direct and indirect ways, my grandparents communicated the value of all Native peoples and the need to "stick with your own." So when it came to dating and mating, the message I received was – there is only one option: Native.

On the reservation, everyone called my grandmother Gram, even those who were not related to her. She had a certain way of putting people at ease with her teasing affections, her robust laugh, and her knowing, playful jabs. While I don't remember her preaching or giving a deliberate speech about dating, mating, or selecting a partner, I vividly remember her delivering an unforgettable phrase accompanied by this unmistakable stern look she would throw with a tilt of her head that suggested you better listen and take her seriously. There must have been some conversation between my cousins and I about rez boys, white boys, and boys in general. My Gram looked at us and simply said, referring to white boys: "You can practice on them, just don't bring them home."

I have never forgotten that.

Throughout high school I had just one boyfriend; he was a "skin."[1] As I got older, I always knew that if I was going to settle down and have a family, there was no question, it had to be with a Native man.

My first husband was Skokomish from Washington State. We both wanted children, but we divorced before we got around to having them. At 32 years old, I found myself unmarried and was very much aware of the loud biological clock ticking inside my head. Not just any man would do, though; he had to be a Native man. I wrote about my panic and the challenges of finding a suitable Native man in an article I entitled "Hunting in Indian Country," published in *Aboriginal Voices*. For me, the need and desire for a Native partner had everything to do with the desire for resultant Native children.

As timing, luck, or determination would have it, I found a Mohawk man at – gasp, of all places! – the Salamanca Powwow one summer on the Allegany Territory. We had two children together, a son who is now 16; and a daughter now 13; both, now arguably of dating age. Sadly, I have been left to guide these two on my own as we lost my husband to cancer five years ago. My children and I live on the Cattaraugus Territory.

Three years ago, with a wild grin on her face, my daughter mischievously snitched on her brother and announced his affection for a girl. It would so happen this girl was not Native, not Seneca. I remember breathing deeply and thinking to myself that the time has come to have "the talk." Not the be-responsible-talk that involves sex, love, safety, protection, and condoms, but the talk about choices in partners, dates, and mates, and why it is important to be selective and particular.

I could not help feeling then, as I do now, that this conversation is among the most important and momentous in my children's lives. I feel that way because whom they choose to date, and ultimately mate with, has tremendous consequences. For Seneca people, and for many other Native peoples, who you select as a partner and have children with has a tremendous impact on the children themselves and the Nation as a whole.

The Seneca Nation is matrilineal. This means that according to the long-held custom and traditions of the Haudenosaunee, or People of the Longhouse, Seneca descent is passed down through the mother's line. A child's mother must be an enrolled Seneca in order for that child to become an enrolled Seneca.[3] The children of a Seneca man, however, will follow the lineage of the natural birth mother. A Seneca woman may "mate out"—mate with a non-Seneca or non- Native, but her children will still inherit Seneca citizenship.

When I was 12, my father remarried a non-Native woman, a *honyo 'oh* or white person as we say in Seneca. Apparently he didn't receive or heed the same messages I had gotten from my grandparents. I remember being a little confused by his choice. She wasn't just white. She was as Sherman Alexie might say: "Glow-in-the dark-white," more white than the whitest white person on earth. White or not, she came to live on the rez in a little four-room cabin that lacked running water. She gave birth to my half-sister, who would grow up on the rez, ride the bus to school, get spit on, teased, poked, and prodded for being a "half-breed."

After my father remarried, my brother and I went to live with him and his new wife. We moved into an old house just a corner's bend down the road from my Gram's. We had the longhouse in our front yard and an out-house in the backyard; we heated the house with a woodstove and we drew water from a well. At midwinters, the peak of the ceremonial season, the ceremonies, dances, and lots of friends and relatives came to our house for days at a time.

Through no fault or choice of her own, my half-sister was raised under the rafters of the Longhouse that extended to my father's house. By virtue of being my father's daughter, she had been witness to sacred medicine cer-emonies, dances, songs, masks, and recitations. Yet suddenly when she was 16, she was asked to leave my father's house, because she was *honyo'oh*; because she did not belong.

My father's choice had consequences, searing, painful, unmistakable, lifelong consequences for my half-sister who ultimately has come to feel she was born of a place and a people to which she did not belong. She had come to understand, respect, and appreciate customs and traditions that she was later prohibited from participating in and even being in proximity to.

The person one selects as a mate has myriad consequences to the chil-dren, but there are also consequences, both short and long term, to one's Nation. When Native people were pushed, shoved, and confined to reser-vations, clearly they mated more within their own group or among people of their region. As time has marched on, Native people have become ex-posed to other tribal members in residential schools, urban work programs, and land displacements. It is now commonplace for young Native men and women to leave the territories for school, higher education, work, the mil-itary, and due to a lack of housing, available property and land bases that cannot accommodate increasing populations. We now have generations of urban Indians, who have never lived on the reservation, who may have little connection to their "home" communities, and little interaction with other Native people outside of family.

The likelihood is great that one will marry out or mate out due to geo-graphical proximity to one's community, or lack of exposure or engagement with other Native people, simply for lack of a pool of options.

In 2011 the Seneca Nation Clerk conducted research and generated a report that indicated the increasing rates of out-marriage and mating out and the effect to Seneca bloodlines. The ever-increasing rates of Seneca men and women mating out clearly has resulted in fewer Seneca enrollees and diluted bloodlines. There was a dull roar of dialogue at the time, but a national Seneca conversation about the long-term consequences to the Nation as a whole has yet to occur.

On the Cattaraugus Territory, Seneca children attend one of three contract schools. Our children are a small percentage of Native students at each of those schools, thus being in the minority in comparison to a largely white student population. When our kids go off to college, they may be one of a handful of other Native students at those schools, even when they attend universities with established American Indian programs, student recruitment efforts, and support systems. As they graduate, mature, and seek work, their careers and opportunities can take them to cities and settings further from home with fewer and fewer Native people.

Even when young Native men and women have a preference or predilection for Native partners, the lack of a Native presence or prospects in one's surroundings debilitates good intentions. Unless, I would argue, one has an unswerving commitment to building a Native family, having Native children, and contributing to the sustainability of one's own tribal future.

Three years ago when I had "the talk" with my son – we call him Oshna, a derivation of his Seneca name, Ohnigohdagweh, meaning "He was wished for" – I discussed the consequences of mating out, shared anecdotes and challenges I had seen, outlined the pros and cons, and trotted out the wisdom of my grandmother. In the end, I told him he was still young, and there was plenty of time to "practice," but that ultimately, when the time comes, he should choose Native.

I was so unnerved when his interest in girls first came to my attention, I immediately got on the phone and called up my cousins and girlfriends to ask them what they were saying to their sons and daughters who had reached this critical juncture – if they were saying anything at all, and why. The responses varied.

My cousin and his wife have eight children together – nine, counting one he had from a previous relationship. I asked his wife if they were having a conversation with their kids. She emphatically answered, "Yes! We talk about it just about every other week!" Being Longhouse people, she said that it was not only important to stress the importance of partnering with Natives to keep Longhouse people and traditions strong, but also that they avoid partnering with their clan cousins and close relatives.

My Tuscarora girlfriend has five children and has always maintained a lifelong commitment to Native spirituality, Tuscarora traditions, and mating Native only. She said she has talked with her kids since they were little about "Who we are and where we come from." She considers it her sacred duty to communicate Native values to her kids. "You have to give them a consistent message and not veer from the teachings that keep ourselves, our people, and our ways strong. We have seven generations we have to think of; it is our obligation," she said. Her 15-year-old daughter "gets it," she says. She is gratified that her daughter already has her sights set on a traditional Native boy.

One Seneca girlfriend and her Seneca husband have two kids, a boy and girl. She said they have talked with their kids about the importance of choosing Native mates. But she had an interesting take and said she emphasized the importance for her son to find a Seneca mate, because if he didn't, he would not have the opportunity to own land on the territory. She said it wasn't as important for her daughter to marry or mate with a Seneca or other Native, because her children would be Seneca regardless.

An Oneida girlfriend from Green Bay has four children, two of whom are older and have children with non-Native partners. She said she always tried to communicate her ideals, practice the values that support her traditions, and convey a message that would lead her children to mate Native. But, she said, sometimes the messages we send as parents don't "take"; sometimes kids deliberately rebel. "Sometimes they do the exact opposite of what you would like, just because they can," she said.

My Cheyenne Arapaho filmmaker friend was adopted as an infant and raised by a non-Native family. He said he was only ever attracted to Native women, and for himself it was of paramount importance that he date and mate with Native women only. He summed it up in a profound and powerful way. He said he had an abiding sense of commitment to mating with a Native woman "for what I lost and what I wanted." He says his only daughter is aware of his thinking that places a priority on a Native mate for her, but he said, "She is free to go where she wants."

My Hopi friend married a honyo'oh; they had two boys and divorced. He takes them home maybe once every other year to see family and attend ceremonies. I asked him, given his own choice, if he was having any conversations with them about choosing Native. He shrugged and said in a cavalier way, "Maybe when they're 21." I could not contain myself. "Twenty-one?!" I shrieked. "Twenty-one is too late! You have to start talking to them now!" He was unmoved and shrugged again. "They're going to do what they are going to do and choose who they are going to choose. I can't stop them."

My son has been with the same girl, on and off since he was 13. One time he gave her a pair of $200 Beats headphones. I had a fit. I said something horrible like how could he give those expensive headphones to that white girl?! He cried. I softened. Again, I said, "It's okay, you're still young, you have plenty of time…"

He has shot up several inches since then and has grown into a lanky, handsome young man. My still-mischievous daughter has shared several times that more than a few of her fellow Seneca lacrosse teammates text and giggle over Oshna with interest. Not so jokingly I have suggested that he trade-up and check out one of those lady Seneca lacrosse rock stars. He exclaims, "Mom!" as if to say "How could you say such a thing!" and rolls his eyes at me.

I raised the subject with my non-Native friends and was surprised by their reactions. One friend gave me a look of astonishment and vehemently said I had no right to dictate to my kids whom they should date. I was told that it was not my place to define for them an appropriate mate or establish restrictions for whom they could love.

I had no right? I argue that as a Native parent, I have a responsibility to convey a message to my children that ultimately values all Native people and supports our survival and our continuation in this world. I see it as my responsibility to ensure that my children know that their decisions will have consequences that will impact the lives of their children and color their experiences throughout.

Am I prejudiced? Biased? Overly aggressive on the subject? Maybe. I have actually said to my children that in light of the Nation's study and other tribal findings, that their need to mate Native is not an option; mating Native is an imperative. I like to think of it as being unequivocally in favor of my own Seneca people, or being unabashedly in support of our long-term survival. I believe each and every single Seneca – or other Native individual – has a compelling responsibility to ensure our children receive a message that sustains our Nations.

Will my son eventually embrace the values and ideals I share? Will he follow the path or go off on a different one? Will I be disappointed if he gives his heart to a non-Native and have non-Native children? I cannot tell my children whom to love. I will love them unconditionally. I can only give them guidance and instill values that hopefully lead them in a direction that is healthy for them, their children, and contributes to the health of our Nation.

Like all Native nations with increasingly diluted bloodlines, I dare submit: shouldn't we be asking ourselves, each other, and underscoring the important and obvious questions to our children, who will determine how we carry on: Who are we? Who have we become? And who do we want to be? What do we want our children to resemble? What will the future face of our Nation look like? Will we cease to exist? Are we headed for the cliff? If so, how can we avoid mating ourselves out of Seneca existence as we know it? Whose responsibility is it to help slow the pace of blood dilution? How can we strengthen and refortify the Seneca people?

I actually began writing this article three years ago. But I abandoned the piece after breakfast one morning when a Seneca girlfriend who cautioned me that the Seneca people would not receive such a piece favorably. She told me people would react negatively and view me as a finger-wagging preacher. People, she said, would attack and ask: Who does she think she is, telling us what to do and how to raise our kids?

My non-Native friends suggest that despite my efforts and enthusiasm, sounding the alarm will make no difference. They suggest that Native people, including the Seneca will continue to mate out and mate out and eventually dilute the bloodlines so drastically that Seneca people will be indistinguishable from the general white population. The 2011 Seneca Clerk's study indicated that the Seneca aggregate is already at a one-quarter degree blood, and that is a maximum. At current and sustained out-mating rates, the diminishment of Seneca blood is moving like an out-of-control race car speeding downhill with the brakes cut.

It is virtually impossible to avoid the conclusion that in the case of the strength of our Native nations, and our people's bloodlines, ultimately the actions of the individual have direct consequences to our respective Nations and to Native people collectively. Will our children hear and heed the good guidance of our grandmothers? First, we have to ensure that they receive the message.

Notes

1. "Skin" as I have come to know it, does not refer to the pejorative term "redskin," but among my peers and community members is a reference to another Indian, not necessarily of the same tribe, but as in *same skin.*"

2. When I was in college I had an unplanned pregnancy and gave my firstborn child up for adoption. Not because the father was non-Native, which he was, but because my father would have surely killed me and disowned me, in no particular order. I have a relationship with my daughter now, but because I didn't raise her, I do not impose my traditional Native values on her.

3. Throughout the seventies and at various times over the years, the Seneca Nation of Indians has discussed further qualifying its enrollment policy that would determine Seneca descent matrilineally AND by at least one-quarter degree blood. In the mid-1960s the Seneca Nation Council voted to add the qualifier of one-quarter degree blood, but the motion was later rescinded. Recent considerations have failed to gain traction. Because the enrollment ordinance is not part of the Seneca Constitution, a major policy change to enrollment would not require a referendum vote by the people.

WALKING IN TWO WORLDS: THE NATIVE AMERICAN COLLEGE EXPERIENCE

by Olivia Hoeft

As a teenager, I was fascinated with ways to identify myself. Personality quizzes, what genre of music I listened to, the ones I didn't, the brands I wore, the movies I liked, and all of the things that made me different from everyone else were vital clues to one of life's first and biggest questions: "Who are you?" College admissions offices asked that same question during my junior year of high school, and finally going to college when I was eighteen felt like a prophesized adventure to discover who I was away from everything that had defined me up until that point. And that's what going off to college is supposed to be all about, right? But at the same time, I was starting to explore my identity as a Native American and the idea of belonging to something that felt so much bigger than me and my individual identity. I wasn't sure if I felt like a Native American. I already knew who I was as an Oneida from Wisconsin, the tribe where I grew up, but away at school, no one would know what an Oneida was. I would have to say I was Native American at new student orientation and during the countless introductions to follow, but I just felt like an Oneida. Although no matter what your background is as a young Native student entering college, whether you grew up near your tribal heritage or far, your identity as a Native American student will be part of your experience both before and during college.

When I was seventeen I received my adult Oneida name, and the summer before I left for college I decided that I would only introduce myself as Yakohahi (pronounced yah-go-ha-he), or Yako for short, during my freshman year. If I ever wanted to make the change, the beginning of college felt like the only time it would be feasible. I imagined it would be easy, once everyone from college knew me as "Yako," my friends and family from home would follow suit. However, when I first showed up to my dorm in September, the busy resident staff had already printed "Olivia" on my dorm room sign and name tags. No one knew how to pronounce Yako, and I'm still asked if there is any relation to the evil bird from *Aladdin*, or *Othello*, from the more literary types. Whenever I met someone, it took a full five minutes to explain the name, how to pronounce it, where it (and I) were from, and at the end, most people asked if they could call me Olivia anyway.

There are over 500 federally recognized Native American tribes in the United States, and I actually knew very little about any tribes when I was entering college that weren't part of the Iroquois Confederacy: the Mohawk, Oneida, Onondaga, Cayuga, Seneca, and the sixth nation, the Tuscarora. There isn't enough room on a college application form for over 500 tribes to each have their own box to check, so we are united by the pan–Native American identity we share, which is broad enough to denote all tribes, yet none specifically. It is a true iteration of the movement from the specific to the general. Just like there is no one actual "tree," there are only types of trees. There are maple trees, oak trees, and evergreen trees, but no general "tree." We all belong to tribes, so no Native American is just Native American, and yet we all are. When I was in Oneida, I was Oneida, but the moment I stepped on my college campus, I started being Native American and for the first time I started to understand what that meant.

Because "Native American" refers to all tribes, as a Native American you are tasked with being *a* representative for all tribes, but that doesn't mean you *are* representative of all tribes. Like anything else in the world, there are a variety of different ways to look and be Native American, and yet the most common reaction that I've had to identifying as Native is, first and foremost surprise, quickly followed by doubt. "You're *really* Native American? How *much* are you?" is an almost guaranteed response. This breach of social etiquette is jarring every time. The first time you meet someone, you normally aren't asked to share intimate family details, the relationship of your parents, your upbringing, or why you look the way you do, but somehow identifying as Native American is seen as an invitation into your autobiography. At first, I would quickly jump to my own defense, counting the ways that made me real. But soon, I got tired of treating my ethnic identity like an application for belief, especially when I was still exploring what it meant to me personally. This doubt can seep into our own interactions with other Natives too, creating a competitive culture that measures how much Native you are against someone else's definition. Today, I don't feel an inclination to prove how Native I am during every introduction. I believe that being Native American cannot be summed up by a percentage or quantifiable factor, and that it is something I have found to define for myself. Just like the college admissions process, there is no formula or right way to answer the question, "Who are you?" We are both the general and the specific. I am Native American, I am Oneida, and I am Olivia all at the same time, although I didn't necessarily figure out all of those identities at once.

The history of Native Americans provided in today's high schools unfortunately stops after Thanksgiving. This means that the majority of the peers you meet at college, if it's a non-tribal university, will not have much, if any, knowledge of modern Native American tribes, their history with residential education, their status and rights as sovereign nations, the diversity of the many tribes in the United States, and the implications of the constant misrepresentation Native Americans face in mainstream media. There are usually only one or two images that someone may be familiar with prior to meeting a Native American (probably a mascot, a cartoon, or a historical figure), and they are hard to change. The narratives that Native Americans are found in today are static and almost always based in the past. They are supporting characters in the pilgrims' lofty fight for freedom, helpful guides on someone else's journey in a story that happened a long time ago. That persistent narrative can be hard to shake, in others and in yourself. At college, you are on your own journey, happening right now and you are a modern person like anyone else. It is hard for people to recognize the simple fact that Native Americans exist in the present. We are still here and we are here now. I wear jeans like the next person, but that doesn't mean I stop being Native. I'm not only Native when I wear my regalia or when I practice our traditions. The doubt that we are real and that we are here now can put us in a box, but we have to fight for our right to grow and develop.

The most famous representations and images of Native Americans and Native American culture today are almost entirely from works of fiction. Native Americans are pictured alongside vampires, pirates, and witches, in a lineup of the usual suspects from a magical, nonexistent land. Unlike other minorities, Native Americans have to fight for the acknowledgment that we are even real, let alone for understanding of our complex histories. We face many stereotypes and prejudices as a people, but the most damaging one is that we are extinct.

The week before Halloween during my freshman year, I went with a group of other students from my dorm to a local costume shop and had the surprise encounter of finding two of my acquaintances deliberating over not if, but which Native Princess–themed outfit to buy while standing in one of the crowded aisles. In these instances, it's difficult to see the difference between the specific and the general. Whose fault is it for this misappropriation? Is it the two individuals buying the products? The companies that make them? Or the education and legal systems that didn't prevent it? Do I take on the responsibility of educating a person who may or may not intend to be disrespectful? Due to the lack of education and awareness of Native American history and culture, many people commit these acts of cultural misappropriation due to ignorance, which can make it all the more difficult for someone to flag a seemingly innocuous situation as harmful for fear of being the bad guy. Or does not saying something mean I'm not doing my duty to spread awareness and understanding? Do I even help and will they even listen? I decided to say something and inserted my canned response that I've memorized over many situations like these. It was slightly awkward and uncomfortable of course, but in the end the costumes stayed in the shop. Later that night, I saw someone wearing a giant, dollar store headdress and beige outfit walking ahead of me. Again, a series of questions and scenarios occurred to me. I imagined myself going up to this stranger and confronting them, but ultimately decided against it. There are a number of different ways to react to these situations, and everyone chooses their own way. Now, I normally only feel compelled to say something to people I know and I turn the other cheek to strangers. During my last year at Stanford, a costume store set up a pop-up stand in the middle of campus with hundreds of costumes and had volunteers come and audit the stock to remove any offensive costumes from the racks. It was gratifying to see this change over the course of four years and the expansion of the conversation.

Cultural misappropriation is a challenge that Native American students face while at college, but there are also structural and historical challenges that young Native students will face even before arriving on campus. Native American students are uniquely affected by the historical trauma created by the United States' government boarding school system, which utilized, and often enforced, residential education to assimilate Native American children into American society. These programs helped to eradicate entire generations of cultural heritage, traditions, and languages from being passed down, and not only affect those who went to the schools, but their children and grandchildren as well. The boarding school system left a complicated and painful scar on many tribal communities' memories by associating residential education and higher learning with the loss of tribal identities and traditions. However, positive legacies were also created from the boarding school system. Like the Native communities on college campuses today, the boarding schools enabled youth from different tribes to meet and help forge the beginning of the pan-Indian identity that persists in Indian Country. The Haskell Indian Nations University was originally a boarding school, but was reclaimed and turned into a tribal university. However, despite these progresses, the painful memory of the residential education system remains, which is a challenge to Native American students in both reaching and graduating from college. This troubled history with residential education, along with many other factors, may contribute to the fact that Native American students have the lowest rates of minorities both pursuing and graduating from institutions of higher education.

Secondly, Native Americans are historically place-based cultures, which means that tribal identities are closely tied with residence on tribal land. Today, many tribal traditions and education of tribal culture and language only take place on tribal land. This further challenges Native American students to both participate in higher learning and remain culturally active at the same time. Going away to college can feel like choosing education over cultural and community involvement. Some students may even face discrimination when they return home to their peers. Another Native American student I knew at Stanford grew apart from her friends from home over the four years she was away at school and was often told she had "stopped being Native, and started being white." It is often expensive and time-consuming to frequently travel between school and home; however, advances in technology have made it easier for students to continue to learn their language and about their culture remotely. The language center in Oneida, Wisconsin, offers language classes through Skype so students can participate and attend language classes even while they are away. Additionally, many Native communities on college campuses offer workshops for students or visiting tribal members to demonstrate their crafts, skills, or knowledge of tribal histories to other students. These campus communities can provide vital spaces of cultural involvement that can help students learn about other tribes or even more about their own.

Finally, many Native students also face the added challenge of overcoming the stigma of affirmative action. Before reaching their college of choice, many students may face prejudice from their peers in high school who use a student's Native American heritage as a reason to undermine the student's acceptance. Native American students are in danger of internalizing that idea and believing that they were only accepted due to their ethnicity, which can thus undermine their confidence and success when they arrive at college. This may also discourage students from readily identifying as Native American at school, as they fear the discrimination that may be associated with their acceptance. College acceptances and the admission process is contextual, and often takes in the background of many different types of students. However, students are accepted based on their academic performance and abilities as a whole. No student is accepted for one reason alone, whether Native American or any other background affiliation. Native American students are assured to be the least represented at their schools of choice and thus, should be confident that their presence is a triumph for both themselves and the Native American community at large.

In Indian Country, there is a growing reference to idea of the "two worlds." Purcell Powless, a prominent Oneida leader, once said that as Native Americans, "we have to walk in two worlds and succeed in both." Our identities seem to be split between two different contexts, one that fits into mainstream, modern culture and one that acknowledges our Native identities. As a young person struggling to find their own identity, adding two more can feel like a lot to ask. However, I believe it is possible to balance these identities at once, that they are not mutually exclusive. Through my time at college, I learned I didn't have to compartmentalize my identity. I learned what being Native American meant to me and how to bring my whole self into every situation. I am Native American, I am Oneida, and I am Olivia.

TRICKSTER TEACHES THE PRAIRIE DOGS HOW TO DISENROLL THEIR MEMBERS

by Robert Chanate

Trickster was on his way to the National Gathering of Tricksters when he came upon the Red Whisker Prairie Dog Village.

At the gathering each trickster there would be bragging about their accomplishments and trying to outdo one another. Trickster was embarrassed to be arriving on foot and not in a stretch Hummer like the big timers so he thought he might get a few bragging rights if he was able to fool this little village right before he arrived at The Gathering.

The Red Whisker Village was a small village and everyone got along well so Trickster figured he would get them to fight one another.

Trickster approached the outer perimeter guard, Unafraid of Hawk, and asked to be taken to the leadership council because he had a very important proposal to pitch to them.

Trickster was taken to the village and told he could speak. Trickster transformed into his professional persona, appearing in a suit and carrying a briefcase.

"My friends, I have a proposal for you. In this briefcase I have some cards that will be given to each member. It means you are an official member of the village. They are very fancy cards and each one entitles a Red Whisker Prairie Dog to the goodies I will bring with me when I return this way. All I ask in return is a place to lay my head for the night and half of your plums. Mind you, upon my return, I will give you triple this amount of plums."

The council members were puzzled by this gift but they saw no harm in the proposal.

The next morning they and all the Prairie Dogs gathered to receive their cards. As he was preparing to leave, Trickster said he had another idea he wanted to share.

"Good morning," said Trickster. "I have another idea for your consideration. It appears to me that the great supply I bring back will last for a while, but it can last even longer if it is divided among a smaller number of people."

"This is true," said one of the council members. "But we divide everything here equally. How can some get more?"

"Very simple," said Trickster. "If you have fewer Prairie Dogs in your membership, then there will be more for those who remain."

A larger group of the village who had been silently listening did not like what was being proposed. Though she was still considered a young adult, Quiet Chirper spoke up.

"I don't like this idea. How can anyone be asked to leave? We all made this village what it is and we all deserve to be treated the same."

With that, all the Prairie Dogs began speaking at once and eventually they were arguing with one another, shouting down one another. Quiet Chirper tried to call for calm but it was of no use. Trickster used his giant voice to get everyone's attention.

"My friends, let me tell you how this can be settled. The council gave out official cards to everyone, am I correct? Isn't that the right of a council? And if this is their right, does it not follow that they also have the right to take those cards away? This is a very important power to have. It proves that you are indeed a powerful entity and capable of making decisions like civilized Prairie Dogs. Furthermore, it sends a message that you are a free and independent village with the ability to determine not only your membership but also your future."

Quiet Chirper said, "If we want to prove we are free then why choose this method? Why not prove it by strengthening our defenses so we can keep the hawks from snatching our family and friends? Why don't we build better perimeters so the snakes don't come in unless we let them so we can bury them in the holes? Why did we make a deal with those ferrets that one season when we gave them most of our berries if they promised not to invade us? Why did we relocate our entire village in the time of our ancestors just because some coyotes were lurking nearby? If more plums are so important then why don't we devise a better ways of gathering and storing? Why don't we fight those battles instead of throwing out our own relatives?"

All of Quiet Chirper's protests were of no use. The council decided that Trickster's way was the easiest and best way to get more for their group. The council made a new rule. Only those Prairie Dogs who met certain, new requirements were going to be allowed to stay. All Prairie Dogs who had been critical of some council decisions didn't make the members list. Some Prairie Dogs who were related to them didn't make the list either.

The banished Prairie Dogs packed their belongings and prepared to leave. Quiet Chirper and the others who had opposed the new rule exchanged hugs and tears with their relatives and friends who were asked to leave.

They all walked to the edge of the village together and those who were still members stopped while those who had been excluded continued on in search of a new home. Their future was uncertain.

"I will see you again Unafraid of Hawk," said Quiet Chirper as he walked away. "Trickster won't get away with this."

"Well," said Trickster, faking a tear. "That was downright touching. The sadness and gravity of the departure shows that your traditions are still as strong as ever and we are all indeed related. This council is the wisest one I've ever encountered and should be congratulated for having to make such important decisions."

The council members smiled at one another and shook hands. What Trickster said was true, they thought. They were very wise.

"Friends, I must be on my way now," said Trickster. "I promise to return with plums, gamma grass, buffalo grass, alfalfa and some casino tokens. I will see you shortly."

As he cart-wheeled away, Trickster was very pleased with himself. He had a nice little story to share at the gathering. As he skipped along, he began tossing the plums away one by one saying, "I tricked them, I tricked them not."

"That was one trick but I think I will pull three more before I make it to the gathering," said Trickster. "Four is a sacred number and I need to complete it so I get my medicine man trickster badge."

And so along Trickster went, skipping, spinning and dancing. He didn't notice Quiet Chirper was following him.

Acknowledgment

This story was previously published in *Indian Country Today*, February 7, 2014, http://indiancountrytodaymedianetwork.com/2014/02/07/trickster-teaches-prairie-dogs-how-disenroll-their-members-153446.

A FRACTION OF LOVE

by Reed Bobroff

A Fraction of Love is an exploration of love and identity in Indian country as shown through the romance and struggle of a Navajo community. Indigenous love stories are rarely as simple as two people falling for each other; the influence of colonization has contributed to an intense pressure in Native communities to continue our legacies through marriage and having children. Often times, people are valued or discounted solely because of blood quantum while children have greater implications and responsibilities from the moment of conception. This play draws on my own experiences and conversations I've had in Native communities and examines what it can mean to be Native and how it affects the ways we fall in love.

Characters

Tia Campbell, Navajo and Mexican woman (on tribal rolls with 1/4 blood) in her early 20s from the Tóhajiléé Indian Reservation

Dennis Campbell, a white doctor in his late 20s from Pittsburgh, Pennsylvania

Mugzi, Registered full-blood Navajo man from Tóhajiléé

Campfire, Choctaw man in his early 20s from Oklahoma who grew up in Tóhajiléé

Ashkii, Navajo man (registered 5/8), in his early 20s, and Tia's high school sweetheart from Tóhajiléé

Nancy Pinto, Tia's mother (registered 1/2), in her 40s who lives and is from Tóhajiléé

Rae, Navajo woman, early 20s, and Tia's best friend growing up in Tóhajiléé

Reuben Markowitz, white Jewish lawyer, mid-30s from New York, married to Cindy

Cindy Markowitz, white Jewish lawyer, mid-30s from New York, married to Reuben

A Fraction of Love **follows the protagonists, Tia and Mugzi, two Navajo people from the Tóhajiléé reservation settling into adulthood. Tia has recently moved to Albuquerque, New Mexico, with her white husband, Dr. Dennis Campbell. And Mugzi is still crashing on his friends' couch.**

ACT I, SCENE 3

Tia and Dennis' apartment: a bare living room with boxes stacked and scattered around the stage. Dennis stands with his arms around Tia.

DENNIS
This place sure is beautiful.

TIA
It's the nicest place *I've* ever lived in.

DENNIS
Our first home... Can you see it? We'll put your grandmother's rug on that wall, my granddad's rocking chair can go right over there, my bookshelf will go here, and yours will go right next to it. And eventually we can put one of those plastic playpens on the floor and watch the babies roll around. We can read to them on your sheepskin rug. We'll take turns: you can read them radical feminist scholars and I can read them the *Gray's Anatomy* textbook. They'll have a nice balance between us.
(He squeezes her tighter and lightly kisses her.)

TIA

And what if they don't look like your books?

DENNIS

Then they'll have a lot of useless knowledge about muscles and bones.

TIA

If it's any child of mine, they won't have a mind for science.

DENNIS

Then it's a good thing they get DNA from both of us.

TIA

They can have your awkward hips and messy hair.

DENNIS

And they can have your knobby knees!

TIA

They can have your hairy knuckles.

DENNIS

They can have your soft skin and sweet lips.
(He kisses her.)

TIA

And if they don't look like me?

DENNIS

And if they don't look like me!

NANCY
(from offstage)

Ayye! Dóóda! You just leave me out by the truck. You think *I'm* moving these boxes?
(A stout Nancy Pinto enters from stage right.
She is dressed in a velveteen dress and her best jewelry.
She leans on her IHS cane for support.)
Go bring some stuff inside!

(Dennis kisses Tia on the forehead and rushes out.)

NANCY
(calling offstage)
With your knees! Your knees! Didn't anyone ever teach you how to lift!
You're gonna pull something!
*(Dennis re-enters, carrying two moving boxes and
takes awkward steps since he can't see where he's going.)*

TIA
Careful of your fingers coming in the door, hon!

DENNIS
Ooooooowwwww! I pinched it! Tia, can you grab me the first aid kit from
that box over there? I should clean this cut before I move any more from
that filthy truck bed.

NANCY
Let me see that.
*(She takes Dennis' hand, spits on
the injured finger and rubs it on her dress.)*
There. Now it's clean. Indian medicine. Now go get the other boxes. This
house won't move itself in.

DENNIS
Blech! Hon! I really need that kit – forget it, I'll go grab the travel case in
the car.
(He exits.)

NANCY
(calling after him)
And this time, lift with your *legs*!

TIA
Mom, what do you have to do that for? This is his first time out west. Go
easy on him.

NANCY
Those East Coast bilagáanas need someone to toughen them up! He better
get used to it if he's gonna be a part of this family.

TIA
Were you this rough on *dad* the first time you brought him here?

NANCY

You better believe your uncles put him in his place. First time I brought your dad to Tóhajiléé, they had him up at 5 a.m. every day to haul water and take care of the sheep.

(beat)

They weren't even our sheep!

TIA

Well, it took enough work on my part to get him to move out here in the first place. I would just appreciate some help to make him stay.

NANCY

Ei dóóda! You tell him that your family's here. Your community is here. You're staying put. That East Coast has made you light enough as it is.

TIA

Dennis is really trying to make things work – he's looking for jobs – we have our one-year lease. This is our life now.

NANCY

Biigha! You should be back at home! Near your family!

(Dennis comes back into the room with a couple more boxes.)

NANCY

With your knees! Your knees!
(Ad-libs more nagging, then rushes around behind Dennis, waving her cane as she berates him.)

DENNIS

Whew! Okay, I hate to quit now, but I have to go to my interview soon. Do you know where my blazers are?

(Tia pulls one out of a box on the couch as Mugzi enters with Rae, bringing their argument with them.)

RAE

I told you: no cash, no crumbs. I'm not payin' for – Tia!!

TIA

Rae!

(They embrace.)

TIA

It's so good to see you! And Mugzi, too! How *are* you?

RAE

We just got into town from Tó'haj'! I woulda been here sooner, but, as you see, I picked up a stray.
                                (beat)
So there's that.

TIA

Come in, sit down! This is my husband, Dennis.

MUGZI

Ayyyee! Good to meet the new hubby!
                            (to Dennis)
How you likin' the desert?

DENNIS

Well, it sure is dry. I was trying to find a job before the move, but there just weren't too many options. I'm actually on my way to an interview at one of the few hospitals and then a few private practices around the city.

MUGZI

Eeeeeee! You're a doctor, huh? I hear that makes good coin!

DENNIS

Hah! We'll see about that. Right now I'm off to meet for a research position at the Cryobank.

RAE

Bank? I thought you said you were a doctor?

DENNIS

I am! I am. The Cryobank is a private practice for embryo and stem cell research as well as a sperm bank.

MUGZI

I used to have a cousin who did that down at the race track! *(He mimes jerking off a horse.)* The old catch and release! She used to make good money doin' it too! Except she ended up with one regular arm and one with biceps the size of a bowling ball.

RAE

You're so gross.

DENNIS

Well you know, human sperm banks aren't such a bad gig. At some of these places you can get two to three hundred dollars for your first donation.

MUGZI

No shit! I was gonna do that anyways!

DENNIS

Uhhhh… yeah. I mean, these places are always looking for more donors. And a Native guy – there aren't too many Native men who donate sperm so I'm sure they'd pay a lot of money for a sample.

MUGZI

No shit... Hey buddy, where did you say your interview was?

DENNIS

Let me pull out the address. Tia gave me directions...

MUGZI

Directions? I know this city like the back of my head. I'll be your navigator – let's go.

RAE

Uh-oh. Nancy, can you go with Dennis and numbnuts to make sure they don't get lost? I'll help Tia unpack.

(Mugzi puts his hand on Dennis' back and starts pushing him toward the door. Dennis gives Tia a kiss on the cheek and grabs his jacket.)

MUGZI

Hey man, you wanna go get somethin' to eat?

(Mugzi and Dennis, Nancy trailing behind, exit stage right.)

TIA

Damn, you sure brought the circus with you.

RAE

Business as usual. You really have been gone too long. Look at you! You're all pale!

TIA

Oh shut up! I'm just as dark as you!

RAE

You got some catching up to do. How's it feel to be back?

TIA

I still can't get over the horizon. It's like it gave me shock – like when I had trouble breathing my first semester of college when I couldn't see the sky. Everything felt like it was closing in: getting darker and darker. But now I'm back. I'm here and I'm having trouble catching my breath all over again. It's like seeing someone you're so in love with after a long trip. And when you're finally reunited, it hurts.

RAE

Damn, look at you being all poetic.

TIA

You know how much I've missed home. When I was away, the only thing that made me feel warm like that was Dennis. After a long shift at the hospital, he'd come home and crawl into bed with me. His long arms would reach around me and... I could breathe easy. When I'd bury my face in his chest, I'd smell the hospital — you know I always hated that smell: it was like IHS... sterile and sick. It smelled like fluorescent lights. And Dennis always had that scent on him. But maybe that's why I fell in love with him. Everything around me was so unfamiliar, I just clung to him like that smell.

RAE

And now you guys are both locked down! You dragged his ass back to New Mexico like a good little ball and chain!

TIA

He knew I needed to come home. Maybe not when we started going together, but I spent two Christmases in Pittsburgh with his whole family. I took the racist jokes from his drunk older brothers and the side-eye glances from his mom and her book club friends. When I wore that pretty white dress, I didn't complain about the starch.

RAE

Your mom was pissed as hell about that.

TIA

And you better believe I held it all over his head when he finished.

RAE

Your dad told me a joke when I was little. He said, "Pueblo women, to show respect, walk behind their men. Lakota women, to show they're equal, walk beside their men. But Navajo women? Navajo women walk all over their men!"

TIA

I like the life I'm living in now. I want this house, I want to be in Albuquerque. I grew up in Tóhajiléé and didn't have this much opportunity. I worked my ass off to get out of there and I deserve to make my life here.

RAE

Hey! I'm not the one putting you on trial. I know when Tia sets her mind to something, she makes it happen.

TIA

I want to start my life with Dennis.

RAE

How's married life treating you?

TIA

You've dated white guys before. You know how it goes.

RAE

Not no more! I've been clean since you last saw me. Washed away my sins! I just couldn't take it no more. They're assholes, all of them! All of them at their core. They're all just racist pricks. They'll fuck you like they hate you. It's hot for a while: sexy, dangerous, but you can tell how they feel, deep down – it got… scary. But on the other hand, the nice guys just kept falling in love with my long hair and dark eyes. They were all goo-goo like I just walked out of a Disney movie. But the worst of them were the ones that thought they understood what it's like to *be* me. Those one-love, drum circle, "I only eat what I can grow" hippies. I'd get with one of them and suddenly he thought he was brown too! "Everyone is related, baby" – quoting Lakota proverbs at me. So I'm sworn offa them. It's strictly Native guys from now on.

TIA

You dating anyone from Tóhaj?

RAE

Hell no! I'm related to *everybody*! And if I'm not related to them, they've slept with someone I'm related to. No, I'm keepin' my eye out for a nice, tall Crow guy. Or maybe a Cree guy from Canada. That way, when I kick him out, I know I ain't gonna run back into him.

TIA

You're sworn offa Navajo guys, too?

RAE

There's 566 tribes out there, girl! And I am a strong proponent of diversity. Now, when I'm ready to settle down, have some babies, I'll find a stable Navajo guy. Someone who won't kill my quantum. What about you? How's that gonna work out with Dennis?

TIA

Well we haven't talked about it – I mean, we have. We both knew we couldn't start a family while he was in med school.

RAE

I'm not tryna have a kid who's not Navajo. I need them to be at least a fourth so I have my ear to the ground for an eligible half-blood or more.

TIA

Is that an old scouting tip?

RAE
(speaks in stereotypical accent)
I ask eagle to listen to the wind and find me husband!

RAE

So if you and Dennis have kids, they're not gonna be registered, huh?

TIA

Not unless tribal government decides to lower how much blood you need to be enrolled.

RAE

Damn. It all ends with you then... Well props to you. Following your heart all the way. You know, I had this girlfriend who wouldn't even date someone if they were less than a fourth. Might as well just have an arranged marriage if you're gonna be like that.

TIA

Did she find anyone?

RAE

You know Chief Manuelito?

TIA

He signed the treaty after the Navajo Long Walk.

RAE

His great-great-grandson.

TIA

Oh wow!

RAE

Yeah, I guess he sells weed outta his trailer. Pretty good stuff too. I hooked her up when we were pickin' up my stash.

TIA

You serious?

RAE

Yup.

(long pause)

TIA

How's Ashkii doin'?

RAE

I knew that was comin'.

TIA

What!

RAE

I always thought you two should have cleared things up.

TIA

Clear things up?

RAE

Look, I love you to death and you know that. But you kind of just... left him. No closure. That's gotta eat you up.

TIA

I was leaving for school; I just didn't know… It's difficult.

RAE

You ever think about him?

TIA

Everyone thinks about their ex every now and again. Maybe I remember the way his hand used to swallow mine. Or I'll remember the way he would look at me from across the room and I would know exactly what he was thinking and we'd burst out laughing, from fifty feet away. Everyone thinks about their ex.

RAE

The difference is that all my exes are just ghosts to me.

TIA

He's long forgotten about me.

(Rae rolls her eyes.)

RAE

Let's get you moved in.

(Rae and Tia grab a couple boxes and exit.)

After Tia returns to the reservation to visit her friends and family, she realizes that she is still in love with Ashkii, her high school sweetheart, and, unbeknownst to Dennis, the two begin an affair. Defiant to live her life in Albuquerque (a place she imagines as the land of opportunity), Tia fights pressure from her community to move back home to teach at the high school.

ACT II, SCENE 2

(Nancy's house. The atmosphere is warm and comfortable as Nancy rocks in her chair while Tia kneels in front of her, both facing the audience. Tia is dressed in professional clothes and accents of Navajo jewelry. Nancy is combing her hair.)

NANCY

Last time I did this was when you graduated high school. Right before you lined up for your diploma. You remember that?

TIA

You took so long tying it up, I thought they were going to start walking without me!

NANCY

I wasn't gonna have you walking out with flyaways. Hold still.
(Nancy licks her fingers and pulls
small hairs away from Tia's forehead.)

TIA

…I'm just nervous.

NANCY

You don't even need to go to this interview! Dr. Yazzie already told me that if you want a job at the high school, they have a classroom open. You're already in Albuquerque, why are you trying to get farther away!

TIA

All the Natives I know who left, came back home. But my whole time in college… I can count how many Natives I met on two hands. I was always the only Native student in any of my classes. Every professor I ever had turned to me with all of their Indian questions and I was always expected to tell everyone else about "the Natives."

NANCY

You should help the students here get to college just like you!

TIA

If some of the Natives who left stuck around to support the rest of us who make it out, maybe it wouldn't be so hard! If those students get to where I was, they'll still have to teach the unit on people of color in their classes! But if I teach at one of these private schools? At a school that sends all of their students to those small liberal arts colleges all over the country? Year after year, that's fewer and fewer people who are making those places harder for people like us.

NANCY

It's all ignorant out there. Everyone already thinks we're extinct. It's not your job to make the world less ignorant. It's their job to be more curious.

It is your job to help where you're needed. The kids at Bosque are going to college. But the kids here, they need someone like you to give them guidance – encourage them. They're *just* as capable as those prep school kids, but no one's taken the time. Quit squirming. You're pulling out your braids.
                                    (pause)
You should come back home. You'll get a house, you'll teach at the school. You wouldn't worry about fixing your apartment no more. All your friends are here! Your family's here. Ashkii's here too.

TIA
I don't want to talk about Ashkii. We're over. I'm with Dennis now.

NANCY
The old chiefs used to have multiple wives. You went to a women's college. It's time we got to have multiple husbands!

TIA
Mom.

NANCY
Men are so lazy. You need four of them just to chop wood, get dinner cooked, and the bills paid.

TIA
I can chop my own wood and I can pay my own bills.

NANCY
But wouldn't you much rather watch Ashkii do it?

TIA
Are you done with my hair?

NANCY
Now that you're home, you should be thinking about the life you're setting down for yourself. What are you going to do away from home that you can't do back in Tóhajiléé? What kind of life do you want for your children? What happens if they start calling Albuquerque their home?

TIA
I'm not moving back to Tóhajiléé! I *want* my life to be in the city. I want the good job, I want to go shopping without making a two-hour drive, I want nice dinners, I want to send my kids to a good school! What can Ashkii give me that Dennis can't?

NANCY

He grew up around the corner. He knows how things go around here. He's a good, Navajo man. He can give you babies.

TIA

I'm not just good for making babies! What's wrong with wanting more opportunity for my kids!

NANCY

You're going to have white babies. And you're going to raise them in the city with your white husband.

TIA

That's not fair! You got to fall in love with no consequences. Who sat you down when you brought Dad home to marry?

NANCY

I went through hell with my family for dating a Mexican!

TIA

You're putting me through the same thing for being with Dennis!

NANCY

I didn't have to worry about you being Navajo. You were registered. You grew up here. You had the culture, you had the community. But if you have kids who can't be enrolled then how do you make sure you aren't just raising white kids? If you stay in the city, with the man that you have, you're giving up your blood, your community, and your people.

TIA

You're just concerned with keeping the bloodline! You didn't have to deal with the consequences. You're lucky I'm registered! But did you ever think about how you falling in love would affect me? You got to fall in love freely but now you want to police the way my heart beats?

NANCY

A white man can't listen to a brown woman the way she needs to be heard.

(Tia stands and faces her mother. Lights dim and Nancy takes her rocking chair and quietly exits stage right. Tia shakes out the braids her mother has been weaving and pulls her hair into a ponytail.)

While Tia struggles to establish herself as an Albuquerque resident and build her life with Dennis (while hiding her affair), Mugzi has been searching for rent money. A conversation with Dennis led him to a sperm bank where, after learning that Native Americans are sought after as donors, Mugzi offered a sample for a quick buck.

ACT II, SCENE 4

(Lights up on an immaculate dinner table with multiple forks and spoons for each place setting. Reuben and Cindy Markowitz sit at the table with a half-full bottle of wine and their glasses half empty. The couple is dressed casually, but still look very proper. They are both nervous and naive, but very earnest. Mugzi and Campfire enter underdressed.)

MUGZI
Heeeeeyyy! I'm Mugzi and this is my lawyer: Campfire David... Ayye! just kidding. He's my ride.

CAMPFIRE
Thanks for havin' me.

MUGZI
I'm here to teach you how to be Navajo!

REUBEN
It's very nice to –

MUGZI
And the first thing you gotta know is how to feed *the people*! Hey! Waiter! Could we get some bread?
(Picking up the bottle on the table)
What do you have here? Wine? That's fancy stuff, huh. Shiraz... That sounds like there's glitter it in. They have any beer?

CAMPFIRE
Forget about it.

MUGZI
You want a beer?

CAMPFIRE

I'm driving.

MUGZI

I'll get us some beer.

*(Mugzi exits the stage and returns with two beers
and a basket of bread: one piece in his mouth.)*

REUBEN

Hi, uhhh... Mugzi. And Campfire? We spoke on the phone; I'm Reuben. Thank you so much for meeting with us tonight.

CINDY

You know, we aren't very impulsive people, but we just had... one of those moments. Oh! Sorry – Cindy.
(She extends her hand.)

MUGZI

So you're the one who's got my little Mugzis swimmin' around in there!

CAMPFIRE

Mugzi.

MUGZI

I'm just callin' it how it is! We all know why we're here.

CINDY
(laughing uncomfortably)
It's fine, it's fine. A little unorthodox, but he's not wrong. Sorry, we're still getting used to the way things go around here.

REUBEN

We're from New York and came down to Santa Fe for a little vacation.

CINDY

There's so much sky and such beautiful art! You all are very lucky to live here.

CAMPFIRE

So how did you... uhhh... decide to... ummmm...

REUBEN

This is new for us too.

CINDY

We've been married for about six years now and have been having trouble... conceiving.

MUGZI

Ahhh! The train don't run or the tunnel's boarded up!

REUBEN

...We were looking at adoption and things like that and it was all very taxing on us so that's why we took the vacation. We're both lawyers back in the city.

CINDY

And we absolutely fell in love with New Mexico as soon as we arrived. We figured, you know, we're away from our stresses, we're putting time into each other, this is... a blessing. Such a blessing.

REUBEN

So I started looking into fertility banks in the area...

MUGZI

And you think you can raise a Navajo baby?

CINDY

We really wanted our child to have a connection to the land. When we saw Mugzi's sample on the list...

REUBEN

Well that's why we wanted to meet with Mugzi. We don't know very much about the Diné, but we've had friends adopt from China and such. They've always taken time to understand the birthplace of the child so we thought we should do the same.

MUGZI

Well let's see that money, buddy!

(Reuben takes out his wallet and places $300 on the table. Mugzi takes a large swallow of his drink and counts the bills.)

MUGZI

First off, tribal enrollment is a tricky bitch. No one wants to see how the sheep gets butchered! But this system's been around... since... since time immemorial!

CINDY

Oh! Hold on, hold on!

(Cindy reaches into her bag and pulls out two legal pads, passing one to Reuben. They ready themselves, sitting in note-taking position.)

CAMPFIRE
(sighs)

I assume you two don't know much about the enrollment process. You know about treaties?

(pause)

MUGZI

The things Indians are always protesting about.

CINDY
(looking at Reuben)

Sounds like something we should have learned in law school.

CAMPFIRE

Treaties between the United States and tribes recognize us as sovereign nations to be dealt with like other nations.

MUGZI

His uncle's an attorney for the Choctaw.

CAMPFIRE

Well you understand that the U.S. was established around a system of laws, starting with the constitution. But Native nations – our beginnings don't start with the Constitution. We had our own laws before America and we still have different ones now.

MUGZI

It's the system that keeps out *fake* Indians!

CAMPFIRE
(to Mugzi)

Shut up.

MUGZI

t's true! Without blood quantum, all of these fuckin' "My grandma was a Cherokee princess" assholes would be coming out of the woodwork to enroll in a tribe. Our governments had to make up something that would make sure our members were real!

CAMPFIRE

Blood quantum is the system of measurement that the *U.S.* used to decide Indian identity. And it was created because of land rights and ownership, not keeping "fake" Indians out.

CINDY

Now, I did do *some* research on blood quantum and I thought the whole idea had roots in slavery – like how slaves used to be quantified by their skin color and features: Quadroons, Octaroons, Mulattos –

MUGZI

(sipping his beer)

Espressos, cappuccinos...

CAMPFIRE

Be serious. She's right: the English and Spanish were completely obsessed with blood and purity. And America adopted that system when politicians tried to claim Indian lands for the U.S.

MUGZI

(takes Campfire's beer)

You know what, if you get at all tipsy you're just going to start spouting more bullshit.

CAMPFIRE

But when Natives and Americans started intermarrying, the government couldn't decide whether mixed-bloods should be given citizenship because of their white heritage or denied because they were Native. They were Indian or citizen, but not both.

MUGZI

(now drinking Campfire's beer)

We never had a choice! That's what I'm sayin': fuck those fake Natives!

CAMPFIRE

That was back in the 1800s, Mugzi!

MUGZI

My great-great-grandparents would have said "fuck 'em," too! But in Navajo.

CAMPFIRE

Go ahead then! Why don't you tell Reuben and Cindy how Navajo would have decided membership back in the day.

MUGZI

The traditional way! Clanship!
(Standing up, he speaks to the audience.)
Navajos have their own system. Everyone has a clan that was passed down to them from their mother: your clan is your mom's clan, is her mom's clan, all the way back to Changing Woman, who created the first four clans. But now there are over ninety. And everyone has four clans when they introduce themselves: their clan, their dad's clan, their mom's dad, and their dad's dad. And that's how you tell who you're related to when you meet other Navajos. So when *you* have that baby, its clans will be Ma'ii tó, Coyote Springs, from me and Lok'aa' Diné, the Reed People, from my dad.
(pause)
And you're white so it'll be bilagáana and bilagáana: White people.

CAMPFIRE

Navajos eventually just got lazy makin' up clans for folks.

MUGZI

What do you know!

CAMPFIRE

White people have ancestry too!
(to Reuben and Cindy)
Where are you two from?

MUGZI:

(to Campfire)
He's bilagáana! *She's* bilagáana. They're *bilagáana.*

CAMPFIRE

You want to give some respect to the people who are going to be raising your blood? Or for all you care is this kid they're gonna raise just bilagáana and bilagáana?

MUGZI

No kid that comes from me is just bilagáana. They got roots in Tohaj on both sides.

CAMPFIRE

And now they got roots somewhere else too.
(silence)

MUGZI

...So where are your families from?

CINDY

Well my family is Dutch, but we're also French, English, Welsh, and I heard my great-grandmother was Scottish? But that was a long time ago. I'm fifth-generation American.

REUBEN

My grandparents emigrated from Poland during the Holocaust. But we're both pretty removed from our roots. There's a lot of mixing in my family. So we're both mutts.

(They chuckle.)

CAMPFIRE

When the government started recording tribal members on reservations, you either fell into white, black, or Native. Agents would record mixed-bloods as full-blood, light-skinned Natives as whites; sometimes Indians would be recorded as blacks and lose tribal status completely. Sometimes agents would go to a reservation and record everyone who showed up as a full-blood. The government decided that an "Indian" could only be registered in one tribe to keep track of the number of Indians in the country, so plenty of mixed-bloods had to pick which tribe to be enrolled in despite having multiple backgrounds. Sometimes one family could be enrolled in two or three different tribes just because members might visit another reservation and get registered in a tribe they weren't even a part of. The whole system is arbitrary! And when tribes started to take control over their membership, there were already records of documented members. So most of them just kept the system and determined membership by blood. So now *we're* obsessed with it.

CINDY

So does it even matter if we register the child?

MUGZI

If the kid is coming from my seed, it'll be Navajo. It should be registered.

REUBEN

Well how do we go about that? And what are some of the benefits of being registered?

MUGZI

...I don't really get tons of benefits from the Navajo Nation. Not like per cap or anything – no money from the casino.

CAMPFIRE

They have too many members for them to divvy up those funds. Not like those Pueblo tribes or some of the big casino tribes. Tribes that have money for members have to protect their funds or anyone with a sixteenth of Indian blood would try to get their paws on those handouts.

REUBEN

So what's the big deal with being registered?

MUGZI

It's just the principle of the matter.

CAMPFIRE

I will say that if being Native is important to your kid, being enrolled can go a long way in Indian Country.

MUGZI

It proves that my kid ain't a fake.

CAMPFIRE

Because they'll likely meet people like him.
(indicating to Mugzi)

CINDY
(to Mugzi)
What did it mean for you to grow up being Diné?

MUGZI

I just grew up in Tohaj all my life. Never not been around Navajo people. I guess I never really thought about it. My mom, she would take me to the Shiprock fair every year and sometimes we'd go to Yei bicheii dances. My dad was in and out: scene-by-scene kind of guy. He made me listen to a lot of country music. I never really thought or tried to be Navajo. I was around it all the time: going to ceremonies when they were happening, knowing the place where I was from. I mean, Navajos have a long-ass history of being on our land. I've just always been Navajo. When I go into the city, people see I'm different. They look at me funny. And I know I'm Navajo. So maybe it's that people see that I'm something else and I know who I am. Maybe that's what makes it. I've always been registered so I never even questioned it. My tribe says I'm a member. I say I'm a member. That's just who I am.

(The dinner party stands and Cindy and Reuben take the table off stage right. Campfire and a drunk Mugzi wander the streets of Santa Fe. Mugzi lights a cigarette and stalls their walking.)

CAMPFIRE

You're an asshole.

MUGZI

And you're the stick up my ass.

CAMPFIRE

That couple gave you a lot of money to talk to you about how to raise a Navajo kid and you just spit in their face, telling them that they can't do it.

MUGZI

They don't know what they're doing.

CAMPFIRE

That's why they invited you to dinner!

MUGZI

They should have thought about what it means to raise a Navajo baby before taking a sample.

CAMPFIRE

Your sample. *You* should have thought about what you were doing when you donated your sperm. That's *your* kid, Mugzi! Whether you like it or not. That couple don't have no Navajo blood in 'em. They're getting it from you.

MUGZI

They took it! They thought about my sample and they took it!

CAMPFIRE

Because it's your fault too! No one told you to walk into a sperm bank and jack off into a cup for anyone one in the world to use.

MUGZI

You'd think people would have some common sense before choosing a donor.

CAMPFIRE

You'd think some people would have some common sense before becoming a donor!

MUGZI

Are you jealous of me?

CAMPFIRE
What?

MUGZI
That's what this is! You're jealous that I happen to find a good opportunity that made me more money in a day than you've made this week.

CAMPFIRE
That's not what this is about and that's not true.

MUGZI
Here! Take some money! Take what you want!
*(Mugzi pulls out a wad of cash out of his pocket
and starts throwing it at Campfire.)*

CAMPFIRE
I don't want any of your damn money! I want you to be responsible for once!

MUGZI
How's this for responsible? This is for the rent! This is for gas! And this is so you can buy some more goddamned Cokes!

CAMPFIRE
Grow up! I'm tired of you giving shit away and telling us it's charity. You think you're doing that couple a favor by giving them your seed? You treat the whole thing like a joke. That kid's not gonna think it's funny when they don't know where they're from and don't know who their community is. And it's all because you're a fuck up jerk-off!

MUGZI
I'm a fuck up. My dad's a fuck up. And if this kid has so many problems it's because they're a fuck up, too! Guess it's just in my blood.

CAMPFIRE
You think this is all fun and games, but I'm tired of your crap. Keep your money. You can hitch your way back home. I'm not giving you any more advice about this mess you got yourself into.
(Campfire exits stage left, kicking some of the stray bills on his way out.)

MUGZI
Go ahead then! I can get home without you! I got two legs! I got four legs! I got nine lives and 300 bucks!

(Silence. Mugzi scurries to pick up the loose dollar bills. He sits, counting his money.)

MUGZI

This could have been the next house party. Or a road trip. This could have been money for my garden. Psssssh. He'll get over it. He'll swallow his pride and come back for me. I know you will!

(silence)

MUGZI

I know you will...

(Lights dim)

Mugzi continues to struggle with his identity and deal with the implications of his actions. Meanwhile, Tia learns that she has become pregnant with Ashkii's child and must decide whether to tell Dennis (and risk her stable life in Albuquerque) or be forced to keep the child's father (and, thus, its true blood quantum along with her ability to enroll it in the tribe) a secret.

ACT III, SCENE 3

(Nancy's house. Nancy, Rae, Mugzi, and Campfire are standing about the room with cups. A banner reading CONGRATULATIONS! hangs above the couch. Rae raises her cup to make a toast.)

RAE

Girl, everyone in this whole damn town always looked up to you. Everyone had the highest expectations for your life and we were all so excited to see what lay on your path and what came out of you. And now that you're having a baby and we're all *still* excited to see what comes out of you! You've always made us so proud. I know your baby's gonna do the same for you. To Tia and Dennis!

MUGZI and CAMPFIRE

Tia and Dennis!

(Nancy takes Dennis by the ear into the kitchen. Mugzi sits on the couch next to Tia as Rae and Campfire quietly exit.)

MUGZI

I got a lot of respect for you.

TIA

Respect? Why's that?

MUGZI

You're carrying around a baby!

TIA

You get to a certain age and you start thinking about all of this... Kids, the future. Hell, it's not even this age. I remember in first grade on the playground, all of the girls gossiped about which boy they were going to marry. When I started dating Ashkii, mom treated it like she had made it to the promised land. I swear, somewhere in the garage she has cradleboards for all of the children she expected me to have. I've just been... this thinking is bred into us. It's self-preservation. Literally, they treat us like we're the last of the bloodline. And it's worse when you are. Even if your parents tell you that you can fall in love with whoever you want, somewhere in your ear the past is whispering genocide.

MUGZI

Man, carrying a white baby gives you dark thoughts, huh? That's why I don't listen to the past, I just have to remember to look behind me all the time.

TIA

It's just something we always have to think about. When you're Native, falling in love is an act of revolution.

MUGZI

It's kinda funny – I always looked up to you in high school. You were always Tia-with-a-plan. Goin'-off-to-college Tia. I spent so much time just tryna get by. I didn't have no plans after graduation. I figured it would all work out. And still I ain't have no plan. Just bouncin' from couch to couch. Tryin' to figure out what I'm gonna do next.

(pause)

You know how many people from high school got kids now? Seems like almost everyone graduated and decided they were gonna be parents. Or ended up that way. So I didn't think too much about nothin' when I was down there at the sperm bank. Now here we are both about to be parents. I mean, you more than me. I'm just a donor. But I been thinkin' about it and, in a few months, there'll be a kid in the world with my blood, my DNA, and not know shit about where they're from. They'll be somewhere in New York, registered Navajo, but learning about Lady Liberty and eating bagels and lox. What's so Navajo about that?

TIA
They'll still have your blood.

MUGZI
I thought that was enough, too! But growing up away from Navajo? Who knows what they could end up like? Just think about how different Albuquerque is from Tóhajiléé. A kid from there don't understand about us – about where we're from. They're urban. Now think about a Native kid in New York. They're URBAN. That's a whole different type of Indian. Shit, I don't even know if Coyote stories travel that far.

TIA
Are you gonna try and adopt that kid away from the couple now?

MUGZI
No. I was just thinking that while my kid is growing up on hotdogs and baseball, you're gonna raise a bilagáana and they'll know more stories, more culture, more everything than my bloodline will ever understand. I don't mean to throw it around, I just been thinkin' about it. Because... well you know I'm more Navajo than you. And whatever kid those lawyers have from my sample has more claim to this culture and community. But they just won't know. Not without being from here. That kid still has my blood, my history, and this land in its DNA. That's gotta count for something. If they don't tell our stories, that's their fault. But if they don't have someone to teach them, that's on us. Somewhere, there'll be a Navajo who don't know their stories and don't know their history. And that's my fault. But your kid... They're not registered. Not even that Navajo anymore. But they'll have more culture than my kid can ever hope to learn. And that's just the way it is. I don't know how to think about this stuff anymore.

BLOODFLOW

by Reed Bobroff

I.
Your hair had notes
of honeysuckle and your
lips were supple as sand.
(Notice how the softest places
are those filled with blood.)
I have written red pages
and pages of wholehearted attempts
to say I love you
without sounding like everyone else.
I have odes to your armpits,
toes, cuticles, your taste
in roadtrip playlists, the days spent
engulfed in conversation—
your rose-tipped tongue
that paints sunsets on syllables
until we are late into the night
and forgot where we started.

II.
Born on the fringes
of my Certificate of Indian Blood,
My cousins would joke
that without a Navajo wife,
my veins would be dammed
up and my lineage would dry out.
I have grown up in a desert
all my life.
Like a gold miner,
I have been sifting through my body
for those pieces of Indian identity:
shiny flakes in a river
I can point to
as evidence that the work is worth
the grief.
All water is not the same.
Some rivers have gold
and some rivers have mud.
Sometimes there is mica in clay.

III.
I remember our fights soon after we held hands
in public
about whether I loved
you
or just the idea
of you.
How hard I fought
to convince you that my love wasn't
something clinical:
I wasn't enamored with what your body could do,
wasn't smitten with the stories we could pass
on to someone who looked like us—
who might have dark hair and skin and
my last name.
I did feel songs unravel
in my lungs and butterflies
dancing fancy shawl in my stomach

whenever you came near.
You wouldn't believe me
if I told you,
I donated my tribal enrollment at a blood drive.
Sitting in that doctor's office,
I told the nurse what clans to mark
down on my O Negative.
After 3 pints,
they told me I wouldn't be Navajo
for 24 hours
(until the blood cells regenerated)
so not to drink any excess of alcohol
or operate heavy machinery,
but that I could help myself to the orange juice and cookies.

IV.
For a full day,
I still wrote love poems.
I still felt dancing in my gut.
I'm still counting
the hours until I feel Navajo again.
I think the doctors may have lied
and missed some corn pollen
in my veins (not that there was much).
I'm still waiting to feel those songs and stories
get pumped back into me.
If I don't feel different without that blood
then I must have been searching for gold
in all the wrong places.

*"I cut myself into sixteen equal pieces,
keep thirteen and feed the other three to the dogs."*

– Sherman Alexie
Spokane–Couer d'Alene

Part 2

DECOLONIZING HISTORY

"The First Americans" courtesy of **Sam English**

VAMPIRE POLICY IS BLEEDING US DRY – BLOOD QUANTUMS, BE GONE!

By Suzan Shown Harjo

Native Peoples have the traditions, openness and patience that come from measuring time and possibilities against the entirety of our ancient cultural continuum. That's why we, collectively, have gotten so many things right – we have tried things out for myriad generations, incorporating those that work and discarding those that do not.

We like to observe something new from a distance and circle around it for a while. We don't hate or love the new thing – we just show it respect. It could be dangerous, like a rifle, a tool of destruction and of providence. It could be charming, like cut-glass beads, a good way of sharing a vision.

We may want to admire it from afar and we may want to invite it to our camp, either to stay as family or to come and go as a friend.

Oftentimes, decisions about societal incorporation have been forced upon us. Our ancestors did not get to make a leisurely decision about "civilization," for example. From 1880 to 1936, the federal government banned our traditional religions and made outlaws of our spiritual leaders. While American Indians were starving and eating rancid rations, the coffers of Christian denominations were fattened by annual congressional appropriations for civilizing the Indian. Children were taken to prison schools, parents were held hostage at home and no one had a choice in this new thing.

This new thing was a way for the white man to keep Indian land without keeping treaty promises. Some white men had a theory that went roughly this way: savages could be tamed and taught to be God-fearing and English-speaking at the government schools and their allegiances to their families and tribes would diminish. Cross-tribal and non-Indian alliances should be encouraged until Indians value pan-Indianness and white values.

The federal government calculated it would take three generations for American Indians to breed themselves out as tribal people. By 1900, the terms "full-bloods" and "half-breeds" were commonly used on reservations and in popular culture.

Eligibility for most federal Indian programs was made dependent on a quarter-degree-Indian-blood-quantum requirement. The idea was that the United States would continue to uphold treaty promises for health, education, land protection and the like, but only until the Indians were down to one-quarter Indian blood. At that point, the government could stop paying for their new lands, water, gold and silver.

In the 1930s, the BIA forced many tribes to codify this slow genocide policy in tribal constitutions, declaring that once their people were down to a certain level of tribal blood, they would cease being tribal citizens and Indian people. In the 1940s, the BIA made lists of those tribes whose people had low tribal blood quantums and few cultural attributes, who could be sent sailing down the mainstream, and of those whose people spoke their tribal language and practiced their traditional ways, who still needed the government to take care of them.

Congress, in the 1950s, started terminating ties with tribes whose people were the most deculturated. Some tribes even raised their blood-quantum requirements to one-half to escape being targeted for termination.

Now, the blood-quantum requirements are having exactly the pernicious effect on many Native Peoples they were intended to have. Lots of children and grandchildren of tribal citizens do not qualify for enrollment, because their parents and older ancestors married outside their nation. We are not talking about the pseudo-Indians who have zero Native ancestors or cultural ties. These are real Indian kids and many of them speak their language, practice their traditional religion, contribute to their nation and, in fact, are the future of their nation.

So, what federal laws are forcing us to keep these blood-quantum requirements? None.

In the mid-1970s, the Supreme Court ruled that no federal agency or any entity except an Indian tribe could determine who its people are. For even longer, the high court has held that Indian nationhood and tribal citizenry are political, not racial matters. If we cling to these blood standards, which are solely about race, some clever neo-terminationist is going to try to unravel the Indian political status doctrine by using the fixation on and fiction of tribal blood. (The BIA draculas make us particularly vulnerable in this regard by their continuing use of CDIBs – certificates of degree of Indian blood).

For the past 25 years, we have been free from any federally imposed standards for tribal citizenship. While some nations dropped the blood-quantum nonsense, most have not. This is an excellent (and sad) example of internalized oppression. We don't need the federal government to breed us out of existence – we are doing it ourselves.

I talked with some tribal leaders this year who do not know that tribes have had the power for a quarter of a century to drive a stake in our constitutions' vampire clauses. Some want to do it, but are worried about fakes flooding the tribal rolls and siphoning off precious tribal monies and benefits.

Native Peoples have traditional ways of defining citizenship, ways that worked for millennia before there were any non-Natives or pseudo-Indians in our countries. Those ways begin with family. If one or both parents are tribal citizens, frauds are automatically eliminated.

For those leaders whose nations have lost their traditional ways of deciding citizenship, there are more than 560 Native nations today with governmental relations with the United States. Ask a leader of one of those what kind of citizenship standards they have. Shop around – compare tribal citizenship requirements to those of France, India, China, Zimbabwe, South Africa, Mexico or the United States.

Blood quantums are not new things and they are not our things. We have circled them and been surrounded by them for more than a century, easily long enough to know that we do not respect them, need them or want them. Doing something about this is almost as easy as one, two, three – blood quantum, begone!

Acknowledgment

Previously published in *Indian Country Today*, February 14, 2001, http://indiancountrytodaymedianetwork.com/2001/02/14/vampire-policy-bleeding-us-dry-blood-quantums-be-gone-87119.

BLEEDING OUT: HISTORIES AND LEGACIES OF "INDIAN BLOOD"

by Doug Kiel

"It seems to me one of the ways of getting rid of the Indian question is just this of intermarriage, and the gradual fading out of Indian blood; the whole quality and character of the aborigine disappears, they lose all of the traditions of the race; there is no longer any occasion to maintain the tribal relations, and there is then every reason why they shall go and take their place as white people do everywhere."

– Senator Anthony C. Higgins (R–DE), 1895[1]

For three hundred years, between the seventeenth and nineteenth centuries, two paradigms for assessing Native personhood coexisted. One paradigm regarded Indianness as membership in an Indigenous community defined in terms of kinship and social relations. Another set of ideas, originating with the Spanish and gradually adopted by the French and English, emphasized inherited blood and purity of ancestry, as well as a nascent conception of race. These European ideas fostered a second paradigm that came to regard Indianness as a quantifiable attribute that could be computed on the basis of one's lineage or bloodline. By the twentieth century, blood quantum had become not only the predominant measure of Indianness, conceived in terms of race, but also the prime criterion for citizenship in a particular Indigenous nation. The incongruence between these paradigms has created some familiar but nonetheless strange situations.

Consider, for example, the case of Dr. Lillie Rosa Minoka-Hill. One of the best-known and most important figures of the Oneida Nation of Wisconsin during the twentieth century was not actually Oneida—at least not by blood or citizenship. Lillie was born in 1876, and her mother, from the Akwesasne (St. Regis) Mohawk reservation in New York State, died shortly afterward. A Quaker physician named Joshua Allen adopted Lillie and raised her away from her tribal community, and she eventually went on to enroll at the Women's Medical College of Pennsylvania. In 1899 she became the second Native woman to earn a medical degree. Not long after, Lillie met an Oneida man from Wisconsin, Charles Hill, who had attended the Indian Industrial School in Carlisle, Pennsylvania. Lillie and Charles fell in love, and in 1905 they married. Lillie went to live with Charles on his farm on the Oneida reservation in Wisconsin, where they raised six children in the Native community that she called home for most of her life, but she never became a formal tribal citizen.[2]

Dr. Hill, as most Oneidas called her, practiced medicine in the community for decades. In 1916, Charles died suddenly. That same year, the sole Oneida physician on the reservation, Josiah Powless, left to serve in World War I, where he would die just five days before the armistice that ended the war. In Charles's absence, Hill earned a living to support her family by filling the void that Powless had left. Oneidas throughout the reservation sought medical services in her "kitchen clinic," often paying in barter when harsh economic conditions left them without money. In 1947, the Oneida Nation's executive committee recognized Hill's service to the community by adopting her as an honorary member of the Oneida Nation. They gave her the name "Youdagent," meaning "She Who Carries Aid." At last she was a member of the community—sort of.[3]

The community recognized Hill's membership on social and cultural levels, but the constraints of blood quantum (which disqualifies from citizenship anyone who does not possess a minimum degree of tribal-specific blood) and enrollment policy barred her from political citizenship. Although she was a descendant of the Mohawk Nation – "older brother" to the Oneida Nation in the Haudenosaunee (Iroquois) Confederacy – and although she had spent most of her life on the Oneida Reservation prior to being adopted and also married an Oneida man, Hill could only become an *honorary* member. She could neither vote at tribal meetings nor hold an elected position. The nation that her children and grandchildren would one day lead did not—*could* not—fully recognize her as an Oneida person because she did not meet the blood quantum criterion.

Dr. Hill's story, in short, embodies one of the paradoxes of blood quantum that all of Indian Country lives with to the present day: even an Indigenous person married in and adopted from a related community cannot gain political rights within her new community. Vexing as it is, the notion of "Indian blood" (and even community-specific blood) is entangled with Indigenous life and nationhood as a result of settler colonial domination. Despite the many ways in which academic and popular discourse about race has gradually shifted away from biology and toward understanding race as a social construct, biological notions of race (and even racial registration) remain rigidly in place in Native America. Blood quantum is a colonial invention with oppressive intent and effect, yet it has also offered a source of solidarity for some Native people. This chapter aims to make some sense of what is largely not sensible by demonstrating how conceptions of Indigenous belonging have historically been more fluid than the rigid system of blood quantum permits, and by describing some of the consequences of the continued reliance on blood quantum as a measure of citizenship.

Blood as Symbol and Practice

The idea that the proportion of community-specific "Indian blood" in a person's veins determines her or his tribal citizenship and claims to cultural membership and legitimacy is so widespread and familiar that it has become common sense. To understand blood quantum and its historical origins, one must ask certain fundamental questions: Of all the potential tools for determining membership and citizenship, why blood? Anthropologist Janet Carsten's work, for instance, serves as a powerful reminder that blood carries with it a symbolic value and effect. As she notes, blood "is visually striking, it can be seen inside and outside the body – both routinely and in exceptionally dramatic circumstances – and it can be obviously associated with life or life's cessation."[4] Sociologist Karen E. Fields and historian Barbara J. Fields further note that blood "can consecrate and purify; it can also be profane and pollute. It can define a community and police the borders thereof."[5]

But thinking more broadly, if relation is to be marked by the physical transmission of substance between bodies, why blood? Why is the immutable substance of kin not signified by saliva, sexual fluids, breast milk, or even organ transplants? Why should kinship be signified by any bodily fluid or by the body at all? What of, for instance, place of birth, or landscape and language, which anthropologist Keith Basso has so beautifully explored as the root of Western Apache being? Indeed, the coupling of blood and nationhood is by no means natural. Blood only carries social meaning as a medium through which inheritance is transmitted because it has been assigned this meaning, whose roots are ancient in Western thought.[6]

The idea of "pure" Christian blood, along with certificates documenting such purity, emerges from the Spanish Inquisition and anxieties about the contaminating effects of Jewish and Muslim blood. As historian María Elena Martínez notes, "by the middle of the sixteenth century, the ideology of purity of blood had produced a Spanish society obsessed with genealogy."[7] The Spanish imported these obsessions to their first settlements in North America, and over the course of two centuries the distinction between Christian and non-Christian blood gradually morphed into ideas of immutable racial difference. Blood quantum eventually became the US federal bureaucracy's preferred instrument for determining who was entitled to an allotment of reservation land under the Dawes Act of 1887, a policy that President Theodore Roosevelt hailed during his 1901 State of the Union address as "a mighty pulverizing engine to break up the tribal mass."[8] The blood quantum standard was, by most scholarly estimations, a product of colonial pseudoscience that joined ideas about biological substance with Victorian typologies of social evolution. In essence, racialization was a mechanism that could accelerate the disappearance of Indigenous peoples. If there is one problem that plagues all of Indian Country, it is the prospect of shrinking tribal enrollments due to a blood quantum system that frames Native communities as isolated racial groups first and sovereign nations second. Blood quantum figures as a peculiar schema of authenticity, a set of social practices and interventions that is policed not only by legal institutions of the state, but also by Indigenous nations themselves. Blood quantum, however, undermines the authority of tribes, as sovereign nations, to grant citizenship to individuals regardless of their ancestry.

The effects of the adoption of blood quantum as a measure of Indianness are hard to overstate. Native being became distilled in a biological identity. Once a fluid, open-ended concept defined primarily by cultural participation and embeddedness in kinship relations, being Native became less and less flexible as it came to be defined by the immutable properties of blood. Reliance on blood quantum to determine tribal membership has often resulted in arbitrary forms of exclusion. Like Dr. Hill, someone who belongs to an Indigenous nation socially and culturally may be denied the full political rights of citizenship because of their biological heritage. This was not always the case. Native identities were in fact fluid and porous before blood quantum became the predominant criterion – and they remain so, whether this is fully admitted or not. The blood quantum system is not broken, however. It is doing exactly what it was intended to do: reinforce binaries.

Histories beyond Blood: Adoption, Performance, and Symbol

The blood quantum policy brought an end to fluid forms of incorporation for members of different Indigenous nations and hardened the division between Native and non-Native. The famous story of Eunice Williams's adoption in the eighteenth century reminds us that even European settlers had once been incorporated into Haudenosaunee communities. Eunice was born into a prominent New England family. She counted among her kin the influential Puritan ministers Increase Mather and his son, Cotton Mather. In the winter of 1704, Mohawk warriors from Kahnawake, near Montreal (along with additional French and Native forces), raided an English frontier settlement at Deerfield, Massachusetts, taking young Eunice and more than one hundred others captive. She served as a replacement child for a grieving Mohawk woman who had lost one of her own. Despite later having the opportunity to return to her biological family and community of origin, Eunice chose to remain in Kahnawake, living most of her nearly ninety years as a Mohawk Catholic.[9]

Eunice Williams's case is by no means unique. Frances Slocum (or Maconaquah), born into a Quaker family in Pennsylvania, was also taken captive as a child. She lived her life as a Miami woman and raised Miami children. Like Eunice, she chose to remain in her adoptive community. In fact, when many Miamis were removed from Indiana to the Kansas Territory in the 1840s, Slocum successfully petitioned Congress for exemption from removal, and she, along with twenty-one of her relatives, remained in Indiana.[10]

The stories of Dr. Hill, Eunice Williams, and Frances Slocum highlight the dramatic shift in ideas of Indigenous belonging, race, and kinship that occurred between the eighteenth and twentieth centuries. For Williams in the eighteenth century, blood did not present a barrier to her assimilation into the Kahnawake community, where she gained full standing, including clan membership. A century later, Slocum used her whiteness to shield a village from removal, though half a century after that, the Miamis of Indiana would lose recognition as a tribe. Fifty years later, Hill was limited to honorary Oneida membership because she lacked Oneida blood. These seismic shifts point to the expanding significance of blood as the key criterion of tribal membership and collective recognition between the eighteenth and twentieth centuries.

Native American history provides a multiplicity of examples – far beyond stories of captive whites – that highlight the contingent nature of Indigenous identity over time. In some cases, granting Native identity to outsiders served a strategic purpose. Native communities routinely assimilated non-Native people to secure military alliances and economic partnerships and often positioned people of mixed blood as cultural brokers in diplomatic situations.[11]

Sometimes, in addition to conferring Native identity on Europeans, Natives themselves assumed a European identity. In French Louisiana, prior to the crystallization of rigidly biological notions of race in the mid-eighteenth century, a Native woman could become "Frenchified" – that is, legally recognized as French by colonial authorities. In such cases, conceptions of identity and belonging were closely associated with material culture and lifestyle. As historian Sophie White notes in *Wild Frenchmen and Frenchified Indians*, "For an Indian woman, wearing a French-style gown was a defining act when the woman in question was an Illinois convert to Catholicism, sacramentally married to a French husband and living within a French colonial village."[12] This ability to effectively "put on" Frenchness by donning a garment points to the fluid and socially constructed nature of identity in French Louisiana. As White indicates, identity was temporary, reversible, and performed on a daily basis in part through the act of dressing. Moreover, assuming a new identity was not necessarily a one-way process of colonial assimilation: according to White, just as "Indians had the potential to be converted and 'civilized,' the French could themselves be transformed as a result of their physical presence in the territory they sought to colonize."[13]

To be sure, racial ideology did exist in eighteenth-century Louisiana, and support for Frenchification would gradually lose ground to notions of inherent Indigenous difference based on skin color and transmitted through blood, a difference that could not be neutralized simply by wearing laundered linen.[14] Nonetheless, as White argues, "how Indian wives of Frenchmen and children of Frenchmen in the Illinois Country practiced Catholicism, how they furnished their homes, and how they deployed dress . . . influenced how colonists in Upper Louisiana interpreted ethnicity and race."[15] The co-existence of malleable indigeneity and Frenchness alongside emergent ideas of race indicates that identity formation was not a simple binary process in which European cultural influence eroded "pure" Indigenous authenticity.[16]

A shift toward understanding identity based on skin color, however, would cement racial categories. Nonetheless, Native people did not receive racial ideology passively. They maintained some degree of agency in the process. As Nancy Shoemaker highlights, the marker of "red people" originated within southeastern Native communities (particularly Cherokees) and their own color symbolism; it was English colonists who later applied it as a generic label for Native people. In the early eighteenth century, as the English abandoned older binaries between Christians and "pagans" in favor of language that positioned whiteness in relation to blackness, Native people responded by calling themselves "red." In the symbolism of the Indigenous Southeast, red and white were opposites, and as Shoemaker notes, "metaphors for moieties, or complementary divisions, within southeast societies."[17] Elsewhere, "red" carried different significance. Houmas in Louisiana and Chakchiumas in Mississippi took their names from the red crawfish in their creation stories, while the Meskwakis in the Great Lakes region called themselves "red earths" in reference to their own creation story. Although "red" did not have a fixed meaning, as Shoemaker explains,

> By the end of the [eighteenth] century, the color-based categories that grew out of Cherokee color symbolism had become racial categories because the Cherokees described the origins of difference as being innate, the product of separate creations, and they spoke of skin color as if it were a meaningful index of difference. But they persistently molded what race meant to fit particular contexts.[18]

Over the course of the eighteenth century, a Cherokee articulation of difference grounded in color symbolism would come to serve as a marker of race, transforming into an instrument of systematic Indigenous oppression under the hegemony of white Americans.

Creating Legal Indians

Throughout the nineteenth century, the US courts, Congress, and Indian affairs bureaucracy each sought to define who was and was not an Indian and tribal member; Indian blood became an increasingly common measure of legal recognition. Racially classifying people by degrees of blood was, of course, not a nineteenth-century invention, as is evidenced by earlier Spanish notions of purity of descent. The Southern Colonies defined the rights of mixed-ancestry people at least as early as 1705, declaring some individuals ineligible to marry whites, hold public office, or testify in court depending upon their amount of Indian or black blood, or rather, their proximity to perceived Indianness or blackness.[19] The federal government drew on such precedents in colonial law to position Indian blood as marking one's relationship to the US state in order to determine civil and criminal jurisdiction, in addition to eligibility for treaty payments and other material entitlements.

The federal criteria associated with recognition as a tribal member during the nineteenth century were inconsistent, to say the least. In 1879, for instance, the US District Court for the Western District of Arkansas applied a rule of patrilineal descent in *Ex Parte Reynolds*. The case involved two Euro-American men, Reynolds and Puryear, both of whom had married into the Choctaw Nation. Reynolds, the defendant, had been accused of murdering Puryear. Reynolds's attorney argued that both men had become naturalized citizens of the Choctaw Nation, thus the Western District of Arkansas lacked jurisdiction, and Reynolds should be tried in a Choctaw tribunal as stipulated in Article 38 of the 1866 treaty with the Choctaw and Chickasaw Nations, which stated:

> Every white person who, having married a Choctaw or Chickasaw, resides in the said Choctaw or Chickasaw Nation, or who has been adopted by the legislative authorities, is to be deemed a member of said nation, and shall be subject to the laws of the Choctaw and Chickasaw Nations according to his domicile, and to prosecution and trial before their tribunals, and to punishment according to their laws in all respects as though he was a native Choctaw or Chickasaw.[20]

For the Choctaw Nation to have jurisdiction in this matter, both Reynolds and Puryear would have to be Choctaw citizens, which would depend on both of their wives possessing such citizenship. So, the court asked, "were the wives of Reynolds and Puryear Choctaw Indians?" The court noted that Mrs. Puryear's paternal grandfather was a white US citizen from Mississippi, and on the basis of her "blood," and citing "natural law," determined that she inherited the status of her father and grandfather, and was thus not a Choctaw citizen. In this decision, the federal court invalidated a Choctaw woman's tribal citizenship for the purpose of extending jurisdiction over the Euro-American man who murdered her husband.[21]

Ex Parte Reynolds points to several important features of Native racial status. First, it operates differently from the "one-drop rule" of African American hypodescent, according to which individuals of mixed ancestry only inherit the status of their black kin, with "African blood" polluting all other types of blood. According to the US court that determined Mrs. Puryear's status, "white blood" has the capacity to fully absorb "Indian blood." In this particular instance, denying Mrs. Puryear recognition as a Choctaw citizen on the basis of a white paternal grandfather was a direct affront to the jurisdiction of the Choctaw Nation's legal authority. What makes *Ex Parte Reynolds* even more curious is that throughout the nineteenth century, federal authorities granted or denied individuals recognition as Indian according to wildly inconsistent criteria. As legal scholar Paul Spruhan notes, if tribal communities recognized individuals of mixed or non-Native ancestry as tribal members, federal authorities tended to as well. On the other hand, federal authorities might recognize mixed-ancestry people as Indian because of their mothers, and sometimes their fathers. In other cases, place of residence became a determining factor, and at times anthropologists were called upon to assess Indianness on the basis of physical features. In *Ex Parte Reynolds* itself, the court raised the following questions:

> Does the quantum of Indian blood in the veins of the party determine the fact as to whether such party is of the white or Indian race? If so, how much Indian blood does it take to make an Indian, or how much white blood to make a person a member of the body politic known as American citizens? Where do we find any rule on the subject which makes the quantum of blood the standard of nationality? Certainly not from the statute law of the United States; nor is it to be found in the common law.[22]

Examining *Ex Parte Reynolds* alongside inconsistent federal criteria throughout the nineteenth century demonstrates that within US legal frameworks, the notion of Indian blood could be deployed either to position an individual as an Indian ward of the federal government or to deny their indigeneity to undermine the authority of Indigenous nations. Indian blood was a flexible tool of domination.[23]

It was not until the Indian Reorganization Act of 1934 that the federal government formulated a standard for determining who would be recognized as Indian:

> All persons of Indian descent who are members of any recognized Indian tribe now under Federal jurisdiction, and all persons who are descendants of such members who were, on June 1, 1934, residing within the present boundaries of any Indian reservation, and shall further include persons of one-half or more Indian blood.[24]

For the federal government's purposes, a clear definition of tribal membership was essential to ensure the proper distribution of federal resources to Indigenous wards. One of the sponsors of the act, Senator Burton K. Wheeler of Montana, expressed his concerns about setting a federal benchmark at anything less than one-half Indian blood, lest Indigenous people seeking welfare overwhelm the government:

> I do not think the government of the United States should go out there and take a lot of Indians in that are quarter bloods and take them in under [the Indian Reorganization Act]. If they are Indians in the half blood then the government should perhaps take them in, but not unless they are. If you pass it to where they are quarter blood Indians you are going to have all kinds of people coming in and claiming they are quarter blood Indians and want to be put on the government rolls, and in my judgment it should not be done. What we are trying to do is get rid of the Indian problem rather than add to it.[25]

Senator Wheeler's suggestion that defining Indigenous status by blood offers a way to "get rid of the Indian problem" is perfectly candid. Blood quantum was invented and imposed as part of a colonial project designed to subvert the sovereignty of Indigenous nations. The construction of indigeneity as a racial category based on degree of blood is a fiction that helps to sustain white supremacy and normalizes disregard for Native nations as legitimate sovereigns. In its practical implementation through the Dawes Act (1887) and Indian Reorganization Act (1934), blood quantum served the aim of dispossessing Native peoples by limiting the number of individuals who could claim Indigenous identity.[26] Enforcing a strict biological definition of "Native" reduces the number of Native people who demand individual and collective rights, seek continued recognition of treaties, and serve as a reminder that the United States still exists in a state of colonial domination.

Contemporary Dilemmas

Historical examples of the construction of Native identity by Indigenous peoples as well as colonial powers have profound implications for the present. They demonstrate that blood is no more natural a factor than language and material culture in determining cultural transmission and markers of belonging. Yet blood quantum has so thoroughly permeated ideas of race and citizenship in Indian Country that even the most common alternative to the blood quantum system – enrollment by lineal descent – largely adheres to the same racial logic.[27] The Cherokee Nation, for example, grants citizenship based not on degree of Cherokee blood but on the ability to prove biological descent from an individual listed as Cherokee by blood on the Dawes Rolls generated in the late nineteenth century. Importantly, this reckoning excludes thousands of Cherokee Freedmen, the descendants of African slaves whose history within Cherokee society traces back to the late eighteenth and nineteenth centuries.[28] Configuring identity on the basis of descendance recycles the concept of indigeneity as biology and posits that sociocultural belonging in Indian Country – along with ties and claims to Indigenous lands – is on some level transmitted genetically.

In some cases, a biological concept of indigeneity couples with the erasure of matriarchal traditions and their replacement with imposed patriarchal structures to create new problems. A sufficient degree of "Indian blood" flowing through one's veins is not necessarily enough to claim membership in some communities. For some tribes, one must receive that blood from the right parent. The 1978 US Supreme Court case *Santa Clara Pueblo v. Martinez* highlighted an enrollment policy that denied citizenship to the children of female tribal members who married outside the tribe, even though the same policy granted citizenship to the children of male members who married out. Similarly, Mohawk women who have married non-Natives are routinely expelled from the Kahnawake community near Montreal, and their children can likewise be denied citizenship – even in cases where they have been raised in the community.[29]

When tribes whose enrollment practices adhere solely to the logic of blood descent refuse citizenship to members within their communities, they effectively perpetuate the federal government's use of blood quantum to fight a war of attrition against Indigenous nations. According to the colonial logic of the federal bureaucracy, "Indian" as a racial category can be gradually eliminated.[30] Broadening citizenship requirements to include standards that extend beyond blood quantum would be a step toward reversing the attrition of Indigenous nations, while emphasizing the sovereign powers to naturalize whomever they choose.

Why do Indigenous nations hesitate to take that step? Are Native communities willingly participating in injustice? How can we explain the persistence of blood quantum as a mechanism for determining tribal membership in a way that does not shame or blame the colonized? Critics of blood quantum such as Joanne Barker have pointed out that the practice indirectly works to destroy Indigenous nations by creating a dilemma of identity: Native nations must either racialize themselves or risk losing recognition as "authentic" Indians.[31] This colonial double bind leaves Indigenous communities to exemplify notions of authenticity that are not entirely of their making, yet have become central to Native self-identity. This painful situation is exacerbated by the fact that the system of racial registration – along with the unscientific notion that race and purity even exist as biological realities – is a remnant from an era of eugenics and theories of white racial superiority.[32]

Ultimately, the perpetuation of blood quantum systems in Indian Country emerges from a historically grounded sense of peril – a persistent worry that the only way to preserve the sovereign powers of Indigenous nations is to present Indigenous communities in a way that appears most authentically Native to non-Native people. Indeed, Native people are not paranoid or pessimistic to worry that their collective rights may be extinguished if they no longer qualify as "real" Indians.[33] And "real" Indians, in the popular imagination, are scarce. It is also important to remember that the US Congress maintains plenary power over Indian affairs – that is, the US Supreme Court decided in 1903 that Congress has the authority to abrogate treaties with Indian nations, dissolve reservation lands, or even terminate federal recognition at will.[34] Moreover, there is a long history of Euro-Americans "playing Indian" – that is, self-identifying as Indigenous without recognition from Native communities themselves – as well as the deployment of genetic science as a tool to reframe Native Americans as recent arrivals, making them less entitled to indigenous land.[35] Native communities use blood quantum to draw a bright-line distinction between tribal citizens and individuals who would appropriate an Indigenous identity for their own gain, unfortunately cutting out kin the process.

To reject blood quantum as the sole measure of belonging is to decolonize Native communities' own sense of Indigenous personhood and nationhood. Yet the high stakes associated with blood quantum make it a problem that cannot be approached with a one-size-fits-all solution. It is for each tribal community to navigate its own route through the treacherous shoals of ceaseless, unrepentant colonialism rooted in law and expectation. Some scholars, such as Glen Coulthard, have called for rejecting the very rubric of recognition; others have argued for a conception of peoplehood that is not rooted in blood, but instead originates through common bonds of language, sacred history, place, and ceremonial cycles.[36] The latter position poses a new set of problems for those who live with the legacies of assimilation and no longer speak their Indigenous languages or participate in ceremonial life, or who, like the vast majority of Native people (78 percent according to the 2010 census), live beyond their reservation territory.[37] After all, stripping Native people of their relationships to their Indigenous land and epistemologies has been a precise goal of forced assimilation. Lumbee historian Malinda Maynor Lowery has offered a more inclusive vision of peoplehood: "A People can encompass different names, bloods, residences, and ideologies; a People need not be biologically or culturally homogeneous. A People can become a nation when it exercises self-determination, when it engages its members' identities to create change in their society."[38]

Conclusion

By today's standards, many of the most celebrated individuals in Native American history would not be considered citizens of the tribes that continue to honor them. Even quite recently, the US Supreme Court has remained fixated on questions of Indian blood. In *Adoptive Couple v. Baby Girl* – a

2013 case about the adoption of a Cherokee child into a non-Native family – US Supreme Court Justice Samuel Alito opened the majority opinion by stating, "This case is about a little girl (Baby Girl) who is classified as an Indian because she is 1.2% (3/256) Cherokee."[39] Alito's decision was focused primarily upon percentage of blood rather than nationality, flattening all of the rich complexity of indigeneity and Native nationhood into a simplistic, one-dimensional calculus of blood.[40] Under the logic of blood quantum, the answer to a deeply complicated question such as "Who carries the burden of Indigenous history and intergenerational trauma?" is seemingly a simple matter of determining shared bodily matter. The body does matter in Native history, in a variety of ways that extend far beyond the limited notion of blood quantum. After all, racially marked Indigenous bodies have been the targets of state violence. They have been enslaved, displaced, murdered, raped, brutalized in boarding schools, forcibly sterilized, and disproportionately incarcerated as bodies that look, sound, and in some imaginations even smell Indian. The violence of racialization, however, has sometimes been reproduced within Indigenous nations themselves, as evidenced by the disenrollment of black Cherokees. So long as blood quantum alone confers citizenship, Indian Country will remain bound to an enrollment system that reifies biological categories that were originally founded upon the hierarchical presumption of white supremacy.

Notes

1. 27 Cong. Rec. 2614, quoted in Paul Spruhan, "A Legal History of Blood Quantum in Federal Indian Law to 1935," *South Dakota Law Review* 51 (2006): 32, fn 263.

2. The following is the most thorough account of Dr. Hill's life: Roberta Jean Hill, "Dr. Lillie Rosa Minoka-Hill: Mohawk Woman Physician" (PhD diss., University of Minnesota, 1998).

3. Hill, "Dr. Lillie Rosa Minoka-Hill," 426–427; "Oneidas to Adopt Doctor Who Tended Them 40 Years: Tribe to Fete Mohawk Woman Today," *Milwaukee Sentinel*, November 27, 1947, 12.

4. Janet Carsten, "Substance and Relationality: Blood in Contexts," *Annual Review of Anthropology* 40 (2011): 24.

5. Karen E. Fields and Barbara J. Fields, *Racecraft: The Soul of Inequality in American Life* (Brooklyn: Verso Books, 2012), 51.

6. Melissa Meyer, *Thicker Than Water: The Origins of Blood as Symbol and Ritual* (New York: Routledge, 2005).

7. María Elena Martínez, *Genealogical Fictions: Limpieza De Sangre, Religion, and Gender in Colonial Mexico* (Stanford: Stanford University Press, 2008), 1.

8. Theodore Roosevelt, "First Annual Message: December 3, 1901," *American Presidency Project*, http://www.presidency.ucsb.edu/ws/index.php?pid=29542.

9. For sources on the Deerfield raid and Eunice Williams' life, see the following: John Demos, *The Unredeemed Captive: A Family Story from Early America* (New York: Alfred A. Knopf, 1994); Evan Haefeli and Kevin Sweeney, *Captors and Captives: The 1704 French and Indian Raid on Deerfield* (Amherst: University of Massachusetts Press, 2003); Audra Simpson, "From White into Red: Captivity Narratives as Alchemies of Race and Citizenship," *American Quarterly* 60 (2008): 251–257. Eunice's grandson, Eleazer Williams, played an important role in facilitating the relocation of many Oneidas from New York to Wisconsin during the 1820s. See Michael Leroy Oberg, *Professional Indian: The American Odyssey of Eleazer Williams* (Philadelphia: University of Pennsylvania Press, 2015).

10. Susan Sleeper-Smith, *Indian Women and French Men: Rethinking Cultural Encounter in the Western Great Lakes* (Amherst: University of Massachusetts Press, 2001), 116–141.

11. See in particular Richard White, *The Middle Ground: Indians, Empires, and Republics in the Great Lakes Region, 1650–1815* (New York: Cambridge University Press, 1991); James F. Brooks, *Captives and Cousins: Slavery, Kinship, and Community in the Southwest Borderlands* (Chapel Hill: University of North Carolina Press, 2002); Lucy Eldersveld Murphy, *Great Lakes Creoles: A French-Indian Community on the Northern Borderlands, Prairie du Chien, 1750–1860* (New York: Cambridge University Press, 2014); Ann McGrath, *Illicit Love: Interracial Sex and Marriage in the United States and Australia* (Lincoln: University of Nebraska Press, 2015); Claudio Saunt, *A New Order of Things: Property, Power, and the Transformation of the Creek Indians, 1733–1816* (New York: Cambridge University Press, 1999).

12. Sophie White, *Wild Frenchmen and Frenchified Indians: Material Culture and Race in Colonial Louisiana* (Philadelphia: University of Pennsylvania Press, 2014), 5.

13. Ibid., 6.

14. Ibid., 7, 11, 19.

15. Ibid., 12.

16. For additional sources on race and performance, see Joshua David Bellin and Laura L. Mielke, eds., *Native Acts: Indian Performance, 1603–1832* (Lincoln: University of Nebraska Press, 2011); David J. Silverman, *Red Brethren: The Brothertown and Stockbridge Indians and the Problem of Race in Early America* (Ithaca, NY: Cornell University Press, 2010); Claudio Saunt, *Black, White, and Indian: Race and the Unmaking of an American Family* (New York: Oxford University Press, 2005).

17. Nancy Shoemaker, "How Indians Got to Be Red," *American Historical Review* 102 (1997): 632.

18. Ibid., 643.

19. Spruhan, "A Legal History of Blood Quantum," 4–5.

20. "Treaty with the Choctaw and Chickasaw, 1866," in Charles J. Kappler, ed., *Indian Affairs: Laws and Treaties, Vol. II: Treaties* (Washington, DC: Government Printing Office, 1904).

21. *Ex Parte Reynolds*, 20 F. Cas. 582 (C.C.W.D. Ark. 1879).

22. Ibid.

23. For legal histories of Indigenous racialization, see Bethany R. Berger, "'Power Over This Unfortunate Race': Race, Politics, and Indian Law in *United States V. Rogers*," *William and Mary Law Review* 45 (2004): 1957–2052; Bethany R. Berger, "Red: Racism and the American Indian," *UCLA Law Review* 56 (2009): 591–656.

24. *Indian Reorganization Act*, 73d Congress, Sess. II, ch. 576, 48 Stat. 988, § 19.

25. Quoted in Paul Spruhan, "A Legal History of Blood Quantum in Federal Indian Law to 1935," *South Dakota Law Review* 51 (2006): 46, fn 414. For similar reasons, the Hawaiian Homes Commission Act (HHCA) of 1921 set Native Hawaiian blood quantum at 50 percent, see J. Kēhaulani Kauanui, *Hawaiian Blood: Colonialism and the Politics of Sovereignty and Indigeneity* (Durham, NC: Duke University Press, 2008).

26. Barker, *Native Acts*, 3–6.

27. For an examination of one tribal community's adoption of enrollment by lineal descent, see Jill Doerfler, *Those Who Belong: Identity, Family, Blood, and Citizenship among the White Earth Anishinaabeg* (Lansing: Michigan State University Press, 2015).

28. On the disenrollment of the Cherokee Freedmen, see the following: Jodi A. Byrd, "'Been to the Nation, Lord, But I Couldn't Stay There': American Indian Sovereignty, Cherokee Freedmen and the Incommensurability of the Internal," *Interventions: The International Journal of Postcolonial Studies* 13 (2011): 31–52; Circe Sturm, *Blood Politics: Race, Culture, and Identity in the Cherokee Nation of Oklahoma* (Berkeley: University of California Press, 2002). See also, Tiya Miles, *Ties That Bind: The Story of an Afro-Cherokee Family in Slavery and Freedom* (Berkeley: University of California Press, 2005).

29. On *Santa Clara Pueblo v. Martinez* (1978), see Joanne Barker, *Native Acts: Law, Recognition, and Cultural Authenticity* (Durham, NC: Duke University Press, 2011), 98–145. For more about Kahnawake and enrollment, see *Club Native*, directed by Tracey Deer (Montreal: Rezolution Pictures, 2008); Audra Simpson, *Mohawk Interruptus: Political Life Across the Borders of Settler States* (Durham, NC: Duke University Press, 2014).

30. Patrick Wolfe, "Settler Colonialism and the Elimination of the Native," *Journal of Genocide Research* 8 (2006): 387–409. 31. Joanne Barker, *Native Acts: Law, Recognition, and Cultural Authenticity* (Durham, NC: Duke University Press, 2011). See also, Paige Raibmon, *Authentic Indians: Episodes of Encounter from the Late-Nineteenth-Century Northwest Coast* (Durham, NC: Duke University Press, 2005); Jessica Cattelino, "The Double Bind of American Indian Need-Based Sovereignty," *Cultural Anthropology*, Vol. 25, No. 2 (2010), 235–262.

32. In particular, see Robert Wald Sussman, *The Myth of Race: The Troubling Persistence of an Unscientific Idea* (Cambridge, MA: Harvard University Press, 2014).

33. For examinations of Indigenous recognition struggles as a result of mixed race, see the following: Brian Klopotek, *Recognition Odysseys: Indigeneity, Race, and Federal Tribal Recognition Policy in Three Louisiana Indian Communities* (Durham, NC: Duke University Press,

2011); Arica Coleman, *That the Blood Stay Pure: African Americans, Native Americans, and the Predicament of Race and Identity in Virginia* (Bloomington: Indiana University Press, 2013).

34. The basis of plenary power is *Lone Wolf v. Hitchcock*, 187 U.S. 553 (1903).

35. For sources on non-Natives appropriating Indigenous identities, see Philip J. Deloria, *Playing Indian* (New Haven, CT: Yale University Press, 1998) and Circe Sturm, *Becoming Indian: The Struggle over Cherokee Identity in the Twenty-first Century* (Santa Fe, NM: School for Advanced Research Press, 2010). On the use of genetic science, see Kim TallBear, *Native American DNA: Tribal Belonging and the False Promise of Genetic Science* (Minneapolis: University of Minnesota Press, 2013).

36. Glen Sean Coulthard, *Red Skins, White Masks: Rejecting the Colonial Politics of Recognition* (Minneapolis: University of Minnesota Press, 2014); Tom Holm, J. Diane Pearson, and Ben Chavis, "Peoplehood: A Model for the Extension of Sovereignty in American Indian Studies," *Wicazo Sa Review* 18 (2003): 7–24.

37. The 2010 US Census figures report 22% of "American Indians and Alaska Natives, alone or in combination, who lived in American Indian areas or Alaska Native Village Statistical Areas in 2010. These American Indian areas include federal American Indian reservations and/or off-reservation trust lands, Oklahoma tribal statistical areas, tribal designated statistical areas, state American Indian reservations, and state designated American Indian statistical areas." "American Indian and Alaska Native Heritage Month: November 2012," accessed July 8, 2016, https://www.census.gov/newsroom/releases/archives/facts_for_features_special_editions/cb12-ff22.html.

38. Malinda Maynor Lowery, *Lumbee Indians in the Jim Crow South: Race, Identity, and the Making of a Nation* (Chapel Hill: University of North Carolina Press, 2010), 254.

39. *Adoptive Couple v. Baby Girl*, 133 S. Ct. 2552, 570 U.S., 186 L. Ed. 2d 729 (2013).

40. For more on the complex components of indigeneity, see Pamela D. Palmater, *Beyond Blood: Rethinking Indigenous Identity* (Saskatoon, SK: Purich Publishing, 2011).

DECOLONIZING COLONIAL CONSTRUCTIONS OF INDIGENOUS IDENTITY: A CONVERSATION BETWEEN DEBRA HARRY AND LEONIE PIHAMA

by Debra Harry and Leonie Pihama

Debra Harry (Kooyooe Dukaddo/Numu) and Leonie Pihama (Te Ātiawa, Ngāti Māhanga, Ngā Māhanga a Tairi) have worked together for the past fifteen years on a range issues, including issues of biocolonialism and the impact of genetic engineering on Indigenous Peoples. To contribute to this publication, Debra and Leonie met in 2015 and discussed a need to have a conversation about identity and the ways in which colonial constructions of identity such a blood quantum need to be viewed in the wider context of colonial invasion and subjugation of Indigenous Nations. What follows is a transcription of that conversation.

Debra: In our language, we refer to ourselves as Numu, or The People, and that is further defined by our regional localities, and our major foods. For instance, I am Kooyooe Dukaddo, or a kooyooe-eater, a fish endemic to Kooyooe Pah (Pyramid Lake in Nevada). What we know is that any time there was contact with the colonizers, they sought to claim and rename our world through discovery. This included the implementation of a federal process to reorganize our traditional governance system, label [us] as tribes with elected tribal councils, define who can be a member of our nations, and ultimately to rename the individuals themselves with English names. It is the ultimate in intrusion into our very being. Central to the colonial project was a process to redefine our people through assumptions about pedigree using labels such as "full-blooded" or "half-breed." Over a century later, we see these colonial vestiges still being used to define our very identities.

As you know, it is an old standard here in the context of US federal policy, instituted through the Indian Reorganization Act of 1934. For most tribes, this act replaced traditional forms of governance with elected tribal governments through a boilerplate constitution and bylaws. An aspect of this act includes criteria for determining tribal membership based on notions of blood quantum. It's clearly developed as an assimilationist strategy designed to diminish the number of individuals who can claim citizenship with a particular tribe. It is an extremely problematic methodology for determining membership on many fronts. It assumes an individual, beginning at an arbitrary point in time, is 100% of a particular tribe. If their child has a non-member parent, the child is considered to have a 50% blood quantum. If that individual has a child with a non-member, their child is considered to have only 25% blood quantum. So for many Native Peoples in Turtle Island, once an individual falls below the 25% or other established threshold, they are no longer consider[ed] eligible for membership or citizenship. If you follow the strategy to its intended conclusion, in as little as three generations it is possible for Indigenous individuals to be denied an opportunity to be a recognized member or citizen of their nation.

Leonie: I think that by way of introduction, it is important to note that prior to the invasion of our lands we always identified ourselves by our *whānau* (extended family of at least three generations), *hapū* (subtribal group) and *iwi* (tribal groupings). The term *Māori* actually means "pure" or "normal." So our *tūpuna* (ancestors) chose to use a term that highlighted the centrality of our positioning in these lands and which identified us collectively as being of here. We did not see ourselves as "other" to anyone, in the way that the colonizers viewed us, we saw ourselves as the norm. The naming of the colonial immigrants that came here as *Pākehā* (white people) was also a way by which to identify those white people who came from elsewhere. So we have always named ourselves in ways that affirm our Indigeneity as *Tangata Whenua* (People of the Land). What we see, however, with *Pākehā* definitions is a constant marginalisation of our people, and a reductionist approach that is based on removing both us and our rights as Indigenous Peoples.

There is a whole range of legislation that sought to define Māori. In some contexts they said "Native," in other documents they referred to "Aboriginal Inhabitant," and in others "Māori." In the early writings and colonial documents the implication was that they were referring to what were considered a *"full-blooded"* Māori person. If that was not the case, then they would further define the individual by adding comments such as "that would include half-castes and their descendants by natives." So historically, if we look back to the early legislation there were many references to Aboriginal Natives or Aboriginal Inhabitants. So those kinds of definitions go back to the early 1800's and I expect that they probably learnt that they needed to do that quite early from what they did on Turtle Island and other continents that were invaded by our colonizers.

Debra: Historically, federal policy to determine who is Indigenous goes back to those first counts of our people during the early wars and Indian Agent period in the latter half of the 1800's. It was a military process in which they needed to count, and name, our people and place them on reservations, or in prisons/forts, or to forcibly remove them to some remote reservation. These initial lists are called base rolls and create the baseline for subsequent membership or citizenship determinations. The individuals on the initial base rolls are artificially considered to be full-blooded or 100% of a particular tribe. However, these base rolls were created during the time of intense wars and conflict. Our people had been subjected to capture by the military, others had to flee to other locations, some were forcibly removed to remote localities. These base rolls are based on an arbitrary process of issuing our people a number, a new name (because they couldn't understand our real names in our own languages), and an identity. It fails to take into consideration that our peoples have always been fluid, and we moved about, traded, and intermingled with other tribes throughout our history.

Leonie: There were a range of attempts early on to do population counts, and then in the Census Act in 1877 it was noted that the census did not apply to Māori, and that Māori was defined as *"any person of the ab-*

original native race, and includes half-caste persons of that race living as members of any tribe." So very early on you have people talking about Māori of pure descent or half-caste. That was a dominant way of referring to Māori up to the 1970's. I remember as a child being asked if I was half-caste or quarter-caste. It was so entrenched that people would refer to themselves as a 1/8th or 1/16th. It was a fragmentation of identity. Making our people think in terms of fractions, where we become a part person. It is a means by which colonization works to make us less and less human, less Indigenous. It works its way to a point of making us invisible. Colonial processes of fragmenting our identity, our Indigenous identity and replacing it with a lesser version of themselves. That is connected directly to the denial of our fundamental rights. To deny everything about us, to deny our existence.

Debra: In the initial descriptions, that's how they were describing you as Māori?

Leonie: In terms of defining for the registration of births and deaths in 1858 our people were not included; however, it did note that *"Half Castes and other persons of Mixed Race, living as members of any Native tribe, shall, for the purposes of this Act, be deemed to be persons of the Native Race."* In the Qualification of Electors Act in 1879, Māori was defined as *"an original habitant of New Zealand includes any half-caste living as a member of a native tribe according to their customs and usages and any descendants of such a half-caste by a Māori woman,"* so consistently there's a notion of a "pure" Māori and then there's a notion of a "half-caste," and at the end is the added qualifiers of a descendant of a half-caste by a Māori woman, which is an example of how notions of race and gender intersect at different times in terms of colonial definitions of who we are.

In terms of the census it was really around being "half-blood" Māori; i.e., "half-caste" or "pure." Added to the quantum definitions we also saw that when it suited the colonial regime to affirm their patriarchy, then they would also define Māori in terms of gender hierarchies. This was the case in the 1867 where Māori in that act was defined as a "male aboriginal native inhabitant of New Zealand of the age of twenty-one years and upwards and shall include half-castes." The intersection of race and gender is seen through a number of acts, including in terms of education where the establishment of Native Schools was dependent on agreement of a majority of *"male adult native inhabitants."*

In 1953 The Māori Affairs Act noted "Māori" means "…a person belonging to the aboriginal race of New Zealand; and includes a half-caste and a person intermediate in blood between half-castes and persons of pure descent from that race." So it wasn't that long ago, up until the Māori Community Development Act 1962, which then defined Māori as "*a person of the Māori race of New Zealand; and includes any descendant of such a person.*" This was then further embedded in the Māori Affairs Act 1974, by which time there was a clear movement from a racial blood quantum, blood degree definition to a definition of ethnicity and self-definition.

Debra: So much of these identity politics are shaped by federal policy, and how the federal government wants us to define ourselves. Those early racist and arbitrary policies instituted in the late 1800's and early 1900's are still being carried out today, insidiously integrated into tribal membership policies that we now implement for and against ourselves. These determinations of who is or is not a member or citizen are based on these false constructs.

Leonie: In Aotearoa (referred to as New Zealand), now it's by *whakapapa* (ancestral lines) and self-identification alongside that, or some would say ethnicity. But I guess that's the thing around the renaming ourselves when we think about the title of this discussion. Renaming is actually about a return to our own naming, of our own selves, our own identity as *whānau, hapū, iwi, Māori. Māori* is a generic term used to identify us collectively and I see that we use it as a unifying term. One of the things we talk a lot about in the work we do is the term *Māori* itself. It is a term that is used to collectivize and it has certain things about that that work for us and certain things that don't. We have been cautioned in the past by elders to be aware of how the colonizer strategizes both through fragmentation and also through seeking to universalise our identity so that our iwi identities are subsumed by a national one. That is something that I hear across Indigenous Peoples. That we are also iwi and nations and tribes and we have a distinctiveness that comes with where we come from and from our historical experiences and languages. The definitions in the early legislation and census are about the term *Māori*, and it was not until much more recently that adding your iwi was included, which has been an outcome of our people asserting our definitions of identity.

Debra: The movement to reclaim our right [to] use our original names has gained momentum here on Great Turtle Island, as well. Many Indigenous Nations have reclaimed their original nation names in their own languages and tossed the colonial mislabel to the wayside. The process of renaming also extends to our homelands because almost no aspect of our homelands have escaped colonial definition. Our mountains, valleys, lakes, waterways, now carry colonial labels. Many Indigenous Nations have also worked hard to reclaim the original names of our homelands. One thing I've always been impressed with as I've traveled in Aotearoa is the fact that so much of your homelands have Māori names. If you understand a bit of the language it is possible to see that the Māori names transmit a deep knowledge and special features of the place. That is true for our people as well. Our names for place carry special meaning and need to be reclaimed and used so our children will carry that knowledge forward. So how would you define the relationship between the *iwi* level as compared to any definition advanced at the government level?

Leonie: In a contemporary sense our people still tend to, in daily interactions, adhere more to our traditional ways of introducing ourselves. So we will often ask *"nō hea koe?"* which is "where do you belong?" That is a very Māori way of engaging people and understanding our relationships. So I will say things such as *"ko Taranaki te maunga, ko Waitara te awa, ko Te Ātiawa te iwi, ko Ngāti Rāhiri te hapū,"* which is *"Taranaki is the mountain, Waitara the river, Te Ātiawa the tribe, Ngāti Rāhiri the subtribe."* Immediately people know who I am through their knowledge of those connections. So whakapapa, for me, remains the most appropriate way by which to identify ourselves. Whakapapa is often defined as genealogy but it is more than that. Western genealogy is very reductionist, in the same way that contemporary science of DNA as identity is reductionist. Western genealogy is based on a dualistic structure of the colonial nuclear heterosexist family unit, and so using that as a defining way of who we are then positions us in a colonial structure again. *Whakapapa* means to have layers. So it is as broad and deep as we determine. It is enabling of multiple relationships and acknowledges those relationships across generations. So for example, all of the female members of my generation are my children's *whaea* (aunties) and my grandchildren's *kuia* (grandmothers). *Whakapapa* also links our connections to *Papatūānuku* (Earth parent) and *Ranginui* (Sky parent), to all living things that we share this planet with and to all of our wider Indigenous relations.

In a contemporary context now we find *iwi* are having people register if they wish to access resources that are held by the *iwi* organizations.

With my *iwi*, you need to give at least three or four generations back in terms of your *whakapapa* link, and then generally they will have someone within the *iwi* who know *whakapapa* lines and they will affirm or otherwise your connections.

Debra: Well, obviously just the very act of creating those initial head counts and rolls [is] just riddled with colonial ideology because first of all they assume the power to rename our people. They impose their patriarchal ideologies upon us by organizing family units by male heads of household, despite the fact that most Indigenous societies are traditionally matrilineal. Our family relationships are also much broader than the so-called nuclear family. Our *Numu* relationships are very similar to what you describe for Māori. While we differentiate maternal and paternal lines, I am either a mother, auntie, or grandmother to all of our family's children, not just my own. Western genealogies makes reference to cousins, but in our way, they are also brothers and sisters. So you can see that our definition of family includes multiple layers of relationship, each playing an important role in the well-being of each family member. The patriarchal restructuring and renaming ultimately carries over to matters relating to how we relate to the natural world. The natural world becomes reframed in terms of resources and property. It is the imposition of a domination framework based on the doctrine of discovery.

The doctrine of discovery is based on European beliefs that Indigenous peoples are uncivilized, non-Christian pagans, and childlike in nature, to justify the genocide, slavery, and taking of the lands and territories of Indigenous Peoples throughout the Americas, the Pacific, Asia, and Africa. In the US, these racist beliefs are unjustly embedded in federal law and policy, primarily through the Marshall Trilogy. Since they consider Indigenous people to be wards of the government, they claim dominion over us, and extend this domination to determine our very identities. This includes how we determine our citizenry, who has ties to our traditional territories, and who has entitlements to social and governmental services such as housing, educational grants, or other social services. It has now developed into a complex network of reservation-based politics, economic, and social organization based on federal mandate. We've been living within and under that construct for decades now, and most people have not questioned its origins because the status quo seems normal. Our original nations now have tribal constitutions, bylaws, and membership codes. Some tribes still determine their citizenry and membership using the false construct of blood quantum. Others have developed other policies based on some form of lineal descendancy.

Leonie: Part of the issue in terms of how things are constructed in terms of being able to register onto an *iwi* role is actually determined by the process of seeking redress in regards to our treaty rights. So, there is a government-imposed process of mandating, processes of registering numbers of tribal members, *iwi* members, processes of democracy in terms of one person vote, government structures, who gets elected on, how they get elected that's all predetermined in the treaty settlement process. So we can't really separate out this notion of quantum or notion of identity from those imposed processes that are embedded within the system of treaty settlements, because if *iwi* don't appear to be providing the mandate or the votes or whatever that the governments have determined is required in the process, they won't settle with them. So here you have the colonial oppressors who are using their system and supposedly working to some kind of resolution on treaty claims, but actually the whole mechanism is put in place that means that the counting has to be done, the individual registrations have to be done, all those processes that we now see that iwi are doing have become a part of what the government has determined as required to be in the claim process.

Then on top of that we are still living with the consequences of the early colonial constructions of identity in terms of their race ideas and their gendered ideas and all those things they brought with them. They fragmented Māori communities in the beginning in terms of how we understood ourselves, then there is the whole way in which they defined us through legislation, and it continues on to this day where they continue to define how we should be identifying ourselves and how we should be grouping ourselves and how we should be governing ourselves and how we should be breathing the air that we breathe.

In terms of historical event[s] such as those constructions of the "doctrine of discovery" and how colonial imperialism created and utilised that as the means to legitimate genocidal acts against Indigenous Peoples, then clearly that is the basis for these systems that came to our lands. We have monuments in Aotearoa that speak of *"soothing the pillow of a dying race."* So the imposition of ways of defining us through blood quantum was another colonial assimilation tool to remove those generations that did survive and continue to live as Indigenous Nations. I see the notion of defining people by blood as to whether or not we are

Indigenous as a part of the longer-term genocidal act as a way of ensuring that in time there will be no one able to legally define as Indigenous, define as Māori, or define as Native, and that's one of those intentions of notions of blood quantum or degrees of blood, half-caste, quarter-caste.

Debra: It is definitely masterminded as an assimilation tool to ultimately fractionate us out of existence once and for all. This is a biological weapon, similar to what was done in eugenics in which they try to breed out the so-called "bad blood."

Leonie: The eugenics intention was really clear here too in the early 1800's, the seeking to breed us out to deny our existence. In terms of a medical field it was really about ensuring that we didn't survive as a population of people. That too is another part of the definition of what constitutes genocide, which is to deny rights to children having children. So can you clarify the ways in which blood quantum link[s] to the wider issues of biocolonialism, and in particular how genetic testing is utilised in the process and the issues with that.

Debra: They are two very different processes that are used for determining identity. Blood quantum looks at your degree of descendancy and tribal affiliation numerically, based on intergenerational relationship to a specific ancestor. DNA analysis requires a comparative analysis of genetic markers against some baseline DNA sample or samples. They both have the same problem in that the determinations and assumptions made about the identity of the baseline sample(s) are based on arbitrary constructs. Additionally, not all markers are known in terms [t]hat are considered Native American markers. There can be contamination of DNA samples, and false positives and negative results depending on what kind of genetic analysis is being done. Finally, we know that tribes are political, social, and cultural constructs, and are not distinct biological units. So genetic analysis has no useful role in determining matters related to Indigenous identity.

These are false constructs because there is no such thing as [a] full-blood person because the very nature of human beings is to have relationships with each other. So unless you can get go back to the beginning of time, it is completely arbitrary to say this ancestor is a full-blood representative of any group and everybody measures their degree of Indigenousness against that arbitrary standard. So we can assume that our people have had a continuous presence here for many thousands of years. What we don't know is how much genetic exchange with other peoples took place over the course of our human history. Culturally, we were/are 100% *Numu*, but any assertion of pure biology is pure assumption.

We need [to] ask ourselves why are we playing out this script over and over again against ourselves, against our future generations, harming our own people, and our own future well-being? A bit of critical analysis community by community, nation by nation, will help us decide that we are not doing this anymore. It is not conducive to who we are as people, and where we want to be in the next seven generations and beyond.

Leonie: The other term that I have heard more and more is "mixed-blood." It's disturbing to me that our people continue to define and be defined through ideas of blood or caste. How do you separate blood? Who else does this to themselves, talks about themselves as fractions and then denies other people like them who have less fractions than them? So our colonizers don't refer to themselves in fragments, they only refer to us in that way, and that kind of fractionalization and fragmentation of not only us as people but us in ourselves. People would come and they'd say, *"Oh well I'm half-caste"* or *"I'm part Māori,"* and I would say, *"Well which part? Is it your right leg, your left leg? Or which half, because if you are going into a Māori hui which half do you leave outside?"* Often they then see how ridiculous that kind of definition is. But those kind of ideas are so deeply embedded and ingrained and it's reproduced in each generation through a whole range of mechanisms. And until we see this is not healthy, that its fundamental intention is to eradicate us, then we will continue to have debates within our communities about who is or is not a part of our people. Those ways of seeing ourselves are biological reductionism that does not affirm our ancestral lines, but rather those terms are about watering down our *whakapapa*.

Debra: Absolutely, and people are using it against each other. It is not uncommon to hear our own folks describe themselves or their relatives as being full-blood or mixed-blood. We have internalized these terms and concepts and use them to describe ourselves. Fortunately, not all Indigenous Nations are using blood quantum as their means of determining their citizenry. Most nations use some form of descendancy, but we shouldn't forget that many Indigenous Peoples have historical and cultural processes of adoption. The determination of tribal membership is considered an internal matter, and tribes can use whatever processes and criteria that are appropriate to them.

Indigenous peoples have a right to determine their own citizenship based on their right of self-determination. If you look at the Martinez Cobo's definition of who is an Indigenous Person, he describes it as a twofold process: that an individual may choose to self-identify as Indigenous, but the group that they claim to belong to must also recognize them as one of their members. I'm not advocating his criteria, as there are some problematic aspects [there]. For instance, he says that Indigenous Peoples are non-dominant sectors of the society in which they live. Does that mean that you will always have to be in a state of domination to be Indigenous?

Leonie: So one of the things in the blood quantum discussion is that often it overrides us being able to talk about those *iwi* or nations who don't buy into that. You know, the tribes that don't use that mechanism because the focus becomes on that, on blood quantum, but as you are saying, there is a whole range of nations that don't use those colonial definitions in terms of how they define themselves. And you have talked about the differences in Turtle Island and also the differences between the ideas of membership and citizenship. Can you share a bit about that here?

Debra: I would say that I am a citizen of my nation which acknowledges its nationhood, and my nation recognizes me as a contributing citizen of the nation. A nation is defined as a people with a common heritage, common language, common history, who see themselves as linked culturally, socially, and politically. Membership sounds like a club. It is easy to forget that we are the original, free, and independent nations of this land when we adopt such demeaning terminology.

Leonie: Notions of citizenship and membership and how they are used [are] really interesting. We have seen an increasing use of terms here such as "tribal beneficiaries," and that means that you are able to receive the benefits from the tribe. Terms like that add another layer of identifying our people, but they are very limited and located within a very economic capitalist manner. Beneficiaries here, in terms of the government, are those that are receiving some form of state assistance such as the "unemployment benefit." It's a very kind of economic capitalist frame to define people as "beneficiaries" and not as citizens of your nation.

Debra: Some of the current settlements are doing the same here and using the settlement process as a means to forever quiet any future claims to lands and resources. The net effect is that those inherent and prior rights as nations become usurped and abandoned in exchange for the benefits offered in the settlement.

Leonie: Yes, we have some similar issues. Then we have also some great initiatives that are challenging daily these colonial constructs that have been imposed upon our people. We have language revitalisation initiatives such as *Te Kōhanga Reo* (Māori Language Nests) and *Kura Kaupapa Māori* (Māori Language Immersion schools), Māori radio, and Māori Television. We see a generation of young people emerging with a powerful sense of who they are and who constantly challenge the dominant deficit thinking. So a part of the decolonizing project for us has always been about questioning the power relationships both in terms of cultural and structural inequalities and pushing back to regenerate our own ways of defining ourselves. A part of that is the resurgence of *whānau, hapū*, and *iwi* identities that sit with our collective Māori identities. Where we can come together collective[ly] for the well-being of all and simultaneously protect and enhance our *iwi* ways of being. That is very exciting. And those are little wins that we have, little victories in the bigger movement of *tino rangatiratanga*, of regaining our sovereignty. So we have to challenge those things that limit us and that reposition us into a colonial frame, we have to challenge the colonizers and we have to challenge our own internalization and the hegemony of those things. Graham Smith has always advocated that we celebrate the small victories along the way, and so we can do that, we can celebrate our *tamariki* (children) and *mokopuna* (grandchildren) who now carry ancestral names and bring those ways of being back to this and future generations. And having a conversation like this together is really important. So that we can work together on the struggle and also share together those transformative ways of being.

Debra: There is some great work and thinking going on in the Indigenous world. There are both Indigenous strongholds that are protecting and perpetuating our original laws and lifeways, and there is amazing work going on to decolonize our worlds. I think about the Indigenous Nations that travel on their own passports. Or the Indigenous Nations that intellectually, spiritually, and culturally define themselves as a nation. They hold an unwavering belief in themselves as nations, and that informs the nature of the development they do for their peoples. It is possible to break out of that tribal membership colonial framework. Like anything else, if you inherited a system that wasn't designed by you, then the first challenge is to think critically about that system: Where did it come from? What was its purpose? Who designed it? Who does it benefit? I think that is the starting point for Indigenous People who want engage in the process of decolonizing our constructions of Indigenous identity. We have to reclaim our right to name ourselves. Most Indigenous People know this intellectually, but it also takes deliberate action to deconstruct from the colonial framework that has become so invasive in our lives, and I think that's the biggest challenge.

RACE AND SOVEREIGNTY

by Julia Coates

In March 2007, the citizens of the Cherokee Nation voted for a proposed constitutional amendment to limit citizenship to those who are able to demonstrate descent by Indian "blood," a vote which impacted about 2,800 newly incorporated descendants of freedmen. Only a couple of months earlier, the Cherokee Nation established several "satellite" organizations in California, the state that contains the most citizens of the Cherokee Nation outside of Oklahoma. Although the formation of these new satellite organizations had been planned for some time, and although their "kickoff" events were intended as membership drives rather than political forums, given the timing of the upcoming referendum, freedmen descendants from a family that resided in Compton appeared at all four of the southern California events, seeking to speak and make their case to the crowds of Cherokee Nation citizens in attendance.

Some of the statements of Cherokee history made by the freedmen descendants at these events evidenced many of the popular misconceptions that researchers of the deep history know to be incorrect. As an instructor of Cherokee history for many years, I was afterward questioned by one of the family members about the amount of time given to the specific history of the freedmen in the course I teach. But in addition, as part of their challenge to me, I was asked what gave me the right to be calling myself Cherokee, questioned on the point of my blood quantum, and ultimately asked, as it was worded by a young man of the family, "Why do white people get to be Cherokees and black people don't?"

It was clearly futile given the heightened emotions of the moment to debate the intricacies of Cherokee identity at that time. But the questions he posed brought into sharp focus the divergence in understandings of race and identity construction, both in Native America and in the United States today, that lead to the different perceptions of the current issue of the inclusion of freedmen descendants into citizenship in the Cherokee Nation. One perspective believes that the "exclusion" of the descendants of freedmen is based in racism. This perspective understands "race" in popularly held American conceptions as primarily about skin color, and thus it is a perspective that is easily grasped by American media and the American public. America understands the acceptance of whites and the denial of blacks in the historic context of the United States, hence the perception that "whites get to be Cherokees while blacks cannot" resonates as racist.

Cherokee voters, however, likely had a different perception of what they were voting on, and didn't see it as a matter of race, but rather of more complex historic, cultural, and traditional components that have often come into play as the Cherokee Nation and its citizens have navigated determinations of who is and is not a Cherokee. Identity construction and the contests around it are not new issues for the Cherokee people and government, and seen in the light of the Cherokees' specific history, the 2007 vote was fairly consistent with historic patterns of determining identity, and the way race has (or has not) played into those patterns over the past three centuries since intensive contact with Europeans and Americans. Americans, American media, and American lawmakers have little knowledge of this specific history, of course. In addressing some of the most prevalent misconceptions around this issue that have been spread by both the media and some academics, I will draw on the historical outlines of how Cherokee identities have been constructed over the past two centuries and how race has factored in – or not. It is not intended to take a position on the question of the inclusion or exclusion of freedmen into the citizenry of the Cherokee Nation but rather to enlighten as to how and why many of the Cherokee people understand the issue differently from Americans, as well as most of the freedmen descendants. My hope is that in doing so the subject will acquire not only more depth but also a more balanced presentation of the issue that includes additional Cherokee perspectives that have not been prominent thus far in the media or scholarly work.

Misconception #1: *The freedmen descendants have been citizens of the Cherokee Nation throughout the 20th century and were disenfranchised by the 2007 vote.*

Commonly misunderstood by the media and others as a vote that "disenfranchised" freedmen descendants from citizenship that had been continuously exercised since the 1866 Treaty, the 2,800 who are currently citizens of the Cherokee Nation had in fact been citizens of the Nation for only about nine months at the time the constitutional amendment was voted. Previous to that time, they had not voted in 20th-century tribal elections and had not been eligible for tribal benefits. That brief period of citizenship had come after a ruling by the Cherokee Nation Judicial Appeals Tribunal, the highest tribal court, that the language of the 1975 Cherokee Constitution was too ambiguous to specifically deny citizenship to freedmen descendants. Contrary to popular rhetoric, the Cherokee court did not state that the descendants of freedmen should be incorporated, only that it was a matter that the Cherokees needed to clarify, and until they did, there was no legal basis to deny the petitions.

After the ruling in July 2006, an aggressive registration effort began in which the citizenship applications of freedmen descendants were moved to the top of the pile as ordered by the court. Applicants who were Cherokees by blood, often children whose parents were registering them for the first time, typically waited about 9 to 12 months for their applications to be approved. But freedmen descendants were now seeing theirs approved in record time, often a matter of weeks. The Cherokee Nation government, under the leadership of Principal Chief Chad Smith, did not resist the order of its highest court, nor did it appeal to a federal court, which would have severely compromised Cherokee Nation sovereignty in the view of the Smith administration. Instead it moved immediately to effect the tribal court's order, even as a citizen petition drive was implemented (which was their constitutional right) to resolve the constitutional ambiguity with the addition of clarifying language. In its prompt adherence to the court order, as well as the implementation of a citizen petition, the Cherokee Nation actually demonstrated its long-held self-image as a people who created and abide by their own legal structures.

Historical Background: In the early 1800s, the Cherokee Nation offered a nationalistic response to federal encroachment. Throughout the 1810s and '20s, a system of courts, laws, and ultimately, a constitution were established. Having been militarily overwhelmed during the major wars of the 1700s, the Cherokees began to think that a legal and political resistance might be more effective. Adapting the legal processes of the American nation was seen by the Cherokees as a way to meet, and hopefully prevail against their greatest adversary on terms that adversary would understand and respect. As a new nation, the United States, was proclaimed and developing in front of them, some Cherokees seemed to wonder why the Cherokee Nation could not assert the same kind of national status. Beginning in the 1790s, the language of "nation" began to appear in Cherokee treaties and a more centralized governing system began to emerge. Continuing throughout the next 40 years, the Cherokees engaged in an entirely self-directed process of significant governmental reform. The change to written statute and constitutional government was opposed at first by traditionalists, and instances of rebellion and internal violence occurred in the 1810s and early 1820s. But by the 1820s, a remarkable coalition of traditionalists and more acculturated members of the national political body strategized together to develop effective governmental reforms for countering US power and asserting their own sovereign authority.

Out of their burgeoning sense of nationality, the Cherokee Nation insisted that it would set the criteria for a new political category – "citizen." A series of written statutes was passed by the Cherokee National Council that defined criteria for political citizenship. Intermarried whites were incorporated as citizens only so long as the marriage lasted, or if there were children of the marriage, in the case of the death of the Cherokee spouse. In short, the citizenship of outsiders depended on familial relationship to Cherokee(s) by blood. Intermarriage with blacks was prohibited by Cherokee law, and the children of any such intermarriages were not recognized as citizens. Some interpret this simply as Cherokees adopting American racism. But others suspect[1] more complex motivations and believe the anti-miscegenation statutes reflected a strategic Cherokee maneuver in a time when "free persons of color" laws prohibited landholding by blacks and Indians in the southern states originally occupied by the Cherokees. At the time, the Cherokees were fighting to keep their lands and did not want to be categorically associated with landless blacks. This is an ugly pragmatism, but it is not necessarily racist. Nevertheless, Cherokee land was lost and the nation was removed to the Indian Territory in 1838–39.

In February 1863, midway through the Civil War, the Cherokee Nation, a society in which slaveholding had been legally allowed, emulated the United States and passed an Emancipation Proclamation freeing any slaves who were held by Cherokee slave owners and outlawing slavery forevermore in the Cherokee Nation. But the proclamation also stated that the "freedmen," as they would now be called, were not to be incorporated into Cherokee citizenship. This was likely because they did not conform to the familial requirements long established in Cherokee law for incorporation of outsiders: the majority of freedmen were not spouses or parents of Cherokees by blood, nor did they themselves have Cherokee parentage.

In 1866, after the conclusion of the Civil War, the Cherokee Nation entered into a treaty with the United States that reestablished the federal relationship the Cherokees were desperate to secure, since they had broken it after being militarily cornered by the Confederates. The Cherokee Nation in 1863 had quickly repudiated the Confederate treaty it had made 16 months earlier as a means of strategic political survival. But in 1866 the United States treated the Cherokee Nation as though it had been an enemy combatant and insisted that curtailments of Cherokee sovereignty be included in the treaty made that year. One imposition in Article 9 of the treaty overrode the Cherokees' own determinations about freedmen citizenship made three years earlier, and insisted that the Nation must include freedmen as citizens, a right that for some time, the United States did not even grant to southern blacks under its own government. Again, in their reverence for law and having entered into this treaty, the Cherokees brought their constitution into conformity with the treaty by passing an amendment that extended citizenship to freedmen and their descendants.

Nevertheless, Cherokees chafed under the imposition and resisted equitable inclusion of the freedmen for decades afterward. Was this an exercise of racism on their part, or was it their resistance to the incursion on their sovereignty to set their own citizenship criteria? Or both? This question is, and always will be, open to interpretation. We weren't there; we can't know for certain. But we can be certain that racism is not the only possible explanation for Cherokee resistance to freedmen citizenship, even in the late 1800s.

No one disputes that the freedmen were constitutionally citizens in the late 1800s, but did they legally continue to hold Cherokee citizenship throughout the 20th century? Although the arguments are riddled with complexity, this is still the fundamental legal question in front of the federal court today.

Misconception #2: *The Cherokees are breaking a treaty.*

Although the recent federal and tribal court cases have twisted into the extremely complicated minutiae of law, there are still fundamental positions that can be generally understood. One has been prominent in media and academic circles: in voting the 2007 constitutional amendment, the Cherokees are breaking a treaty. Period.

This is the fundamental argument of the freedmen descendants, and on the surface it seems self-evident. Article 9 of the 1866 Treaty indeed sets out parameters under which freedmen will be acknowledged as having all the rights of Native-born citizens of the Cherokee Nation. The argument seems very straightforward, at least to the public and many academics.

The public has little awareness of the legal counterarguments, and so it may be difficult to comprehend how, thus far, the Cherokee Nation has actually been the prevailing party in the federal legal cases. The 2006 decision by the three-person Cherokee court was not the first case filed by freedmen descendants. In fact, lawsuits had been filed for almost 30 years beginning in 1979, first in federal courts, and then in tribal courts after their reestablishment in 1988. In perhaps half a dozen such suits, the legal arguments of the freedmen descendants have never succeeded, not even in 2006 when the Cherokee court decided the constitutional language was too ambiguous. The federal courts had always taken a decidedly hands-off perspective on tribal sovereignty, essentially declaring that this was a matter for the Cherokee Nation to determine. Governments get to set their own citizenship criteria, the courts effectively stated, and the Cherokee Nation was no different.

Historical Background: There is a counterargument that rests in the crevices of federal law, but those crevices have had tremendous impact on the sovereignty of the Cherokee Nation nevertheless. First, although there is a provision in the 1866 Treaty that seems to grant citizenship to the freedmen, there is also a US Supreme Court decision from 1870, informally known as the Cherokee Tobacco case, that gives Congress the ability to strip specific provisions from treaties. All Congress has to do is pass a contradictory law and voilà! – the treaty provision is nullified. One argument is that Congress did exactly that in 1906 when it passed the Five Tribes Act, a law that contained a specific provision for the legal and political continuance of the Five "Civilized" Tribes, even as it included another counterintuitive provision stating that the citizens on the Dawes Rolls would be the last citizens of those governments. The argument is that by passing this law, Congress itself nullified the treaty right guaranteeing freedmen citizenship. Only after the piecemeal restorations of political sovereignty that occurred in the late 20th century could anyone be considered citizens of these Five Tribes. Those tribes have set the criteria themselves that usually did not include the descendants of freedmen, but they were not in violation of a treaty as any citizenship rights represented a restoration to citizens after the abrogation of citizenship by Congress in 1906.

There is also a more straightforward argument. Treaties are agreements between two or more governments. They are not generally the place where one government defines its internal governing criteria, such as citizenship requirements. That is done in a document specific to the one government, such as a constitution. The Cherokee Nation clearly did that in a constitutional amendment in 1866 that granted citizenship to the freedmen. The argument is that by superseding its own constitution in 1975 and passing additional amendments in 2007, the Cherokee Nation has done what it is legally able to do in its constitutional continuum.

The Bureau of Indian Affairs (BIA), counter to the position of the federal courts thus far, has repeatedly inserted itself into sovereign determinations of various kinds, and has taken up the cause of the freedmen descendants. In its resistance to removing itself from the approval process of the Cherokee Nation's constitutions, the bureau failed to sign off in timely fashion on a 2003 vote of the Cherokee people superseding their 1975 constitution, even though various Assistant Secretaries of the BIA had promised to do so, including Kevin Gover and Neal McCaleb, the latter of whom had issued a letter of intent to the Cherokee Nation. Because the BIA delayed until 2009 in taking care of that housekeeping task, it is now their contention that the 2007 vote cannot be put into effect because they have not approved it as they assert was required.

The case has been ongoing for almost a decade, and there is no indication that it will be resolved anytime soon. This rendering is actually the simplified version, but if you have followed it, or even if you have not, I hope you are convinced that it's not as straightforward as "the Cherokees are breaking a treaty." The Cherokee Nation may prevail yet again in the current case, which may seem incomprehensible to the public when all they've heard is the cant of racism and broken treaties. We could only wish the pubic was as concerned about the fact that the United States has broken every treaty it has made with Indian nations.

Misconception #3: *This was a racist vote on the part of the Cherokees.*

The March 3, 2007, vote was a landslide among the Cherokees. In all, 77% of the voters favored the addition of language to their constitution that required that one be an Indian "by blood." On March 4, Cherokees awoke to negative headlines in major metropolitan dailies across the country above stories in which spokespersons for freedmen descendants were proclaiming that the Cherokees were "racists." In the weeks and months afterward Cherokees took a psychic beating as bloggers, good liberal folks, and academics picked up the cant. By summer, the Cherokee Nation was facing, for the second time in a hundred years, the proposed termination of their government through legislation spearheaded by Diane Watson, an African-American legislator from Los Angeles, and backed by the entire Congressional Black Caucus, with the exception of Rep. John Lewis, a prominent civil rights veteran, who had made a prolonged visit to the Cherokee Nation and had gained a more in-depth understanding of the issue.

"Racism" fits on a bumper sticker, while the sovereignty of an Indian nation to determine its own citizenship requirements is not even on the radar of most Americans, who view Native Americans primarily in racial or ethnic terms, rather than as governments. It was a struggle to try to rapidly educate a population and a Congress who didn't know very much about Indian sovereignty or this particular issue, and who probably didn't care that much, but who certainly didn't want to be seen as supporting "racists." Even those who did support the Cherokee Nation citizenry's right to decide still will likely view the decision as race-based, at least, if not indeed racist.

Are there individuals among the Cherokees who hold racist sentiments toward blacks? Yes, unfortunately, there are. Do 77% of the Cherokee people hold racist sentiments toward blacks? Emphatically, they do not. So if not voting racism, then what was the basis for this landslide referendum?

For some who know the history of imposition of freedmen citizenship on the Cherokee Nation, it may have been a principled vote in resistance to what they anticipated would be a continuing federal imposition. For some it may have derived from a suspicion that this was only about benefits that could be accessed through citizenship. For some who knew that political opponents of Principal Chief Chad Smith were using the issue in an election year to try to oust him from office, it may have been a vote in defense of his administration. But most probably voted the more limiting language because it only seemed logical that in order to be a citizen of the Cherokee Nation one ought to have Cherokee ancestry. They thought it was already that way, but apparently it wasn't, and so they voted to rectify that oversight. And there are other possibilities. There are numerous complex reasons that go far beyond simple racism as to why the Cherokees may have voted as they did.

Historical Background: As stated above, the Cherokee Nation passed anti-miscegenation laws in the 1820s, and with the Cherokees' noted reverence for their system of laws, the best evidence is that relationships between Cherokees and blacks were much more limited throughout the middle and late 1800s than comparable relationships within the others of the Five "Civilized" Tribes. Although often treated as though the customs and laws of these tribes were almost interchangeable in this regard, this tendency on the part of some academics and others is problematic. In the middle and late 1800s, each of these tribes had a very distinct dynamic with their former slaves.

Slavery was permitted in the Cherokee Nation in the early to mid-1800s and was likely viewed as an adaptation of customs that had existed for centuries. Cherokees had long practiced the capture and "enslavement" of Indians of other tribes. These "slaves" (the meaning conveyed by the English word probably does not mirror Cherokee perceptions of their aboriginal practice) were not used as chattel labor, but rather to trade for Cherokees who had been captured, or to perform light chores mainly as a manner of expressing and maintaining a visible boundary within the tribe between those who are "us" and those who are not. In time, many Indian slaves were ultimately adopted into Cherokee society through incorporation into clans, and many made marriages with Cherokees. In the view of the Cherokees, a marriage in itself did not make the former slave a Cherokee. It was the adoption into a clan that was the defining act.

By the late 1700s, a handful of Cherokees instead were beginning to acquire blacks as slaves as a hunter-warrior culture diminished in favor of an agricultural system for the marketplace. In the early 1800s the practice expanded somewhat, but in total, very few Cherokees were plantation slaveholders. A federal census taken among the Cherokees in 1835 indicated that additional families had one or two slaves each who were mostly household help rather than used as chattel labor, as these families did not operate plantations. They likely had a more traditional view of their slaves that mirrored the practice from earlier times of holding other Indians as slaves.

There were more families holding one or two slaves than there were plantation owners, but plantation owners held more slaves overall than did the families with one or two. The overwhelming majority of Cherokees did not hold any slaves at all. The 1835 census indicated about 1,600 slaves held by Cherokees in the years just prior to the forced removal, the Trail of Tears of 1838–39. One claim often heard by freedmen descendants is that their ancestors, too, were on the Trail of Tears. However, the wealthier slaveholding families did not subject themselves or their slaves to the hardships of removal. They had the means to remove independently and in greater comfort, and they did. About ¾ of the slaves immigrated to the Indian Territory with these families previous to the Trail of Tears. The ¼ who were on the trail, about 400 people among the 16,450 Cherokees who were also removed, were those who were owned as one or two by the smaller subsistence households who had no means to transport either themselves or their slaves more comfortably. These 400 indeed suffered the same rigors of the march as the Cherokees, but it's very difficult to know exactly which ones they were or who their specific descendants are.

Following the voluntary emancipation of the former slaves by the Cherokee Nation in 1863, the 1866 Treaty suggested areas within the Nation's boundaries where freedmen could establish new communities of their own families. This was not segregation – the freedmen were able to live wherever they wanted to. It was instead a provision for areas where land would be made available for new settlements within the Cherokee domain. Many new communities were established, and although there were relationships between them and the neighboring Cherokee communities, the freedmen communities often developed their own distinct identities as "black towns" that were among the first in what would later be the state of Oklahoma.

Freedmen were incorporated politically to a degree. Many of the new towns were in the area where the southern Cherokees (those who had sided with the Confederacy) had been strongest, and were also the areas where many of the plantations had been and where the slaves had long lived. But ironically – and deliberately – the concentration of freedmen communities in areas where their former masters had reigned meant that those former slaveholders now had to court the freedmen voting bloc in their political districts, which was numerous enough to push a close race one way or the other. Several freedmen also served as members of the Cherokee National Council in the late 1800s.

By the time of the allotment era and the creation of the Dawes Rolls (1898–1906), the base roll used by each of the contemporary Five Tribes, the population of freedmen and their descendants among the Cherokees had grown to just under 5,000 in a nation of about 40,000 that also included intermarried whites as well as Delaware and Shawnee Indians who had been politically incorporated after the Civil War. Each of these groups, as well as Cherokees "by blood," had a separate roll within the Dawes. Anecdote has it that anyone who was black was automatically placed on the freedmen roll, and thus was the Indian identity of freedmen and their descendants erased. There may be some basis in truth in some cases. But the anecdote can also be easily deconstructed. Even a cursory review of the Cherokee-by-blood roll evidences those who are listed as having freedmen parentage along with Cherokee parentage. It certainly appears that descent from freedmen did not eliminate anyone from the Cherokee roll, as long as a Cherokee parent could also be demonstrated. Today, several thousand Cherokee citizens who are descended from freedmen and Cherokees are citizens and have been all along because of their demonstrated Cherokee ancestry as well. Their citizenship has never been in question, they have never been disenfranchised, and they never will be, notwithstanding the "black" phenotypes of many.

Likewise, many Cherokee citizens who are descended from Cherokees and (non-freedmen) blacks are citizens and always will be. Their citizenship is not questioned either. In this instance, one drop of black blood does not eliminate anyone from citizenship, but one must have at least one drop of Cherokee blood to be "in." In 1898–1906, the majority of freedmen could not demonstrate that drop. I have heard many questions from people wondering why their ancestors chose to be on the freedmen roll rather than the Cherokee roll, and some unlikely explanations. The most probable explanation, however, is fairly straightforward. They chose the freedmen roll because they weren't Cherokee.

The genealogies of descendants of slaves in the United States are notoriously difficult to construct, and it may be that the same is so among the Cherokees. But in this country, there are three times as many people of all races and phenotypes claiming Cherokee heritage as there are those who can actually prove it. The Cherokee Nation doesn't accept hearsay and anecdote in considering applications for citizenship, nor does any tribe. And yet many Cherokees feel as though that's exactly what is expected in the case of the freedmen, even though genealogical evidence is lacking and historical evidence would tend to indicate otherwise.

Misconception #4: *The freedmen descendants are culturally and linguistically Cherokee and have been a part of Cherokee communities throughout the 20th century.*

Unquestionably, whether cognitively or intuitively, the main reason Cherokees voted as they did in 2007 is because they didn't know who the descendants of freedmen were. They didn't know where they came from. They didn't know how to place them into Cherokee family lineages. They didn't know how to situate them in Cherokee communities, either traditional communities or the more diverse communities of interest. Despite the assertions of a prominent academic, Circe Sturm, writing in the early and mid-1990s, the evidence she found of freedmen descendants who were culturally and/or linguistically Cherokee, or members of communities identified as "Cherokee" was very limited and existed primarily among elderly people. Twenty years later, most of those people have probably gone on. And yet her analysis was presented as though this was a widespread reality among the Cherokees and became the foundation of further theoretical musings on the part of other academics.

Most Cherokees in 2007 had never met a freedmen descendant. Today, most still haven't. The suspicion, therefore, about a group that seemed to come from nowhere demanding citizenship and rights appeared to be little more than the typical claimant who is most interested in benefits and per capita payments from casinos. The Cherokees have seen a multitude of such individuals in recent decades and to many, the freedmen descendants appeared no different.

Historical Background: The elders of the 1990s who may have retained some cultural and linguistic affiliation with Cherokees were perhaps among the last. By the 1930s, many of eastern Oklahoma's black towns were diminishing as younger generations headed for the cities during the Depression that had hit so hard in the rural communities of the state. Many Cherokees did the same, migrating west to California and other states. World War II solidified the diasporic populations of both Cherokees and freedmen descendants, some in nearby urban areas such as Tulsa, Oklahoma City, Dallas, and Kansas City, and others as far flung as Bakersfield, Los Angeles, and the San Francisco Bay Area. At home in the Cherokee Nation, Cherokees, Shawnees, and Delawares who stayed behind banded together in community and ceremonial activities that continued throughout the 20th century. Although some communities retained distinct identities as Shawnee or Delaware, intermarriages with Cherokees were commonplace, and community interrelatedness was even more so. But the descendants of freedmen increasingly seemed to have gone their own way.

Misconception #5: *This is only 2,800 people out of more than 325,000. What's the issue with just letting them in?*

Within the nine-month period between the court decision and the vote on a constitutional amendment, only 2,800 contemporary freedmen descendants actually even applied for citizenship. Those 2,800 remain citizens to this day while the court cases are still pending. They vote and they access tribal resources and benefits. The concern is not as much about the present 2,800 but rather the estimates that somewhere between 25,000 and 40,000 descendants would be eligible for citizenship if the Cherokee Nation does not prevail in the legal arena. Any tribe would be concerned about a group of that size, but with little overall knowledge or experience, suddenly becoming a part of its citizenry. Even at 325,000 citizens, the Cherokee Nation is small. A voting block of even a couple of hundred people can dramatically shift the races for Principal Chief. In Tribal Council races, a dozen votes or less can make the difference. Many Cherokees view the inclusion of tens of thousands of freedmen descendants as a potentially overwhelming force. It may or may not be a realistic fear, but it is not an unreasonable concern. The impact of those already registered as citizens likely has already shifted the outcome of political races, particularly the race for Principal Chief in 2011 in which the federal court ordered an additional two weeks of voting in order to accommodate freedmen descendants. The voting was carried out in a district where they were demographically well represented, but which also happened to favor one candidate over the other. Other districts were not provided easy access to additional voting. It was not difficult to predict who would win under those new circumstances, even as the race had previously been extremely close.

In Conclusion

This chapter has, for the most part, favored a particular perspective. It has not been my intent to write a "fair and balanced" piece, since one perspective has already been very prominent in the media and academic circles for many years. My hope is that another perspective, one that analyzes the 2007 Cherokee vote and the resistance to freedmen incorporation from a deeply internal tribal position, can claim a little bit of the air in the room. To cast this issue as exclusively an issue of race violates a most basic principle of research. One cannot make a pronouncement of cause until one has eliminated all other possible causes, and no one has even attempted thus far to do that. The blind acceptance that racism is the only possible explanation for the vote, or at best some kind of racial "false consciousness" on the part of the Cherokees, is simplistic.

Is racism one of the contributing factors? Without question, unfortunately, it is. Are the 77% of the Cherokee voters who expressed a desire to keep Cherokee familial lines as part of the definition of their tribal citizenry therefore racist? Adamantly they are not. It is frustrating when academics weave elegant literary analyses of the issue, debating philosophical meanings of race and sovereignty while dismissing as mere colonial constructs the realities that tribal governments and populations deal with. It is hurtful and infuriating to hear social scientists and the media describe my nation and people as racists and greedy. The tribal population is not living theoretical lives based on claims of heritage. These are real political and cultural existences lived, yes, under colonial constructs, but the constructs we nevertheless must deal with on the ground. Cherokees have real concerns about their political system, their cultural identities, and their sovereignty as expressed in their ability to make governmental decisions without outside interference. These are concerns that impact their lives far more immediately than American-based perceptions of race, and I believe that in the main, this is what the citizens of the Cherokee Nation voted in March of 2007.

Note

1. Theda Perdue, *Mixed Blood Indians, Racial Construction in the Early South* (University of Georgia Press, 2003), and Fay Yarbrough, *Race and the Cherokee Nation: Sovereignty in the Nineteenth Century* (University of Pennsylvania Press, 2007).

*"Indian identity is not about
being part something,
it is about being part of something."*

– Angela Gonzales
Hopi

Part 3

DECOLONIZING BIOLOGY AND DEMOGRAPHY

TWENTIETH CENTURY TRIBAL BLOOD POLITICS: POLICY, PLACE, AND DESCENT

by Kim TallBear

I have spent my entire life as an "enrolled" member (we often like to say "citizen") in one or another federally recognized US tribe (we often like to say "Native nation"). I've spent significant episodes in my life as both a reservation-based and urban Indian. I have spent nearly twenty-five years working for tribal governments, federal agencies, national Native American organizations, in private consulting, and now as an academic on issues that intersect the environment, science, technology, and Native American cultures. I also pay attention to how Native American citizenship and identities are conditioned by political economic circumstances.

In other words, I look at how policy and material realities shape and are shaped in return by concepts of "tribe," "race," and "nation." These realities do not completely precede one another, but – like M. C. Escher's *Drawing Hands* – policy, economic realities, and Aboriginal peoples' identities are mutually constructive. That is, federal policy, resource allocations, and concepts of race and nation loop – always building and tweaking one another simultaneously – although not as evenly as the image of the hands indicates. Colonization, of course, is power imbalance.

US Tribal Citizenship and Blood Rules

"Tribal" or "Native Nation" citizenship, as we call it in the US, is incredibly confusing. We did not have a monolithic piece of legislation historically, like the Canadian Indian Act. We have, in some ways, ideological equivalents to the Indian Act, in which nearly everyone assumes that "blood" matters very much, but it matters in different ways to different people. Indeed, things are confusing in the US because we have had 100 years to construct, revise, and revise again – in response to ever-shifting political economic circumstances – circuitous rules about who gets to belong and who does not to the tribal body politic. We've also had no national conversation to discuss the pros and cons of particular concepts and criteria.

In the late nineteenth and early twentieth centuries, US tribes and federal agents together constructed "base rolls," or lists of "Indian" individuals living on reservation (and often their supposed blood quantum) who eventually became members of those tribal entities. One can imagine the kinds of discrepancies that came into play, which have been documented by scholars. If individuals were absent from the reservation when the rolls were compiled, for example, they might have been left off, leaving their descendants ineligible for enrollment. Or, an individual may have been judged on sight and according to phenotype to be "half-blood," while their full sibling was judged to be "full-blood." Thus, their respective descendants would have different rights to citizenship in tribes that use a blood quantum (and not simply lineal descent) rule. Additionally, during the past century, tribes have variously allowed enrollment according to reservation residence, simple parental enrollment, legal adoption of children, and marriage. All of these complex rules, worked together differently in different tribes, have resulted in confusion and disparity regarding who has citizenship rights in tribal nations.

Different scholars characterize federal intervention in tribal enrollment differently. Some characterize the federal role as "imposing" dominant "racial ideologies" and biologically essentialist criteria, particularly blood quantum, onto Native American tribes.[1] Other scholars – with extensive empirical evidence – characterize the federal role in more complex terms as a "conversation" between Indians and federal agents throughout the twentieth century. Historian Alexandra Harmon explains:

> In the [Coleville] enrollment councils, federal agents did not brainwash or impose their will on Indians; neither did Indians resolve to draw an economically strategic, racially defined boundary around themselves. Rather, officials and Indians participated in a prolonged discourse that I would characterize as incomplete mutual education and accommodation.

Harmon refers to the commissions as "an unprecedented conversation – one that would take place in many tribal communities and continue for decades – about what it meant to be Indian in the twentieth-century United States."[2]

Throughout the twentieth century and into the twenty-first, Native American tribes have shown that they are deeply attached to kinship, much of it biological, in determining citizenship. Interesting exceptions of non-biologically based tribal citizenship are the Seminole and Cherokee Freedman cases. Descendants of freed slaves – and not necessarily "blood" relations of the tribe – have long been eligible for tribal enrollment due to post–Civil War treaty provisions. Nonetheless, Freedman descendants continue to struggle against the privileging of blood rules within the tribe and broader society, with their tribal citizenship either at risk or recently revoked.

The following chart (see Figure 2) often shocks audiences when I display it during presentations. I often hear audible gasps and comments about "antiquated ideas of race." But in "Indian Country," as we call it in the US, we are accustomed to blood talk and visuals. The above chart is from a 1982 Bureau of Indian Affairs (BIA) enrollment manual. The visuals in today's guidance documents, whether they be generated by the Bureau or a tribal government itself, are probably computer generated, but the general concept still prevails. We know such conceptual frameworks are problematic, but familiarity lessens our surprise. Even critics of blood quantum in the US, who tend to privilege concepts of "citizenship," "nation," and "decolonization," do not eschew altogether biological bases for Native American identity. They advocate concepts of tribal citizenship that ultimately extend beyond biology, such as reservation residence, cultural requirements, adoption, and other allowances for naturalization. But they also argue for the more inclusive blood rule of lineal descent. According to the concept of lineal descent, a would-be tribal citizen would need only to document his or her biological descent from an individual named on the tribe's "base" roll. In a very few tribes that use descent rules, the ancestor must be strictly maternal or paternal, according to traditional modes of clan affiliation, but for most tribes such a rule would apply to either line. I find it interesting that lineal descent is portrayed by scholars as less biologically focused because it is more inclusive than say a one-quarter blood quantum rule. However, it facilitates an identity claim reckoned through a single ancestral line. Indeed, without any blood quantum rule, we are likely to have claims to citizenship based on fewer and more distant Native American ancestors – a thin ancestral connection granting access to the tribe for those with little or no experience with the tribe, whereas a higher so-called blood quantum is likely to be the product of recent and ongoing lived relations within the Native American community. Lineal descent does not de-emphasize biology. It emphasizes it differently, making a distant relative more like to stand for social relations.

Moving from blood quantum to descent rules also does not free us from colonial ideas. Notions of blood quantum may seem to fall into the same conceptual pot as racial ideas such as "mulatto," "quadroon," and "octoroon." But lineal descent—that multigenerational lineal blood relationship (real and true, whatever the legal framework decrees)— has also been shown to be a dominant US (European) American mode of reckoning kin and identity (Schneider 1980). Indeed, it helps us understand the genetic ancestry testing craze among non-Native Americans as they give biological samples in order to have their maternal (mother's mother's mother's) or paternal (father's father's father's) lineages traced to certain populations and geographic locations in the distant past (Lee et al. 2009, 38–39).

Alternatively, the blood quantum concept can also be seen in more "traditional" terms in that it foregrounds genealogical links between individuals and an extant group via biological links to a multiplicity of named and tribally affiliated ancestors (Medicine 2001). Native American studies scholar Elizabeth Cook-Lynn, a vocal advocate for the rights of Native American tribal citizenship and sovereignty, sees being "Indian" or a member of a particular tribal nation as being precisely about citizenship, but one based in part on blood. She acknowledges that "relationships based on blood have been a tenet of survival and identity in native enclaves from the beginning and continue to be" (2007, 145). Blood quantum can be seen to stand in for probabilistic social links between an individual and a land-based group; for example, the higher the blood quantum, the more relatives one has that are Native American or of that specific tribe (depending on the way that blood is calculated), and the greater the probability of actual group affiliation.[3] There are problems with blood quantum, but the concept does not only reflect an uncritical take-up of Eurocentric and racist ideas that cause us to focus on biology over culture; ideas about relatedness that go to the heart of what is unique about the tribe also ground its continuing use.

CHART TO ESTABLISH DEGREE OF INDIAN BLOOD

PARENTS ▶

	N·I	1/16	1/8	3/16	1/4	5/16	3/8	7/16	1/2	9/16	5/8	11/16	3/4	13/16	7/8	15/16	4/4
1/16	1/32	1/16	3/32	1/8	5/32	3/16	7/32	1/4	9/32	5/16	11/32	3/8	13/32	7/16	15/32	1/2	17/32
1/8	1/16	3/32	1/8	5/32	3/16	7/32	1/4	9/32	5/16	11/32	3/8	13/32	7/16	15/32	1/2	17/32	9/16
3/16	3/32	1/8	5/32	3/16	7/32	1/4	9/32	5/16	11/32	3/8	13/32	7/16	15/32	1/2	17/32	9/16	19/32
1/4	1/8	5/32	3/16	7/32	1/4	9/32	5/16	11/32	3/8	13/32	7/16	15/32	1/2	17/32	9/16	19/32	5/8
5/16	5/32	3/16	7/32	1/4	9/32	5/16	11/32	3/8	13/32	7/16	15/32	1/2	17/32	9/16	19/32	5/8	21/32
3/8	3/16	7/32	1/4	9/32	5/16	11/32	3/8	13/32	7/16	15/32	1/2	17/32	9/16	19/32	5/8	21/32	11/16
7/16	7/32	1/4	9/32	5/16	11/32	3/8	13/32	7/16	15/32	1/2	17/32	9/16	19/32	5/8	21/32	11/16	23/32
1/2	1/4	9/32	5/16	11/32	3/8	13/32	7/16	15/32	1/2	17/32	9/16	19/32	5/8	21/32	11/16	23/32	3/4
9/16	9/32	5/16	11/32	3/8	13/32	7/16	15/32	1/2	17/32	9/16	19/32	5/8	21/32	11/16	23/32	3/4	25/32
5/8	5/16	11/32	3/8	13/32	7/16	15/32	1/2	17/32	9/16	19/32	5/8	21/32	11/16	23/32	3/4	25/32	13/16
11/16	11/32	3/8	13/32	7/16	15/32	1/2	17/32	9/16	19/32	5/8	21/32	11/16	23/32	3/4	25/32	13/16	27/32
3/4	3/8	13/32	7/16	15/32	1/2	17/32	9/16	19/32	5/8	21/32	11/16	23/32	3/4	25/32	13/16	27/32	7/8
13/16	13/32	7/16	15/32	1/2	17/32	9/16	19/32	5/8	21/32	11/16	23/32	3/4	25/32	13/16	27/32	7/8	29/32
7/8	7/16	15/32	1/2	17/32	9/16	19/32	5/8	21/32	11/16	23/32	3/4	25/32	13/16	27/32	7/8	29/32	15/16
15/16	15/32	1/2	17/32	9/16	19/32	5/8	21/32	11/16	23/32	3/4	25/32	13/16	27/32	7/8	29/32	15/16	31/32
4/4	1/2	17/32	9/16	19/32	5/8	21/32	11/16	23/32	3/4	25/32	13/16	27/32	7/8	29/32	15/16	31/32	4/4
1/32	1/64	3/64	5/64	7/64	9/64	11/64	13/64	15/64	17/64	19/64	21/64	23/64	25/64	27/64	29/64	31/64	33/64
3/32	3/64	5/64	7/64	9/64	11/64	13/64	15/64	17/64	19/64	21/64	23/64	25/64	27/64	29/64	31/64	33/64	35/64
5/32	5/64	7/64	9/64	11/64	13/64	15/64	17/64	19/64	21/64	23/64	25/64	27/64	29/64	31/64	33/64	35/64	37/64
7/32	7/64	9/64	11/64	13/64	15/64	17/64	19/64	21/64	23/64	25/64	27/64	29/64	31/64	33/64	35/64	37/64	39/64
9/32	9/64	11/64	13/64	15/64	17/64	19/64	21/64	23/64	25/64	27/64	29/64	31/64	33/64	35/64	37/64	39/64	41/64
11/32	11/64	13/64	15/64	17/64	19/64	21/64	23/64	25/64	27/64	29/64	31/64	33/64	35/64	37/64	39/64	41/64	43/64
13/32	13/64	15/64	17/64	19/64	21/64	23/64	25/64	27/64	29/64	31/64	33/64	35/64	37/64	39/64	41/64	43/64	45/64
15/32	15/64	17/64	19/64	21/64	23/64	25/64	27/64	29/64	31/64	33/64	35/64	37/64	39/64	41/64	43/64	45/64	47/64
17/32	17/64	19/64	21/64	23/64	25/64	27/64	29/64	31/64	33/64	35/64	37/64	39/64	41/64	43/64	45/64	47/64	49/64
19/32	19/64	21/64	23/64	25/64	27/64	29/64	31/64	33/64	35/64	37/64	39/64	41/64	43/64	45/64	47/64	49/64	51/64
21/32	21/64	23/64	25/64	27/64	29/64	31/64	33/64	35/64	37/64	39/64	41/64	43/64	45/64	47/64	49/64	51/64	53/64
23/32	23/64	25/64	27/64	29/64	31/64	33/64	35/64	37/64	39/64	41/64	43/64	45/64	47/64	49/64	51/64	53/64	55/64
25/32	25/64	27/64	29/64	31/64	33/64	35/64	37/64	39/64	41/64	43/64	45/64	47/64	49/64	51/64	53/64	55/64	57/64
27/32	27/64	29/64	31/64	33/64	35/64	37/64	39/64	41/64	43/64	45/64	47/64	49/64	51/64	53/64	55/64	57/64	59/64
29/32	29/64	31/64	33/64	35/64	37/64	39/64	41/64	43/64	45/64	47/64	49/64	51/64	53/64	55/64	57/64	59/64	61/64
31/32	31/64	33/64	35/64	37/64	39/64	41/64	43/64	45/64	47/64	49/64	51/64	53/64	55/64	57/64	59/64	61/64	63/64

TO DETERMINE DEGREE OF BLOOD OF CHILDREN, FIND DEGREE OF ONE PARENT IN LEFT COLUMN AND OF THE OTHER PARENT IN TOP ROW. READ ACROSS TO RIGHT AND DOWN THE COLUMN TO THE PROPER DEGREE. "N·I" MEANS NON·INDIAN. EXAMPLE: CHILD OF ONE PARENT 1/16, THE OTHER 5/8, WOULD BE 23/32 DEGREE INDIAN.

Fig. 1. Chart from 1984 Bureau of Indian Affairs (BIA) Enrollment Manual. US Department of Interior. Bureau of Indian Affairs. Tribal Enrollment. Phoenix: Phoenix Area Office, 1984.

Shifting Political Economy, Shifting Rules: From "Race" to "Tribe"

In addition to US histories of race, federal government heavy-handedness to varying degrees, and Native American concepts of kin and tribe, shifting political-economic conditions prompted demographic changes that shaped tribal citizenship rules throughout the twentieth century. The majority of tribes in the early twentieth century used parental enrollment, residency, marriage, and adoption. But, by the mid-twentieth century, tribal enrollment rules changed in order to account for shifting patterns of residence, exogenous marriage – that is, to non-Native people – and the resulting lower "blood quantum" of their offspring.

During this period, federal government thinking emphasized individual Indian development and assimilation rather than tribal economic and governmental development. Federal policy focused on urban relocation programs and tribal termination policies. During World War II, a mass migration of Native Americans from the reservations swelled as approximately 50 percent of "able-bodied Indian" men left for military service (Gover 2008, 286). Economic conditions, federal policy, and war prompted profound demographic shifts that led to changes in enrollment rules. In 1940, 5 percent of Indians lived in urban areas. By 1970, 50 percent lived in cities. Legal scholar Kirsty Gover (2008) explains that parental enrollment and residency rules that dominated pre-World War II became unsustainable:[4]

> The effect of these migrations of tribes was to disrupt or weaken the demographic continuity of tribes and also to interrupt the intergenerational "transmission" of legal membership from parents to their children... Membership design decisions made by tribes after 1970 are influenced not just by the new opportunities and resources provided by federal self-determination policy, but also by the legacy of termination-era policies and migrations... Lineal descent and tribal blood rules can therefore be seen as part of a tribal response to the disruptions caused by shifts in federal policy and changes in tribal demography... They are forms of self-help that are intended to reconstitute a tribe as a historically continuous community. (248)

Many tribes used enrollment criteria to try to "repair the historic continuity of the communities" (Gover 2008, 248) in part by shifting from what Gover calls the "racial mechanism" of "total Indian blood" to the "genealogic mechanism" of "tribe-specific blood." In her survey of 330 tribal constitutions, Gover describes the emergence of a new "genealogic tribalism" in the second half of the twentieth century (2008). Tribal nations increasingly coupled either Indian blood quantum or a tribe-specific blood quantum (all calculated symbolically through documentation of ancestors) with the concept of lineal descent to produce the "genealogic tribe." It is genealogic in that it traces a genealogy of ancestors, and it is tribal in that it increasingly prefers tracing ancestors to one tribe rather than Indian ancestors more broadly.

Today, 70 percent of tribal constitutions surveyed use a blood quantum rule, with 40 percent still using total "Indian blood" and 33 percent using a "tribe-specific blood rule." Tribe-specific blood rules are on the increase. An example might help. I was previously enrolled in the Cheyenne & Arapaho Tribes of Oklahoma (C&A), which require one quarter "Cheyenne and Arapaho blood" to be enrolled, a tribe-specific blood rule. The tribe in which I am currently enrolled is the Sisseton-Wahpeton Oyate (SWO). SWO also uses a blood quantum rule, but requires one-quarter total Indian blood with a genealogical trace to the base roll. Most tribes in the US that use blood quantum use a one-quarter blood quantum rule. Some tribes use a blood rule as exclusive as one-half tribe-specific blood. Others use no blood quantum rule, but rather use simple lineal descent.

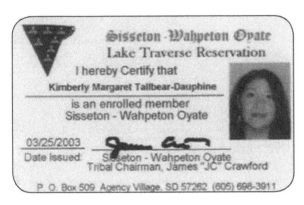

Fig. 2
Sisseton-Wahpeton Oyate Enrollment Card

On the reverse of my tribal enrollment card, shown above, is the following:
- Degree of SWO Indian Blood: 1/32
- Other Sioux Blood: 1/16 Flandreau Santee
- Other Indian Blood: 1/4 Chey-Arap., 1/16 T. Mt/Chpw
- Total Indian Blood: 13/32

Because SWO rules require one-quarter total Indian blood plus lineal descent from their base roll, I am eligible to be enrolled, even though my SWO blood quantum is the lowest of any I am seen to possess. I happen to identify most strongly with my SWO and Flandreau Santee heritages as those are the places where I spent formative time in my life. I lived recently on the reservation of the Sisseton-Wahpeton Oyate. It is also the place where two of my three siblings are enrolled, and where my mother is enrolled and lives periodically. So, I am grateful that SWO has regulations that allow me to mesh my lived experience with my tribal citizenship.

Not all the enrollment changes of late have been to my advantage, or those of other Native Americans with strong personal and cultural ties to specific tribes. Since the passage in 1975 of the Indian Self-Determination and Assistance Act, the frequency of descent and blood-quantum rules in tribal constitutions has increased rapidly. It seems ironic that in an era of increased tribal economic development, reduced federal oversight, increased formal tribal autonomy, and the administrative devolution to tribal governments of programs previously managed by the BIA (e.g., health care, education, housing), that tribes moved away from policies of dual enrollment, residency, and adoption. Enrollment of legally adopted children and enrollment through residency are two mechanisms that critics of blood rules often put forward as more in keeping with traditional concepts of kin. They are almost never allowed in tribal enrollment post-Self Determination. This cannot be explained by federal government heavy-handedness.

For example, even though I spent practically my entire childhood in Flandreau, South Dakota, that tribe won't enroll me because I am eligible to be enrolled elsewhere. It's worth noting that this additional enrollment rule came into being only after gaming started. SWO engages in gaming too, but they don't pay out dividends to individual members, as Flandreau does. Gaming and per capita payments, increasingly, are driving forces changing enrollment rules: in my view, for the worse, but that is a topic to be treated in detail elsewhere. In general, we see in the enrollment rules of both tribes central to my family, C&A and SWO, a transition from total Indian blood to tribe-specific blood rules that Gover observes in tribes across the country post-World War II. Changes to "citizenship criteria" (maybe you're beginning to understand why I have mixed feelings about using that term) in tribes across the US are not best understood by thinking of simply imposed federal criteria or simple conceptual self-colonization. Shifts in tribal enrollment regulations have plenty to do with managing numbers, of both people and dollars, in changing political-economic circumstances. I quote Gover's pithy summary of the significance of tribal enrollment shifts at the end of the twentieth century:

> Increased tribal preference for lineal descent and blood rules
> ... challenge the assumption that the characterization of tribes
> as "ethnic" or "racial" groups (rather than political or cultural
> ones) is a colonial artifact, imposed and perpetuated by the fed-

eral government, that would be shed by the tribes as their autonomy increased.... [T]heir membership practices are not becoming more "liberal," in the sense of using racially and ethnically
neutral criteria. They are moving away from a race-based model
of tribal membership (which conceives of Indians as a racially
undifferentiated albeit tribally organized population), but are
not moving toward a classically liberal "civic polity" model.
Instead ... tribes are evolving their own ... construction of membership, in the form of a "genealogic" tribalism. (2008, 249)

In other words, lineal descent coupled with tribal-descent rules enables
both continuity (children of urban Indians can be enrolled) and imposes
limits on the number of potential enrollees, especially post-1970s, when
tribes became wealthier. I hear from tribes all over the US that they are
inundated with enrollment applications from individuals whom they have
never heard of, who may have no real personal connection to the tribe, and
who may seek enrollment primarily for economic benefit. Thus, tribal blood
rules may not be "traditional," but neither are they simply "imposed." Gover's findings agree with other scholars' assessments that the older model of
"total Indian blood" is characteristic of federal government thinking and of
dominant US race thinking that focuses on Native Americans as members of
an undifferentiated racial mass. But, she also demonstrates that the concept
of tribe-specific blood quantum is "a tribally endogenous concept," meaning
it emerged as a response from within tribes (2008, 251).

The most difficult challenges to US tribal citizenship – and I would suspect it is similar with First Nations' citizenship – will not be in any measure
to simply throw off the ideological yoke of colonialism. Political economic
pressures very much condition Indigenous citizenship responses. It is true
that political economy is part and parcel of a broader history of colonialism
and its institutions, but the relationships are not linear, nor are tribes simply
on the receiving end of intervention.

Fortunately, we in the US do not have an Indian Act that officially
regulates our citizenship practice. But, I think it is fair to say that, in both
practical and ideological terms, we have an Indian Act that profoundly
shapes our ability to govern and to determine who is part of the "we." It is
true that the federal government sometimes throws its weight around, for
example in tribal federal recognition processes, where the US has great
leverage in determining (according to dominant racial criteria) who legitimately constitutes an Indian (Gover 2008; see also McCulloch and Wilkins

1995). On the other hand, US tribes have varied and complex tribal citizenship ordinances that we have considerable legal control over (some of us more than others, depending on how we were recognized by the federal government). We all have enrollment or citizenship cards. Yet, the ideal of citizenship among US tribes remains questionable, and economic power and real control over our lands and resources have everything to do with the practical limits we see on tribes as nations governing citizenries. With all of our "reparative" efforts throughout the twentieth and early twenty-first century, we still produce something that does not look quite like citizenship.

I have one final insight to share. It comes from a young man from Saskatchewan named Howard, who sat quietly next to me at the 2011 Assembly of First Nations (AFN) gathering hosted by the Enoch Cree Nation, near Edmonton, Alberta. Unlike the speakers, panelists, and vocal citizens, Howard was unusually soft-spoken. He turned to me when there was a short break, and said something akin to the following: "What I don't understand is, why 'citizen'? And why 'nation'? Are those concepts ours? Are they in our languages? Are they the best translations for what is in our own languages?" He said this in a humble rather than accusing way. He was concerned that his fellow First Nations' people were seizing on concepts that, while they may go some ways (one hopes) towards political sovereignty, seemed to be taken up too readily as if they easily represent Aboriginal concepts of peoplehood and self-determination. A discussion of assumptions at that fundamental level, such as Howard spoke about with me, was never approached in the broader conversation those two days in Enoch. Perhaps these questions were also on the minds of other quiet folk in the room.

I've come back several times to Howard's words. He made such an impression on me. I too share his concerns. Like him, I think hard on these things and I wonder sometimes, are these the best conceptual frameworks for organizing our decolonization and how we govern? Will we think of something better, especially as these concepts are increasingly undermined or come to lack coherence in nations much more powerful than ours? I am a pragmatist, however. We cannot invent anew governing structures as if 1492 never happened, as if the Indian Act and 1876 never happened, and thinking as a Dakota now, as if the 1862 war in Minnesota never happened. Those pivotal moments in the histories of all our peoples re-circumscribed the geographies, political economies, family relations, governance, and identities of our ancestors. All Indigenous peoples have similarly crucial historical narratives – those pivotal moments in colonial history that re-shaped our ancestors' lands and now ours, and thus our land-based identities. We go on from here.

Notes

1. See Churchill (1999; 1994); Edmunds (1995); Edmunds and Jaimes (1992); Neath (1995); Yellow Bird (2005).

2. Also see, for example, Gover (2008); Alexandra Harmon (2001, 179, 200; 1998); Carole Goldberg (2002); Carole Goldberg-Ambrose (1994).

3. There is a genetic test that complements blood quantum called the DNA profile, also known as a "DNA fingerprint" or the common "paternity test." Unlike tests that trace one's genetic lineage to a continent or region of the world long ago, the DNA profile confirms genetic connections between closely related and named individuals, and it is increasingly used by tribes with lineal descent rules.

4. I rely to a great extent in this section on the recent empirically rich work of law scholar Kirsty Gover (2008). Gover's analysis confirms my anecdotal experiences with shifting tribal enrollment rules in the multiple tribes that I am descended from, and in the many tribes that I've had the good fortune to work with as an environmental planner and consultant.

Acknowledgment

This chapter was published in an earlier version as "The Political Economy of Tribal Citizenship in the US: Lessons for Canadian First Nations?" *Aboriginal Policy Studies* 1 (3) (2011): 70–79.

Bibliography

Churchill, Ward. 1994. *Indians Are Us? Culture and Genocide in Native North America.* Monroe, ME: Common Courage Press.

———. 1999. "The Crucible of American Indian Identity: Native Tradition versus Colonial Imposition in Postconquest North America." *American Indian Culture and Research Journal* 23 (1): 39–67.

Cook-Lynn, Elizabeth. 2007. *New Indians, Old Wars*. Urbana and Chicago: University of Illinois Press.

Edmunds, R. David. 1995. "Native Americans, New Voices." *American Historical Review* 100: 733–34. http://dx.doi.org/10.2307/2168602

Edmunds, R. David, and Annette M. Jaimes. 1992. "Federal Indian Identification Policy: A Usurpation of Indigenous Sovereignty in North America." *In The State of Native America: Genocide, Colonization, and Resistance*, ed. M. Annette Jaimes, 123–38. Boston: South End Press, 1992.

Goldberg, Carole. 2002. "Members Only? Designing Citizenship Requirements for Indian Nations." *University of Kansas Law Review* 50: 437–71.

Goldberg-Ambrose, Carole. 1994. "Of Native Americans and Tribal Members: The Impact of Law on Indian Group Life." *Law & Society Review* 28 (5): 1123–48. http://dx.doi.org/10.2307/3054025

Gover, Kirsty. 2008. "Genealogy as Continuity: Explaining the Growing Tribal Preference for Descent Rules in Membership Governance in the United States." *American Indian Law Review* 33 (1): 243–310. http://dx.doi.org/10.2307/20455382

Harmon, Alexandra. 2011. "Tribal Enrollment Councils: Lessons on Law and Indian Identity." *Western Historical Quarterly* 32: 175–200.

———. 1998. *Indians in the Making: Ethnic Relations and Indian Identities around Puget Sound*. Berkeley and Los Angeles: University of California Press.

Lee, Sandra Soo-Jin, Deborah Bolnick, Troy Duster, Pilar Ossorio, and Kim TallBear. "The Illusive Gold Standard in Genetic Ancestry Testing." *Science* 325 (5936): 38–39.

McCulloch, Anne Merline, and David E. Wilkins. 1995. "'Constructing' Nations within States: The Quest for Federal Recognition by the Catawba and Lumbee Tribes." *American Indian Quarterly* 19 (3): 361–88. http://dx.doi.org/10.2307/1185596.

Medicine, Beatrice. 2001. *Learning to Be an Anthropologist and Remaining "Native."* Urbana: University of Illinois Press, 2001.

Neath, Mark. 1995. "American Indian Gaming Enterprises and Tribal Membership: Race, Exclusivity, and a Perilous Future." *University of Chicago Law School Roundtable* 2 (2): 695–702.

Schneider, David. 1980. *American Kinship: A Cultural Account*. Englewood Cliffs, NJ: Prentice Hall.

Yellow Bird, Michael. 2005. "Decolonizing Tribal Enrollment." In *For Indigenous Eyes Only: A Decolonization Handbook*, ed. Waziyatawin Angela Wilson and Michael Yellow Bird, 179–88. Santa Fe, NM: School of American Research Press.

WHO COUNTS? INDIANS AND THE U.S. CENSUS

by Russell Thornton

From early contact, Europeans were curious about Indian populations encountered. Later, more practical interests encompassed slavery; religious conversion; trade and exploitation of natural resources; wars, possible wars and peace; diplomacy, negotiations and treaties; and of course Indian-free territory. Sizes of Indian populations were relevant to each interest and numerous estimates were made.

The British Board of Trade was particularly interested in Indian populations and advocated for numerous censuses. It might even be said, "The British Board of Trade was the originator of census taking in America."[1] At least 38 censuses were conducted in various colonies before the national census began in 1790, the first in 1641, the last in 1789, 1 of 11 between then and 1774.[2]

The Constitution and the First U.S. Census

The colonists eventually thought of themselves as Americans, not Europeans, and desired their own country. To create one, they needed to establish America and themselves as Americans, different from England and Englishmen. Indians as a symbol of America emerged, a unique people of a unique land: "The Indian-as-American-icon played directly into the new national narrative, reinforcing the morality and integrity of the New World and demonstrating that the New Republic possessed a distinctive history – a spirit that defined America as unique and divinely favored."[3] Indians remain as icons of America, but the nature of the icon has changed as America has changed.

With the U.S. Constitution, the Congress of the United States was established, a bicameral congress replacing a unicameral one in 1789. After some debate about how representation of states would be established, it was decided each state would be represented equally through two senators in a Senate and by a variable number of representatives based on population size in a House of Representatives.

Enumeration: Who "Counts"?

Representation and taxation for states would be determined not by overall population but rather "by adding to the whole number of free persons, including those bound to service for a term of years, and excluding Indians not taxed, three fifths of all other Persons."[4] The Constitution declared an "Enumeration shall be made within three Years after the first Meeting of the Congress of the United States, and within every subsequent Term of ten Years, in such a manner as they shall direct by law."[5] Thus, the U.S. continued the colonial practice of using "numbers to describe both the continent and their activities upon it."[6]

The first census act was passed in 1790. After debate, Congress modified population characteristics considered important in the Constitution. The census would describe the population as: free white males under and over 16 years of age, free white females of all ages, other free persons and slaves. Therefore, relevant categories became: free; race, or at least "whiteness" and other (defined as non-whites by default); "adultness" (over or under 16 years); and slave.

The first census was conducted under Secretary of State Thomas Jefferson on August 2, 1790, with responsibility assigned to marshals of the U.S. judicial districts. It encompassed the 13 states; the 3 districts of Kentucky, Maine and Vermont; and Southwest Territory (Tennessee). The total U.S. population was 3.9 million. President Washington and Thomas Jefferson thought the figure too low, which it surely was.

Indians in the Census

The census was to become America's quantitative expression of itself through definitions, enumerations, categorizations, representations and publications. As Indians were a part of America's self-expression, the census became a portrait of Indians in American society painted every ten years.

Tribes and the number of tribal members were important in 1790, but were outside the United States and therefore not relevant for representation or taxation. Only Indians not living as Indians "in tribal relations" but as part of the U.S. population and therefore to be taxed were relevant; however, they were not reported as a separate category.

Both before and after the 1890 Census, *who* was enumerated as Indian and *how* they were reported varied from census to census. *Why?* Changes in the Indian population certainly, but also because of changes in how the U.S. related to Indians, and the images American society had of Indians and the ways these images fit into larger society's image of itself. "Indian" as an individual *racial* characteristic was relevant, but because it was non-white, not Indian. Who were and remained most important were white males, females (to a lesser extent), and the free. White was the important race, though only assumed in the Constitution; however, (other) races were not — they were important only as *other*, categorized as "free" or "slave." In the future, census categories would be changed as *who* and *what* were important to the fledgling nation, and how numbers might influence policy. Censuses became increasingly elaborate in delineating population characteristics.

Censuses: 1800 to 1890

The 1800 Census elaborated on age of whites. The separate categorizations of "other free" and "slave" remained. There were few changes made for the 1810 Census. In 1820, however, "free white males" between 16 years and 18 years were distinguished, and there were now age groups for both male and female "free *colored*" and "slaves." By this time, the U.S. population reported in the census had grown to 9.6 million, of whom 1.5 million were slaves. No information on Indians was obtained; the category "colored" stated that Indians not taxed were to be excluded, meaning, I assume, that Indians paying taxes were included.

The U.S. became particularly concerned about Indians around this time. Americans were expanding into the interior Southeast, and large tribes there – the Cherokee, Choctaw, Chickasaw, Creek and Seminole – were barriers to expansion. By 1830, confrontation loomed on the horizon. Changes in the census occurred for Indians and "others," ones reflecting a *racialization* of the census.

The 1830 Census enumerated "Indians out of their tribal relations" and exercising rights of citizenship. Further, age groups were expanded, and "other free persons" became "free colored persons"; a "white-other" category in census reports was replaced by a "white-colored" one; and age and sex categories for the non-white population(s) emerged.

Midway between the 1830 and 1840 Censuses, the Indian Removal Act of 1836 provided for an "exchange" of Indian lands east of the Mississippi River for lands west of it. Special censuses and rolls subsequently were conducted to assess the magnitude of the "exchange." By the decade's end, nevertheless, large Indian populations still languished on tribal lands. The result was forced removal commencing before the next census, but extending afterwards for some tribes. Yet, the 1840 Census closely followed the 1830 Census. In 1846, an appropriation called for an Indian census.[7] As reported in the 1850 Census, there were 400,764 Indians in the U.S., but 279,130 of the total was estimated.

The "mixed person" emerged in the 1850 Census, perhaps "due to lobbying by so-called 'racial' scientists."[8] Racial categories were now threefold: "White, black, or mulatto." (Only "white" was capitalized.) Indians were identified on a few schedules by enumerators; for example, Pueblo Indians in Taos County, New Mexico, were listed as "copper."

The 1860 Census was similar, but capitalized "Black" and "Mulatto" as well as White. The growing Chinese population in the West produced a new category for California only.[9] Chinese became the first nationality classified as a "race" for census purposes. (An argument could be made that Indians were the first, as tribes were "nations.")

This census also clearly identified "Indian." Instructions read: "Indians *not taxed* are not to be enumerated. The families of Indians who have renounced tribal rule, and who under state or territory laws exercise the rights of citizens, are to be enumerated."[10] The census counted 44,021 Indians, along with 459 "half-breeds."[11] (Indians "retaining their tribal character" totaled 295,400.)

In 1870, "Indians not taxed" were listed in the column "Color" as "I" or "Ind." The Superintendent of the Census, Francis A. Walker, pondered how to "classify" offspring of mixed unions: Was a person White? Indian? Black? Should race be assigned as that of mother? Or father? Should "superior or inferior blood" be taken into account? Should, in the final analysis, race be determined by "the habits, tastes, and associations of the half-breed?"[12] Walker concluded the latter was the most logical – those who lived as "white" were white, and those who lived as "Indian" were Indian. This contrasted greatly with mixed Blacks, who remained Black no matter what, or mulatto, which basically also meant Black.[13]

The 1870 Census included a "Table of True Population," with Indians subdivided into "out of tribal relations" and "sustaining tribal relations." (The latter were enumerated and/or estimated). The "true" population of the United States was 38,925,508, including 357,981 "tribal" Indians, whereas the "official" population for reapportioning representatives to Congress was 38,558, 371.[14]

The 1880 Census described "Indians not taxed" as "living on reservations ..., or roaming individually, or in bands, over settled tracts of land." Indians to be enumerated were "not in tribal relations ... who are found mingled with the white population ... or living in huts or wigwams on the outskirts of towns or settlements." While instructions requested first and surnames of those enumerated, what was written varied widely. "Sometimes there are what appear to be names in an Indian language or the probable Indian name translated into English."[15] There were "924 enumerations in which the surname is 'Indian' and 560 entries in which 'Indian' is recorded as the given name with no surname.[16] Even "papoose," "squaw," or a number was listed for given names! In all, 66,407 "civilized" Indians were enumerated.

There was a question on racial mixture and enumerators were "to specify what fraction of each person's 'blood' was white or black, and whether white, black or mulatto persons had been adopted into a tribe."[17]

The 1890 Census was the first to enumerate all Indians, though a special census was conducted for Indians not taxed. (Most census records were destroyed by a fire in 1921.) It did so under the Census Act of March 1, 1889. It followed the Dawes Act of 1887, "granting American citizenship to full and mixed-blooded Indians who 'civilized' according to the terms laid out by the state."[18] As such, the government needed "to clearly define the boundary between white and Indian."[19] To do so would involve "blood quantum data" which proved problematic, especially for those still residing east of the Mississippi, many of whom had little Indian "blood," as judged by their appearance, according to the official report. The report notes individuals with small amounts of Indian "blood," or none at all might wish to call themselves Indian, sometimes for "pecuniary advantages," and who might be called "Indians for revenue."[20] The special report was prepared by the Census Office, and entitled *Report on Indians Taxed and Indians Not Taxed in the United States (except Alaska) at the Eleventh Census: 1890* (1894). It was 683 pages, and contained numerous illustrations, maps and portraits, some in full color. It is a magnificent volume! As reported, the Indian population was 248,253; 58,806 being Indians Taxed, 189,447 being Indians not Taxed. This is a very significant decrease from the 400,764 Indian population of 1850!

1900 to 1970

After 1890, all Indians were more or less included in the census. The 1900 Census enumerated a total population of 76 million, 237,196 were enumerated as Indian. (Based on census data this was the American Indian population nadir.) For the first time "race" was used along with "Color," to become "Color or race" for the "personal description" category. This census is especially important because it was the first to enumerate Indians on and off reservations as part of the regular enumeration. Both were to be designated under the "Color or race" column. Instructions were given to write 0 if no white blood, and ½, ¼ etc. of "whatever fraction is nearest the truth."

The 1910 Census enumerated a population of 92.2 million, of whom 265,683 were Indians (plus another 25,331 in Alaska). This was the first increase in the Indian population since initial European contact! A determined effort was made to enumerate Indians completely, particularly mixed Indians, as racial mixture was increasing. It was indicated that "all persons of mixed white and Indian blood who have any appreciable amount of Indian blood are counted as Indians."[21] Some increase in the Indian population was due to these procedures; however, some was due to natural increase. It was noted that given the increasing amount of white "blood" in the Indian population, the numbers of Indians could increase from census "without necessarily any increase in the total amount of Indian blood in the country."[22] Why was so much information collected about Indians in this census, and why so much emphasis on "blood"? There were advocates of "solving the Indian problem" through assimilation.[23] Both Indians and the government needed to decide ways to include them within tribe or nation. Governmental issues were reflected in the decennial censuses as questions of how to categorize Indians. As things developed, America was still struggling with assimilating Indians by the end of the century. A result was the Dawes Act of 1887, allotting many Indian lands and providing citizenship for those giving up or losing "tribal relations." According to one scholar, this "required the government to clearly define the boundary between white and Indian."[24] Under the Act, restrictions were placed on Indians of one-half or more Indian blood, as it was thought they were not capable of "handling their own affairs." Not long after, science was beginning to backlash against the "scientific racism" of the 19th century, or at least investigate issues empirically.[25] Of concern, was the nature of "mixed Indians." Many thought them inferior; others were not so sure. Franz Boas, a leading anthropologist, thought census data would help investigate the issue.[26] A special census on Indians was conducted under the direction of another anthropologist, Roland Dixon of Harvard, a polygenicist. But what data should be collected? Obviously, information on Indian-white and/or black mixture should be collected; it was. Instructions were elaborate: A "full-blood" Indian was simply designated "full" in the Indian column, though it should be verified by the "old men of the tribe." For "mixed bloods," two additional columns were provided, one for "white," another for "negro." In the Indian column, amount of Indian blood should be designated; likewise amounts of white and/or "negro" blood should be designated in the same manner: the total should be 1.[27] Of the 265,683 Indians enumerated, 150,053 (56.5per cent) were "full blood"; and 93,423 (35.2 percent) were mixed, mostly with white 88,030 (33.1 percent). (No information was collected on 22,207 enumerated [8.4 percent].) There were tremendous differences among tribes in percentage "full blood," for example, 98.6 percent of the Pima versus 34.5 percent of the Ojibwe.

To provide comparisons between the "full bloods" and the others, information on age, sex, fertility, location, education and vitality were collected. Of particular relevance was an analysis of fertility: Mixed marriages were more fertile in several ways, for example, producing more children and children were more likely to survive. This was particularly the case for children with a white parent. It could be concluded, therefore, that intermarriage was advantageous. Given the findings, there arose concern that the "full bloods" were disappearing, increasingly replaced by "mixed bloods" producing more and healthier children.[28] Arthur C. Parker, an Indian anthropologist, thought the census monumental for depicting "what the Indian is and is becoming and how he is progressing."[29]

The 1920 Census was not nearly as elaborate. It enumerated 244,437 American Indians, a decline from 1910, in part because not-so-extensive efforts to enumerate Indians were used but largely the result of the 1918 influenza pandemic that killed 21 million people worldwide.

The 1930 Census placed some emphasis on Indians. It obtained information on "full-blood" and "mixed-blood" Indians and tribal affiliation; these data were compared with those from 1910, and a picture of changes in the two groups was obtained. Interestingly, guidelines for classifying "Color or race" now included Mexican separately, who had prior to this mostly been included as white. This was a result of political pressure pertaining to increased numbers of Mexican immigrants (and a decreased number from Europe,) and growing hostility toward them.[30]

A significant development between the 1920 and 1930 enumerations was the passage of the one-sentence Indian Citizenship Act of 1924, making citizens of all noncitizen Indians born in the United States, whereas previously those living on reservations were citizens of their tribe, not the U.S. (They *could* become citizens if they left their tribe, accepted allotments and so forth.) Under the Act, approximately one-third – 125,000 or more – of the Indian population was granted citizenship, with most Indians already citizens. However, tribal affiliation could remain as could claims to tribal property; in a sense many Indians had "dual citizenship."

Instructions were to enumerate white and Indian as Indian, except where the amount of Indian blood is minor, and/or the person is regarded as white. Both "Negro" and mulatto were to be enumerated as "Negro," as were Indian and "Negro" mixed individuals "unless the Indian blood predominates and the status as an Indian is generally accepted in the community." There were also instructions to enumerate other mixed races according to the non-white parent if mixed with white, and according to the father if mixture was between two "colored" groups, except "Negro-Indian" mixture. The Indian population was 332,397, with 153,933 (46.3 percent) being "full blood," 141,101 (42.4 percent) being mixed blood, and the rest not having a designation.[31] While some of the difference was influenced by census procedures and increased rates of intermarriage, differences in the rate of "natural increase" between "full" and "mixed bloods" was definitely involved.

The 1940 Census "Color or race" categories were the same as previously, except there was no separate Mexican designation because of a backlash following the 1930 "racial categorization" of Mexicans: There were protests from the Mexican government, Mexican Americans and the League of United Latin American Citizens (LULAC) and earlier advocates backed off. The Census Bureau responded:"[O]ur classification must always be in accordance with the policy of the Federal Government"; thus, "Mexicans are Whites and must be classified as 'White.'"[32] As one scholar[33] concludes, "Racial ideology ... brought 'Mexican' onto the census. International political pressure took it off."

It is hard to ascertain how the Indian Reorganization Act of 1934 impacted the 1940 Census. The Act strengthened Indian tribes; tribal membership became important as tribal members were "Indian" irrespective of the amount of blood the tribe required, as were nontribal members having at least one-half Indian blood. The Census enumerated a total population of 132.1 million; of these, 345,252 were Indians. Following the IRA of 1934, only nontribal members of one-half or more Indian blood were considered Indian, but this was eased in the Census. Enumeration procedures for the first time limited Indians as Indians to a blood quantum requirement, although only for nontribal members. Instructions were to enumerate someone as Indian "if enrolled on an Indian agency or reservation roll" and those others if "Indian blood is one-fourth or more" or considered Indian by the community.

What the 1940 Census lacked in enumerating certain Indian-mixed groups was partially made up for in 1950, as both the former "Color or race" column and some of the designation for it changed. The column only read "Race." Specific designations for Hindu and Korean were dropped; Indian was changed from Indian ("In") to American Indian ("Ind"); Japanese was changed from "Jp" to the derogatory "Jap," reflecting, perhaps, World War II. Instructions more or less remained the same except for a couple of important additions. One, special care should be taken in enumerating Indians where "there were many Indians living outside of reservations." And, two, mixed white-"Negro"-Indian individuals "living in certain communities in the Eastern United States" should be designated as "all other races" by their local name, for example, "Croatian" (in Virginia and the Carolinas), "Jackson White" (in New York and New Jersey) and "We-sort" (AKA Wesort in Maryland). Given all of the above, the 1950 Census enumerated an Indian population of 357,499, a slight 3.5 percent increase from 1940.

1960 to 2010

The 1960 Census brought about numerous changes. For one, forms similar to today were used, and mostly mailed to households, then picked up by census workers. "Color or race," was indicated by simply filling in a circle under the appropriate category for each person in the household. This was done sometimes by the census worker but many respondents self-identified. If classification was in doubt for mixed children of nonwhite or nonblack and Indians, they were enumerated according to their father's "race." People of Indian-white mixture were Indian if on rolls or considered Indian by the community. If mixed with Black, then they were Indian only if predominantly Indian or recognized as Indian.

A separate schedule was used for Alaska (and Hawaii); the Alaskan schedule enabled the identification of Eskimos and Aleuts as well as American Indians (and the Hawaiian one allowed for identification as "Hawaiian" or "Part-Hawaiian").[34] The 1960 Census enumerated a total U.S. population of 179.3 million, including 523,591 Indians in the United States and 22,000 Eskimos (Inuit) and 6,000 Aleuts in Alaska (and 11,000 Hawaiians and 91,000 Part-Hawaiians in Hawaii). This was a 46.5 percent increase from 1950, attributed in large part to the possibility of self-identifying as an Indian. (The increase in the total U.S. population was 18.5 percent.) Thus individuals identified by census workers in previous censuses as non-Indians became self-identified Indians. Much has been written about this increase, thought in part to be a result of *some* lessening of prejudice toward Indians as well as changes in enumeration procedures, although there was some natural increase of Indians from 1950 to 1960.[35]

The 1970 Census "Color or Race" question ("Race" now capitalized) was much the same as for 1960, though Indians appeared as "Indian (Amer.)" with an adjacent blank designated "Print tribe" and an arrow pointing to the blank. Importantly, for the first time "Color or Race" was determined solely by self-definition. (Those in doubt were to be designated as father's identification.) An individual simply filled in a circle next to the appropriate color/race. Here again, there was a large increase in the Indian population from the previous census. Of the 203.3 million Americans enumerated, there were 792,730 Indians, an increase of 51.4 percent, while there was an increase of only 13.4 percent for the total population.

The 1980 Census reflected an increased Indian population of 72.4 percent from 1970, to 1.37 million, with the total U.S. population increasing by 11.4 percent. This was influenced by changes in the schedule and enumeration procedures. Importantly, "Color or Race" disappeared entirely, and there was no heading for the category. It was simply asked: "Is this person—." For the first time, Eskimo and Aleut designations appeared on the schedule for all states.[36] A separate question was added asking if a person was "Spanish/Hispanic origin or descent. If so, then they were self-designated either "Mexican, Mexican-American, Chicano"; "Puerto Rican"; "Cuban"; or "other Spanish/Hispanic." Thus, this was not a racial designation but a nationality one; however, as it was a separate question (No. 7), these individuals would also be designated (No. 6) as "White," "Black or Negro," "Indian (Amer.), or whatever.

The 1990 Census counted 1.9 million Indians, 57,152 Eskimos (Inuit) and 23,797 Aleuts. This 38 percent increase from 1980 to 1990 was not nearly as large as the one from 1970 to 1980, but still a very large increase. Natural increase occurred but as in the two previous censuses additional forces were operating, viz:

Other factors that may have contributed to the higher count of American Indians, Eskimos, and Aleuts such as: improvements in the way the Census Bureau counted people on reservations, on trust lands, and in Alaska Native Villages; continued use of self-identification to obtain information on race; greater propensity in 1990 than in earlier censuses for individuals (especially those of mixed Indian and non-Indian parentage) to report themselves as American Indian; and improved outreach programs and promotion campaigns.[37]

The total census enumeration for the United States was 248.7 million, an increase from 1980 of around 10 percent.

As the 1960–1970 enumeration procedures for Indians (and all others) changed the nature and number of the Indian population, so did those of the 2000 Census. For the first time, one could be enumerated as more than one race. There were some modification of the categories as well, but the real change was regarding "racial" enumeration. The question now was "What is Person 1's race?" (Numbers were changed as family members were enumerated.) Following this was "Mark x one or more races to indicate what this person considers himself/herself to be." Thus, racially mixed people were designated as such with their races indicated.

The 2000 Census enumerated a population of 281.4 million, an increase of 13.2 percent. Only 6.8 million (2.4 percent of the population) indicated they were of more than one race. A total of 4.1 million said they were American Indian or Alaskan Native (AIAN), which was 1.5 percent of the population. Of the 4.1 million, 2.5 million (0.9 percent of the U.S. population) indicated only American Indian as "race," while 1.6 million (0.6 percent of the U.S. population) said they were American Indian and another race, mostly white (1.1 million of the 1.6 million, or 0.4 percent).[38] The 2010 Census categories had some slight modifications. Importantly, there was a space to write "Some other race." The total population in the United States was 308.7 million, an increase of 9.7 percent in 10 years. There were 5.2 million who identified as AIAN, an increase of 26.7 percent form 2000; 2.9 million self-identified as AIAN only, an increase of 18.4 percent from 2000; and 2.3 million reported themselves as AIAN and another race, an increase of 39.2 percent from 2000. Over three-fourths of the 5.2 million (78 percent) lived outside of tribal areas.

Conclusions

The formulators of the U.S. Census desired a picture of the American population as a numerical representation of segments of the population deemed important. As stated in the Constitution, objectives were to assess state populations for representation and taxation. Only 6 of the 13 states had definite boundaries, as boundaries were disputed and territories claimed. At the time of the first census the total area of the U.S. encompassed 820,377 square miles, with only 239,953 square miles considered "settled area."[39] All segments of the population were not equal, although the situation was complicated. Slavery had been recognized by law everywhere, although most states recognized "free Negros." By 1790 things weren't so clear; at that time "laws providing for the extinction of slavery had been put into operation in all states north of Maryland, with the exception of New York and New Jersey."[40] By this time Indians living in the census area were few and scattered. Reservations existed in New York and Pennsylvania, but tribal Indians overwhelmingly existed west of the colonies and any settlements. One estimate is that only about 76,000 Indians lived on all the land claimed by the U.S., and all but a few lived in what would come to be called "tribal relations."[41]

In the initial census act, the relevant population was free persons – enumerated by sex and color, and free males of age 16 years and over distinguished from those younger (supposedly because of the relevance of the older group to industrial and military strength) – distinguished "from all others" (slaves). "Indians not taxed" and other categorizations were irrelevant for constitutional and census purposes. "Indians not taxed" would remain outside the official census for decades, although results of a special census were reported in the 1850 Census. And an effort was made to include Indians on reservations in 1870 in a special memorandum, but they were not counted as part of the "True Population." Indians "in tribal relations" as falling officially outside the U.S. prevailed until the ICA of 1928.

Meanwhile, race had entered the census extensively. "Free colored" replaced "other free" in 1820, then in turn was replaced by "color." And "white-other" was replaced by "white-colored."

Gradually the idea of the "mixed person" found its way into the census, with the 1860 Census and the threefold "White, black or mulatto." Then, this was replaced by "White, Black, Chinese, or Indian," and so on. Meanwhile, mixed Indians became especially complicated to enumerate. In 1870, there was discussion about the fate of Indians, especially mixed bloods: Were Indians capable of being assimilated? Were mixed Indians inferior to "pure" Indians? Gradually blood quantum entered censuses by recording degrees of Indian blood, and how to differentiate between an Indian mixed with white blood and an Indian mixed with Black blood. Basically Indians with white blood and "appreciable" Indian blood were Indian, whereas those with Black blood were not. Coinciding with all of this was the idea that mixed Indians of any type who lived as Indians (or recognized as Indians) were Indians, no matter what. With the IRA of 1834 and its emphasis on tribal membership to determine Indians and one-half blood quantum to determine nontribal Indians, but used in the census (and government) as one-fourth, the 1940 Census probably limited the enumeration of Indians, especially as it was determined visually by enumerators. This became increasingly problematic as intermarriage increased. Enumeration by self-definition eliminated this but opened the possibility of being Indian existing only in the mind. This was a step away from reality, as "race" was now anything a person says. The 2000 Census represented, in turn, a step toward reality with the recognition that one could be and often is of more than one race, which is particularly true of Indians.

The U.S. Census became increasingly racialized, for others as well as for Indians. While "living as an Indian" remained important as recently as 1940, then lingered around until the 1960 census as "recognized by the community," Indian blood quantum never stopped being important. Started partially in 1960, self-identification changed everything. Now "Indian" simply exists in someone's mind. Nothing else matters in terms of the census. The census has used encompassing criteria to define Indians as America changed – geographical (where one lived), social (formal members of a tribe), cultural (living in tribal relations as an Indian), biological (blood quantum) and now psychological (self-identification). What's next? Who knows? It only seems certain that the U.S. Census has stopped considering Indians as Indians in any real sense, and that geographical, social, cultural and/or biological Indians are irrelevant, though indicators such as reservation residence and the like will show up in tables. Now that the "Indian problem" has lessened, are Indian characteristics or experiences irrelevant to larger society, at least in describing Indians as a segment of American society? Does "Indian" exist only in one's mind as a self-definition?

Notes

1. W. S. Rossiter, "Population in the Colonial and Continental Periods," pp. 3–15 in U.S. Bureau of the Census, *A Century of Population Growth from the First Census of the United States to the Twelfth, 1790–1900* (Washington, DC: Government Printing Office, 1909), p. 3.

2. W. S. Rossiter, "Introduction," pp. 1–2 in U.S. Bureau of the Census, *A Century of Population Growth from the First Census of the United States to the Twelfth, 1790–1900* (Washington, DC: Government Printing Office, 1909), p. 4.

3. David Hurst Thomas, *Skull Wars: Kennewick Man, Archaeology, and the Battle for Native American Identity* (New York: Basic Books, 2000), p. xxix.

4. U.S. Constitution, article 1, section 2.

5. Ibid.

6. Margaret M. Jobe, "Native Americans and the U.S. Census: A Brief Historical Survey." *University Libraries Faculty & Staff Contributions*, paper 28. Boulder: University of Colorado, 2004. The idea of basing politics and policy on quantitative data was emerging among Western nations as they realized, according to Jobe, "numbers were inherently more objective, and thus truer, than qualitative descriptions of people and events."

7. U.S. Bureau of the Census, *Report on Indians Taxed and Indians Not Taxed in the United States (except Alaska)* (Washington, DC: U.S. Government Printing Office, 1894), p. 15.

8. Erin Blakemore, "How the U.S. Census Defines Race." SmartNews Keeping you current, Smithsonian.com, November 9, 2015.

9. U.S. Census Bureau, "The Asian Population: 2010," *2010 Census Briefs*, issued March 2012, p. 2.

10. U.S. Bureau of the Census, *Population of the United States in 1860* (Washington, DC: Government Printing Office, 1864), p. 14.

11. James P. Collins, "Native Americans in the Census, 1860–1890." National Archives, Vol. 38 (2006), p. 1.

12. See Francis Amasa Walker, "Report of the Superintendent of Census to the Secretary of the Interior," pp. ii–xlviii in U.S. Bureau of the Census, *Ninth Census of the United States: Statistics of Population*, vol. 1 (Washington, DC: Government Printing Office, 1872), p. xiii; see also Jobe, *Native Americans and the U.S. Census*, 2004.

13. Jennifer L. Hochschild, and B. M. Powell, "Racial Reorganization and the United States Census, 1850–1930: Mulattoes, Half-Breeds, Mixed Parentage, Hindoos, and the Mexican Race," *Studies in American Political Development*, Vol. 22, pp. 1–65, 2008.

14. U.S. Bureau of the Census, *Ninth Census*, 1872, p. xvii; see also Jobe, *Native Americans and the U.S. Census*, 2004.

15. James P. Collins, "Native Americans in the Census, 1860-1890." National Archives, Vol. 38 (2006).

16. Ibid., p. 2.

17. Hochschild and Powell, *Racial Reorganization*, 2008, p. 31; U.S. Bureau of the Census, *Population and Housing Inquiries in the U.S. Decennial Censuses, 1790–1970*, U.S. Department of Commerce Working Paper 39. Washington, DC: U.S. Government Printing Office, 1973. This interest apparently was related to federal policy (see Hochschild and Powell, *Racial Reorganization*, 2008, fn. 133), especially regarding intermarriage, including discouraging intermarriage near reservations and encouraging mixed Indians to separate from their tribes and relinquish tribal status (see Thomas Ingersoll, *To Intermix with Our White Brothers: Indian Mixed Bloods in the United States from Earliest Times to the Indian Removal* [Albuquerque: University of New Mexico Press, 2005, pp. 243–44]).

18. Hochschild and Powell, *Racial Reorganization*, 2008, p. 31.

19. Ibid.

20. See Russell Thornton, *American Indian Holocaust and Survival: A Population History since 1492* (Norman: University of Oklahoma Press, 1987), pp. 215–16; U.S. Bureau of the Census, *Report on Indians Taxed and Not Taxed*, 1894, p. 131; see also Hochschild and Powell, *Racial Reorganization*, 2008, pp. 31–32.

21. U.S. Bureau of the Census, *Indian Population of the United States and Alaska, 1910* (Washington, DC: Government Printing Office, 1915) p. 10.

22. Ibid.

23. See, for example, Kenneth Prewitt, *What Is Your Race? The Census and Our Flawed Efforts to Classify Americans* (Princeton and Oxford: Princeton University Press, 2013), p. 36.

24. Hochschild and Powell, *Racial Reorganization,* 2008, p. 31.

25. Ibid., p. 32.

26. Franz Boas, "The Census of North American Indians," pp. 49–53 in *The Federal Census: Critical Essays by Members of the American Economic Association*, Publications of the American Economic Association, No. 2 (New York: Macmillan, 1899), p. 51; see also Jobe, *Native Americans and the U.S. Census*, 2004.

27. U.S. Bureau of the Census, 2002, p. 56.

28. See U.S. Bureau of the Census, *Indian Population of the United States and Alaska*, 1915, pp. 176–80.

29. Arthur C. Parker, "The Status and Progress of Indians as Shown by the Thirteenth Census," *Quarterly Journal of the Society of American Indians*, Vol. 3 (1915), p. 185; see also Jobe, *Native Americans and the U.S. Census*, 2004.

30. Hochschild and Powell, *Racial Reorganization*, 2008, pp. 34–35.

31. U.S. Bureau of the Census, *Indian Population of the United States and Alaska* (Washington, DC: United States Government Printing Office, 1937). These percentages are different from the 1910 Census: 56.5 percent full blood and 35.2 percent mixed blood.

32. Quoted in Hochschild and Powell, *Racial Reorganization,* 2008, p. 36.

33. Ibid.

34. Campbell Gibson and Kay Jung, *Historical Census Statistics on Population Totals by Race, 1790 to 1990, and by Hispanic Origin, 1970 to 1990, for Large Cities and Other Urban Places in The United States,* Working Paper No. 76 (Washington, DC: U.S. Census Bureau, February 2005).

35. Thornton, *American Indian Holocaust and Survival,* 1987, pp. 159–76.

36. If there was doubt, children were to be designated according to mother's designation; if more than one race was reported, designation was the first race listed.

37. Edna L. Paisano, *We, the First Americans* (Washington, DC: Bureau of the Census, issued September 1993), p. 1.

38. See U.S. Census Bureau, "Overview of Race and Hispanic Origin," *Census 2000 Brief,* Issued April 24, 2001.

39. U.S Bureau of the Census, *A Century of Population Growth,* 1909, p. 17.

40. Ibid., p. 37.

41. Ibid., p. 40.

NDN DNA

by Jessica Kolopenuk

Introduction

My name is *wâpiski-mîkwan*. I am a bear clan *Iyiniw* (Cree) woman, descendant of Chief Peguis' people from the Red River region north of what is now called Winnipeg, Manitoba, Canada. While my father is of Ukrainian and Polish descent, maternally, I belong to the McCorrister and Spence families of Peguis First Nation. I am an Indian – according to Canada, anyway – and its legal framing of what it calls its three "Aboriginal peoples": "Indian," "Inuit," and "Métis." Specifically, I became a section 6(2) Indian as defined by Canada's *Indian Act* – legislation used to govern (some) Indigenous peoples in Canada. Additionally, I have learned that I am "Native American" – another label I've been recently given, this time not by decree of federal policy makers, but by another set of historically colonial agents: scientists. Let me explain: whereas I am classified as an Indian according to Canadian state racial logics, my DNA has been classified according to population geneticists and their logics as being "Native American," and more specifically, that my mitochondrial DNA is deemed to fall into a category called "haplogroup B."

I have introduced myself according to some of the names and categories that mark my body and which contribute to arranging my relationships as a Cree person. *Iyiniwak* (Cree peoples) often position our bodies in terms of our relationships to place (where we come from), to people (who we come from), and to other human and non-human relatives (who sustain us), all of which are constituted by and constitutive of our peoplehood. In doing so, we demonstrate that as a people, each of us is uniquely individual, but also and importantly, connected to and through a system of relationships. We belong through kinship.

In the second, as an Indian, I am additionally identified racially in legal state-based language based on criteria of birth and a perception of my genealogical proximity to my registered status ancestors. Finally, as an *Iyiniw* woman, who also happens to be a so-called genetically verifiable "Native American," my body and those of all the women in my direct maternal lineage are reduced to biological organisms, and, as such, the geneticist understands our bodies and bodily relationships to one another according to what he believes is a truth about who we are revealed by a genetic mutation. While scientists may agree that a person's identity is far more complex than genetic analysis may understand, their act of naming (some) Indigenous people as "Native American" is also a powerful act of representing us as something other than how we necessarily understand ourselves. While blood politics rely on the erasure of the Indigenous person's social, cultural, and political complexities, genetic science does not deny their existence, but rather, deems them unnecessary for the genetic study of physical bodies.

I've introduced myself for the sake of *Iyiniw* custom, but also, and importantly, to acknowledge something that Indigenous people already know and live with daily; that is, that our identities are made out of knotted-up configurations of how we are understood by others (e.g., our family, our community, our clan, our First Nation, the nation-state, scientists, etc.) and how we have come to understand ourselves. We have been subject to outsiders' definitions of who we are, whether it be through law, religion, Hollywood and popular culture, academia, and so forth. These definitions have helped to facilitate the colonial nation-state's attempts to sever us from our land bases while complicating and, in many instances, damaging our own self-conceptions as particular place-based peoples connected to our ancestors. There is much at stake in the act of analyzing from Indigenous standpoints the language and processes through which outsiders name and categorize us and how we either consciously or unconsciously buy into their meanings. After all, the naming of Indigenous peoples as Indian, American Indian, Native American, or Aboriginal has been fundamental to colonial projects and the making of nation-states because such categories contribute to our intense regulation (if not outright erasure) as peoples. Genetic science is the newest and potentially fastest growing field that may do just that.

Genetic science is deeply political as it generates the power to tell a certain story about who we are as place-based Indigenous peoples. Regardless of the popular perception that science is about objectivity and neutrality, reliability and validity, and a pursuit of "truth" for the "greater good," genetic research among Indigenous peoples is about the power to advance a particular way of understanding the world and our existence in it. And it's about the power to tell the stories that make us who we are. In this context we may well ask: Who do we want telling our stories and how do we want them to be told? Will we let geneticists and the language of genomic and genetic science (re)tell our stories?

Kim TallBear (2013), Dakota scholar and leader in the study of genetics[1] as it relates to Indigenous peoples, insists that in order to understand the potential implications of genetic science and Native American DNA for Indigenous people, we have to consider the broader contexts of race and colonialism within which Indigenous peoples live. Accordingly, how Canada legally defines (some) Indigenous people through the *Indian Act* is connected to the practices of genomic science, although this may not be immediately obvious. In Canada, as codified in the *Indian Act*, one official formulation of Indigeneity has been typically expressed as "Indianness" through the symbol and presumed materiality of "Indian blood" and used to measure degrees of Indigeneity through stratified categories (6(1) and 6(2)) that unevenly distribute the juridical ability to transmit status to one's children. As the first *Indian Act* to amalgamate all previous legislation regarding Indians, the 1876 *Act* defined Indians as "[a]ny male person of Indian blood … any child of such person … [or] any woman who is or was lawfully married to such person" (*Indian Act*, 1876, s. 3(3)). Historically (and to some degree today), criteria of birth have determined Indian status for those tracing their Indianness through paternal lines (through one's legal father), while making vulnerable those who trace it matrilineally (through one's legal mother). Indian status, while having been transmitted in this gendered and heteronormative manner (through the status of one's father and then husband) has also been highly dependent on a racialized conception of the Indian, expressed through the symbol of "Indian blood." The racialized logic of *Indian Act* registration posits the "truth" of Indian existence as lying in Indigenous peoples' notional bodily material – our *alleged* "Indian blood" and then ties rights or entitlements (as limited and problematic as they are) to those the Canadian state deems as embodying enough of that imagined characteristic.

The logic of *Indian Act* registration implicitly denies the fuller complexities and richness (i.e., the multiple and entangled realities) of Indigenous lives and cultures, and rather posits the authenticity of identity as lying in Indigenous peoples' *symbolic* bodily material – our "Indian blood."

What I mean by "symbolic" is this: Indian blood, in the way that it is used in the *Indian Act*, is not biologically real. One could not take a blood test and decipher which proportion of the blood is "Indian." Instead, Indian blood, as defined by the *Indian Act*, is an idea that came out of the late nineteenth century Western science, which asserted that biological characteristics, however non-real we now know they are, can indicate inherent human difference and, as such, are a rational way to determine identity and forms of (non)citizenship (Sturm 2002). It was this science that deemed Indigenous people primitive and less evolved than our white counterparts. As such, Indianness, as measured by the notion of Indian blood, becomes a racialized and racializing way of categorizing Indigenous peoples. Through its reliance on a notion of blood purity, the *Indian Act* attaches official legal categorization to the Indian's notional bodily material: her blood and to the exclusion of the (other) ways that Indigenous peoples determine identity and belonging (e.g., kinship, family, clan, names, hereditary positions, etc.).

Additionally, and importantly, Canadian Indianness has been constructed as a racially dilutable category. Meaning that *it* (Indianness) can be thinned out over generations and eventually eliminated in children who are born to legally defined Indians and non-Indians. Although its specific meaning has changed over time, Indianness has become a powerful symbol representing Indigeneity extending beyond any perceived limits of the legal world into the common language and ideas of both Indigenous and non-Indigenous people(s) as well as into the official membership codes of First Nations and Métis[2] peoples themselves (Andersen 2014; Simpson 2014; Palmater 2011; Green 2007). In this way, Indian blood and Indian status have been used to determine the degrees of legal relatedness between family members (Indian and also Métis) according to *symbolically* biological criteria in ways that have rearranged our systems of kinship and belonging.

Critically analyzing these frames of purity that define Indigeneity in racially restrictive ways is important because they are not only produced alongside Indian status regulation that has removed Indigenous people and peoples from their land bases (Palmater 2011; Barker 2006; Freeman 2005; Napoleon 2001), but non-Indigenous ideals of bodily or species purity have always conditioned the very practice of Indigenous removal *as* natural and therefore legitimate. In the making of colonial nation-states, Indians were not seen as sufficiently evolved (be that culturally or biologically) to be fit for full state citizenship (Reardon and TallBear 2012). Neither are some perceived as racially pure enough to retain their Indian status. For example, until 1985, according to the *Indian Act*, a status Indian woman who married a non-status man was stripped of her Indian status and, with it, the right to take up residence on reserve and inherit family-held land.[3] Her children suffered the same consequences, and neither divorce nor spousal death guaranteed her or her children's return to their community in life, or in their own death, as formally, their bodies were not permitted to be buried on reserve land (Suzack 2010; Jamieson 1978). As a result, *Indian Act* registration, through its patriarchal and racial standards, has reduced the number of individuals eligible for Indian status and thus the need for reserve land and government spending on Indians (Freeman 2005, 51).

While it originated as an imposed colonial legal category, the term "Indian" has become powerfully embedded within many Indigenous communities in Canada. In many instances, racially defined legal categories and logics have come to disrupt what are already intricate systems of relationships that make up Indigenous families and peoples – and these categories, additionally, have played a significant role in dispossessing Indigenous people and peoples from territory and community. So while Indian blood, as I stated, is not a literally physical substance, it retains very *real* effects because (some) people have bought into the idea that the Indigenous person's body via a perceived purity of Indian blood (opposed to, for instance, her particular ancestral family lineage(s) and relationships) should be the main consideration for defining oneself and others. This way of thinking is common and we can see it in such expressions as "Well you don't *look* Indian" or "I'm full blooded" or "How much Native are you?" As the state has intended, Indigenous people have, *to some degree*, come to racialize ourselves – to think of ourselves in racial (i.e., Indian) terms instead of in terms of ancestral peoplehoods (i.e., *Iyiniwak*).

Breaking Down Some Basics: What Is Native American DNA?

While blood politics continue to play a significant role in the dispossession of Indigenous peoples in Canada, scientific understandings of Indigeneity have moved from the idea of blood to an understanding that relies on genes.

Genetic science understands Indigeneity according to the molecular group-ings of genetic building blocks, which make up our DNA. These building blocks are known as chemical bases, and they are called adenine (A), gua-nine (G), cytosine (C), and thymine (T). What is imaginary (i.e., Indian blood), is becoming physically real in the minds of some people and they are calling this allegedly real substance, Native American DNA. Genetic testing of Native American DNA is the newest force that Indigenous peoples have to contend with when it comes to outsiders' definitions of Indigeneity, and, for the most part, it is not being done on our own terms. Knowing this, I sequenced my own mitochondrial DNA in the lab. What follows is an ex-planation about why I decided to subject myself to scientific classification.

The study of human genomics and genetics has grown significantly in the last decade. Within this scientific field, the bodies of (some) Indigenous people have been sought out and studied for the alleged purpose of gain-ing insight into humanity's collective past and present (Tallbear 2013, 1). Following the completion of the Human Genome Project in 2003 in which scientists mapped the entire human genome, geneticists broadcasted a joint message – that the results of the study disproved any genetic basis for the existence of human races (Koenig, Soo-Jin Lee, and Richardson 2008, 1). Race, they said, does not genetically exist. Human genomic research claims, then, that humans are practically all the same. Such a claim makes the al-leged existence of Native American DNA puzzling since geneticists have differentiated (some) "Native American" people from other human popula-tions (sub-Saharan African, European, and East Asian) based on biological genetic markers (i.e., DNA) alone and to the exclusion of other forms of physically and socially determined group membership.

What is DNA, anyway? Most simply, deoxyribonucleic acid (DNA) is a tightly wound molecule – a small portion of almost all of our body's cells, that holds the information that makes our species uniquely what it is. In my understanding, DNA is like the seed of a tree. You can look at the seed and predict what kind of tree it will be – that seed is the tree's road map – but until that seed grows, you don't know *exactly* how it will look or if it will be healthy, how tall it will be, or how much shade it will provide. No matter how good the map is, all kinds of factors can impact its growth: the amount of sunlight it gets, how much rain falls in any given year, whether an animal eats it or cuts it down. The same is true for human genetics. While it is com-mon to think that our DNA determines who and what we are, at least biolog-ically, numerous environmental factors affect how our DNA is expressed. DNA does not tell the *whole* story.

While for the most part all humans do share the same genetic make-up, there are small areas within the genome where individuals may differ, and it is important to note that most markers denoting these differences are non-coding, meaning that they do not actually amount to observable differences in physical characteristics (Tallbear 2013, 40). These differences, called "mutations," are normally passed down and inherited by biological relatives. Through the identification of mitochondrial DNA mutations (the DNA that we all inherit from our biological mother) and Y-chromosome DNA mutations (the DNA that biological males inherit from their biological father), scientists have declared the existence of Native American DNA. These mutations have been identified as "haplogroups." Scientists have named mitochondrial haplogroups A, B, C, D, and X, and Y-chromosome haplogroups C and Q as being distinctively Native American as they are believed to distinguish genetic mutations that some 21st century Native American people have inherited from the founding populations of the Americas.

This method of classifying Native American DNA begins by removing a sample from the organism (in this case, a human). This means that the scientist takes a piece of your body, containing your cells, to analyze. Usually, this happens through a cheek swab (which was the case when I did the test, but can also be done through the extraction of blood). This sample is then processed in a lab and manipulated through systematized procedure. Specifically, the scientist separates the DNA from the other cellular contents surrounding it: the cytoplasm, the proteins, the organelles, and the membranes. The scientist needs to get the DNA on its own in order to make sense of it. Since I sequenced my own DNA in a lab, it was at this point in the test where I could look at a piece of myself in the form of a colourless liquid inside of a test tube. The feeling, for me, was unsettling because it was the moment that I realized that, to the scientist, other than those little molecules inside of the test tube, nothing about who I am mattered – yet he felt prepared to classify me. I felt dehumanized and I wanted that little piece of me back. I was confused about how they could understand anything about me through something that felt so disconnected, physically and culturally, from my body and my own understanding of self. I felt like I had lost control and I was left with a sense of distress. The stripped down DNA can now be analyzed. The DNA gets what is called amplified meaning that it is multiplied into millions of copies in order to get a statistically more accurate picture of the DNA. Following this process, a DNA sequence is revealed.

The sequence is like a face that allows scientists to determine the individual's place in relation the world's other faces. In the field of population genetics, this is done by comparing the genetic sequence to a "standard" face, referred to as the Cambridge Reference Sequence. Ironically, this sequence, that *all* sequences are compared against (at least when testing mitochondrial DNA), is that of an individual of northern European decent: an average ordinary white person, one might say (although this is not a scientific claim). The mutational differences between the organism (human) under analysis and the standard face enable the scientist to categorize the DNA into a grouping called a haplogroup. As noted, mitochondrial haplogroups A B, C, D, and X as well as Y-chromosome haplogroups C and Q have been identified as being Native American.

While these categories contribute to scientifically backed claims about the genetic identities of Native American individuals and populations, mitochondrial and Y-chromosome haplogroup tests are limited. They test only single genetic lineages. In other words, when being sequenced for, say, the mitochondrial DNA test as I was, you are only testing *one out of many hundreds of thousands* of independent genetic lineages that are contained in your DNA.

Let me be clear, the mitochondrial DNA and Y-chromosome DNA tests respectively examine *less than one percent* of your entire genetic makeup to decipher whether or not you are Native American. In the mitochondrial DNA test, for example, this means that even a single *non*-Native American ancestor (defined genetically) in your entire direct maternal lineage (this means your mother's mother's mother's mother and so on to the beginning of your lineage), will result in a finding of *no* Native American DNA. As a consequence, and in a similar way that an Indigenous person in Canada who is accepted by an Indigenous people might not allegedly have *enough* "Indian blood" to qualify for Indian status, an Indigenous person might not, and in many cases, won't have Native American DNA. When I was sequenced amongst a group of other Indigenous people, for example, only two out of about a dozen of us actually had Native American DNA in the very specific lineage being tested. The group was left with the impression that Native American DNA is quite rare and not in the sense that science has perceived us as a disappearing race on the threshold of extinction. Instead, we were left with the understanding that such a measure of Indigeneity (i.e., Native American DNA) is so narrow that most Indigenous people just don't have it.

Taking the Test:
The Day I Became "Native American,"
and My Friend Didn't

In 2013, I attended the Summer Internship for Native Americans in Genomics (SING) workshop hosted by the Institute for Genomic Biology at the University of Illinois at Urbana-Champaign. This is an annual one-week intensive workshop geared at introducing and training Indigenous students and other community people in the sciences of genomics and bioinformatics. I wanted to learn everything I could about Native American DNA. What exactly was it? What was it going to mean for my family and my community? What would it mean for Indigenous people generally? Who's in and who's out? How could this potentially be used against us? As part of the workshop, we had a choice to sequence and analyze our own mitochondrial DNA. I decided to go all in – not to find out if I have Native American DNA (although I would discover that as well): instead, I wanted to find out what it *felt* like to be told whether or not I have it.

I've seen what it does to Indigenous people who are struggling to figure out who they are and where they fit. Admittedly, I've experienced it myself: many of us labour internally – emotionally even – to find a comfortable place somewhere between the way that we know we belong to our family and our community, and the way that we either "look the part" or don't, or the way we live "traditionally" enough or don't, or the way we fit into official recognition systems or not (e.g., enrolment, status registration, band membership, etc.). How these things all interact and play out has enormous impacts on how we are seen as Indigenous people and how we see ourselves.

Identity, as I understand it from my own experience, is made through relationships to our own selves, to territory, to humans and non-humans, to the living, to those since passed, and to the ones that have yet to come. Colonial forces have worked hard to destroy who we are, and reconnecting with our relational identities is an important part in peeling off the wet jacket of colonial naming and the clinging self-doubt that accompanies it. With the understanding that issues concerning identity are significant to Indigenous people, I sequenced my mitochondrial DNA in order to find out if this test carries a similar emotional weight – something that can make you *feel* more or less Indigenous – to the weight that legal definitions have for a lot of Indigenous people in Canada.

My worries were confirmed. What I learned from this experience, though, did not only come from learning my own genetic classification. The more telling lesson came from watching a peer of mine, I'll call him Jackson. When I met Jackson, I got the impression that he is very connected to his community, enrolled, and traditional in what I saw as all the obvious ways: he can speak his language, he is ceremonial, and he displays a humble pride in his in-depth awareness of his genealogy. In my mind, he has no reason to be insecure about his self-identification as a specifically tribal man. As the week went on, we teamed up and questioned a lot of what the scientists were telling us about their research. In the evenings when we retired from the lab and classroom, Jackson and I would mull over the day recovering from our scientific encounters and the labour that it takes to critically analyze and question "experts" and their "expert knowledge" about who they think we are. It became very clear to us that there is more about the human genome that geneticists don't understand than what they do (e.g., until a few years ago, geneticists generally thought that at least 75 percent of our genome was "junk" and that it did nothing significant), and this added to our skepticism about the legitimacy of these DNA tests.

On the last day of the workshop, we were given our results. I was one of the last to find out what my haplogroup is because, at that time, I was illiterate in reading DNA sequences – honestly, I mostly still am. A teaching assistant helped me understand my result. "Haplogroup B," is what she said. "So what does that mean?" I asked. "It means you have Native American DNA," she replied. "Oh, ok, so what does THAT mean?" I questioned further. As she pointed to a map, she responded, "Well, it means that your ancestors have lived in this particular area in Canada from as long back as humans have inhabited North America." "Right," I said, "but I could have told you that on the first day of the workshop," I concluded.

I already knew that because that is where my family is from. If this test told me what I already knew, what *is* the point of it? In that moment, I questioned the relevance of testing for Native American DNA. I felt like it was also an insult because it was as if science was "validating" the stories that my people have known and told for thousands and thousands and thousands of years. Why is our oral and physical connection to territory not enough? Why do we need to be legitimized through scientific measures? We don't.

Some Indigenous people may not have knowledge of where their families are from due to the ways that colonial processes have disconnected them from their communities – indeed, I myself, although always having known and been connected with my family, have done a lot of learning, as an adult, about the history of our people. But here's the thing: a Native American DNA test cannot tell you what community you are from. Instead, the test can tell you if you fit into a homogenous grouping that genetic scientists have said exists with no tribal specificity and no accountability to any specific people. It also can't reconnect you to your community. There are more fulfilling ways, in my opinion, to heal from colonial dispossession and disconnection, which involves finding and spending time with actual family members rather than claiming a relationship to some abstract Native American population based on a DNA test. In my frustration, I looked over at Jackson who was still hunched over the computer screen looking at his result. He was going over it again and again asking the lead scientist if there was any way it could be wrong. He did not have Native American DNA in the lineage we had sequenced.

Jackson's appearance was deflated. Even after spending a week learning about the limitations of this test (i.e., that it accounts for less than one percent of all of our DNA), it still has the potential to elicit an emotional investment that can, at most, make someone question who they are as an Indigenous person or, at least, the level of their attachment to the things that make them Indigenous. As far I could tell, Jackson knows who he is, he knows his family, why does it matter what the test says? Would it matter if one of his ancestors turned out to be non-Native American (defined genetically)? While I don't know exactly what he was thinking, by watching Jackson, I learned that genetic science has the potential to make people question the stories of our families and peoples in ways remarkably similar to what state legal categories have done.

The dangers of genetic science are existential, but they may also turn out to be material on a large-scale basis as well. Because genetic testing is so new on the historical stage, we haven't even begun to understand how this type of science might be used to limit our citizenship and, in turn, further minimize the amount of land and self-determining authority that is ours. What we do know is that the language of genetics is quickly permeating popular language and culture. We also know that thousands of (non-Indigenous) people are flocking to genetic ancestry testing websites (instead of to Indigenous communities) and sending in their cheek swab samples in hopes of proving to themselves (and probably to others) that they are, in some way, Native American. Genetic science has the potential to further complicate our self-conceptions, but also our relationships to place through the controlling of our status and entitlement to territory and by inviting non-Indigenous people to potentially claim belonging on the basis of a DNA test.

Additionally, it throws off the balance in the making and maintaining of strong Indigenous self-hoods, potentially adding more self-doubt and confusion than previously existed.

Conclusion

The world continues to change quickly. Fast-paced change is not new to Indigenous people, but what is new – to everyone – is the language of genetics. DNA is being used to express perceived degrees of relatedness between Indigenous bodies across time and space. But Indigenous peoples already have conceptions of relations with each other, with ancestors, and with the land and water and cosmos and its inhabitants – all of which contribute to understanding who we are and the responsibilities we owe to our relatives. Science is over-coding this knowledge with and through gene talk.

I sequenced my DNA. I can tell you that from what I experienced, I don't believe that this course is safe yet. I don't know if it ever will be. I am fearful that in our attempts to wriggle out of the tight-fitting hold of colonial nation-state naming, we will put on yet another wet jacket in the form of genetic science. Watching Jackson lower his head as he reads the results of his DNA test makes me think that the damage of Native American DNA has already been too great.

Acknowledgments

I would like to thank Dr. Chris Andersen and Dr. Kim TallBear for their comments on an earlier version of this paper and Kirsten Lindquist for her creative input regarding the title of this chapter. Additionally, I am thankful to Rick Smith who helps me understand the science behind Native American DNA. Lastly, I would like to thank the organizers of the Summer Internship for Native Americans in Genomics (SING) for giving me the opportunity to participate in their program.

Notes

1. Genetics research refers to the study of one or multiple isolated genes whereas genomics research refers to the study of all the genes in a genome.

2. In contrast to definitions of 'Métis as mixed', Giokas and Chartrand (2002) describe the Métis Nation as having "form[ed] a provisional government, establish[ed] civil order, and defend[ed] their territory through arms, [and] the fact that they obtained diplomatic recognition from Canada and constitutional recognition in the Constitution Act, 1871, fuel[ed] the perception both inside and outside of the historic Red River and Rupert's Land Métis/Half-breed community that they were a…people" (Giokas and Chartrand 2002, 86).

3. For chronological descriptions of the legislative and judicial events whereby the sexist determinations of Indian status have been contested by Indigenous women see Eberts (2010) and Palmater (2011).

References

Andersen, Chris. (2014). *"Métis": Race, recognition, and the struggle for indigenous peoplehood.* Vancouver and Toronto: UBC Press.

Barker, Joanne. (2006). "Gender, sovereignty, and the discourse of rights in native women's activism." *Meridians: Feminism, Race, Transnationalism*, 7(1), 127–161.

Eberts, Mary. (2010). "McIvor: Justice delayed – again." *Indigenous Law Journal*, 9(1), 15–46.

Freeman, Victoria. (2005). "Attitudes toward 'miscegenation' in Canada, the United States, New Zealand, and Australia, 1860–1914." *Native Studies Review*, 16(1), 41–69.

Giokas, J. and P. Chartrand. (2002). "Who are the Métis? A Review of the Law and Policy." In P. Chartrand (Ed.), *Who are Canada's Aboriginal Peoples? Recognition, Definition, and Jurisdiction*, (pp. 83-125). Saskatoon, SK: Purich Publishers.

Green, Joyce. (2007). "Balancing strategies: Aboriginal women and constitutional rights in Canada." In Joyce Green (Ed.), *Making Space for Indigenous Feminism* (pp. 140–59). London and New York: Zed Books, 2007.

Indian Act. R.S.C. 1876, c.18. (39 Vict.).

Jamieson, Kathleen. (1978). *Indian women and the law in Canada: Citizens minus.* Ottawa: Advisory Council on the Status of Women/Indian Rights for Indian Women.

Koenig, Barbara A., Sandra Soo-Jin Lee, and Sarah S. Richardson, eds. (2008). *Revisiting race in a genomic age.* New Brunswick, NJ, and London: Rutgers University Press.

Napoleon, Val. (2001). "Extinction by number: Colonialism made easy." *Canadian Journal of Law and Society*, 16(1), 113–45.

Palmater, Pamela D. (2011). *Beyond blood: Rethinking indigenous identity.* Saskatoon, SK: Purich Publishing Limited.

Reardon, J., and K. TallBear. (2012). "Your DNA is *our* history": Genomics, anthropology, and the construction of whiteness as property." *Current Anthropology*, 53(S5), S233–45.

Simpson, Audra. (2014). *Mohawk interruptus: Political life across the borders of settler states.* Durham, NC, and London: Duke University Press.

Sturm, Circe. (2002). *Blood politics: Race, culture, and identity in the Cherokee Nation of Oklahoma.* Los Angeles: University of California Press.

Suzack, Cheryl. (2010). "Emotion before the law." In Cheryl Suzack, Shari M. Huhndorf Jeanne Perreault, and Jean Barman (Eds.), *Indigenous women and feminism: Politics, activism, culture.* Vancouver and Toronto: UBC Press.

TallBear, Kim. (2013). *Native American DNA: Tribal belonging and the false promise of genetic science.* Minneapolis and London: University of Minnesota Press.

(RE)BUILDING THE LĀHUI (HAWAIIAN NATION)

by Maile Taualii

An examination of blood quantum and Native Hawaiians requires a review of historical and continued colonization. In a nutshell, the first Native Hawaiians, or *kānaka 'ōiwi*, arrive from the south around AD 400, celebrate nearly a century and a half of booming population growth, experience "first contact" with infectious disease in 1778, and subsequently suffer a 90 percent population drop in the 150 years following (Blaisdell, 1993). A foreign greed for sugar wealth, built upon a foundation of devastating life loss (and therefore land loss) among kānaka, throws open a door of opportunity for foreigners to hoard land and displace kānaka (Kame'eleihiwa, 1992).

In the wake of the illegal overthrow of the Kingdom of Hawaii, coupled with a 90 percent population loss, kānaka suffer gravely. Fear that Hawaiians would die off, efforts to rehabilitate kānaka and return them to land rise in the form of the Hawaiian Homes Commission Act (HHCA) of 1920. Earlier land allotment programs for American Indians introduced the concept of setting 50 percent blood quantum influenced the HHCA hearings (Kauanui, 2008). Scholars also agree that blood degree allotments were intended to "phase out" obligations to native people (Barker, 1995).

Many brilliant kānaka 'ōiwi scholars have established foundational work on issues surrounding blood quantum and its impact on kānaka. In 2008, Dr. J. Kehaulani Kauanui authored *Hawaiian Blood, Colonialism and the Politics of Sovereignty and Indigeneity*. This fundamental work provides a thorough and thoughtful examination of blood quantum and the Native

Hawaiian Homes Commission. Another fundamental contribution to scholarship is *Native Land and Foreign Desires*, authored in 1992 by Dr. Lilikalā Kame'eleihiwa, which excellently presents the kānaka 'ōiwi relationship, both spiritual and political, to the land. These two essential works are critical to understanding the relationship between kānaka and land and how blood quantum divides the Hawaiian people.

This chapter aims to build on their work and expand on the discourse in two critical areas: (1) proposed legal changes to reduce the blood quantum requirements to qualify for Native Hawaiian homeland and (2) the use of DNA testing to determine eligibility. These areas are timely, due to both proposed legislation in Hawai'i and increased national attention to genomics, biobanking, and precision medicine. Finally, this chapter presents an idea of embracing bloodlines for nation building for Native Hawaiians, considering suggestions to develop a Native Hawaiian sperm and ovum bank and other possibilities to embrace genealogy and common cultural connections.

Piko I, Piko O, Piko A: Past, Present, and Future

Since the very first voyaging canoes landed on the shores of the most isolated place on earth, *kānaka 'ōiwi*, Native Hawaiians, have focused intently on building the Lāhui (nation). Early settler needs included the basic necessities to cultivate land and thrive. Building from a handful of voyagers to nearly a million people required major nation-building efforts. Traditional knowledge of child rearing demonstrated the importance of protecting the growing nation. Women who were with child were separated from others, put on special nutrient-rich diets to aid in child rearing, and given much attention to ensure the life of the child she was carrying (Pukui, 1942). In addition to traditional birth practices, there were efforts of the Hawaiian monarchy to encourage the growth and health of the Hawaiian people. King David Kalakaua was credited with the decree "*E ho'ola lahui,*" which translates to "Give life to the Hawaiian race," the founding phrase that encouraged the establishment of the Ahahui Ho'oulu a Ho'ola Society and the Kapi'olani maternity home (Kapiolani Health Foundation, 2009).

Upon first contact with foreign infection, efforts to build and sustain the Lāhui would be thwarted. First to cause devastation would be gonorrhea, syphilis, and tuberculosis, later followed by dysentery, pneumonia, measles, influenza, mumps, and typhoid, with progressive depopulation (Blaisdell, 1993). Infamous British captain James Cook, who is attributed with the "discovery of Hawaii" in 1778, reports in his captain's log that he was aware that his men carried with them many diseases and the impact contact would have on the Hawaiian people (Cook, 1778).

From 1778 to 1922 the Lāhui would dwindle from one million strong to only 24,000 with only Hawaiian ancestry (Noyes, 2003). While the numbers of those with only Hawaiian ancestry became frighteningly small, those with mixed heritage increased. Today those who carry any quantum of Hawaiian blood are nearly half a million strong throughout the Hawaiian Islands and the U.S. continent (U.S. Census Bureau, 2010). In the state of Hawai'i, Native Hawaiians are the greatest percentage of births (36% of births are Native Hawaiians) (State of Hawai'i, 2012). Efforts to build the Lāhui are continuing.

Invisibility Is the Ultimate Hallmark of Colonization

Despite every effort to build the Lāhui, kānaka 'ōiwi face many challenges to be successful in their native homeland. The State of Hawai'i has the highest cost of living, most expensive housing market, highest cost for electricity, and highest cost of doing business (CNBC, 2017). While Native Hawaiian traditional homelands serve as playgrounds for the wealthy, Native Hawaiians depend on programs and services to assist in meeting basic needs. One of these essential programs is the Native Hawaiian Home Land Program, which requires 50 percent blood quantum in order to be eligible to apply for land (discussed in more detail later in this chapter).

To demonstrate the need for programs and services, Native Hawaiians depend on data to describe the disparities seen among the population. Data produced by demographers and statisticians are helpful for advocacy and education. However, that data is limited because funding for programs is determined by national data reports, which do not accurately depict Native Hawaiians.

Native Hawaiians have struggled to educate the broader society in the United States about their unique cultural underpinnings and historical relationships and their health and wellness issues. This has been complicated by the fact that in 1977, the Executive Office of Management and Budget (OMB) created for the first time racial and ethnic categories for federal data collection and reporting, one of which was "Asian and Pacific Islander," or

"API." This aggregated identifier brought together in one category multiple populations of Asians, Native Hawaiians, and Pacific Islanders despite the fact that all three groups have immense and distinct cultural, socioeconomic, political, and historical differences. These complexities were further complicated by the formulation of a number of organizations that initially began as distinctly Asian but because of the OMB API aggregation, expanded their name to include "Pacific" or "Pacific Islander." Yet they neither altered their services nor substantially enhanced their staffing or board representation to include Pacific Islanders.

In 1997, the OMB revised its standards for identifying ethnic and racial populations in the United States (Federal Register Notice, 1995). It split the API aggregation into two distinct groups: those of Asian descent (A) and those of Native Hawaiian and other Pacific Islander descent (NHOPI).

The major reasons for disaggregation were:

1. The need for identifying health disparities and issues within Native Hawaiian and Pacific Islander populations apart from Asian populations within the United States, and
2. The need for recognizing and protecting the unique and distinct relationships and political status that Native Hawaiians and specific Other Pacific Islanders have with the United States.

Today, the implementation of this policy continues, with difficulty, both within the federal government and with private sector organizations and institutions that undertake and report on research involving populations within the United States. The former API category has continued to be used along with a newer "AAPI" (Asian American/Pacific Islander) identifier, yet neither category is recognized by OMB as an appropriate federal definer of a class of people or a racial grouping. The negative impacts of the continued use of an API or an AAPI category are considerable for Asian, Native Hawaiian, and Pacific Islander populations.

In its 1997 determination, OMB differentiated "Native Hawaiians" from "Other Pacific Islanders." This was explicitly done as Native Hawaiians, unlike other Pacific Islander populations, are Indigenous Peoples to what now is a state of the United States: Hawai`i. This recognition is afforded only to two other population groups in the United States, American Indians and Alaska Natives, and is based on a political rather than a racial or ethnic relationship.

When the AAPI or API identifier is used, not only is the data blurred or completely inaccurate as it relates to NHOPI, but it also eliminates the ability of NHOPI populations with these special relationships to address their specific health issues through accepted political mechanisms, such as existing treaties and/or agreements.

The relationship between lack of representation in data and blood quantum is simple. Native Hawaiians are struggling to exist in our homelands. There are countless barriers: economic barriers in the form of highest cost of living in the country; political barriers in the form of no Hawaiian authority over state lands and programs (Rice v. Cayetano, 2000);[1] physical barriers such as low education rates and highest mortality rates; and spiritual barriers in the form of the protection of our most spiritual place, Mauna a Wakea, from the construction of the largest telescope on earth. The data to tell these stories is hidden. It's hidden because of agencies lack of creativity to meet their own federal mandate to separate Native Hawaiian data from others. It's hidden because of ignorance that believes and reports that separation of Native Hawaiian data from other races isn't possible. It's hidden because despite what we tell the courts, when our sacred places are destroyed, it harms our health. It's hidden because they don't want to know. Lack of representation in data is another way of making us disappear. Blood quantum rules makes many Native Hawaiian people disappear from eligibility. Invisibility is colonization. Invisibility is another way of denying our existence.

Pandora's Box: Genetic Testing or Paternity Testing

Through legislation, the United States sets blood quantum rules for Native Hawaiians. The Hawaiian Homes Commission Act as amended, provides for "the rehabilitation of the native Hawaiian people through a government-sponsored homesteading program." To qualify for this program, Native Hawaiians are defined as "individuals having at least 50 percent Hawaiian blood." If a Native Hawaiian meets this blood quantum rule and is at least 18 years old, they can apply for a 99-year homestead lease at an annual rental of $1. Homestead leases are for residential, agricultural, or pastoral purposes. There is language in the act to allow for aquacultural leases; however, none have been awarded to date. The intent of the homesteading program is to provide for "the economic self-sufficiency of native Hawaiians through the provision of land."

The homesteading program definition of Native Hawaiian (any descendant of not less than one-half part of the blood of the races inhabiting the Hawaiian Islands previous to 1778) has remained unchanged since the HHCA's passage in 1921. However, in August 2012, a lawsuit against the Department of Hawaiian Home Lands (DHHL) resulted in a proposed change to the federal rules. The lawsuit was filed on behalf of a homestead applicant (Pang Kee v. DHHL, 2012) who unsuccessfully applied for a DHHL lease using DNA test results to prove his relationship to his biological father, who was not listed on his birth certificate. Pang Kee applied for a DHHL lease and submitted his DNA results as evidence to prove his paternity. Denying his application, DHHL informed Pang Kee that it lacked a policy about whether to accept DNA results as genealogical evidence for the purpose of qualifying applications for a DHHL lease.

While DHHL states that this proposed rule change might "open up the possibility that more Hawaiians can qualify for Hawaiian Homelands," there might be an unexpected consequence that could result in the proposed language for a change in the administrative rules. The proposed DHHL language states "Genetic tests. (a) 'Genetic test' means the testing of inherited or genetic characteristics (genetic markers) and includes blood testing." The proposed language aims to allow those who do not have birth certificate proof of 50 percent or greater to use DNA paternity testing, which is more like a DNA profile or fingerprint that determines whether two individuals are biologically parent and child. While this proposed language of genetic testing to determine parent-child relationship is well-intended, it could lead to genetic testing requirements. Genetic testing for eligibility would be like opening Pandora's box. For anyone who has sought to know their "genetic ancestry," one only need look as far as the internet to find a number of companies wanting to tell someone their ancestry based on their DNA. These companies will charge anywhere from $99 to $199 to tell a willing shopper their "ancestry." While the technology is advancing and becoming more accessible to the average person, it has not gotten so precise as to tell you if you are indeed a member of "race" group or how much of that race (blood quantum) you truly are. This is not because of the technology but rather because of the nature of genes and, more specifically, recombination. Recombination is the rearrangement of genetic material, especially by crossing over in chromosomes (King, 1998). It is the process or act of exchanges of genes between chromosomes, resulting in a different genetic combination and ultimately to the formation of unique gametes with chromosomes that are different from those in parents (King, 1998). While DNA paternity testing can tell you if you are the child or parent of an individual, genetic testing for ancestry cannot definitively identify one's race, and even more elusive would be one's blood quantum.

It is for this reason that great care must be made in the introduction of terms such as "genetic testing" in rule making. DHHL would have been more accurate, as well as more sensitive to possible risks, had it used the language of "DNA paternity/maternity testing" rather than the more broad term "genetic testing." Many scholars, such as Kim TallBear (TallBear and Bolnick, 2004), have already outlined the harm that can come to Native Peoples if we are forced to use genetic testing over Native title to determine eligibility for land and enrollment.

Reducing Blood Quantum

The 2016 session of the Hawai'i State Legislature held hearings in both the House and Senate to reduce the blood quantum requirement from one-quarter to one-thirty-second Hawaiian required in order for a homestead lessee's husband, wife, children, grandchildren, brothers, or sisters to succeed to the lessee's lease (Department of Native Hawaiian Home Lands, 2016).

Arguments on both sides were persuasive. Native Hawaiian families who have been homesteading for generations testified that reducing the blood quantum would allow for land to be held in perpetuity within the family. Equally as heart-wrenching was testimony from those who represented the 44,217 applications waiting for decades to be awarded land (Department of Native Hawaiian Home Lands, 2015).

Once again, the divide-and-conquer strategy of blood quantum is used to distract Native people from fighting the true battle. In this case, the shortage of designated homesteading land has taken precedence over ensuring all Native Hawaiian families, regardless of blood quantum, the right to afford to live in their Native homeland.

Expanding the Genetic Information Nondiscrimination Act

Concerns of genetic discrimination caused by the proposed administrative rule changes to the Hawaiian Homes Commission Act of allowing genetic testing to determine eligibility, as well as the requirements of a blood quantum, could be avoided if federal legislation contained language to prevent discrimination. The Genetic Information Nondiscrimination Act of 2008, also referred to as GINA, is a federal law that protects Americans from being treated unfairly because of differences in their DNA that may affect their health (H.R. 493). If one considers the intent of the HHCA to create economic self-sufficiency for Native Hawaiians a health-related issue, one could make a case that discrimination based on genetic testing would in fact affect the health of Native Hawaiians. Equally so, if the Native Hawaiian Health Care Systems or even the Indian Health Service required genetic testing to determine eligibility, it would be discriminating against Native Americans by preventing access to health care services. While the GINA is federal law intended to protect all Americans from genetic discrimination in the workplace and by health providers, its expansion to protect Native peoples from genetic testing that would limit access to benefits would provide some respite, as new rulemaking casually throws around terms such as "genetic testing" without consideration for the possible interpretation and implementation.

On the Brink of Extinction

In 2040 they say we gone away,
Could never let them control Hawaiian man,
take back your Hawaiian land.

— 'Aipōhaku, "Controller"

Popular culture and scholars alike speak to the prediction of the extinction of the Hawaiian race (Noyes, 2003). This "all or nothing" mentality assumes that only full-blooded Hawaiians will ensure the continuation of the Hawaiian people. This ideology is intended to limit who can be considered a Hawaiian. Blood quantum sits at the center of this notion and is perpetuated in the Hawaiian Homes Commission Act and rhetoric spewed by those who are in opposition to the survival of the Hawaiian people.

The Hawaiian word for genealogy is *mo'okū'auhau* and is made up of smaller words that help to explain the importance of bloodlines to the Hawaiian people. *Mo'o* is a lizard but also means "succession." Mo'o are also connected to places on our lands. Hawaiian people were identified by the places they lived just as they were identified by their names. Mountains, valleys, passages, areas all had names. The genealogy of the land is a genealogy of the people.

For Hawaiians, moʻokūʻauhau is several things. It is a genealogy, or the study of your family and your history. It traces your lineage back to your ancestors. Moʻokūʻauhau set the social order in Hawaiian society. The inherited *mana* (spiritual power) from your moʻokūʻauhau and the people in your moʻokūʻauhau is what made an *aliʻi* (chief) an aliʻi and a *makaʻāinana* (commoner) a makaʻāinana. Mana determined a person's place in society and was an indicator of abilities and talents. Reciting one's moʻokūʻauhau to others would demonstrate connections and relations. This practice has diminished somewhat, and is often replaced with the ignorant question of "How much Hawaiian blood you get?" In Hawaiian thinking, it wasn't how much Hawaiian blood you had, but how your blood is connected to others. Bloodlines are the foundation of our people; blood quantity wasn't a concept we valued.

Native Hawaiian Sperm and Ovum Bank

Imagine these scenarios…

- A 12-year-old Native Hawaiian boy is diagnosed with testicular cancer. His lifesaving treatment will leave him sterile. For him to preserve his family name, his right to pass homestead land to his children and his ability to send his kids to Kamehameha schools will depend on his ability to bank his own sperm prior to receiving cancer treatment.
- A Native Hawaiian woman is concerned she will be past her biological prime to have children by the time she chooses a partner and starts a family. She decides to have a child on her own, but needs to find a sperm donor with high enough Native Hawaiian blood quantum to allow her to pass on her family homestead land.
- A young Native Hawaiian woman of 22 is diagnosed with ovarian cancer. Her survival depends on immediate removal of both ovaries. Her ability to ensure benefit to her future children depends on the collection and banking of her eggs. After banking her eggs, she decides not to have her own children

and wishes to donate her eggs to a Native Hawaiian family not able to conceive on their own.

- A Native Hawaiian woman of one-quarter Hawaiian blood has been living on her family homestead land which has been in her family for three generations. She fell in love with her high school sweetheart who is not Native Hawaiian. Both agree that keeping the family home for their children is critical to them; they decide to have artificial insemination with a Native Hawaiian sperm donor who has also one-quarter Hawaiian blood quantum to ensure their child meets the qualification to retain the family homestead.

Reproductive justice exists when all people have the social, political, and economic power and resources to make healthy decisions about our gender, bodies, sexuality, and families for ourselves and our communities (Asian Communities for Reproductive Justice, 2017).

Native Hawaiian cultural master and pioneer in the resurgence of Hawaiian practices and pedagogy Dr. Pualani Kanaka'ole Kanahele, is a renowned *kumu hula* (grand master and teacher of the traditional dance and culture of Hawai`i) and is held in the highest esteem among Native Hawaiians and Indigenous people worldwide. Speaking at conferences and community forums, Dr. Kanahele is the leading advocate for the establishment of the Native Hawaiian sperm and ovum bank. The previous outlined scenarios could all be addressed with the creation of this reproductive justice solution. Akin to the effort to preserve the native ōhi'a lehua forests, preserving the seed of the Native Hawaiian people would ensure the continuation of the Hawaiian bloodlines in perpetuity. While some may view this possible solution as a radical step in preservation, the center focus of the issue is choice. The right to choose to continue your family line and create an open sharing of Native Hawaiian seed may not seem like a radical solution to those facing a reproductive challenge that is so tightly woven to Native rights.

Conclusion

Consider for a moment, children speaking the language of their ancestors, understanding how to perpetuate their culture by applying ancestral knowledge to lived practices of growing native foods, gathering traditional medicine, and celebrating ceremonies of life and wellness. Those children, raised in Hawaiian immersion, raised guided by ancestral knowledge, will seek out those with shared value systems. This is not a discourse about race or that of blood quantum. This is a vision of a thriving healthy people, whose choices in life may help to build the Lāhui. And who knows, maybe one day they will laugh that we ever worried about qualifying for land because of dwindling blood quantum.

Ho'ola Lāhui
E Ola, E Ola, E Ola O Na Kini E
Live, live, live the multitudes of the Hawaiian People!

– Pavao, 1994

References

'Aipōhaku. (2009). "Controller." Moku o Keawe, Hawai`i.

Asian Communities for Reproductive Justice. (2017). Accessed from http://strongfamiliesmovement.org/what-is-reproductive-justice.

Barker, Joanne Marie. (1995). "Indian Made: Sovereignty, Federal Policy, and the Work of Identification." Qualifying essay, History of Consciousness, University of California, Santa Cruz.

Blaisdell, R. K. (1993). The Health Status of the Kānaka Maoli (Indigenous Hawaiians). *Asian American and Pacific Islander Journal of Health*, 1(2): 116–160.

CNBC. (2017). America's Top States for Business 2016: A Scorecard on State Economic Climate. Accessed from http://www.cnbc.com/2016/07/12/americas-top-states-for-business-2016-the-list-and-ranking.html.

Cook, James. (1728–1779). *A Voyage to the Pacific Ocean. Undertaken, by the Command of His Majesty, for Making Discoveries in the Northern Hemisphere, to Determine the Position and Extent of the West Side of North America; Its Distance from Asia; and the Practicability of a Northern Passage to Europe*, vol. 2. London: W. and A. Strahan, for G. Nicol, & T. Cadell, p. 456.

Department of Native Hawaiian Home Lands. (2015). Accessed from http://dhhl.hawaii.gov/applications/application-wait-list/.

Department of Native Hawaiian Home Lands. (2016). House Bill 1931, Senate Bill 2868. State of Hawai`i.

Federal Register Notice. (1995), "Standards for the Classification of Federal Data on Race and Ethnicity," Office of Management and Budget, Federal Register, 60FR44674-44693, August 28, 1995.

Kapiolani Health Foundation. (2009). "100 Years of Caring for Children." Honolulu.

Kame'eleihiwa, Lilikalā. (1992). *Native Land and Foreign Desires: Pehea Lā E Pono Ai? How Shall We Live in Harmony?* Honolulu: Bishop Museum Press.

Kauanui, J. Kehaulani. (2008). *Hawaiian Blood: Colonialism and the Politics of Sovereignty and Indigeneity* (Narrating Native Histories). Durham, NC: Duke University Press Books.

King R. C., and W. D. Stransfield. (1998). Dictionary of Genetics. New York/Oxford: Oxford University Press.

Noyes, Martha. (2003). *Then There Were None.* Honolulu: Bell Press.

Pang Kee v. Jobie Masagatani. (2012). In her official capacity as Chairperson of the Hawaiian Homes Commission and the Director of the Department of Hawaiian Home Lands, Hawaiian Homes Commission, and the Department of Hawaiian Home Lands. State of Hawai`i. First Circuit Court, Honolulu.

Pavao, Dennis. (1994). *All Hawai'i Stand Together.* Poki Records, Honolulu.

Pukui, Mary Kawena. (1942). *Hawaiian Beliefs and Customs during Birth, Infancy, and Childhood,* vol. XVI. Occasional Papers of Bernice P. Bishop Museum of Polynesian Ethnology and Natural History. Honolulu: Bernice P. Bishop Museum.

Rice v. Cayetano, 528 U.S. 495 (2000), Supreme Court

State of Hawai'i Primary Care Needs Assessment Data Book 2012. (2012). Family Health Services Division, Hawai'i Department of Health.

TallBear, K, and D. A. Bolnick. (2004). "Native American DNA Tests: What Are the Risks to Tribes?" *The Native Voice.*

U.S. Census Bureau. (2010) American Community Survey 1-Year Estimates; generated by Maile Taualii, using American Fact Finder. http://factfinder2.census.gov, 6 September 2016.

Notes

Rice v. Cayetano, 528 U.S. 495 (2000), was a case filed in 1996 by Big Island rancher Harold "Freddy" Rice against the state of Hawai'i and argued before the US Supreme Court. In 2000, the court ruled that the state could not restrict eligibility to vote in elections for the Board of Trustees of the Office of Hawaiian Affairs to persons of Native Hawaiian descent.

"Who is an Indian? Who decides?
What is a full blood? Half blood? Quarter blood?
What part of you is Native? Is it your head?
Your heart? Maybe it's just your thoughts.
But it is not just your blood. We are the sum
of all our parts. All human. One hundred percent.
And fully Native."

– Jolene Richard, guest curator
and Gabrielle Tayac (NMAI signage 2004)

Part 4

POLICY,
LAW, AND
NATION BUILDING

MAKING OURSELVES WHOLE WITH WORDS: A SHORT HISTORY OF WHITE EARTH ANISHINAABEG TRIBAL CITIZENSHIP CRITERIA

by Jill Doerfler

*"We are touched into tribal being with words,
made whole in the world with words and oracle gestures."*

– Gerald Vizenor
White Earth Anishinaabe scholar

Native people across the United States and in Canada are working to rebuild their nations, which often includes establishing governance structures and practices that enact traditional values. Scholar Eric Lemont argues that "the wave of constitutional reform sweeping Indian Country will represent a critical starting point in American Indian nations' journey to retake ownership of their governments."[1] Many nations see this as an opportunity to embed core cultural values within their governing documents. A constitution is a foundational governing document that sets out the framework for the governance structure of a nation. While a constitution is a governing document, it should also be a reflection of the goals, principles, and values of a nation.

On November 19, 2013, the citizens of the White Earth Nation (WEN) voted to approve a new constitution, by an overwhelming majority of nearly eighty percent. This historical moment created a new governing structure and requires lineal descent for tribal citizenship. The new constitution represents a major shift in citizenship requirements from blood quantum to lineal descent.

In this chapter, I will discuss two significant moments with regard to White Earth Anishinaabe identity and tribal citizenship. I will first explore why the Minnesota Chippewa Tribe implemented a one-quarter Minnesota Chippewa Tribe blood quantum for tribal citizenship in 1961. I will then focus on the 2007 to present effort for constitutional reform at White Earth, concentrating on why and how the decision to return to lineal descent as the requirement for tribal citizenship was made. Part of my consideration here is if/how constitutions and citizenship requirements play a role in "making ourselves whole." I want to be clear that I'm not saying that a constitution will solve all the infighting; that all of a sudden all people will treat one another with respect and follow our teachings, or that an elected official will never embezzle another dollar if a strong constitution is in place, but, what I am suggesting is that a governing document like a constitution can be part of the process of reconstituting Native nations – and that the words in those documents are one step in the larger process of "making ourselves whole."

It's also important to note that citizenship is only one component of Anishinaabe identity. It is the official, legal recognition of one's identity. It brings legal responsibilities and protections. For many, being Anishinaabe goes beyond legal status and also includes myriad other aspects, including kinship relationships, clan identity, actions, cultural values, language, spiritual beliefs, residency, and worldview. Nishnaabeg scholar Leanne Simpson has argued:

> If we are to continue on a Nishnaabeg pathway, we must choose to live as Nishnaabeg, committing to mino bimaadziwin, and committing to building resurgence. We have a choice and that choice requires action, commitment, and responsibility. We are not simply born Nishnaabeg, even if we have "full-blood." We must commit to living the good life each day. We must act. We must live our knowledge.[2]

As Anishinaabeg we create our identities, families, and nations. We must take responsibility for our actions and choose to practice our core values. Citizenship requirements should enact core values and empower families and individuals to create their identities.

We create and re-create ourselves and our nations through stories. In *Wordarrows*, White Earth Anishinaabe scholar Gerald Vizenor writes: "We are touched into tribal being with words, made whole in the world with words and oracle gestures."[3] Indeed, we have a long and rich literary tradition.[4] Stories have served several important functions in Anishinaabe communities, including illustrating appropriate behavior and actions as well as views on life, death, and religion since time immemorial.[5] Anishinaabeg have utilized narratives to argue political agendas and to subvert the colonial histories created by dominant society.[6] In recent years, Anishinaabe scholar John Borrows has argued that stories express law and share a close relationship with common law asserting that Native nations can "look to their stories as a body of knowledge that fulfills many of the same functions as common law precedent."[7]

Stories were and are in constant motion. They are often changed to fit particular audiences and contexts continually being told and retold, edited and re-edited, published and republished. Constitutions are also a form of a story and are, as Vizenor suggests, a way that we create ourselves. Nishnaabe scholar Leanne Simpson writes:

> Storytelling is at its core decolonizing, because it is a process of remembering, visioning and creating a just reality where Nishnaabeg live as both Nishnaabeg and peoples. Storytelling then becomes a lens through which we can envision our way out of cognitive imperialism, where we can create models and mirrors where none existed, and where we can experience the spaces of freedom and justice.[8]

A constitution and citizenship requirements are opportunities to tell stories, to re-create ourselves and our nations.

The Minnesota Chippewa Tribe: A Reluctant Acceptance of Blood Quantum

In the late nineteenth and early twentieth centuries there were myriad complex systems and social regulations that Anishinaabeg used to determine who was and who was not a member of their tribe.[9] It would be a mistake to think that these systems functioned without any conflict – undoubtedly, there were disagreements and power struggles. However, Anishinaabeg controlled these systems and they worked out conflicts or agreed to disagree, as was their sovereign right; they determined who was and who was not a member/citizen of the nation, but the US would soon interfere in an unprecedented fashion.[10]

After the passage of the Indian Reorganization Act (IRA) in 1934, six Anishinaabe nations in Minnesota, including White Earth, joined together to create the Minnesota Chippewa Tribe (MCT) in 1936.[11] The MCT Constitution has some similarities to other IRA-era constitutions. For example, it is a one-branch governing structure and it gives broad powers to the US Secretary of the Interior, but the governing structure is entirely unique and has changed over time. Originally there was an annual election at which citizens elected up to two tribal delegates from the designated districts, which were not fixed and changed over time. Tribal Delegates then selected two people from each nation/reservation to compose the Tribal Executive Committee (TEC), and these groups worked in tandem to govern along with the reservation level governments.[12] Each nation has a Reservation Tribal Council or Reservation Business Committee, which is composed of a chairman, secretary/treasurer, and district representatives and serves as a local governing body. In 1964, several major constitutional changes were approved by the Secretary of the Interior. The practice of electing tribal delegates ceased, and the TEC was from that time on composed of the chairman and secretary/treasurer of each nation.[13]

The IRA was an important crossroads for tribal citizenship; it was not uncommon for the Bureau of Indian Affairs (BIA) to push tribes to enact racial requirements for citizenship. Legal scholar L. Scott Gould has argued that the IRA "helped entrench race as an essential requirement for tribal membership."[14] While enrollment within the Minnesota Chippewa Tribe is generally spoken of as *membership*, I employ the term the *citizenship* in this chapter with the intention of evoking the political status of the MCT. The original MCT constitution states: "...the governing body of the tribe shall have power to make rules governing the qualifications required for enrollment in the tribe and descendants of members of the tribe...."[15] Initially, all Anishinaabeg who had registered on the approved roles of any of the six nations participating in the MCT were citizens and children of these individuals and were subsequently qualified to enroll as citizens.[16] However, I have been unable to find any official MCT policies or procedures governing the citizenship process. It seems as though a system of lineal descent was used as the method for determining citizenship, but there is some indication that residency might have been required.[17] The historical record reveals that the BIA wanted the MCT to pass an amendment relating to the exact requirements for tribal citizenship and strongly asserted that blood quantum would be an excellent requirement.

Citizenship was discussed on several occasions during Tribal Executive Committee meetings. For example, at a meeting in May of 1940, Mr. Morrell, from the Leech Lake reservation, stated that he believed everyone with Indian blood should have the same privileges. He urged the TEC to be "guided by the love of children, your little grandchildren, even they are mixed-bloods."[18] Morrell's comment is reflective of a communal focus and attention to the future of the nation. He recognized that a growing portion of the younger generations were "mixed-bloods" and was aware that many of them would be ineligible for tribal citizenship if a blood quantum requirement was instituted. In addition, he asserts that love should guide the decision-making process. Love is a core value of the Seven Teachings.[19]

One year later at TEC meetings in May and July of 1941, tribal citizenship was once again a prominent issue. Mr. Rogers began the discussion on citizenship at the meeting in May of 1941 with a summary of the discussion from the previous year. He noted that there was agreement that everyone who was a descendant from the "Treaty of 1889," known as the Chippewa in Minnesota Fund as established under the Nelson Act, should be able to enroll "regardless of blood degree, place of residence, etc."[20] He reminded the group that they had discussed citizenship several times over the last five years and so he drafted some regulations based on those discussions. Rogers explained,

> These rules throw the gate wide open. Any descendants of the original members who were entitled to enrollment under the treaty or agreement of 1889 are entitled to enrollment. These rules provide that any descendant, no matter what degree of blood he possesses or where he lives, or where he is born, so long as he can prove that he is a descendant or issue of one of the original families, is entitled to enrollment under these regulations.... We want to enroll everybody who is entitled to enrollment. We didn't consider the quantum of Indian blood, nor we didn't [sic?] consider the place where they were born or where they lived.[21]

The discussion continued and William Anywaush from White Earth was very vocal on the issue. He began, "Friends and Relatives – The reason I say 'relative' is that you are Indian and so am I."[22] By noting that they are all both friends and relatives Anywaush was highlighting their unity and responsibility to each other. He said that he believed they were dealing with a "very dangerous" issue because of the implications it would have on future generations. He asserted,

> There was never in the past any mention of drawing any line; relationship was the only thing that was considered in the past. Even though the child had very little Indian blood, in considering the relationship, he was still an Indian. One thing that these old folks over there urged me to do was to have mercy on my Indian people. Don't ever, as long as you live, discriminate against your fellow Indians.[23]

Anywaush appeals to the TEC to use relationships (kinship/family) as the way to determine if an individual should be able to become a tribal citizen, noting that this is what the "old folks" want. In doing so, he reminds TEC members of their responsibilities both to children and to elders. In addition, he declares that they had never used blood quantum before, implying that it goes against Anishinaabe values, and using it would discriminate against their "fellow Indians."

Finally, after years of discussions, a resolution on tribal citizenship was passed on July 26, 1941. It required lineal descent from the Act of January 14, 1889. The resolution passed unanimously among the TEC, and easily, 35 to 12 among the Tribal Delegates. [24] After the passage of the resolution, Superintendent Scott wrote to the Commissioner of Indian Affairs submitting the resolution for approval. He took care to note that it was the result of five years of thoughtful discussion. Scott wrote, "[I]t is hoped that the rules governing enrollment as adopted by the governing body of the Minnesota Chippewas [*sic*] be given approval and I so recommend."[25]

In 1942, Oscar Chapman, Assistant Secretary of the Department of the Interior Oscar Chapman wrote to the MCT rejecting the resolution. He wrote:

> If the Minnesota Chippewa Indians desire to share their property with a large number of persons who are Indians neither by name, residence, or attachment but merely by the accident of

a small portion of Indian blood ... [t]he Minnesota Chippewa
Tribe must realize that every new name which they add to the
membership roll will by that much decrease the share every
member now has in the limited assets of the Minnesota Chippewa Tribe.[26]

Here Chapman's direct implication is that the fewer citizens there were
the more resources there would be for each individual, using economics as
an attempt to sway the MCT into passing a citizenship resolution that would
be more restrictive.

The Tribal Executive Committee continued to discuss the issue and, on
December 11, 1948, passed a new resolution relating to tribal citizenship.
The tribal delegates voted unanimously to approve the resolution on May
21, 1949. This new resolution was very similar to the previous one in that
it again required individuals to prove descendancy from a member of the
Tribe in order to become a citizen.[27] The resolution was sent to the BIA for
approval. The MCT anxiously awaited approval of the resolution, writing
the Commissioner of Indian Affairs, John R. Nichols, indicating their desire
to have the matter settled as soon as possible. To their disappointment, the
Secretary of the Interior, William Warne, rejected the resolution on December 9, 1949. He felt the resolution was too similar to the 1941 resolution in
that it allowed all descendants to enroll with no blood quantum or residency
restrictions, noting that the new resolution was "for all practical purposes
almost identical" to the previous resolution and "will accomplish the same
purposes."[28]

Getting the MCT to pass a resolution on tribal citizenship that would be
approved became of increasing concern. In 1951, the Commissioner of Indian Affairs specified that the MCT should be urged to pass a more restrictive
resolution, offering ideas such as requiring that "both parents are recognized
members of the tribe, or that the residence of the parents is within the reservation, or that the child is of a certain degree of Indian blood."[29]

The MCT continued to fight against blood quantum over the next decade, but then, in a dramatic turn, in 1961 the TEC passed an ordinance that
required a minimum of one-quarter Minnesota Chippewa blood for tribal
citizenship.[30] This requirement allowed "blood" from all of the participating
MCT nations to count towards the one-quarter requirement. Two days later
at the delegates meeting, the president of the MCT was called upon to explain the ordinance. He rationalized, "[I]t was necessary to set the ¼ degree
blood quantum in the ordinance in order to receive approval of the Depart-

ment of the Interior which defines an Indian as being ¼ or more degree Indian blood."[31] He went on to uphold the ordinance stating that "if the MCT does not set up enrollment rules, than [*sic*] the Department will make their own rules."[32] It is likely that both the TEC and the Tribal Delegates felt they had few options. The ordinance passed among the Tribal Delegates 29 for and 15 opposed. The Secretary of the Interior approved. The blood quantum requirement was added to the constitution along with other constitutional changes voted on and approved by voters in 1963 and by the Secretary of Interior in 1964.[33]

The White Earth Nation: Moving Forward by Returning to Lineal Descent

Many have been unsatisfied with the blood quantum citizenship requirement because, in part, families have literally been divided between those who are eligible for enrollment and those who are not. There have been a number of efforts at constitutional reform, including changing the blood quantum requirement, during the past few decades. The most recent effort formally began in 2007 and culminated in the citizens of the White Earth Nation voting to approve the then-proposed constitution by a margin of nearly eighty percent in 2013.

On March 1, 2007, at the annual State of the Nation address at the Shooting Star Casino in Mahnomen, Erma Vizenor, Chairwoman of the White Earth Tribal Council, declared that among the issues she wanted address in the upcoming year was constitutional reform of the tribal government. Vizenor urged that a clear separation of powers of the tribal government should be considered as well as the requirements for citizenship, stating, "[A]s tribal membership continues to decline under the present one-fourth blood quantum requirement, we must decide eligibility for enrollment."[34] Vizenor carried through her priority over the next few months, and forty Constitutional Delegates were sworn in at the first of four Constitutional Conventions in October 2007.[35]

Throughout the reform process, citizenship would prove to be an emotional issue that caused strong feelings in many Constitutional Delegates. As legal scholar Carol Goldberg has observed: "Indian nations' constitutional reform efforts encounter some of their most paralyzing conflicts over criteria for membership."[36] Defining citizenship requirements is one of the most fundamental activities a nation must engage in. This is a difficult task for any nation, but colonization and the US government's use of blood quantum to define American Indian identity makes this an especially difficult question for Native nations.[37] Based on a study of 322 current and historic tribal constitutions, legal scholar Kirsty Gover found that blood quantum requirements for tribal citizenship peaked between 1960 and 1970.[38] She argues that citizenship decisions made after 1970 are "influenced not just by the new opportunities and resources provided by federal and self-determination policy, but also by the legacy of termination-era policies and migrations."[39] Scholars argue that the implementation of blood quantum for tribal citizenship in the mid-twentieth century was a form of termination because it was designed to eventually eliminate American Indian nations.[40] As already discussed, the elected leaders of the MCT only approved a minimum of one-quarter MCT blood for tribal citizenship in 1961 after resolutions requiring lineal descent were rejected by the Secretary of the Interior and letters containing thinly veiled termination threats were sent from the Bureau of Indian Affairs.[41] Grover notes that in response to termination-era policies, Native nations are electing to employ a genealogical approach to citizenship requirements, and they are increasingly likely to use lineal descent as a requirement for tribal citizenship because lineal descent is often seen as a way to repair or reconstitute nations that have been split under blood quantum requirements.[42]

Creating and agreeing upon the criteria for citizenship at White Earth was a challenge. Constitutional Delegates discussed citizenship on several occasions during the four conventions. They grappled with the concepts of blood quantum and race and the various ways in which they have been used. While they voiced a wide range of ideas and opinions, many of them came back to core Anishinaabe values and our families as the most significant factors related to citizenship. They questioned the accuracy of blood quantum. For example, one delegate stated, "No one really knows how much Indian blood they have and the only way to know would be to go back to the beginning." Many in the room nodded in agreement. The history of how the various White Earth blood rolls were created in the early 1900s was discussed.[43] Several delegates noted the inconsistencies among these rolls as well as irregularities, such as siblings listed with different blood quanta on the final official roll.[44] While some delegates questioned the validity of blood quantum entirely, others questioned what they saw as inaccuracies that could never be corrected. Another delegate noted that s/he favored the use of lineal descent because it includes all family members and is also a way of taking care of our families. It was also noted that lineal descendants would go on forever, but that if blood quantum were to continue, White Earth's sovereignty would be in jeopardy because the day would come when no one would have the required blood quantum. A different delegate added, "Everything we do – all the hard work, love, respect, etc. – should be pointed toward future generations. Core values should be used to take care of future generations." The core values and sentiments discussed closely parallel the Anishinaabe Seven Teachings, which emphasize the importance courage, truth, respect, love, honesty, wisdom and humility as guiding principles of Anishinaabe life.[45]

At the second convention delegates were asked to examine a list of citizenship options that had been generated in a constitutional reform effort during the late 1990s. The options included: lineal descent and several different options based on a variety of blood calculations. Once again, the issue of family surfaced in many of the delegates' comments. One delegate noted that he favored the use of lineal descent because it includes all family members and, therefore, it is also a way of taking care of our families. Some delegates were apprehensive that more citizens would put an increased strain on already limited resources. Another delegate stated, "No one is happy with blood quantum" but was unsure how White Earth should regulate citizenship. The wide diversity of comments and opinions reflect both a desire for change as well as trepidation about what change might really mean. Even though delegates had easily identified core values in a previous exercise, some were having a difficult time conceptualizing how to practice those values in a citizenship requirement(s).

At the third convention, delegates again examined the list of citizenship options with the addition of several questions designed to help them effectively evaluate these options. Questions included:

- What kind of citizenship requirement will put our beliefs, values, and culture into motion?
- How might our values of love and family be expressed in citizenship regulations?
- Which citizenship requirement will strengthen our nation?

During the presentation and discussion of the options a few people began talking loudly to each other, which was disruptive. Clearly frustrated, one of the delegates stood up and interrupted to ask if a motion could be made. The Chairwoman agreed. The delegate made a motion requesting that no options for tribal citizenship that required blood quantum be discussed any further. The motion passed.[46] There was only one option on the list that did not include blood quantum: "Lineal descendants of enrolled members of the White Earth Ojibwe Nation." Consequently, the issue of citizenship was decided.

After the convention, Chairwoman Vizenor designed a Constitutional Proposal Team to draft a constitution based on the three Constitutional Conventions. She asked Constitutional Delegate Gerald Vizenor[47] to be the principal writer and to draft the document. I was also a member of the team.

As agreed upon by the delegates, lineal descent was included as the sole requirement for citizenship. The first article reads: "Citizens of the White Earth Nation shall be descendants of Anishinaabeg families and related by linear descent to enrolled members of the White Earth Reservation and Nation, according to genealogical documents, treaties and other agreements with the government of the United States."[48] There is no mention of blood quantum. Instead, family and relationship are at the center of this requirement. This is not to say that lineal descent is a perfect system. Biological relationship is privileged here – someone who has an Anishinaabe father but never met him would still be eligible for citizenship. It would be up to that person to decide if they wanted to become a White Earth citizen or not. Genealogical documentation is required, which may be a barrier for some. It relies upon a base roll(s), which is never 100% accurate. Yet, delegates decided that it was the best option they had, and I agree it is a better determiner than blood quantum. This new requirement gives individuals a much stronger role in choosing whether or not they want to become a citizen of the White Earth Nation, much like the personal autonomy that our ancestors exercised in the past. Lineal descent brings us a step closer to uniting our families, as the elected leaders fought so hard for during the mid-twentieth century.

The most pressing concern that arose regarding lineal descent was entitlements. For example, at one of the conventions a delegate stated: "How can we cut this pie any smaller? It scares me." During the drafting process, Gerald Vizenor recognized that it was necessary to clearly state that not all citizens will receive entitlements and/or services in order to address the concerns about resources that were raised by delegates. The second article clarifies that services and entitlements "shall be defined according to treaties, trusts, and diplomatic agreements, state and federal laws, rules and regulations, and in policies and procedures established by the government of the White Earth Nation."[49] All nations have to be responsible in the management of resources and prioritization of services. Simply being a citizen does not mean that an individual "gets" anything except the right to vote and the protections provided in the constitution. Currently, a citizen must meet the various qualifications (e.g., income, residency, age) for any of the numerous social service programs that the WEN operates, and that practice will continue under the new constitution. Programs that experience increased pressure may add new qualifications, including those with cultural significance, to ensure that those most in need are served.[50]

On April 4, 2009, the draft constitution was presented to the delegates. After hours of discussion and some amendments, they voted 16 to 8 in favor of ratifying the draft constitution.[51] Many clapped and cheered. Chairwoman Vizenor reminded everyone present that the document would still have to be voted on by all White Earth citizens in a referendum vote. She thanked the delegates for their hard work and perseverance with the process. The convention was adjourned.

White Earth spent the next several years exploring options for a referendum vote and navigating an array of politics, including issues with the MCT.[52] In December 2012, the WEN was awarded a substantial grant from the Bush Foundation[53] to move ahead with a citizen education and engagement effort that would culminate in a referendum on the proposed constitution. Educational materials were created to provide critical information for voters to make their decision. During the summer and fall of 2013, more than fifty community-education sessions were held at various locations on and off the reservation. In addition, there was a daylong symposium (which was available via livestream), a special edition of the *Anishinaabeg Today* newspaper, educational videos, and more.[54] These informational outreach efforts were successful in getting more than twice the typical number of voters to vote in the referendum.[55]

The referendum was held on November 19, 2013. The citizens of the WEN voted by a margin of nearly eighty percent to approve the proposed constitution. A total of 3,492 ballots were accepted, with 2,780 approving the new constitution and 712 rejecting it.[56] "I am very gratified that the people of White Earth have spoken," said White Earth Tribal Chairwoman Erma Vizenor.[57]

"We Voted, What Happened?"

As of the summer of 2015, the CWEN has not been implemented. The referendum was challenged in White Earth Tribal Court. Chief Judge Robert

Blaeser upheld the referendum in a decision issued on February 12, 2014.[58] The elected leaders of White Earth did not adopt a formal transition plan, and elections were held under the MCT constitution during the spring/ summer of 2014. Three new elected leaders were sworn into office on July 16, 2014.[59] Even though White Earth citizens approved the CWEN by a landslide, all three new leaders oppose the implementation of the CWEN.[60] Chairwoman Vizenor continues to fight for implementation, writing:

> The people made their voice heard in the referendum on Nov. 19, 2013. Despite the current roadblocks at the local and MCT levels of leadership, I remain committed to carrying out the will of the people.... We have a rich history of persistence, determination, and resiliency at White Earth, and I carry that history forward with my actions today.[61]

This is an ongoing political issue that I do not expect to be fully resolved for some time.

The new constitution and the requirements for tribal citizenship reflect Anishinaabe values and cultural practices. Grand Traverse Band of Ottawa and Chippewa citizen and legal scholar Mathew L. M. Fletcher has written, "Indians and Indian tribes must recognize that the space to 'make their own laws' is equivalent to the right of preserving and making their own culture."[62] He has also argued, "Fundamental questions, such as who Indian people are in a legal sense under tribal law, must be answered in light of the modern experiences of Indian people; not the laws and traditions imposed by outsiders."[63]

Anishinaabe identity remains complex and diverse. At White Earth we wait for implementation and what changes the new constitution will bring. The new citizenship requirement based on Anishinaabe values will not solve all social conflict in the nation. Undoubtedly, there will always be a diversity of viewpoints on Anishinaabe identity and the best ways to live out our values. There will always be family divisions, political factions, and differing strategies for how best to build a strong nation, but I believe that the new citizenship requirement is a powerful starting point that carries the power of transformation. How might our youth be changed now that they are accepted not on the basis of their blood, but on the basis of their relationships, which come with both rights and responsibilities? What will happen now that the WEN has rejected the externally imposed ideas of race and blood and, instead, rested its foundation on our families? I hope that a new political reality will emerge, that an influx of citizens committed to upholding their responsibilities will help us (re)build a strong Anishinaabe nation. The Constitution of the White Earth nation echoes Anishinaabe traditions and envisions a perpetual future where the succession of families form nation. The referendum was an act of survivance, one step toward "making ourselves whole" – by placing family at the core of citizenship.

Notes

1. Lemont, Eric D. "Introduction," in *American Indian Constitutional Reform and the Rebuilding of Native Nations,* ed. Eric D. Lemont (Austin: University of Texas Press, 2006), 5.

2. Leanne Simpson. "Our Elder Brothers: The Lifeblood of Resurgence," in *Lighting the Eighth Fire: The Liberation, Resurgence, and Protection of Indigenous Nations*, ed. Leanne Simpson (Winnipeg, Manitoba: Arbeiter Ring Publishing, 2008), 74.

3. Vizenor, Gerald. *Wordarrows: Indians and White in the New Fur Trade* (Minneapolis: University of Minnesota Press, 1978), vii.

4. Scholar Maureen Konkle has noted during the first half of the nineteenth century Anishinaabe writers produced and published the largest body of American Indian narratives (162). She also notes that many nineteenth-century American Indian authors "maintained that Euro-Americans' knowledge about Indian's racial difference was politically motivated…." (5). Maureen Konkle, *Writing Indian Nations: Native Intellectuals and the Politics of Historiography, 1827–1863 (*Chapel Hill: University of North Carolina Press, 2004).

5. Johnston, Basil. *Ojibway Heritage* (1976; reprint; Lincoln: University of Nebraska Press), 1990, 7; Schoolcraft, Henry R. *The Hiawatha Legends* (reprint; AuTrain, Michigan: Avery Color Studios, 1984), 23–24.

6. In fact, as Maureen Konkle has noted in her groundbreaking work *Writing Indian Nations*, Anishinaabe writers produced and published the largest body of American Indian narratives during the first half of the nineteenth century. Konkle observes that Anishinaabe writers of the nineteenth century "make the same arguments that other Native writers make in the period: they write to counter misrepresentation, they reject

the notion of inherent difference, they insist on Native authority for traditional knowledge, and they denounce European Americans' claims to know their own knowledge better than they themselves do." Konkle, p. 162, quote at 166.

7. John Borrows, *Recovering Canada: The Resurgence of Indigenous Law* (Toronto: University of Toronto Press, 2002), 13–14.

8. Leanne Simpson, *Dancing on Our Turtle's Back: Stories of Nishinaabeg Re-Creation, Resurgence and a New Emergence* (Winnipeg, Manitoba: Arbeiter Ring Publishing, 2010), 33.

9. In many ways, the type of government-regulated official membership/citizenship comes after the IRA (Indian Reorganization Act).

10. For a fuller discussion of the nineteenth and early twentieth centuries see Chapter 1 of *Those Who Belong: Identity, Family, Blood, and Citizenship among the White Earth Anishinaabeg* (East Lansing: Michigan State University Press 2015).

11. *Constitution and By-Laws of the Minnesota Chippewa Tribe*, Minnesota Chippewa Tribe, official website, http://www.mnchippewatribe.org/excomandsub.htm, accessed August 16, 2009.

12. *Constitution and By-Laws of the Minnesota Chippewa Tribe*, Article IV, Section 2, 24 July 1936, Minnesota Chippewa Tribe Archives, Cass Lake, Minnesota.

13. Jill Doerfler, *Those Who Belong: Identity, Family, Blood, and Citizenship among the White Earth Anishinaabeg* (East Lansing: Michigan State University Press 2015), 33–35.

14. Scott L. Gould, "Mixing Bodies and Beliefs: The Predicament of Tribes," *Columbia Law Review* 101, no. 4 (May 2001): 720–721.

15. *Constitution and By-Laws of the Minnesota Chippewa Tribe*, Article II, Section 3, 24 July 1936, Minnesota Chippewa Tribe Archives, Cass Lake, Minnesota.

16. *Constitution and By-Laws of the Minnesota Chippewa Tribe*, Article II, Section 2, 24 July 1936, Minnesota Chippewa Tribe Archives, Cass Lake, Minnesota.

This issue was further clarified in Article 1 of the By-Laws, which states: "In the determination of membership under Article II, Section 2, of the constitution, the Government annuity rolls, as such rolls may be

corrected under this Constitution, shall be used to determine the enrollment status in the Tribe and the same shall be conclusive, the said rolls
being the Government official register of the recognized members of the
Tribe." *Minnesota Chippewa Tribe By-Laws*, Article I, "Determination
of Membership," n.d., Minnesota Chippewa Tribe Archives, Cass Lake,
Minnesota.

17. I have not found a resolution requiring residence for tribal citizenship
within the MCT, but the Department of the Interior might have required
it. At a TEC meeting in July 1941, Mr. Rogers noted, "The present policy of the Department is to enroll only those who were born or are born
in the Indian country." Quoted in Memorandum to Mr. Flanery Chief
(signature illegible), 31 March 1942, NARA-DC, RG 75, CCF, Consolidated Chippewa, File 32610-1941, 053.

18. Minnesota Chippewa Tribe, Minutes of Special Meeting of Tribal Executive Committee, May 17–20, 1940, Minnesota Chippewa Tribe Archives, Cass Lake, Minnesota, 22.

19. "Elders direct our people to live their lives in a way that promotes positive relationships with the land, their families and all of Creation. This
is preformed by individuals within the web of the Kokum Dibaajimow-
inan. These teachings include: Aalde'ewin, the art of having courage;
Dbadendiziwin, humility; Debwewin, truth or sincerity; Mnaadendiwin,
respect; Nbwaakawin, wisdom; Gwekwaadiziwin, honesty; and Zaaige-
win, love…" Simpson, *Dancing on Our Turtle's Back*, quote at 68, see
also 124–127.

20. Ibid.

21. Ibid.

Here we see further evidence that the residence requirement was instituted by the BIA.

22. Ibid.

23. Ibid.

24. Resolution No. IV, Rules Governing the Qualifications for Enrollment
in the Minnesota Chippewa Tribe, 26 July 1941, NARA-DC, RG 75,
CCF, Consolidated Chippewa, File 32610-1941, 053.

25. F. J. Scott to Commissioner of Indian Affairs, 5 August 1941, NARA-
DC, RG 75, CCF, Consolidated Chippewa, File 32610-1941, 053.

26. Oscar L. Chapman to Ed. M. Wilson, December 23, 1942, NARA-DC, RG 75, CCF, Consolidated Chippewa, File 32610-1941, 053.

27. Resolution No. 14, Minnesota Chippewa Tribe, May 21, 1949, NARA-DC, RG 75, CCF, Consolidated Chippewa, File 32610-1941, 053.

28. William Warne to Lyzeme Savage, December 9, 1949. NARA-DC, RG 75, CCF, Consolidated Chippewa, File 32610-1941, 053.

29. Meyer, D. S. Commissioner of Indian Affairs, letter to Don C. Foster, Area Director Minneapolis. United States Department of the Interior, Office of the Secretary, September 19, 1951. NARA CCF Minnesota Agency, file 1220-1961, 054.

30. An Ordinance Relating to Enrollment and Membership in the Minnesota Chippewa Tribe, May 12, 1961, Minnesota Chippewa Tribe Archives, Cass Lake, Minnesota.

31. Minnesota Chippewa Tribe, Delegates Meeting, May 13–14, 1961, Minnesota Chippewa Tribe Archive, Cass Lake, Minnesota.

32. Ibid.

33. Ibid. MCT citizens voted 1,761 for and 1,295 against the constitutional amendments proposed in 1963. "Revised Constitution and Bylaws of the Minnesota Chippewa Tribe, Minnesota," Certification of Adoption.

34. Erma J. Vizenor, "White Earth 2007 State of the Nation Address," *Anishinaabeg Today* (March 7, 2007), 10–14.

35. Prior to the first Constitutional Convention in 2007, an open call to all White Earth citizens went out in the tribal newspaper inviting them to apply to be Constitutional Delegates. Additionally, Community Councils were asked to select two delegates and one alternate. The sole requirement for becoming a delegate was enrollment as a White Earth citizen. In an effort to encourage as much participation as possible, everyone who applied was accepted. The delegates were a very diverse group. Although the vast majority were over the age of forty, there was a relatively broad age range represented. They came from a variety of educational and professional backgrounds and family situations.

36. Carol Goldberg, "Members Only: Designing Citizenship Requirements for Tribal Nations," in *American Indian Constitutional Reform and the Rebuilding of Native Nations*, ed. Eric D. Lemont (Austin: University of Texas Press, 2006), 107.

37. For example, Martha Berry, delegate to the 1999 Cherokee Nation Constitution Convention, has noted: "Of all the cruel and subtle gifts bestowed upon the Cherokee by colonization, this [blood quantum] is perhaps the cruelest and most subtle of them all." Martha Berry, "Firsthand Accounts: Membership and Citizenship," in *American Indian Constitutional Reform and the Rebuilding of Native Nations*, ed. Eric D. Lemont (Austin: University of Texas Press 2006) 183.

38. Kirsty Gover, "Genealogy as Continuity: Explaining the Growing Tribal Preference for Descent Rules in Membership Governance in the United States," *American Indian Law Review* 33, no. 1 (2009): 295.

39. Ibid., 248.

40. In her interdisciplinary study of American Indian identity, *Real Indians*, sociologist Eva Garroutte notes: "The original, stated intention of blood quantum distinctions was to determine the point at which the various responsibilities of the dominant society to Indian people ended. The ultimate and explicit federal intention was to use the blood quantum standard as a means to liquidate tribal lands and to eliminate government trust responsibility to tribes, along with entitlement programs, treaty rights, and reservations." Eva Marie Garroutte, *Real Indians: Identity and the Survival of Native America* (Berkeley: University of California Press, 2003), 42.

41. Doerfler, *Those Who Belong*, 35–54.

42. Gover, "Genealogy as Continuity," 248.

43. For a detailed history see: Doerfler, "No, No There Was No Mixed Bloods" in *Those Who Belong: Identity, Family, Blood, and Citizenship among the White Earth Anishinaabeg* (East Lansing: Michigan State University Press 2015), 1–30.

44. Consequently, there are families today who go through a process to have their blood quantum "corrected," which can result in new generations qualifying for enrollment under the one-quarter MCT blood-quantum rule.

45. Simpson, *Dancing on Our Turtle's Back*, 124–127.

46. The vote was made by a simple show of hands by the delegates. The motion was not adopted unanimously, but there was a clear majority in favor.

47. Gerald Vizenor and Erma Vizenor are related by marriage. Erma's late husband was Gerald's father's cousin. Gerald Vizenor and James MacKay, "Constitutional Narratives: A Conversation with Gerald Vizenor," in *Centering Anishinaabeg Studies: Understanding the World through Stories*, ed. Jill Doerfler, Heidi Kiiwetinepinesiik Stark, Niigaanwewidam James Sinclair (East Lansing: Michigan State University Press, 2013), 138.

48. Constitution of the White Earth Nation, Chapter 2, Article 1, White Earth Nation official website: http://www.whiteearth.com/programs/?page_id=523&program_id=24, accessed June 1, 2014.

49. Constitution of the White Earth Nation, Chapter 2, Article 2, White Earth Nation official website: http://www.whiteearth.com/programs/?page_id=523&program_id=24, accessed June 1, 2014.

50. For example, to receive a scholarship a student could be required to take a course on White Earth/Anishinaabe history, or to volunteer a specific number of hours at one of the Head Start programs. The requirement for housing assistance could be attending language classes or, for those who are already fluent, volunteering a certain number of hours teaching the language. Requirements like these would create reciprocity, one of our fundamental Anishinaabe values. As Anishinaabeg we all carry a responsibility to give back to our families, communities, and nation. These classes and volunteer requirements would facilitate relationships among citizens. These activities are also empowering. They give people an opportunity to find their place and to feel good about helping others. There are endless ways that the WEN can work to build a strong nation with citizens who practice Anishinaabe culture and know our history. Jill Doerfler, "Weaving Cultural Requirements into Services," *Anishinaabeg Today: A Monthly Chronicle of the White Earth Nation*, February 6, 2013, 2, 28.

51. Delegates who were present at the final convention and voted include: Pam Aspinwall, Michael Bellanger, Gabriel Brisbois, Bev Carlson, Celeste Cloud, Julie Doerfler, Sharon Enjady-Mitchell, Ralph Goodman, Marcy Hart, Jerry Helgren, Joe Holstien, Louie Johannsen, Alice M. Johnson, Charlotte Lee, Peggy Lewis, Ken Perrault, Gerald Roberts, Lucile Silk, Karen Solberg, JoAnne Stately, Leonard Thompson, Donald Vizenor, Gerald Vizenor, and Roberta Wind.

52. It is beyond the scope of this chapter to detail the complex political issues surrounding White Earth's relationship with the Minnesota Chip-

pewa Tribe, but I will note here that during the conventions, delegates commented that White Earth does not have equitable representation in the MCT. White Earth has nearly one-half the MCT population, but each member nation has two votes at the MCT. Delegates also expressed a desire to have White Earth exercise increased independence with the creation and implementation of a separate constitution, but some did not want to fully withdraw from the MCT. Several delegates saw a degree of strength and solidarity with the MCT. The discussion continued, but there were no clear answers to how White Earth's relationship with the MCT would change with the implementation of a new constitution. Indeed, these questions remain unanswered and continue to be a source of anxiety for some.

53. The Bush Foundation funding was critical to the process moving ahead. The foundation also provided important resources and networks. The Bush Foundation "support(s) the self-determination of the 23 sovereign Native nations that share the same geographic area as Minnesota, North Dakota and South Dakota. Our goal is that, by 2020, all 23 Native nations are exercising self-determination to actively rebuild the infrastructure of nationhood." http://www.bushfoundation.org/native-nations-building/overview, accessed May 12, 2014.

54. White Earth Nation, Constitutional Reform, History. http://www.whiteearth.com/programs/?page_id=547&program_id=26, accessed July 27, 2015.

55. White Earth held the election and conducted the referendum as mail-in ballot only. I believe that this highly convenient format also had a positive impact on voter turnout because it gave citizens ample time to vote in addition to eliminating barriers such as transportation.

56. While this is only about twenty percent of eligible voters, it is more than double the number of votes cast in an average election at White Earth.

57. "White Earth Voters Approve New Constitution," *Anishinaabeg Today*, December 4, 2013, 1.

58. *Frank Bibeau v. White Earth Election Board* (2014) AP12-1236 (White Earth Nation Tribal Court).

59. "2014 Elections: Eligible Candidates Can Begin Filing for Office Jan. 21," *Anishinaabeg Today*, January 8, 2014, 1, 23, and "It's Official: Mason, Goodwin, Clark Are New Tribal Council Members," *Anishinaabeg Today*, August 6, 2014, 1.

60. For example, see: "News from Secretary-Treasurer Tara Mason," *Anishinaabeg Today*, November 5, 2014, 4; "News from Chairwoman Erma J. Vizenor," *Anishinaabeg Today*, December 3, 2014, 2; "News from District I Representative Steven "Punky" Clark," *Anishinaabeg Today*, April 1, 2015, 2.

61. "News from Chairwoman Erma J. Vizenor," *Anishinaabeg Today*, April 1, 2015, 2, 20.

62. Matthew L. M. Fletcher, "Looking to the East: The Stories of Modern Indian People and the Development of Tribal Law," *Seattle J. Soc. Just.* 5:1 (2006), 3.

63. Ibid., 21.

BLOOD QUANTUM: THE MATHEMATICS OF ETHNOCIDE

by David E. Wilkins and Shelly Hulse Wilkins

Blood quantum is a familiar term in Indian County whereby an individual's indigenous identity is directly associated with genetic descent. It is not a traditional notion, but rather one created in the late 19th century by a US federal government intent on assimilating and colonizing surviving Native peoples with as little investment in the venture as possible. By applying this arbitrary measurement, US officials were able to trim the rolls of Tribal Nations and claim fulfillment of their treaty obligations at a much reduced cost. Blood quantum was created to be nothing less than mathematical ethnocide, defined here as the killing of a people's cultural identity.

Since that time, this concept has been adapted and taken up by many Tribal Nations as a simple, definitive means of self-identification. The ideology has evolved to include the use of genetic testing, an allegedly more scientifically elegant approach to Native identity, that is plagued by substantial problems, as Kim TallBear's research has shown. Whether a traced line of descent or a DNA test, the continued reliance on blood quantum formulas is a deadly, slow-growing cancer, which weakens, and sometimes even replaces, traditional clan and kinship systems that have been essential to Indigenous survival for millennia.

The current practice of the termination of existing tribal memberships – disenrollment – is a symptom of this deeply embedded disease. Disenrollment is a dramatic and visible manifestation of reliance upon this colonial tool, which exists, in part, to expedite Indigenous assimilation.

In this chapter, we examine the recent surge of tribal disenrollments of otherwise bona fide citizens across Indian Country underpinned by zealous calculations of individual and family blood quantum, which, for these purposes, includes genetic testing. While formal dismemberments occur for variety of reasons, the most common factors associated with the practice are political dissent, criminal activity, and competition for economic resources.

This expedient, bloodless means of silencing dissent and consolidating resources is the latest manifestation of the philosophy of blood quantum. Unless this lethal shared mindset is rejected in favor of tending and healing traditional relationships, Native peoples will continue to struggle with self-definition until they mathematically cease to exist according to the standards they, themselves, have chosen to embrace.

All Our Relations

Human societies have always invented ways to organize themselves – language, religion, social class, and geography, to name but a few. But, for many Indigenous peoples, genealogical connections as expressed through the kinship system were paramount. As Ella Deloria, a prominent Dakota anthropologist put it, "[A]ll people who live in a community must first find some way to get along together harmoniously and with a measure of decency and order.... The Dakota people of the past found a way: it was through kinship."[1]

Deloria went on describe in great detail how the three interrelated Dakota kinship systems – blood, marriage, and social – worked to create a web of responsible interrelationships culminating in this simple, yet profoundly important, concept:

> I can safely say that the ultimate aim of Dakota life, stripped of accessories, was quite simple: one must obey kinship rules; one must be a good relative.... To be a good Dakota, then, was to be humanized, civilized. And to be civilized was to keep the rules imposed by kinship for achieving civility, good manners, and a sense of responsibility for every individual dealt with.[2]

Deloria was not speaking simply of genetic ties, but was invoking instead a broader and highly sophisticated genealogical framework that has enabled families to retain a vividly and "assiduously traced" recollection of their ancestors, both immediate and distant.

While each Native nation continues as a self-defined social group with defining factors that vary from nation to nation, there are three general criteria that many would agree are central to what constitutes a Tribal Nation. The first is the notion that community members are related to one another, either biologically, socially, or by marriage. Members must also share a cultural affiliation. Finally, they must inhabit, or spend considerable time on, particular lands often deemed vital to their spiritual history. Thus, Native nations may be broadly characterized as communities of kinfolk who view the world through a shared perspective and are tied to a specific sacred or meaningful territory.

Given the complexity and significance of such connections, it stands to reason that severing them would be extremely difficult, if not impossible. That is why banishment or termination has occurred so rarely within Indigenous communities. These actions were only undertaken with the knowledge that cutting someone out of the nation would likely be a death sentence for that individual. It was also understood that banishment for any but the most flagrant of offenses would have ultimately led to the literal social disintegration and depopulation of a community.

We see this today when even a single person with authority can destroy a nation from within when allowed by their community to use this deadly tool to disenroll or banish members for political revenge or economic gain. Community survival is hard work. Native nations have learned across the millennia that there are no shortcuts or quick solutions to successful coexistence. Colonial methods of dealing with conflict do not sustain the relationships needed for long-term survival.

Banishment and Disenrollment

Political strife and disagreement over economic benefits realized through gaming and claims – particularly with the way those dollars are dispensed through per capita distribution programs – typically lead to *disenrollment,* defined as the legal and political termination of an individual's tribal citizenship. Civil violations or criminal activity, such as drug trafficking or gang activity, tends to be addressed by *banishment,* which is simply the physical expulsion of an individual from tribal lands without a complete loss of citizenship.

Disenrollment is a legal term of art that arose during the Indian Reorganization Act (IRA) in the 1930s. Banishment is an ancient concept that has been utilized by societies and states throughout the world. The earliest known written record dates back nearly four thousand years ago when the Code of Hammurabi in ancient Mesopotamia called for banishment for the crime of incest.[3]

Native peoples have existed in the Americas for tens of thousands of years, guided by oral traditions passed down through generations. As sovereign governments, they have the power to practice banishment or exile, although documentary evidence suggests that, given the family-oriented nature of Indigenous societies, permanent expulsion of tribal citizens has rarely been practiced. Rather methods like restitution, mediation, and compensation were used to restore and maintain community harmony. Given the kinship system described earlier, along with the fact that most Native societies refused to employ centralized and coercive methods of dispute resolution, tribal citizens generally acted with great care in how they behaved. The fear of being socially ostracized was generally sufficient to maintain relatively peaceful interpersonal behavior.[4]

Thus, while Native nations have always had the power to exile members, it was, and is, a power rarely used, given the spiritually cohesive nature of tribal societies and the wide ineffective assortment of informal sanctions that were in place to ensure social order and maintain community harmony. For example, the five nations of the Haudenosaunee Confederacy, as well as the Cheyenne people, maintain institutional practices that help them deal with individuals whose behavior – typically murder – calls for banishment.[5]

Interestingly, fifteen US states have clauses in their constitutions that explicitly prohibit banishment or exile, including Alabama, Arkansas, and Kansas. Several – Alabama, Mississippi, and Georgia – allow for intrastate banishment; that is, banishment within the state's borders.[6]

Tribal Constitutional Provisions

Beginning in the 1930s, Native policy makers, as federally recognized leaders, began in earnest to enshrine in their governmental documents the capacity to establish membership criteria, as well as their inherent power to decide who could remain on tribal land. There was, at least until the brief termination period of the 1950s, no question that Native peoples would decide the fundamental question of both citizenship and residency requirements for their nations.

A number of Native nations, including the Iroquois Confederacy and the Creek, Cherokee, Choctaw, and Chickasaw, had adopted written constitutions long before the 1934 IRA, and another sixty or so tribal communities had written constitutions or constitution-like documents before the IRA became law. In the decade following its passage, approximately 133 Native nations adopted constitutions and charters of incorporation. The number of Tribal Nations with formal constitutions (IRA, pre-IRA, and non-IRA types) has since increased to approximately 331. The 236 remaining Indigenous communities operate with an assortment of governing arrangements, some are simple legal charters or town council structures, others like the Pueblo are theocracies. The Navajo Nation has a sophisticated four-volume code detailing their three-branch governmental apparatus.[7]

A comprehensive search of 320 American Indian and Alaskan Native constitutions reveals that the word *exile* does not appear in any of these documents. *Banish* appears in only one document—the constitution of the Pleasant Point Passamaquoddy Tribe—which categorically declares that "notwithstanding any provision of this Constitution, the government of the Pleasant Point Reservation shall have no power of banishment over tribal members."

The word *expel* appears in thirty constitutions, and the term *expulsion* is found in fourteen documents – typically for neglect of duty or misconduct. The term *disenrollment* is found in only ten constitutions: Grand Traverse Band, Little River Ottowa, Shoalwater, Te-Moak, Elk Valley, Lumbee, Koyukuk, Huslia, Kaw, and Quinault. The three reasons given for disenrollment were dual membership, failure to maintain contact with the tribe, and fraud in obtaining enrollment. The term *exclusion* is also present, but it is usually reserved for the removal of non-Indians.

The most common phrase describing how a person can be deprived of membership is *loss of membership*, which appears in 173 documents. Tribal members can *lose* their membership in various ways – excessive absences, failure to visit or maintain contact with the tribal community, non-participation in the tribe's economic activities, or dual-enrollment in more than one nation.

These terms typically are found in those sections of constitutions dealing with the legislative powers of the councils and membership provisions.

Of the 173 provisions addressing loss of membership, almost one-half appear in Alaskan Native constitutions, nearly twenty percent are lodged in California tribal constitutions, and about ten percent are found in the organic documents of several Native nations now based in Oklahoma.

As noted, there is a significant amount of diversity in the rationales used by tribal officials to disenroll or expel tribal members – typically either a majority of the tribal council or the community as a whole could expel tribal citizens for "good reason," which generally meant for such offenses as neglect of duty or gross misconduct. In some cases, expelled persons were entitled to a hearing so they could learn the reasons they were being disenfranchised, and they were given an opportunity to muster a defense against the tribe's decision.

More often, provisions in the IRA constitutions regarding loss of membership tended to emphasize the "voluntary" aspect in which tribal members might decide to emigrate in order to permanently separate themselves from their birth nations. In some cases, governing officials allowed for readmission; in other situations, tribal officials informed voluntary émigrés that they would not be allowed to rejoin the nation if they removed themselves.

Many of the IRA and other tribal constitutions contain clauses that refer to the power of the tribal council to remove or exclude "any non-members of the Tribe whose presence may be injurious to the people on the reservation."[8] Importantly, until the late 20th and early 21st century surge of banishments and disenrollments, provisions addressing a Tribal Nation's power to exclude non-Indians from tribal lands are far more prevalent in constitutions than language regarding the expulsion of bona fide tribal members.

So, while the concept of banishment as a consequence for destructive behaviors was part of the cultural framework of most communities, the permanent, formal severance determined by blood quantum was a concept first imposed upon Native peoples by the US government and then incorporated, as constitutions and other governing documents were formalized under the IRA.

Federal Origins of the Blood Quantum Formula

By the 1870s, US federal lawmakers had concluded that Indigenous peoples and their lands and resources were to be absorbed into the body politic, notwithstanding the determined efforts of Native nations to retain their separate governments and what remained of their territories. The end of treaty making in 1871, along with the subsequent land allotment policy, boarding school system, imposition of the Western legal system, and interference by Christian denominations and interest groups had combined to wreak profound havoc on Tribal Nations.

Even as the US federal government was ramping up its assimilation campaign throughout the late 19th and early 20th centuries, it was also looking to find ways to cut costs associated with fulfilling both its constitutionally obligated treaty commitments to Tribal Nations and its increasing self-imposed policy choices designed to civilize, Americanize, and individualize the property Natives. It was at this time that federal officials, driven largely by economic concerns, began in earnest to apply the blood quantum formula with the sole purpose of reducing tribal rolls.

In 1908 Congress enacted legislation declaring that the allotment of any deceased tribal member of the Five Civilized Tribes of one-half or more Indian blood would remain protected, provided of course, that the Secretary of Interior decided not to remove the restrictions.[9] Section 3 of this statute acknowledged that the tribal rolls, as approved by the secretary, were to be "conclusive evidence as to the quantum of Indian blood of any enrolled citizen or freedmen...."[10]

The issue, however, transcended the Five Civilized Tribes of Indian Territory. Indian education had long been considered a crucial step in the assimilative process of Natives into the mainstream of American society. In 1912, Congress incorporated., for the first time, a one-quarter blood decree limit.[11] In an effort to save federal dollars, extensive hearings were held on the merits of excluding Indian children of one-quarter or less Indian blood "where adequate school facilities exist in their own state, thus permitting Indian children now deprived of school facilities an opportunity to secure an education under the laws of the state wherein they live.[12]

During these hearings, Representative Charles Burke engaged Assistant Commissioner of Indian Affairs E.B. Meritt in a discussion on the merits of this plan, as follows in this transcript:

> *Representative Burke: In case the committee should conclude to limit this appropriation so as to exclude from the Indian schools children of less than one-quarter blood, to what extent would it reduce the number of pupils that are now being educated...?*
>
> *Assistant Commissioner Merritt: It would be largely a guess for me to attempt to answer that question without looking into the*

matter carefully. I should say that if you excluded absolutely all children of less than one-quarter Indian blood it would reduce the attendance 15%.

Representative Burke: *Would that enable you to get along with 15% less in the appropriations?*

Assistant Commissioner Merritt: *I do not believe that it would materially reduce the appropriation at this particular time, because the department would be required to keep up the school plants and continue the teachers.*

Representative Burke: *Why could not the appropriation be reduced somewhat then?*

Assistant Commissioner Merritt*: This general item does not cover the reservation schools.*[13]

In the end, Congress adopted an amendment to exclude children of less than one-quarter blood whose parents were citizens of the United States and the states they resided in from Indian day and industrial schools (except for those children whose appropriations had been made pursuant to treaties).[14] The Five Civilized Tribes were excluded from this measure.

On April 17, 1917, Commissioner of Indian Affairs Cato Sells pushed the issue of blood degree even further, and combined it with "competency." Sells advocated in his annual report "A declaration of policy which contemplates the release from governmental supervision, with all of their property, of practically all Indians having one-half or more white blood." However, having more than half Indian blood alone was no longer an adequate protection. The Commissioner went on to include "those with more than one-half Indian blood shown to be as capable of transacting their own affairs as the average white man, also all Indian students over 21 years of age who completed the full course of instruction in the government schools," among those to be released from federal trusteeship. In essence, the federal government actively sought, in disregard of treaties, agreements, and countless statutes to rid itself of its financial and moral obligations to those Native individuals it considered "white Indians."[15]

The appropriation act of May 25, 1918,[16] contained a number of "economy" provisions that have been considered by some writers as the effects of the federal government's desire to break up tribes and their remaining property.[17] Section 28 empowered the Secretary of Interior to apportion on a pro rata basis the tribal funds in trust by the government. Apparently, stimulated by the United States' involvement in World War I, and hence its need for massive amounts of minerals and other raw materials, this appropriation act ignored any tribal voice in the disposition of tribal property. Further, its provisions were intended to mean the ultimate dissolution of Indian tribes, the division of tribal funds, and the parceling out of tribal lands among tribal members.[18]

The Secretary of Interior's inappropriate power over Native peoples received an additional impetus in 1919 when, once again, an appropriation act was the legal mechanism used by Congress to further dissipate remaining tribal sovereignty. This act harbored a provision that enabled the Interior Secretary "at his discretion," and with the "best interest of the Indians in mind," to "cause a final roll to be made for the membership of any Indian tribe; such rolls shall contain the ages and quantum of Indian blood, when approved by the said secretary are hereby declared to constitute the legal membership of the prospective tribes for the purpose of segregating the tribal funds...."[19] These rolls, the Congress declared, "shall be conclusive both as to ages and quantum of Indian blood."[20]

Although the distribution feature of the final rolls and distribution of tribal funds was repealed by section 2 of the act of June 24, 1938,[21] the impact throughout his eighteen-year history was devastating. The secretary's exclusive ability to determine a tribe's final roll curtailed an essential feature of a tribal governing core powers. It was apparent by this juncture that with congressional understanding and awareness of Native concerns at such a low level, the Congress often enacted general legislation that gave the Interior Department and the Commissioner of Indian Affairs enormous authority over tribal matters.

Use of the blood quantum formula, authorization to create final tribal rolls, and the right to distribute tribal funds on a per capita basis evidenced the striking amount of control the secretary and Commissioner had assumed over tribal nations. Such administrative power would continue to increase over the following two decades.

Native peoples faced a deluge of judicial, legislative, and administrative actions during this period. As they struggled under these enormous pressures, white reformers advocated for improvements. This widespread nationwide commitment to a new approach led to the Meriam Report, a study by the Institute for Government research completed in 1928 which provided a comprehensive survey of tribal social and economic conditions across the country. The report graphically noted how the economic base of traditional Native cultures had been virtually destroyed by the encroachment of white civilization.[22]

The Meriam Report's authors viewed Indigenous peoples as "incompetent," and they completely disregarded the distinctive, treaty-based political relationship between tribal nations and the federal government. However, the survey team conceded that "he who wants to remain an Indian and live according to his old culture should be aided in doing so."[23]

Even as the Indian Bureau was being chastised for providing insufficient and substandard services to Native peoples, as well as for monopolizing control of Indian affairs, other agencies were in the process of establishing entirely subjective defining criteria aimed at limiting the number of Natives eligible for federal services and benefits.

Executive Order 4948, signed into law August 14, 1928, transferred several positions in the Indian Affairs department to the classified civil service. Shortly thereafter, the Civil Service Commission approved, and the Bureau of Indian Affairs (BIA) accepted, a limitation on Indian hiring preference to those Natives with one-quarter or more Indian blood. In addition, the individual Indian had to be registered with an Indian agent on a reservation in order to be eligible.[24]

A blood quantum requirement was instituted even though none of the previous hiring preference provisions, dating back to the first one in 1834, or any accompanying definition of *Indian* referred to blood quantum or reservation status. Prior to this administrative decision in 1928, all references to Indian preference relied solely on Indian *descent*. The new blood and residency rules also conflicted with the statutory language of the Snyder Act, enacted in 1921, which simply referred to "Indians throughout the United States."

Two months before the enactment of the Indian Reorganization Act on April 14, 1934, President Franklin D. Roosevelt, by Executive Order 6676, amended the civil service rules to exempt Indians from competitive examination for certain jobs. The order incorporated a one-quarter blood quantum for applicants. The exemption of Indians from competitive examination had little effect on the number of jobs available for Natives, because the qualifications under the noncompetitive examinations were generally the same as for the competitive service. Nevertheless, this order is significant in that it codified into federal law an administratively created, and presidentially sanctioned, quarter-blood degree criteria.[25]

President Roosevelt's acceptance of the one-quarter blood quantum in relation to Indian preference evidences the inconsistency of the federal government. Particularly when it is clear that the majority of Native nations had no such established requirement for tribal membership at that time, and that

Congress itself sometimes enacted legislation recognizing as Indian individuals with less than one-quarter blood.[26]

During the New Deal era, following the recommendations of the Meriam Report Congress enacted two statutes to codify the gradual shift from the excessive domination of the Indian Bureau to one of at least limited tribal self-government. The Johnson O'Malley Act[27] was designed to implement on a national scale the provisions first enunciated in the Snyder Act of 1921[28] pertaining to improvements in education, social welfare, agricultural assistance, and medical care. The Indian Reorganization Act[29] ended the disastrous allotment policy, returned "surplus" lands to tribal nations, restored trust status of Native lands, and recognized and encouraged tribal self-rule by authorizing the drafting of constitutions and charters of incorporation to foster economic development.

The IRA defines *Indian* to mean "persons of one-half or more Indian blood." This provision is the legislative basis for the BIA's Certification of Indian Blood quanta and the rationale for its issuance of Certificate of Degree of Indian Blood (CDIB) cards that many federally recognized tribal members possess.[30]

Tribal Acceptance of Blood Quantum

At first, these blood quantum rules for determining Native identity were not significantly utilized by Tribal Nations themselves, but after 1941, reliance on the measurements by Native nations, with constitutional references began to increase. Today, approximately seventy percent of Native governments in the US rely on some kind of blood quantum system.[31] According to Gover, "[T]he high rate of usage of blood quantum by tribes in the US reflects the long-standing use of the measurement by the federal government in census-taking, but also in legislation and regulations identifying Indians," such as the IRA.[32]

This trend coincides with the federal government's self-determination policy that began in 1970 – a period when inherent sovereign powers were reaffirmed by presidential decree, congressional laws, and Supreme Court precedent.

Ironically, while federal agencies now rely less on blood quantum rules, some tribal governments are invested in its usage, despite the inherent associated problems.[33] "Why," asks Gover, "would tribes increasingly elect to include rules, precisely at a time when the pressure on them to do so has apparently been relaxed?"[34] She answers her own query by noting that "tribes are moving away from a race-based model of tribal membership ... but are not moving toward a classically liberal 'civic polity' model. Instead, findings show that tribes are evolving their own *sui generis* construction of membership, in the form of 'genealogic' tribalism."[35]

By this she means that Native governments are relying more heavily on lineal descent and blood quantum rules and less on residency or parental enrollment both because of the serious problems brought about by federal termination policy in the 1950s and 1960s and because the US still insists that Tribal Nations be able to prove that they are descended from historically recognized Native peoples.[36]

Disenrollment: Blood Quantum Expressed

As of 2016, at least sixty-nine Native nations are, or have been, disenrolling and/or banishing tribal members. Each situation is different, but upon study, some interesting patterns emerge. Twenty-seven of the sixty-nine engaging in disenrollment are located within California. Of these, twenty-six are either currently attempting to disenroll or have disenrolled individuals and families. One has banished some individuals, and three are both disenrolling and banishing persons. In a majority of the California-based cases, the two dominant reasons given by tribal officials for the disenrollments are lack of sufficient blood quantum or fraud in having obtained enrollment.

Formal disenrollment can occur for a number of reasons:

- *Voluntary relinquishment* by a tribal member who "severs tribal relations," "withdraws from," "resigns from," or chooses to "remove" themselves from membership. This voluntary action may then culminate in a tribal order from the governing body that formally revokes or disenrolls that person from the nation.
- *Dual enrollment,* with nearly all Native nations frowning upon simultaneous enrollment in more than one tribe.
- *Deliberate fraud or error* in having obtained enrollment.
- *Failure in maintaining contact with the tribal body* – for those individuals who move away and do not actively keep in touch with the home community.

- *Misconduct*, which is neglect of duty or involvement in activities that may be injurious to the community (i.e., malfeasance, civil violations, criminal acts).
- *Lack of sufficient blood quantum*, which serves as both a justification and a mechanism for dismemberment.
- Alleging insufficient blood quantum is a favorite tactic of those seeking to disenroll multiple individuals. It is a simple, economical method of eliminating entire families with one action. Once a deceased ancestor has been determined to lack the required amount of Tribal blood, all those descended from that individual are automatically ineligible for membership. Often the only historical records used to make these determinations are those catalogued by the federal government, whose sole purpose for decades was to eradicate or incorporate Indians into the dominant society. Even in cases where genetic testing has proven a deceased individual's connections to a tribe, those behind the dismemberment process have continued, undeterred, to pursue termination through other avenues.

Disenrollees have countered, most with a wealth of documentation, that they do, indeed, have sufficient blood quantum and that their membership had not been obtained fraudulently. They assert that family feuds, personal and political reprisals, financial greed, and political power struggles are the real explanations behind dismemberments. Unfortunately, space does not permit us in this chapter[37] to elaborate on all the complexities.

The remaining forty nations engaged in disenrollment or banishment practices are spread over nineteen other states, with most located within the boundaries of Oklahoma, Minnesota, Michigan, Washington, and Alaska. A key difference between these states and California is that the number of banishing tribal nations – nineteen in all – is nearly equal to the number of disenrolling tribes – twenty-one – with most of the banishments occurring because of civil violations or criminal behavior. Of those being disenrolled, nearly one-half are alleged by tribal governments to have insufficient blood quantum.

Thorough, professional research is needed in order to determine whether these sixty-nine tribal governments can verify that their rationale is scientifically and documentarily accurate and just. Such a study has not been completed to date.

Consequences of Dismemberment

Native disenrollees endure profound psychological, emotional, and financial hardships. In some cases, they face substantial physical burdens as well, especially the elderly who are stripped of services and community supports, those with serious health issues who no longer have access to health care, and those facing or enduring homelessness.

Malicious disenrollments are undertaken on the most spurious of grounds – personal vendettas, financial gain, or political power struggles – and do not afford disenrollees even basic due process safeguards. The practice violates Indigenous values, as well as the civil and human rights of those targeted. The problem is compounded and becomes difficult to address because corrupt tribal officials are emboldened to solidify their own economic and political bases by winnowing out opposition from those individuals and families who question or disapprove of their policies and practices.

They are aided by many from outside the community who directly profit from these conflicts. Attorneys, genealogists, and consultants stand ready to encourage chaos and profit from the results. While there is money to be made and power to be gained by a few, ultimately for Indian communities the divisions and fractions lead to cultural and economic disaster.

Once targeted for termination, disenrollees have limited political, legal, or cultural recourse. Tribal courts rarely side with them, and the federal courts, notwithstanding the Indian Civil Rights Act, largely ignore their plight, citing sovereign immunity and the decision in *Santa Clara Pueblo* v. *Martinez*[38] as the precedent that affirms the authority of tribal officials to be the final arbiter of membership decisions.

Disenrollees and those facing legal and political termination, however, are organizing and using various means – lawsuits, social media, complaints to state and federal officials – to make their voices heard outside their specific context. This chorus is beginning to have an impact. In April 2015, the National Native American Bar Association, the largest Native legal organization, adopted a resolution declaring that the "right of tribal citizenship is being increasingly divested or restricted without equal protection at law or due process of law … through a tribal process known as 'disenrollment.'" The resolution then declared that "it is immoral and unethical for any lawyer to advocate for or contribute to the divestment or restriction of the American indigenous right of tribal citizenship, without equal protection at law or due process of law or an effective remedy for the violation of such rights."

The hope is that this action leads to a cascade of similar actions by other leading Indigenous organization, like the National Congress of American Indians and the Native American Rights Fund. It will take considerable pressure from a variety of forces to quell the epidemic of disenrollments that have erupted across Indian Country. And until and unless stronger democratic safeguards are put into place protecting the sanctity of tribal belonging, tribal citizenship will continue to be viewed by an ever increasing number of Native lawmakers as more a privilege than an essential right.

Conclusion

While there is cause to hope that the battle against disenrollment will ultimately be won, our nations will still be left with the larger war with blood quantum. Disenrollment is simply its latest manifestation. The deceptively simple, seemingly neutral approach to determining who is or is not a bona fide Indian will continue to be a tool of colonization, eagerly seized and wielded by those who wish to consolidate their power and spurred on by those who stand to profit from the resulting conflict.

It is critical for Tribal Nations to reject the tainted calculations of blood quantum and other types of genetic measurements and reclaim traditional clan and kinship relationships. Because when communities use methods designed by a colonizing power to sever a people from their origins and means of sustenance, they further their own ethnocide. The cancerous formulas of blood quantum seek to assure that the extinctions will allegedly be scientifically sound, with no physical violence – nothing more than numbers on paper that eliminate a peoples' shared life's blood within a few short years. There is such cruel irony in knowing that, this time, Native peoples themselves are doing the math.

Notes

1. Ella Deloria, *Speaking of Indians* (Lincoln, NE: University of Nebraska Press, 1998. Originally published in 1944): p. 24.

2. Ibid., 25.

3. William Garth Snider, "Banishment: The History of Its Use and a Proposal for Its Abolition Under the First Amendment," *New England Journal on Criminal & Civil Confinement*, vol. 24 (Summer 1998): p. 460.

4. Vine Deloria, Jr. and Clifford M. Lytle, *American Indians, American Justice* (Austin: University of Texas Press, 1983): p. 112.

5. David E. Wilkins, "Exiling One's Kin: Banishment and Disenrollment in Indian Country," *Western Legal History*, vol. 17, no. 2 (Summer/Fall 2004): pp. 239–243.

6. See, e.g., *Beavers* v. *State*, 666 So.2d 868 (Ala. Cri. App. 1995) and *State* v. *Collett*, 208 S.E. 2d 472 (GA, 1974), which upheld the authority of state officials to exclude individuals from certain locations within the state.

7. See Elmer Rusco's *A Fateful Time: The Background and Legislative History of the Indian Reorganization Act* (Reno: University of Nevada Press, 2000): 301, which discusses how the IRA came to be. There are now several studies that examine constitutional developments in Indian Country, including Eric Lemont, ed., *American Indian Constitutional Reform and the Rebuilding of Native Nations* (Austin: University of Texas Press, 2006); Gerald Vizenor and Jill Doerfler, *The White Earth Nation: Ratification of a Native Democratic Constitution* (Lincoln: University of Nebraska Press, 2012); David E. Wilkins, *The Navajo Political Experience*, 4th ed. (Lanham, MD: Rowman & Littlefield Publishers, 2013); and Howard Meredith, *Modern American Indian Tribal Government and Politics* (Tsaile, Navajo Nation: Navajo Community College Press, 1993).

8. Hualapai Constitution & By-Laws, 1955.

9. 35 Stat. 312, 315.

10. Ibid., 313.

11. 37 Stat. 518.

12. House Report 1912, p. 2.

13. Ibid., 22–25.

14. 37 Stat. 518.

15. Annual Report, 1918, p.18.

16. 40 Stat. 561.

17. Felix S. Cohen, *Handbook of Federal Indian Law* (1972): p. 82.

18. Ibid.

19. 41 Stat. 3.

20. Ibid., 3, 9.

21. 52 Stat. 1037.

22. Lewis Meriam, *The Problem of Indian Administration* (Baltimore, MD: Johns Hopkins Press, 1928): pp. 3, 9, and 41.

23. Ibid., 88.

24. Anita Vogt, "Eligibility for Indian Employment Preference in the Bureau of Indian Affairs," *Indian Law Reporter*, vol. 1, no. 6 (June 1974): p. 37.

25. Karl A. Funke, "Educational Assistance and Employment Preference: Who Is an Indian?" *American Indian Law Review*, vol. 4 (1976/1977): p. 9.

26. For example, on March 4, 1931, the Eastern Band of Cherokee in NC were instructed by Congress that "thereafter no person of less than one-sixteenth degree of said Cherokee Indian blood shall be recognized as entitled to any rights with the Eastern Band of Cherokee Indians except by inheritance from a deceased member or members" (46 Stat. 1518).

27. 48 Stat. 596.

28. 42 Stat. 208. This act gave general authorization for categories of Indian expenditures to be dispensed by the Bureau of Indian Affairs.

29. 48 Stat. 984.

30. Kirsty Gover, *Tribal Constitutionalism: States, Tribes, and the Governance of Membership* (NY: Oxford University Press, 2010): p. 83.

31. Gover, *Tribal Constitutionalism*, p. 83.

32. Ibid.

33. Kim TallBear, *Native American DNA: Tribal Belonging and the False Promise of Genetic Science* (Minneapolis: University of Minnesota Press).

34. Gover, *Tribal Constitutionalism*, p. 112.

35. Ibid., 113.

36. Ibid., 8.

37. See David E. Wilkins and Shelly Hulse Wilkins, *Dismembered: Native Disenrollment and the Battle for Human Rights.* University of Washington Press. 2017.

38. 436 U.S. 56 (1978).

WHAT CAN TRIBAL CHILD WELFARE POLICY TEACH US ABOUT TRIBAL CITIZENSHIP?

by Miriam Jorgensen, Adrian T. Smith, Terry Cross, and Sarah Kastelic

When Congress passed the landmark Indian Child Welfare Act (ICWA) in 1978, many Native nations responded with significant legislative work of their own, backing up ICWA's affirmation of tribal authority with tribal law. Some of this work has been enormously innovative: as Native nations have designed rules and systems that reflect *their* preferences, beliefs, and commitments about child welfare, they have developed standards that, for example, promote cultural learning and recognize tribal understandings of the word "family." Nonetheless, a tribe's own citizenship rules can stand in the way of the achievement of child welfare goals: because a Native nation's criteria for citizenship affect the application of tribal policies, there can be a mismatch between a child's qualification for tribal child welfare protections and desired child welfare outcomes.

This chapter first explores the innovative tribal child welfare principles and practices that have emerged in the self-determination era. It then focuses on the impact of a common type of tribal citizenship rules – those based on blood quantum – on the application of tribal child welfare policies. Finally, it explores this point: child welfare policies reflect Native nations' views about citizenship too. Might Native nation child welfare policies and practices also have implications for tribal citizenship standards?

I. A Brief History of Child Welfare Policy in Indian Country

The Indian Child Welfare Act was designed to remedy a long history of abuses by federal and state officials, state court judges, and private adoption agencies that led to widespread removal of Indian children from their homes and communities.

(Atwood 2010, pp. 155–56)

Since the formation of the United States, the assimilation of Native peoples – and especially of Native children – has been a centerpiece of federal Indian policy. Assimilation officially was embedded in U.S. law as early as 1819, when the Civilization Fund Act provided funding to "introduce among [Native children] the habits and arts of civilization" (Prucha 1975, p. 33) in an attempt to "eradicate the 'Indianness'" in young people" (Mannes 1995, p. 266).

In 1882, Congress appropriated funding for boarding schools to be run by the Bureau of Indian Affairs (Atwood, 2010). These large, mission-driven institutions were characterized by military-type discipline and often forbid all expression of traditional culture (Unger 2004). While some American Indian and Alaska Native (AIAN) students were recruited to the schools, many were separated from their families and homes without parental consent (Unger 2004). In addition to "three R's" instruction, most boarding schools provided instruction in domestic and farm skills with the assumption that students' primary labor market opportunities would be in these sectors (Smith, 2007). Some schools' "placing out" programs also assigned Native children to homes and farms owned by non-Indians so that they could learn the "values of work and the benefits of civilization" (Amendments to the Indian Child Welfare Act 1997, p. 303). Brigadier General Richard Pratt, founder and longtime head of Carlisle Indian School, summarized the foundational idea for the boarding schools in his statement: "Transfer the savage-born infant to the surroundings of civilization, and he will grow to possess a civilized language and habit" (Pratt 1892, p. 56), or more succinctly, "kill the Indian in him and save the man" (Pratt 1892, p. 46).[1] U.S. government–funded Native boarding schools existed in various forms until the 1970s (Unger 1977), although the purposes were perhaps less overtly assimilationist.

U.S. government policies created in the mid-twentieth century were equally grounded in biases against tribal culture and child-rearing practices. Between 1958 and 1968, for example, the Child Welfare League of America[2] collaborated with the Bureau of Indian Affairs and social workers across the country to facilitate the Indian Adoption Project (Atwood 2010). This coordinated project sought to place "at risk" Indian children who were "being passed from family to family ... [or] who had spent years at public expense in federal boarding schools or in foster care" in stable, non-Native families (Lyslo 1972, p. 36). By the conclusion of this project, nearly 400 children had been placed for adoption, some quite far from home (Lyslo 1972). The strong interest in adopting Native children shown by non-Native parents throughout the course of the project prompted states to promote these cross-cultural adoptions even after the project ended (Mannes, 1995).

A study conducted by the Association of American Indian Affairs and presented to Congress in 1974 found that in states with the largest Native populations, 25 to 35 percent of AIAN children were removed from their homes by the child welfare system. Eighty-five percent of subsequent foster-care placements were in non-Indian homes, and 90 percent of resultant adoptions were to non-Indian parents (H.R. Rep. No. 95-1386 1978).[3] The report also noted that many decisions to remove children from their families were based in bias or, at least, a lack of understanding (by state child welfare systems, private adoption systems, and mainstream courts) of AIAN cultures and child-rearing practices. In other words, the decisions to remove children frequently were not based on perceived threat or harm. In fact, removal often *caused* harm. Psychologists and other mental health care professionals have emphasized that AIAN children brought up in non-Indian homes may suffer from a variety of adjustment and emotional disorders caused both by the act of removal and by the isolation from family and culture that out-of-community foster placements can create (Jones, Tilden, and Gaines-Stoner 2008).

In 1978, with passage of the Indian Child Welfare Act (ICWA), Congress finally intervened to curtail these aggressively assimilationist policies and practices. ICWA is designed to protect Indian families and, thus, the integrity of Indian cultures. It does so in two ways. First, it establishes requirements and standards that private and public child-placement agencies must follow when Indian children are removed from their homes. Second, it reinforces Native nation sovereignty by providing tribal governments with the ability to intervene or assume jurisdiction in child custody proceedings involving Indian children (Cross and Miller 2009).

II. Reclaiming Native Nation Self-Determination over Child Welfare

> *[ICWA] assumes that a tribal code is the governance mechanism by which a tribe establishes and implements its jurisdiction over all aspects of child well-being.*
>
> (Cross and Miller 2009, p. 16)

ICWA – and a number of federal and state court decisions that followed in its wake – opened the door to greater tribal self-determination over child welfare. In the years since the passage of ICWA, tribal codes have been a key locus of activity in this reclamation of authority (Cross and Miller, 2009). Through lawmaking, Native nations are refining the jurisdiction recognized in ICWA and incorporating their own values concerning child protection. Selected findings from a 2015 review of 107 tribes' child welfare laws conducted by the Native Nations Institute at the University of Arizona (NNI) and the National Indian Child Welfare Association (NICWA) underscore the intensity and diversity of this activity.[4]

Jurisdiction

ICWA formally recognizes and protects Native nations' jurisdiction over child welfare cases involving member children and describes three specific forms of tribal authority:

1. *Exclusive jurisdiction.* In the absence of federal law granting the state jurisdiction (that is, when Public Law 83-280 does not apply), a tribal government has sole authority over cases involving Indian children who reside on its reservation.

2. *Concurrent jurisdiction.* When Public law 83–280 recognizes state jurisdiction, either a tribe or the state may hear cases involving Indian children who reside on the tribe's reservation.
3. *Transfer jurisdiction.* If an Indian child does not reside on a reservation, then the state has jurisdiction, but through ICWA provisions the tribe can transfer jurisdiction back to its court.

In addition to ICWA, federal case law has found that tribes retain general civil jurisdiction (including child welfare jurisdiction) over all members of *any* federally recognized tribe when the case arises on tribal land.

These aspects of Native nations' inherent jurisdiction exist for all tribes regardless of the language in their codes. Nonetheless, many tribes reiterate this jurisdiction in their tribal laws: more than 70 percent of the 107 codes examined included some type of explicit assertion of tribal child welfare jurisdiction.

Alternative Responses

When a child welfare investigation finds evidence to support a claim of abuse or neglect, removing the child from the family home may not be the best next step. Child welfare authorities instead may opt to "wrap" services around family members in an effort to ensure child safety, keep the family together, and avoid formal court intervention.

These alternative responses are beneficial for Native nations not only because they help preserve and strengthen Native families but also because they support ongoing cultural immersion. One-third of the Native nation codes examined by NNI and NICWA included processes that gave tribal child welfare programs authority to pursue such alternatives to removal.

Paternity Provisions

Many tribal child welfare codes define the term "legal father," or indicate who can be presumed to be a legal father. Thirty percent of the tribal codes examined included language about acknowledging or establishing paternity, and 40 percent included language about presumptive paternity.

These tribal statutes have sway both on and off tribal lands. Thanks to ICWA, state judges look first to tribal acknowledgment activity and tribal law – not state law – when ruling in Indian child welfare cases. As a result, if a tribe's code includes definitions of who is or may be presumed to be a legal father, children in whom the tribe has an interest are less likely to be deemed fatherless by state courts and are less vulnerable to separation from the tribe.

Termination of Parental Rights

Termination of parental rights (TPR) is a standard practice for state courts in cases of abuse or neglect because it clears the way to adoption, the preferred permanent placement for children in mainstream child protection systems when family reunification is not possible. Yet the severing of a parent's legal relationships with a child – and, potentially, of extended family, clan, and tribal relationships – is counter to most tribes' cultures and traditions. In fact, because a child's identity may be deeply rooted in tribal culture and connection, TPR has the potential to inflict cultural harm on the child.

In recognition of these concerns, some tribes use their codes to create opportunities for family members to maintain relationships with removed children. A few Native nations' codes reject TPR altogether and provide instead for the "modification," "suspension," or "cessation" of parental rights. These alternatives allow, for example, for a continuing relationship between parent and child even if the child has a different permanent caregiver; for the protection of specific parental rights even when a parent can no longer provide primary care; for the reinstatement of rights and caregiving responsibilities if the parent is rehabilitated; and for tribal enrollment even when a child is no longer considered the child of a tribal-member parent. A full quarter of sampled tribes that *do* have provisions for TPR in their child welfare codes also recognize that parents, children, and extended family may retain "residual rights." Among others, these rights may include reasonable visitation, consent to adoption, and the privilege to determine a child's religious affiliation.

Permanency

Closely related to their modifications of TPR, many tribes are modifying permanent placement practices to reflect their preferences for ongoing family relationships. For example, 95 percent of sampled codes include procedures for some form of guardianship. Guardians have full control over a child's care and are subject to reduced court and child welfare agency oversight, but guardianship itself stops short of the legal finality of adoption and preserves parent-child and extended family relationships. Two other creative approaches used by tribes are open adoptions, where TPR still occurs but contact between children and biological parents is allowed, and customary adoption, where TPR does not occur but new primary caregivers are provided for the child. A few tribal codes required that all minor adoptions under the tribal court's jurisdiction be open adoptions. Eighteen percent of sampled tribal codes provided for customary adoption.

ICWA specifies placement preferences for state courts to follow when approving adoptions for Indian children. It prioritizes family, tribe, and then other Indian families (25 USC § 1915(a)). ICWA also allows tribes to change these placement preferences in their tribal codes, and if a tribe does so, the state court must apply the tribe's preferences in state court proceedings. Thirty percent of the tribal codes studied changed these placement preferences, providing unique tribal placement priorities to be followed in tribal and state court.

Code Development and Administrative Infrastructure Development

Based on the frameworks created by their codes, a number of tribes have built sophisticated, integrated child welfare systems. These systems often include child welfare policies and procedures, community-based child abuse and neglect assessment tools, and culturally relevant treatment models for children and families. Tribal courts have crafted rules for child abuse and neglect cases, drafted bench cards and bench books that guide judicial decision-making, and formed tribal-state judicial forums to train judges and address jurisdictional problems. Prosecutors have convened multidisciplinary teams, built child advocacy centers, and worked to start tribal CASA programs.[5]

In short, since the passage of ICWA nearly 40 years ago, many Native nations have reestablished governance mechanisms to protect member children and families and have built deep child welfare capacity. While not every tribe can afford to develop the systems necessary to fully exercise their child welfare jurisdiction, those that can, do. Native nations also have strengthened their intergovernmental relationships by facilitating transfer jurisdiction, establishing and communicating tribal standards that affect state actions, and otherwise working with states on behalf of Indian children.

Yet these efforts do more than simply reclaim and implement self-determination over child welfare. In developing child welfare codes and child protection systems, Native nations also are reclaiming and bolstering *relationships*. They are establishing processes through which Indian children, regardless of their situations, can have ongoing relationships with their tribes, and tribes can have ongoing relationships with all of their young tribal citizens.

III. Tribal Child Welfare Policy and Tribal Citizenship Rules

Decisions that seek to limit the number of children covered under the statute undermine key remedial aspects of the law. If the statute is to achieve its restorative goals, child welfare workers must take into consideration the effects that almost two centuries of coercive separation and assimilation have had on generations of Indian people.... Courts should not be using the very abuses that caused so many Indian people to be separated from their homes and communities as a basis for ignoring the restorative aspects of ICWA.

(Graham 2009, pp. 85–86)

The catch in this heartening set of policy developments is that Indian child welfare policies do not apply to all Native American children. For the purposes of ICWA, an "Indian child" is a child who is a member of a federally recognized tribe or a child who is eligible for membership in a federally recognized tribe and has a biological parent who is a member (25 USC §1903). Hence, states' Indian child welfare activities focus on tribal-member (or tribal membership-eligible) children and, absent other jurisdictional claims, so do tribes'.

These jurisdictional limits focus attention on tribes' rules for citizenship/membership/enrollment. Every Native nation's rules will cause some children who are connected with the tribal community – whether by lineage or location – to be ineligible for child welfare protections available to "Indian children" under tribal and federal law. For example, in a tribe where citizenship flows through a maternal line, a child born to a tribal-citizen father is not eligible for ICWA protections in state court. Depending on the child's domicile (that is, where the child lives) and the tribal court's statutorily established personal jurisdiction, the child may be ineligible for protection under tribal law as well. To be sure, these children can be protected under state law, but decisions regarding their cases would not be subject to the differential protections that ICWA makes available to Indian/tribal children.

The Intersection of Child Welfare Policy and Blood Quantum Rules

The example provided is not an isolated case. In fact, a variety of tribal citizenship rules lead to similar results. By far the most common are those that require a particular blood quantum in order to qualify for tribal citizenship. For example, one study of 245 non-Alaska tribal constitutions operant in the first decade of the 2000s showed that among these tribes, 70 percent required a particular blood quantum for citizenship (Gover 2008–2009).

Every one of these blood quantum rules creates a sharp division between who is "in" and who is "out" in terms of tribal citizenship. For example, a 2012 analysis conducted by the Pueblo of Ysleta del Sur in preparation for a referendum on enrollment criteria showed an enrolled population of 1,772 and an unenrolled population of 1,595 (Ysleta del Sur Pueblo 2012).[6] Under the enrollment rules then prevailing, the median age among enrolled members was 33 years old; unenrolled descendants' median age was 13. In other words, children composed more than fifty percent of Yselta del Sur's 2012 descendant population but none would have been considered "Indian children" under ICWA alone.[7]

Blood quantum rules for citizenship also can create the curious situation in which a child is 100 percent American Indian or Alaska Native "by blood" but, because of tribal intermixing, does not meet the standard for citizenship in any single tribal community. This clearly is a child that both federal law and tribal law are intended to protect but cannot because of the restrictions of blood quantum rules.

These are worrisome – and not hypothetical – outcomes that can lead to real harms for children and Native nations. As described above, some Native nations have developed multifaceted child welfare programs, such that the decision to remove a child from tribal jurisdiction results in a loss of services. If a state court uses TPR to clear the way for adoption, a child's ties not only with her natural parents but with her extended family, clan, and tribe also are severed. Furthermore, TPR and adoption into a mainstream home places the entire burden of future reconnection to the tribe on the child. For example, if a child opts to open sealed adoption files upon reaching her majority and in this process learns of her tribal affiliation, she must individually and proactively reestablish her tribal connection. Finally, to the extent that severing family, kin, and tribal ties is a cultural harm, the separation diminishes the well-being of both the child *and* the tribal community.

This first problem that blood quantum rules create for child protection – exclusion – also gives rise to a second, more troubling problem. When state courts make decisions about the application of ICWA based on rules for tribal citizenship/enrollment/membership, they are adjudicating the application of jurisdiction based on legal-political status: is the child a tribal citizen (or eligible for tribal citizenship) or not? Unfortunately, the necessity of making a blood quantum finding to determine legal-political status gives the appearance of decision-making on the basis of race, which under federal law, is discriminatory and illegal.

At best, this appearance confuses non-Natives, causing otherwise well-meaning people to suggest that curtailing ICWA's application is necessary for reasons of fairness. At worst, apparently race-based decision making creates an advocacy wedge for entrenched opponents of ICWA (and tribal sovereignty) who use it to support a return to the United States' former assimilationist approaches to Indian child welfare (Will 2015).[8]

A Brief History of Blood Quantum–Based Tribal Citizenship Policy

> *Blood quantum standards are increasingly troubling*
> *for many Native Nations ... because the standards*
> *commonly originate in historic U.S. federal (and U.S. Army)*
> *decisions as to who was subject to federal Indian policy...*
>
> (Kalt 2007, p. 84)

Ironically, just as the opportunities for increased tribal jurisdiction over child welfare are rooted in U.S. policies, so are the challenges created by blood quantum-based citizenship rules. Historically, Native nations relied on customary laws and traditions to determine who their citizens were. Tribes traced membership through a diverse variety of means including clan lineage, residency, marriage, naming, and adoption. Only with the imposition of U.S. federal laws and policies were the original concepts of citizenship shaped by blood quantum. The most influential and far reaching of these was the Dawes Act of 1887 (also known as the Allotment Act). This legislation allotted individual plots of land to Indians, an action expressly designed to break up the collectivist nature of Indian society (Atwood 2010; Washburn 1986). In order for the federal government to determine to whom land should be allotted, it devised a scheme based on blood quantum. In 1934 when the Indian Reorganization Act was passed, the U.S. government built this same scheme into prescribed tribal constitutions and thus entrenched the concept in Native nations' enrollment laws across the country.

Tribal Innovations

Because it excludes people with close ties to the community from tribal citizenship, many Native nations today are working to enact constitutional reforms that address this concern – they are striving to exercise the fundamental sovereign right of determining their own citizenry. In so doing, "it is not unusual for tribal leaders to push for a lowering or abandonment of blood quantum" (Kalt 2007, p. 84) – and they are finding that one of the most important challenging issues to accommodate in that effort is Indian child welfare.

Additionally or alternatively, some tribes have engineered still other solutions to the problem of exclusion from child welfare protections and, in so doing, provided clarification concerning the basis of their decision-making. For example, within their own territories, tribes can address child protection needs through a statutory extension of civil jurisdiction to all reservation residents. More circumscribed versions of this approach are to assert child welfare jurisdiction or emergency child welfare jurisdiction only over all reservation residents. Still more narrowly, a statute could define the tribe's child welfare jurisdiction as inclusive of authority over any Indian children who live on the reservation. Significantly, these jurisdictional arrangements remove the adjudication of citizenship (and concomitant questions of race) as a step in the protection of children living on a Native nation's lands. Protection instead occurs whenever a child falls within the civil, territorial jurisdiction that a sovereign Native nation government has statutorily specified.

Another approach is to parse the meaning of tribal "membership," the specific term used in ICWA. If a tribe can separate the idea of membership from the idea of enrollment, it gains maneuvering room for the protection of more young tribal citizens. As Cross and Miller elsewhere explain:

> Enrollment carries with it the recognition by the federal government of an individual Indian's citizenship in a particular tribe for the purposes of determining eligibility for certain services, rights, and resources. However, membership and en-

rollment are not necessarily the same. The framers of ICWA intentionally used the term "member" instead of "enrolled" for this reason. (Cross and Miller 2009, p. 14)

In contrast to "enrollment-citizenship," "membership-citizenship" acknowledges those individuals who are part of a Native nation's *community*. It is based on the understanding that the ties that bind individuals together in community are important in terms of personal identity and well-being *and* in terms of societal/tribal health and strength. Critically, the idea carries with it the recognition by tribes that they have struggled against the forces of community dissolution – a core goal of colonization – for a very long time. As a result, the individual characteristics that support a reclamation of community and restitution for past harms may not replicate the individual characteristics necessary for enrollment. (In fact, Ysleta del Sur Pueblo's former use of the terms "Enrolled Member" and "Descendant Member" in the materials the pueblo created for a community-wide discussion of citizenship is an example of this difference.)

Following this logic, a tribe can statutorily define "membership for the purposes of child welfare enforcement." This definition of membership allows state and tribal courts to make decisions about jurisdiction based on children's legal status as established in the tribal statute rather than on the basis of race.

Several tribal code examples (from 2015) that demonstrate these options are presented below:

Muscogee Code (Annotated), Title 6, Children and Family Relations/Hopuetake Hvtvm Cukohvmecvlke Empvlsvlke, Section §1–205

The Prosecutor shall provide the following services in state court proceedings: ...B. Intervention on behalf of the Muscogee (Creek) Nation in all Oklahoma state court child custody proceedings within the boundaries of the Muscogee (Creek) Nation involving enrolled Muscogee (Creek) children or Muscogee (Creek) Nation children whose biological parent or parents are enrolled members...

Lummi Nation Code of Laws, Title 8, Children's Code, §8.01.090

(b) an "Indian child" under this Title, is a child who is: (1) a member of the Lummi Nation as defined in (c) of this section or (2) a member of or eligible for membership in another federally recognized Indian Tribe...

(c) a "member of the Lummi Nation" under this Title and for the purposes of the Indian Child Welfare Act shall include: (1) a child enrolled or eligible for enrollment in the Lummi Nation under Title 34 of this Code, or would be eligible for enrollment if the child's eligible parent were enrolled; (2) a child or grandchild of an enrolled member of the Lummi Nation; or (3) a child who is one-quarter or more Lummi blood quantum; or (4) a child who is otherwise recognized as a member of the Lummi Nation community, as determined in accordance with LCL 8.010.130; recognition of membership pursuant to this subparagraph does not, in itself, provide jurisdiction by the Lummi Children's Court over the child or grant the child enrollment member privileges as defined by the Lummi Nation Constitution or by Title 34 of Lummi Code of Laws.

Law and Order Code of the Kalispel Tribe of Indians, Chapter 7, Kalispel Youth Code, §7-4.01

---

(12) INDIAN YOUTH: An unmarried youth who is under the age of eighteen years, including an unborn child, and who is either a member of an Indian tribe or is eligible for membership in an Indian tribe or is recognized by the Kalispel Tribal Community as being an Indian youth...

(14) KALISPEL TRIBAL MEMBERSHIP: The Kalispel Tribe's determination that a youth is a member of the tribe, or is eligible for membership in the tribe, or that the biological parent is a member of the Tribe or that the youth is recognized by the Kalispel Tribal Community as being an Indian youth is conclusive.

IV. Broader Implications for Tribal Citizenship

Together, Sections II and III show how important it is to understand the implications of tribal citizenship rules for the application of tribal child welfare policies: if the children in whom a tribe has an interest are to fully benefit from its child welfare protections and services, tribal policymakers must pay careful attention to citizenship rules that define who those children are and, as needed and if possible, adjust tribal jurisdiction appropriately.

Further, the creativity and commitments that tribes bring to child welfare inspire a reverse question: are there also implications or lessons in child welfare policy and practice for tribal citizenship policy? The answer is yes.

First, tribal child welfare policies suggest a way to soften the multiple exclusions created by blood quantum rules for tribal citizenship. Tribally connected individuals who do not meet the citizenship standard are excluded from more than child welfare protection – they are excluded from all rights and responsibilities that accompany tribal citizenship. Depending on the tribe, these can range from opportunities for homeownership assistance, academic scholarships, health-care access, cultural education, and land inheritance to the responsibility to vote in tribal elections and to abide by the tribe's laws. But just as some Native nations have developed laws that allow membership for purposes of child welfare protection, they might develop other rules that allow "membership for purposes of x."[9]

So the first lesson is this: carefully specified long-arm rules, which extend select privileges and responsibilities of citizenship to non-citizen community members, may be a way to realize tribal goals (such as building community, preserving tribal resources, or protecting tribal members) even in the presence of a blood quantum rule.

Second, fundamental ideas embedded in tribal child welfare policies and practices have an interesting parallel with blood quantum rules. Blood quantum requirements are intended to select individuals for tribal citizenship who have a strong ancestral connection with the tribal community – and increasingly so, as the recent trend is for blood quantum rules to specify *tribal* rather than *Indian* blood (that is, the rules reinforce descent from a particular people as opposed to a pan-Indian identity) (Gover 2008–2009). Child welfare policies are intended to retain a place within the community for children who have an ancestral connection to the tribe but have been removed (or are at risk of removal) from their family homes. In other words, the policies focus on the related ideas of claiming and retaining tribal members.

In general, however, tribal citizenship plays out in a moment in time. If an individual can be shown to meet the standard for citizenship, she will, from one moment to the next, become a citizen of the tribe. By contrast, child welfare practices implicitly emphasize that becoming part of the tribe is a process. As detailed above, child welfare policies and practices support a child's progressive socialization into the tribal community and require the tribe's ongoing enactment of community responsibilities. Over time and through contact, the activities of a tribe's child welfare system embed the reciprocal idea that, regardless of blood quantum, "You are part of us, we are part of you."

Thus, the second lesson is this: tribal citizenship could also be a process, and at least in terms of its purposes and goals, child welfare policy can be a guide for tribes interested in creating a process for "developing citizens," nurturing community, and building the nation.

Notes

1. Remarkably, his was a progressive viewpoint, as "some colonizers advocated outright physical extermination" (Smith, 2007, p. 1).

2. The Child Welfare League of America, founded in 1920, is a coalition of public and private agencies serving vulnerable children and families. See http://www.cwla.org/.

3. The disparity between the removal rates of AIAN children and non-Indian children was even more striking. In South Dakota, for example, the number of AIAN children in foster care was 16 times the number for other children (H.R. Rep. No. 95-1386). In Washington State, the number of AIAN children who were adopted out was 19 times that for other children (H.R. Rep. No. 95-1386).

4. All of the authors have current or past associations with these organizations and have been involved – to one degree or another – in the tribal code analysis project. Other materials associated with this work are

available on the Native Nations Institute website (nni.arizona.edu); see especially Starks, Smith, Jäger, Jorgensen, and Cornell (2016).

5. Court-appointed special advocates (CASA) programs help ensure that children's interests are represented in the child welfare process. CASA volunteers are trained to assess a familial situation, heed a child's opinion, and adequately represent children in court.

6. "Redefining Tigua Citizenship: An Informational Guide for Tiguas to Make an Informed Decision about the Pueblo's Future Enrollment Criteria, Project Tiwahu, Ysleta del Sur Pueblo," 2012, http://www.ysletadelsurpueblo.org/files/spaw/Project_Tiwahu_Survey_Informational_Guide-12-5-13.pdf (accessed March 22, 2016), p. 4.

7. The Pueblo has since shifted to an enrollment rule based on lineal and lateral descent from an original tribal roll. See "Membership Enrollment Application Process" at http://www.ysletadelsurpueblo.org/html_pages.sstg?id=14&sub1=117&sub2=82, accessed March 25, 2016, and "Ysleta del Sur 2014 Year-End Report," http://www.ysletadelsurpueblo.org/files/spaw/2014_Year-End_Report.pdf, accessed March 25, 2016. http://www.ysletadelsurpueblo.org/files/spaw/2014_Year-End_Report.pdf, accessed March 25, 2016.

8. It is worth observing the irony in the latter argument. Opponents of ICWA often argue that race-based policies are unfair and unlawful, but simultaneously posit that their opposition to ICWA arises because the children in the placement dispute are not racially "Indian enough" for ICWA to meaningfully apply.

9. The Assiniboine and Sioux Tribes of the Fort Peck Indian Reservation offer an example. The tribe has a relatively rigorous blood quantum standard for tribal citizenship but allows "Associate Members" to meet a different criterion (admittedly, still a blood quantum standard) (Enrollment Ordinance Section 1e, as amended May 7, 1988). This recognition assures associate members federal status as Indians (and subsequent access to health care and Indian preference in employment applications) but excludes them from the tribal voting franchise and access to tribal revenue distributions. Essentially, Fort Peck's associate membership rule combines welcome and formal acceptance into the nation with tribally regulated standards concerning rights of access to tribal resources.

References

Amendments to the Indian Child Welfare Act: Before the Senate Committee on Indian Affairs, House of Representatives, 104th Cong., 2d Sess. 303 (Statement of Jack F. Trope, for AAIA) (1997).

Atwood, B. A. (2010). *Children, tribes, and states: Adoption and custody conflicts over American Indian children.* Durham, N.C.: Carolina Academic Press.

Cross, T. L. and Miller, R. J. (2009). The Indian Child Welfare Act of 1978 and its impact on tribal sovereignty and governance. In Fletcher, L. M., Singel, W. T., and Fort, K. E. (eds.), *Facing the future: The Indian Child Welfare Act at 30* (pp. 13–27). East Lansing: Michigan State University Press.

Gover, K. (2008–2009). Genealogy as continuity: Explaining the growing tribal preference for descent rules in membership governance in the United States. *American Indian Law Review*, 33, 243–309.

Graham, L. M. (2009). Reparations, Self-Determination, and the Seventh Generation. In Fletcher, L. M., Singel, W. T., and Fort, K. E. (eds.), *Facing the future: The Indian Child Welfare Act at 30* (pp. 50–110). East Lansing: Michigan State University Press.

Jones, B. J., Tilden, M., and Gaines-Stoner, K. (2008). *The Indian Child Welfare Handbook: A legal guide to the custody and adoption of Native American children.* Chicago: ABA Publishing.

Kalt, J. P. (2007). The Role of Constitutions in Native Nation Building: Laying a Firm Foundation. In M. Jorgensen (ed.), *Rebuilding Native nations: Strategies for governance and development* (pp. 78–114). Tucson: University of Arizona Press.

Lyslo, A. L. (1972). Background information on the Indian Adoption Project: 1958 through 1967. In Fanshel, D. (ed.), *Far from the Reservation: The Transracial Adoption of American Indian Children* (pp. 35–49). Metuchen, NJ: The Scarecrow Press.

Mannes, M. (1995). Factors and events leading to the passage of the Indian Child Welfare Act. *Child Welfare, LXXIV* (1), 264–282.

Pratt, R. H. (1892). The Advantages of Mingling Indians with Whites. In *Proceedings of the National Conference of Charities and Correction at the Nineteenth Annual Session* (pp. 45–59). Boston: Press of George H. Ellis.

Prucha, F. P. (1975). *Documents of United States Indian policy*. Lincoln: University of Nebraska Press.

Smith, A. (2007). Soul wound: The history of Native American schools. *Amnesty International Magazine*, http://www.amnestyusa.org/node/87342.

Starks, R.; Smith, A.; Jäger, M.; Jorgensen, M.; and Cornell, S. (2017). *How are tribes enacting their sovereignty to protect children?* Native Nations Institute, The University of Arizona, Tucson, and National Indian Child Welfare Association, Portland, OR.

Unger, S. (1977). *The Destruction of American Indian families*. New York: Association on American Indian Affairs.

Unger, S. (2004). *The Indian Child Welfare Act of 1978: A case study.* Unpublished doctoral dissertation. University of Southern California, Los Angeles.

United States H.R. Rep. No. 95-1386 (1978).

United States House of Representatives (1974). *Indian Child Welfare Program. Hearings on problems that American Indian Families face in raising their children and how these problems are affected by federal action or inaction.* 93rd Congress, 2nd Session (1974).

Washburn, W. E. (1975). *The Assault on Indian Tribalism: The General Allotment Law (Dawes Act) of 1887*. Philadelphia: J. B. Lippincott.

Will, G. (2015). "The blood-stained Indian Child Welfare Act." *Washington Post.* Sept 2. https://www.washingtonpost.com/opinions/the-blood-stained-indian-child-welfare-act/2015/09/02/d3aea62e-50cb-11e5-933e-7d06c647a395_story.html.

Yselta del Sur Pueblo, Project Tiwahu. (2012). "Redefining Tribal Citizenship: An Informational Guide for Tiguas to Make an Informed Decision about the Pueblo's Future Enrollment Criteria." http://www.ysletadelsurpueblo.org/files/spaw/Project_Tiwahu_Survey_Informational_Guide-12-5-13.pdf.

BLOOD QUANTUM: FRACTIONATED LAND, FRACTIONATED PEOPLE

by Richard Monette

I hunkered down within the exterior boundaries of my Peoples' territory – "on my Tribe's reservation," as it were – to write about the hoary monster known as "blood quantum."[1] While perusing the invaluable indigenous law website Turtle Talk, I stumbled across a blog entry quoting from the anti-Tribe pleadings in an Indian Child Welfare case now pending before the United States Supreme Court. The quote read:

> By honoring the moral imperatives enshrined in our Constitution, this nation has successfully shed much of its history of legally sanctioned discrimination on the basis of race or ethnicity. We have seen in vivid, shameful detail how separate treatment is inherently unequal. Brown v. Board of Education, 347 US 483, 495 (1954). There can be no law under our Constitution that creates and applies pervasive separate and unequal treatment to individuals based on a quantum of blood tracing to a particular race or ethnicity. This country committed itself to that principle when it ratified the 14th Amendment and overturned Dred Scott v. Sandford, 60 US 393 (1857), and when it abandoned Plessy v. Ferguson, 163 US 537 (1896). https://turtletalk.wordpress.com/2015/07/07/a-d-v-washburn-icwa-class-action-suit/

I use Turtle Talk's selected quote and its subsequent editorializing because together they help illustrate the dueling notions of identity confronting indigenous Turtle Islanders. On the one hand, American law treats Native identity as being political, as opposed to racial, in nature.[2] In that light, the aforementioned ICWA (Indian Child Welfare Act) pleading entirely misses the point. Federal law in no way recognizes "blood tracing to a particular race or ethnicity"; rather, federal law acknowledges the *political* identity of a person belonging to a federally recognized Tribe, regardless how the Tribe identifies its subjects.[3] But, if political identity provides constitutional cover to Tribes and Indians, then why do Tribes insist on using a race-based blood quantum requirement to determine their membership? Isn't tracing blood lines a racial exercise?

I offer three main answers to that deceptively simple line of questioning. First, the answer is: blood quantum is not necessarily a racial exercise. In your thinking, leave room for the possibility that not all persons on the "base roll" – that list from which all descendant bloodlines run – are indigenous. In fact, some persons on the various base rolls were European, African, and – if we are to heed growing linguistic and genome studies – also Asian along the West Coast and in the Southwest. So, if today's members trace their blood to a person on the base roll, that isn't necessarily an exercise in racial purity; rather, it's an American exercise in keeping the Tribes' numbers to a minimum, in turn keeping to a minimum the territory, water, and other resources the Tribes or their advocates could justifiably claim. At best, it traces to a nationality or developing ethnicity at the time. Second, the answer is: just because Tribes use blood quantum for "membership," with its seemingly racial component, that doesn't necessarily mean Tribes use bloodlines for "citizenship." As Tribes grow and evolve in response to the world around them, they find themselves forced to cling to the imposed race-based membership identifier while experimenting with culture-based political identifiers. Which brings us to the third point: Tribes continue to use blood quantum because the most powerful nation on the planet forced and forces us to. You see, Tribes did not always use blood quantum, and American law did not always view Native identity as polity-based. But somehow they flipped. This chapter will show that, as a young America struggled with its own identity, American law often treated Tribes and Indians on a racial basis, while Tribes often used political and cultural notions to determine their identities. What caused such an ironic turn of events and how do we deal with it now?

Turtle Talk's editorializing illustrates perhaps the most important recent turn in these developments. After quoting from the ugly ICWA brief, Turtle

Talk follows with: "This complaint goes directly at the right of Tribes to determine their tribal citizenry." Citizenry? *Citizenry.* What does Turtle Talk mean by citizenry? Use of the word "citizen" by Natives has dramatically increased in recent years. What does Native America mean by "citizen"? Does the Native meaning of citizenship correspond with the general American meaning? When a Native declares to be a US citizen, do they mean the same thing as when they proclaim to be a Tribe citizen? To indigenous Americans, do State citizenship and Tribe citizenship describe the same type of civic relationship to them? Does Native America's definition of citizenship correspond with its own notions of blood quantum? One thing is certain: membership and citizenship are very different, and the sovereignty and jurisdiction of Tribes will depend upon at least two things: (1) whether American law agrees on their respective definitions, and of course, (2) whether their own citizens and members agree with their respective definitions.

This chapter will provide a stroll through America's judicial history of indigenous identity, and the stroll will consider two lessons in particular: first, if Native America doesn't determine its own identity, someone else will happily, and probably errantly, fill the void. Second, Native America's self-determined identity must find touch points of recognition and agreement with American law in general, or suffer the unintended consequences. This chapter will conclude that Tribes, and American law, have room for utilizing both blood quantum and civic relations in order to determine membership and citizenship. In short, at this point, Tribes should use both membership and citizenship in their constitutions and laws, and keep blood quantum for determining membership, and dispense with blood quantum for determining citizenship.

Blood Quantum Theory

Blood quantum as used by American Indian Tribes is a mathematical exercise whereby proportions or fractions of parts are reduced and then deduced from the whole. Enough has been written elsewhere about the murky origins and machinations of blood quantum to which this chapter will mostly defer. Generally, they all conclude in one way or another that blood quantum and membership were concepts in early European-American law to limit the relationship between Native peoples and the colonies.[4] In my opinion, blood quantum's arithmetic is an exercise in extinction masquerading as a "zero sum game."

I reiterate the first point – that blood quantum was a means to define the relationship between Natives and the new colonies and new states – because it illustrates that European Americans, not Native Americans, first infused the relationship between them with race and racism. While the original states later ratified a federal constitution that steered clear of a racial classification for Tribes and Indians, and instead adopted a political classification, as evidenced in the phrases "to regulate commerce … with the Indian tribes" and "excluding Indians not taxed," still racialization persists. Moreover, nearly seventy years later, the Fourteenth Amendment[5] again included the "excluding Indians not taxed" language, not only reaffirming the role that taxation plays as a benchmark of civic relations in America, but also reiterating that Indians not paying taxes to the states retained a separate political and civic identity from those states.[6] Nonetheless, between the adoption of the federal constitution in 1789 and the advent of the civil war, certain states fought against the notion that Tribes and Indians had a separate political status. This chapter will summarize cases below that illustrate this point and how they inform Native identity today.[7]

I make the second point – that blood quantum is an exercise in extinction masquerading as a zero sum game – because if the game doesn't stop, sometime before it ends, Tribes and Indians are in trouble. Once fractionated, the "whole Native" can never become whole again. The child of a full-blood Native and a "half-blood" is 3/4s Native. The other quarter? Non-Native. That 3/4 blood can then bear children with another full-blood, and yet the child is now 7/8s. And even if that 7/8ths Native bears a child with a full blood, that child will still be only 15/16s. And so on. Indeed, in the game called "blood quantum," unless the fractionated Native can bear a child with a "little more than a full blood," the resulting child will always be only a fraction of the original whole.

If anything, Native blood quantum is nothing but an inverted legacy of colonialism's fascination with racial purity. After all, if that original intermarriage means the original whole Native can never be reconstructed, doesn't it also require the same result for the original whole non-Native? After intermarriage, the child of the full blood non-Native is also now only half, then 3/4 or 1/4, and so on, never to be whole non-Native again. And yet, when all is said and done, we still have a whole person here and a whole person there. We still have a whole human being as filled with life and potential, as challenged by death and sorrow, as steeped in culture, as confronted by reality, as the original whole. How ironic it is that Native America has become the purveyor of the lies that blood quantum and racial purity are.

Picture a heart-rate monitor, where your healthy heartbeat causes the line repeatedly to jut up and drop down. It's called "reactivity." Like the reactivity of a healthy heart, the blood quantum game suggests that every degree of Native blood lost is equal to the same blood degree of non-Native blood gained. Or, in reverse, on the roller coaster of intermarriage, it might also appear every degree of Native blood gained is equal to an amount of non-Native blood lost. And yet, here is where the game ends, for while two whole persons exist, they and their children can never again become a racially "whole Native" or a racially pure non-Native, and in a reality where Natives Americans are vastly outnumbered and intermarriage is inevitable, the total number of full bloods or "whole Natives" will someday "flatline," long before non-Native America's line goes flat. Just like the monitor's decreasing reactivity on a dying heart, Native identity based solely on blood quantum will finally and ultimately flatline altogether. Using blood quantum to determine civic relations between Natives and their Tribes has to stop, before the game is over.[8]

Uncontrolled Identity

Despite the mathematical certainty of harm from using blood quantum, why do most Tribes continue to play the blood quantum game? Despite the complex human stories behind the numbers, perhaps it's because blood quantum seems simple, scientific, and detached from human intervention. Or perhaps blood quantum's false premise of racial purity leads to the false promise of controlling identity. Is it really controlling identity, or is it just using the hand controls for someone else's endgame? That aforementioned ICWA pleading asserts the continued widespread use of blood quantum:

> Most Indian tribes have only blood quantum or lineage requirements as prerequisites for membership. *See* Miss. Band of Choctaw Indians Const. art. III, § 1; Cherokee Nation Const. art. IV, § 1; Choctaw Nation of Okla. Const. art. II, § 1; Muscogee (Creek) Nation Const. art. III, § 2; Gila River Indian Community Const. art. III, § 1; Navajo Nation Code § 701; Guidelines for State Courts and Agencies in Indian Child Custody Proceedings, 80 Fed. Reg. 10146, 10153, B.3 (February 25, 2015) ("New Guidelines"). Consequently, ICWA's definition of "Indian child" is based solely on the child's race or ancestry.

It is difficult indeed to argue against that anti-ICWA conclusion. And the inclusion of "ancestry" even takes into account that not all persons on many base rolls were Native. The only way for Tribes to justify the ICWA approach and to defeat the anti-Native, anti-ICWA argument is to take control of our territories and identities, to stop letting others determine our identities for us, to make the main distinction between "us and them" be not racial, but political, and to steep that political distinction on borders that have legal significance and to fuse the identity with the actual culture in that territory. If that sounds circular, it is intended to. Such is the circle of life.

Perhaps a stroll through America's legal history will shed some light. The greatest historical lesson comes from the US Supreme Court case of US v. Rogers from the mid-19th century.[9] Mr. Rogers' Native blood quantum was 0/0. Mr. Rogers murdered another man whose Native blood quantum was also 0/0. Nonetheless, Mr. Rogers lived in Cherokee Country, consorted with Cherokees, had a Cherokee spouse and children, and was, culturally, Cherokee. Like America's most famous Armenian, Cher – of Sonny and Cher – and the popular hit song "Half-Breed," Mr. Rogers believed he was Cherokee. So, perhaps not surprisingly, Mr. Rogers claimed that the United States had no jurisdiction to prosecute him for his crime. Well, he lost. The court stated flatly that, despite all his Cherokee acculturation, Mr. Rogers was "still a white man, of the white race."[10] In other words, the US disregarded its own Constitution, the political moorings of the US/Tribe relationship, and instead resurrected its colonial mantra and re-racialized the US/Native relationship. According to the court, Mr. Rogers' cultural, social, and political identities were all irrelevant. Mr. Rogers was not Cherokee because his blood quantum was 0/0.[11]

Speaking of infusing identity with race and racism, consider the matter of People v. Hall[12] before the Supreme Court of California. Mr. Hall's criminal conviction was attained in part upon the testimony of a man of Chinese descent, and California had a statute disallowing convictions of a white man upon the testimony of a "negro, mulatto, or Indian." If the statute says Indian and if the witness is Chinese, then, you ask, what's the issue? Well, one need read no further than the opinion's opening paragraphs to see where this was headed: "When Columbus first landed … he imagined that the Island of San Salvador was one of those Islands of the Chinese Sea …." Yes, that's right. Just like Christopher Columbus' referring to those Chinese people lost in the Caribbean Sea as Indians, the California Supreme Court found a way to conclude, for purposes of the statute, that when the legislature used the term "Indian," it meant Chinese. Thus, a statute disallowing a Native's testimony against a white man wouldn't allow testimony of a Chinese witness either, because Columbus thought he was in China, after all.

Every time I re-read the Rogers and Hall cases I'm reminded of the famous Azerbaijan case where the US government argued that the Chinese Exclusion Act of 1882 also implicitly excluded Armenians. Putting two and two together, if Armenians are Chinese and Chinese are Native Americans, then Armenians are Native Americans ... and, voilà, Cher was Cherokee after all. Not to mention that, at least for purposes of California's statute, we have potentially a couple more billion "Indians" on the planet. Add to that the billion or so "real Indians" on the Asian subcontinent and we're talking about a lot of Indians with some real clout. We're also talking about the folly and perils of leaving your identity to someone else.

Connecting two cases involving the Pueblos illustrates the outrageous legal repercussions of leaving your identity to the convenience of others. It also illustrates why Native identity is and should be polity-based rather than race-based. When the issue was whether a federal official had the authority and responsibility to protect Native Pueblo lands from squatting white men – surprise, surprise – the US court protected the white men because the Native Pueblos were not Indians.[13] Here's how the court knew they were not Indians: "In short, they are a peaceable, industrious, intelligent, honest, and virtuous people. They are Indians only in feature, complexion, and a few of their habits; in all other respects superior to all but a few of the civilized Indian tribes of the country, and the equal of the most civilized thereof." Of course they can't be Indians!

Yet, a few decades later, when the question arose whether a federal official could regulate the liquor trade with the Native Pueblos, it turned out they were Indians after all. Here's how we knew: "The people of the Pueblos, although sedentary rather than nomadic, in their inclinations, and disposed to peace and industry, are nevertheless Indians in race, customs, and domestic government. Always living in separated and isolated communities, adhering to primitive modes of life, largely influenced by superstition and fetichism [sic], and chiefly governed according to the crude customs inherited from their ancestors, they are essentially a simple, uninformed, and inferior people." (*United States v. Sandoval*, 231 US 28, 39 [1913]). Well then, they must be Indians after all.

Then there's the case of Standing Bear of the Ponca Nation.[14] Standing Bear insisted on staying in his homelands rather than be "removed" to Oklahoma, even if it meant severing his ties to his Native peoples. Upon arrest and seeking to be released through habeas corpus, the federal court determined that Standing Bear possessed the basic human right to expatriate from his people and become American; thus, for purposes of federal law, Standing Bear was a "person" with the right to habeas corpus relief. Never mind for the moment that as a patriated Ponca, apparently Standing Bear was not a person under federal law. Instead, compare the case with US v. Rogers, who, unlike Standing Bear, evidently did *not* possess the basic human right to expatriate from his peoples. He was white and that was that. Who could have imagined such racism against white Americans? Of course, with the Rogers/Standing Bear decrees, Natives can now leave their peoples and become American, but white Americans can't leave their peoples and become Native. Does that one-way street sounds a bit like the blood quantum game?

Make no mistake, the American people, acting through their federal and state governments, have consistently infused and imposed race and racism into their relations with indigenous peoples. In 1921, the US enacted into federal law the Hawaiian Homes Commission Act. According to the act itself, only Native Hawaiians of 1/2 or more degree are eligible to participate in its programs. In the case of Rice v. Cayetano, the US Supreme Court, based on a challenge by a non-Native citizen of Hawaii, declared that the state of Hawaii cannot implement the racial contours of the relationship.[15] And yet, in 1971 the US enacted into federal law the Alaska Native Claims Settlement Act (ANCSA), a modern experiment in social genocide by which American law imposes upon Alaska Natives corporate structures to replace Native organizations and institutions.[16] ANCSA adopted a blood quantum as a prerequisite to shareholder status. Since under ANCSA these Alaska Native corporations are entirely subject to state law, one wonders if the blood quantum requirement could withstand a Rice v. Cayetano challenge. Except, given the way ANCSA has hamstrung the Natives and separated them from their wealth, no non-Native Alaskan will likely be bringing that suit anytime soon, for it might be against the best interests of his or her non-Native Tribe.

Today's Blood Quantum in Action

Political debate on immigration during the 2016 presidential primary campaign season has resurrected political arguments over "birth citizenship," a peculiarly American concept that, like many others, symbolizes a revolutionary break from the American majority's European roots. As one concise article from NPR explains, "Most of the rest of the world, for example, gives people citizenship based on a concept known as *jus sanguinis*, literally 'by right of blood.'" (The article contextually cites France, Germany, Greece, Italy, Portugal, Spain, and the U.K.) The USA, on the other hand uses "*jus soli*, or birthright citizenship." The article explains: "The other [*jus soli*] notion of nationhood is generally known as a civic notion of nationhood. And this is the idea that folks are bonded together by where they are, by locality and by the ideas that they might share. And that's what we have in the United States."[17]

In that light, the *Rogers* case implies that the Cherokee Nation, or Cherokee,[18] used a variation of *jus soli*, that they naturalized foreign persons into a full civic relation with their nation. To Cherokees, Rogers was apparently one of their citizens regardless of his 0/0 blood quantum. However, as the young USA proceeded to impose its immature, underdeveloped notions of citizenship on Tribes and Indians, it labeled the practice of Native naturalization as "adoption," as though Tribes and Indians were the ones, instead of the USA, attempting to be one big happy uni-racial family. Unfortunately, and ironically, *jus sanguinis* – literally, "right of blood" – and adoption have made their way into Native America's constitutions and laws and cultures. In other words, with their original *jus soli*, separation of powers, and democratic federalism, the Indian Tribes seem to have given America the best they had to offer, and then, by using blood quantum, Native America seems to have adopted the worst that European Americans imported from Europe.

As it becomes increasingly clear that blood quantum is an exercise in extinction, Indian Tribes must pointedly ask themselves what it is they hope to achieve by continuing to use blood quantum. Is blood quantum really necessary for preserving and protecting their sovereignty? Is weeding out those without a minimum blood quantum a "necessary evil" for preserving and protecting their sovereignty, culture, and identity? Is the United States of America any more or less likely to terminate its political recognition of their sovereignty if their racial characteristics become less distinct? Will having a vibrant culture with its own history, language, religion, foods, and clothing be enough to justify recognition of their sovereignty? Or has blood quantum simply become a placebo to treat the sickness of destroyed cultures and lost sovereignty?

All peoples want to maintain their sovereignty and determine their own identity. History has taught us how to succeed with the following truisms.

1. Identity Autonomy. First, the circle of life cannot be complete without the ability to determine our own identity.

2. Cultural Autonomy. Second, we cannot determine our own identity without a substantial measure of cultural autonomy as part of the circle. After all, it is not just the whims and wishes of the individual that determines identity; it is also the forces and perceptions of those around us. We and those around us evolve distinct norms and values, customs and traditions, beliefs and principles – in short, lifeways. If self-determination of identity is to be meaningful, it must follow with the necessary measure of self-determination of culture.

3. Political Autonomy. Third, we cannot attain and maintain a substantial measure of cultural autonomy without a substantial measure of political autonomy as part of the life circle. Political autonomy is determining your own laws and processes based upon your own norms and values, your own customs and traditions, your own beliefs and lifeways, your own culture and identity.

4. Territorial Autonomy. Fourth, we cannot attain and maintain political autonomy without a substantial measure of territorial autonomy as part of the circle. We cannot ensure that our norms and values become the basis of laws and provide guidance to resolve disputes, unless the force of our own law and police power play a role in the enforcement, administration, and execution of those laws and rules and norms.

5. Fifth, and finally, blood quantum accomplishes none of this. Imposing or possessing a level of blood quantum does not indicate in the slightest that the person has lived in the territory, exercised the political processes of the Tribe, navigated the social processes of the tribal society, and has learned the cultural norms and values. Likewise, not having a minimal degree of blood does not mean a person has not experienced all these things. Nothing short of the completed circle of identity, culture, polity, and territory will ensure our survival.

Given the current state of things, Tribes and Indians must utilize both notions of citizenship and membership. Tribes are at a crossroads where the citizenship connotations of *jus soli* birthright citizenship and the membership connotations of *jus sanguinis* both can and perhaps must play a role. In short, Tribes should use membership in disregard of the Tribe's jurisdictional boundaries, and that membership could and maybe should be based on blood quantum – *jus sanguinis*. However, Tribes must evolve a citizenship model for those who are born or who at least reside inside the Tribe's jurisdictional boundaries, regardless of whether the person is a "member" or not, regardless of that person's blood quantum. Instead, the contours of such citizenship can be determined by birthplace, a minimum residency requirement, and cultural proficiency. And it must have civic relations, responsibilities, and participatory rights as its benchmarks.

Conclusion

I remember once listening to an Oneida elder explaining about the Three Sisters, telling an animated story about how corn, squash, and beans depend upon each other to survive and thrive, and how we, the two-leggeds, use our gift of reason to play a necessary role in bringing them together and helping them flourish.[19] The story brought back memories of tribal elders explaining how important it is to maintain our cultural stories and knowledge, and that someday those stories will re-teach us how to live right with each other.

What does blood quantum have to do with the Three Sisters? Tribal sovereignty, like sovereignty for all nations, requires three things: a distinct Peoples with their own culture, a Territory with well-defined boundaries, and recognition by Neighbors. Like the Three Sisters, territory, peoples, and neighbors depend on each other to flourish. And just like the Three Sisters, they require the two-leggeds to use their gift of reasoning to help bring them into harmony and to play a balancing role.

Thankfully, our elders and youth keep alive the cultural knowledge of our stories. The Three Sisters can re-teach us that our territories, our peoples, and our relations with our neighbors must survive together. We must stop trying to be distinct peoples and cultures solely based upon blood degree. Instead, we must strive to make the cultures inside our territories distinct from those cultures outside our territories in spite of blood quantum.

One of the most instructive things I've ever read was boiled down to one sentence in an *Indian Country Today* letter over a decade ago. The letter writer said: "If tribes do not respect their own jurisdictional boundaries, then how can we expect the state to do so?" (*ICT*, 2/24/04, p. A4). In the relationships between our territories, our peoples, and our neighbors, we must use our territories to help define ourselves. While blood quantum may define "membership," our territories define our cultures and our citizenries. While tribal members, wherever they reside, have a shared history, today's culture is evolved and crafted every day in our territories and in our communities.

Like the Three Sisters, we must bring our territories, our peoples, and our relationships together to depend upon each other for survival so that each may flourish in its role.

Notes

1. Please pardon me as I use the word "tribe," at least as it is used in the US Constitution, despite its currently derogatory meanings in the western press referring to every petty cabal in the Mideast or Africa whose loyalties Americans haven't yet discerned or co-opted. Likewise, I will intrepidly use the word "Indian," as that word also is used in the US Constitution, despite that a billion people of an entire subcontinent of Asia want their name back. To control identifiers is surely to control identity, is it not? So imagine my pleasant surprise – especially after recent developments in the anti–Washington Redskins campaign – when I read a Turtle Talk hotlink implying that the popular media had graciously taken up the campaign to stop popular usage of the "R-word." You know the word I mean, right? The "R" word – "Retard." *See* http://www.up-worthy.com/the-next-time-someone-uses-the-r-word-in-front-of-you-quote-nfl-star-joe-haden-he-nailed-it?c=upw1&u=8c3615429073f5b-9fb15f1643ee8590cee0268f8. You see, sometimes all things Native are so subverted into otherness and marginalized into nothingness that, never mind Redskin, I suppose I should consider myself lucky to have even found Turtle Talk, since searching the term brought up only Disney's "Turtle Talk with Crush." If you think the Lightness of Being is Unbearable, try your hand at the weightlessness of not being at all.

2. See generally, *Morton v. Mancari* 417 U.S. 535 (1974); and *United States v. Antelope*, 430 U.S. 641 (1977).

3. American "conflicts of law" or "choice of law" rules often require an American court to defer to a foreign citizen's legal obligations or legal status under their own country's law; so, if American courts were compelled to apply German or Israeli law using *jus sanguinis*, as they do, does that mean American law is participating in that country's "blood tracing"? Of course not. And it shouldn't be analyzed differently for the Indian Tribes. In other words, if American law is compelled to defer to or apply an "Indian Tribes'" law, that doesn't mean American courts are adopting it.

4. When colonial Virginia migrated the concept in from Europe and applied it to Natives, some say it was a restriction on Native "rights"; however, that only makes sense if one had rights in Virginia in the first place, and more importantly, if one *wanted* rights in Virginia in the first place.

5. Ratified July 9, 1868, and granted citizenship to "all persons born or naturalized in the United States," including former slaves recently freed.

6. The "excluding Indians not taxed" clause refers to state taxes, since the section determines apportionment, and the federal government did not have a per person or income tax at that time; the notion of a federal per capita or income tax was not contemplated at the founding and did not happen until almost a hundred years later. Therefore, the clause means that Natives not subject to per capita or income taxes imposed *by the states* could not be counted as *state citizens* for purposes of determining the number of congressional representatives that each state has. The idea arises on the mistaken notion that the 14th Amendment changed all that and turned all Natives into state citizens whether or not they paid state income taxes. While the 14th Amendment may have turned non-territorial, non-reservation Natives into state citizens and assured their rights in the states in which they lived, it nonetheless maintained the notion of "excluding Indians not taxed" – that those Natives living inside their respective Tribe's reservation or territory do not pay state income taxes and thus care not to be counted for purposes of determining apportionment of congressional representation. The only constitutional and logical conclusion to be reached is that they are not state citizens.

7. A much under-studied theme is how some pre–Civil War states, often those that opposed slavery also supported the separate political status for Tribes, as evidenced by the "excluding Indian not taxed" clause, and thus how the civil war reaffirmed this idea with the 14th Amendment reasserting the federal position of a separate polity for Tribes into the Constitution by reinserting the "excluding" clause. Ironically, today many Natives, even tribal leaders, proclaim state citizenship and their right to participate in state politics, despite not paying tax there, and despite the obvious undermining of their separate political and sovereign status, that if you do participate in a state then you will ultimately pay tax to that state.

8. The difference between the final results for applying blood quantum to Natives and non-Natives in America is this: when only the final non-

whole Native and the final non-whole non-Native are left standing, non-Natives will simply call Europe to replenish their supply, as indeed they have before, while the Native will have nowhere to turn, this being one of the ultimate distinguishing characteristics of colonialism.

9. *United States v. Rogers*, 45 US 567 (1846).

10. *Id*. at 573.

11. The flipside is that the blood quantum of a person whose direct lineage descends from the whole, no matter how fractioned, can never become 0/0. Perhaps that explains the temptation of some Tribes' using "lineal descent" to determine membership. Indeed, as long as lineal descendants keep bearing biological children, the membership keeps expanding with a thinner and thinner degree of blood – a wholly different set of problems for some Tribes.

12. *People v. Hall*, 4 Cal. 399 (1854).

13. *United States v. Joseph*, 94 US 614, 616 (1876).

14. *United States* ex rel. *Standing Bear v. Crook*, 25 F.Cas. 695 (C.C.D.Neb. 1879).

15. 528 US 495 (2000).

16. 43 USC §§ 1601-28 (1988, as amended).

17. http://www.npr.org/sections/thetwo-way/2015/08/18/432707866/3-things-you-should-know-about-birthright-citizenship?utm_source=npr_newsletter&utm_medium=email&utm_content=20150823&utm_campaign=mostemailed&utm_term=nprnews.

18. Note how the differences between the *jus soli* civic relationship of "birthright" connotes a place or a territory while the *jus sanguinis* blood right disregards location and implies a peoples. To illustrate: Wisconsin is the place and Wisconsinites the people. America's sad history of displacing indigenous peoples has resulted in their labels and symbols being about a people rather than a place. It feeds the mistaken notion that the Indian Tribes were placeless wanderers and nomads, terms used by no less an authority than the US Supreme Court in its early cases.

19. A portion of this chapter previously appeared in substantially different form in the Oneida newspaper, *The Kalihwisaks*.

RECONSIDERING BLOOD QUANTUM CRITERIA FOR THE EXPANSION OF TRIBAL JURISDICTION

by Rebecca M. Webster

Tribal governments have the ability to determine membership.[1] In turn, members participate in the election or appointment of their leadership. Those elected leaders, with input from the membership, establish laws that apply within their communities. Tribal communities have the power to redefine and reconstruct how they determine membership. This chapter will discuss the impacts that revising current membership criteria could have on tribal jurisdiction. Reconstructing enrollment criteria to allow more individuals to become enrolled would result in an expansion of tribal jurisdiction. This increase in jurisdiction strengthens tribal sovereignty by making the tribe's laws applicable to more people and more lands. With a focus on federally recognized tribes, this chapter places an emphasis on the ability of tribes to make their own laws and apply those laws to people under their jurisdiction. I will analyze identity from a legal and political perspective, and rely on terms most commonly used in federal laws and cases.

Terminology

As other chapters in this book describe, an individual's cultural and spiritual identity is not necessarily linked with blood quantum. The use of blood quantum for tribal enrollment purposes separates people on a legal basis into different categories. Therefore, the terminology used in this chapter warrants a brief explanation.

People use a variety of ways to describe themselves, including terms such as Native American, American Indian, First Nations, and indigenous. Other people prefer to use their specific tribal affiliation such as Oneida, or even more accurately, On^yote?a·ká. The term "Indian" is a legal term used to distinguish between people who are Indian from people who are non-Indian.[2]

Similarly, people use different terms to describe their tribal affiliation. Some people use "member" while others use "citizen." Some people point out that the term "member" feels more appropriate when talking about a club, while the term "citizen" is more appropriate when talking about a government. The term "member" is most commonly used in federal laws and cases. Like the term "Indian," the term "member" is a legal term used to distinguish between people who are members and those who are non-members.[3]

Status as Indian or a member means that individual has certain rights and privileges under the law. It also means the individual can participate in tribal politics as well as in federal, state, and local politics, and the individual is subject to tribal laws in addition to federal laws. Application of state and local laws to Indians and members is a complex subject and will be addressed later in this chapter.

Another distinction under federal laws and cases involves the different status of tribal governments. Tribes fit into one of three categories: federally recognized tribes, state recognized tribes, and unrecognized tribes. Federally recognized tribes are those with a government-to-government relationship with the federal government.[4] These tribes are eligible to receive federal funding to provide tribal services, such as funding from the Department of Housing and Urban Development and Indian Health Services. As of 2015, there are 566 federally recognized tribes (Dept. of Interior).[5] As a general rule, states also maintain government-to-government relationships with federally recognized tribes. State recognized tribes are those tribes recognized by the state, but are not in a government-to-government relationship with the federal government. For example, North Carolina recognizes its government-to-government relationship with the Lumbee Tribe, but the federal government has not yet granted federal recognition, despite the Lumbee's persistent efforts to obtain it. Tribes with only state recognition may be eligible for limited benefits under federal law. Some tribes, like the Brothertown in Wisconsin, are not recognized under federal or state law. Like the Lumbee, the Brothertown have been struggling for decades to obtain recognition. These tribes are not eligible for any benefits under federal law. Aside from eligibility for federal benefits, a tribe's status as a federally recognized tribe has jurisdictional consequences as well.

Before examining the jurisdictional questions, a brief discussion of what jurisdiction is may be helpful. In general, this term is used to determine whether a court can hear a case or to determine whether a government can apply its laws to a person. Both terms are closely linked with tribal sovereignty, the right of tribal governments to govern themselves. A 1959 United States Supreme Court case recognized the rights of tribes to "make their own laws and be ruled by them."[6] Federally recognized tribes have the ability to make their own laws and apply those laws to people under their jurisdiction.

Membership Criteria

In 1934, Congress passed the Indian Reorganization Act (IRA).[7] This act helped tribes regain more control over tribal affairs by reorganizing their governments and adopting new constitutions. The constitutions generally established tribal enrollment criteria through minimum blood quantum requirements.[8] Most tribes determine membership eligibility on having some measure of blood quantum.[9] Indian tribes have blood quantum criteria that range anywhere from ½ blood to $1/_{32}$ blood. Other tribes only require an individual to prove he or she is a direct lineal descendant to an individual on an original tribal list such as an allotment list. As mentioned above, federal law recognizes tribes can establish membership criteria for themselves. However, tribes with IRA constitutions generally need to obtain approval from the federal government to change their constitutions. Since enrollment criteria are often set out in these constitutions, the federal government may need to approve changes to enrollment criteria. Another option that a few tribes have used is to amend their constitutions to remove the requirement that the federal government approve future amendments. In these cases, the membership can vote to change their constitutions without obtaining federal government approval.

Tribal Jurisdiction over Members

Once an individual meets the tribe's requirements and enrolls with the tribe, that individual is then a member and subject to a wide array of tribal jurisdiction on the reservation, and in some cases, off the reservation as well. Tribal jurisdiction over members includes civil and criminal matters, probates, zoning and land use, and licensing requirements. Unless the federal government limits tribal authority over its members, tribal governments have the ability to make laws that govern member activities.[10] A person's status as Indian or as a member may also limit how much states and local governments can regulate their activities. In addition to consequences such as increasing demand for tribal services and resources, lowering blood quantum or finding other ways to expand membership can also have positive impacts, such as increasing a tribe's jurisdiction over a larger number of people and shrinking the number of people subject to state and local jurisdiction.

Tribal Jurisdiction over Non-members

As a general rule, tribes have jurisdiction over non-members only in a limited number of instances. Tribes have jurisdiction over non-members when the non-member enters tribal land,[11] if Congress delegates authority to tribes,[12] if the non-member enters into a consensual relationship with a tribe or member,[13] or if tribal regulation is necessary to protect tribal self-government and internal tribal relations.[14]

State Jurisdiction over Members

Similar to tribal jurisdiction over non-members, states have jurisdiction over members only in a limited number of instances. The general rule is that "state laws generally are not applicable to tribal Indians on an Indian reservation except where Congress has expressly provided that State laws shall apply."[15] The purpose of this general rule is to ensure that states do not infringe on tribal rights to govern themselves.[16]

One of the most well-known (and misunderstood) examples of Congress giving authority to states is Public Law 280 (PL 280).[17] In 1953, Congress passed this law in response to states' concerns that the federal government was not adequately enforcing criminal laws on Indian reservations. PL 280 transferred federal jurisdiction over crimes committed by members on Indian reservations to the following states: California, Minnesota (except the Red Lake Nation), Nebraska, Oregon (except the Warm Springs Reservation), Wisconsin (except the Menominee Indian Reservation), and Alaska. Nevada, South Dakota, Washington, Florida, Idaho, Montana, North Dakota, Arizona, Iowa, and Utah have assumed limited jurisdiction over crimes committed by members on Indian reservations pursuant to PL 280. This meant that in PL 280 states, members that committed crimes in these states would be subject to state criminal laws. In non-PL 280 states, the federal government maintained criminal jurisdiction. PL 280 also opened up state courts for members to use to resolve disputes such as contract issues and divorces. PL 280 allowed members to choose to have their disputes resolved either in tribal court or state court.

One of the common misconceptions about PL 280 is that this law somehow took something away from tribes. This is not the case. PL 280 was a transfer of jurisdiction from the federal government to the named states over certain issues. It did not transfer complete jurisdiction. For example, PL 280 did not grant states the ability to impose their civil regulatory laws on members.[18] PL 280 also did not remove any tribal jurisdiction. In both PL 280 states and non-PL 280 states, tribal governments retained the ability to criminally punish their members.[19]

Variations on Tribal
Blood Quantum Requirements

To make projections of future enrollments, many tribes now consider the rates at which tribal members marry and/or have children with non-members. Many of these projections show a decline in individuals eligible for membership in the future. While families can still certainly hold on to their language and traditional teachings over time, as long as tribes continue to use current blood quantum requirements as a means of determining membership, tribes will be governing a dwindling population.

As an alternative to lowering blood quantum requirements, some tribes are considering or have implemented methods to determine blood quantum that involves counting the blood from other tribes in blood quantum calculation. For example, the Oneida Tribe of Indians of Wisconsin currently requires ¼ minimum blood quantum. In the early 1800s, the Oneida people emigrated from what is now New York State. This migration resulted in three distinct Oneida communities, and each now has its own form of government: the Oneida Tribe of Indians of Wisconsin, the Oneida Thames in Canada, and the Oneida Nation in New York. However, the ¼ minimum blood quantum to be enrolled in the Oneida Nation in Wisconsin does not consider blood from the other Oneida tribes. For many years, members in Wisconsin have been discussing the possibility of counting blood from the other Oneida tribes in the blood quantum calculations for the Wisconsin Oneida enrollment. In addition, the Oneida people are also part of the Haudenosaunee, or Iroquois Confederacy. The Cayuga, Seneca, Mohawk, Onondaga, and Tuscarora people are also Haudenosaunee. Some of those people have similar histories as the Oneida and now have more than one distinct tribal government. In addition to considering blood from other Oneida communities, another possibility is to include blood from other Haudenosaunee people as well. Both possibilities still account for the cultural, spiritual, governmental, and linguistic connections of the Haudenosaunee people, factors many believe are key to tribal identity.

Jurisdictional Ramifications of Expanding Membership

So what does this mean for blood quantum? Recognizing that many Indian tribes still rely on blood quantum to determine who is eligible to become a member, a tribe's decision to raise or lower blood quantum requirements can have a direct impact on its jurisdiction. If a tribe decreases blood quantum requirements or allows for the inclusion of blood from other tribes, their enrollments will likely expand. With an expanded membership, there would be more members that will rely on limited government resources. There would also be more members that will be able participate in tribal government and more members for the tribal government to exercise jurisdiction over. In essence, larger enrollment bases mean an expansion of tribal jurisdiction and sovereignty.

With larger membership bases, tribes could also leverage more federal dollars because tribes would be able to demonstrate a greater need. For example, more members could mean a tribe may end up with more people that are looking for low-income housing assistance. The tribe would then be able to ask for more assistance from the United States Department of Housing and Urban Development. Similarly, with an expanded membership, there are likely to be more individuals that would benefit from assistance from the Indian Health Services, including direct health services and well and septic system assistance for their homes.

One common concern is that adding members will strain limited financial and land resources, particularly for tribes that offer per capita payments or tribes confined to fixed territories on reservations. It is important to remember, however, that the goal of many tribes is to ensure the preservation of their languages and cultures as well as build the financial security of future generations. Sharing limited resources with descendants or people from related tribes fits within these general goals.

Larger membership bases can also be a strain on the administration of tribal governments. Even with increased federal financial assistance, tribes still need internal capacity to manage the administration of tribal programs and assets. It may not be possible to provide governmental services to a suddenly increased population with existing staff. Tribes might need to consider expanding their workforce or even reorganizing their tribal administrative structure. The good news is that with this influx of new members, chances are good that some of these new members may bring valuable education and experience to help through such a transition.

Aside from the expansion of tribal jurisdiction over more individuals, an expansion of membership can also result in the displacement of state authority over those new members. Since states and local governments have limited ability to regulate members on Indian reservations, individuals previously designated non-Indian or non-member could then fall into the category of Indian or member if a tribe decided to modify its blood quantum requirements. That categorization of Indian or member would naturally transfer jurisdiction from state and local governments to tribal governments. Tables 1 and 2 depict the general criminal prohibitory and civil regulatory changes when an individual becomes newly enrolled in a tribe. As with all general rules, there are exceptions. Table 1 is intended to show how tribal jurisdiction changes when a tribe changes its blood quantum requirements and enrolls new individuals. Table 2 is intended to show how state jurisdiction changes.

	Non-member		→	Member	
	PL 280 State	Non-PL 280 State	→	PL 280 State	Non-PL 280 State
Criminal Prohibitory Jurisdiction	No	No	→	Yes	Yes
Civil Regulatory Jurisdiction	It depends	It depends	→	Yes	Yes

Table 1. Changes in Tribal Jurisdiction

	Non-member		→	Member	
	PL 280 State	Non-PL 280 State	→	PL 280 State	Non-PL 280 State
Criminal Prohibitory Jurisdiction	Yes	Yes	→	Yes	No
Civil Regulatory Jurisdiction	Yes	Yes	→	No	No

Table 2. Changes in State Jurisdiction

For tribes concerned with building or maintaining positive governmental relationships with state and local governments, such a change in membership rolls and transfer of jurisdiction away from states could cause concern for state and local governments. Recognizing federal law preserves the ability of tribes to determine membership criteria for themselves; no law requires tribes to consult with these local governments when having internal discussions about membership. However, for a variety of political reasons, elected tribal leaders may want to consider having discussions with local governments despite the lack of a requirement to do so.[20]

Conclusion

Tribal governments, with input from their communities, need to decide for themselves whether and how they will change their membership criteria. While these discussions are not new, they have been gaining more attention in recent years. It will continue to be an intense philosophical debate that will surely have impacts for generations to come. There are many factors for tribes to consider. This chapter focused primarily on the enlargement of tribal enrollment to expand tribal jurisdiction.

Notes

1. *Cherokee Intermarriage Cases*, 203 U.S. 76 (1906); *Roff v. Burney*, 168 U.S. 218 (1897).

2. For example, 18 U.S.C. § 1152 discusses applicability of federal criminal laws to "Any Indian who commits against the person or property of another Indian or other person." This section distinguishes between Indians and non-Indians (other person).

3. The tests to determine whether someone is an Indian and whether someone is a member are different. Tribes determine membership. Courts determine Indian status by considering the degree of Indian blood the person has and whether the tribe or federal government recognizes the person as Indian. *United States v. Keys*, 103 F.3d 758 (9th Cir. 1996). For a discussion on the conflicting ways courts determine Indian status see Luke Emmer Miles, "A Tale of Two Statutes: Zepeda and the Ninth Circuit's Descent into Jurisdictional Madness," *American Indian Law Review* 38, no. 269 (2014): 269.

4. The Department of the Interior regularly publishes a list of federally recognized tribes in the *Federal Register*. See *Federal Register*, vol. 80, no. 9, January 14, 2015, p. 1942.

5. United States Department of the Interior website. http://www.bia.gov/WhoWeAre/BIA/OIS/TribalGovernmentServices/TribalDirectory/. Accessed April 2016.

6. *Williams v. Lee*, 358 U.S. 217, 220 (1959).

7. 25 U.S.C. §§ 461 et seq.

8. For a discussion on tribal constitutions and blood quantum requirements see Kristy Gover, "Genealogy as Continuity: Explaining the Growing Tribal Preference for Descent Rules in Membership Governance in the United States," *American Indian Law Review* 33, no. 243 (2008–2009): 244.

9. For a discussion on tribes enrolling individuals without any Indian blood see Tommy Miller, "Beyond Blood Quantum: The Legal and Political Implications of Expanding Tribal Enrollment," *American Indian Law Review* 3, no. 323 (2014): 323. See also Jeremiah Chin, "Red Law, White Supremacy: Cherokees Freedmen, Tribal Sovereignty, and the Colonial Feedback Loop," *John Marshall Law Review* 47, no. 1227 (2014): 1228.

10. The Tribal Law and Order Act of 2010 limits the jurisdiction of tribes to impose sentences not exceeding three years' imprisonment and a $15,000 fine or both. 124 Stat. 2258, Sec 234.

11. *Water Wheel Camp Recreational Area v. LaRance*, 642 F.3d 802 (9th Cir. 2011). A recent decision out of the Seventh Circuit questioned the holding in *Water Wheel*. *Stifel, Nicolaus & Company, Inc. v. Lac Du Flambeau Band of Lake Superior Chippewa Indians*, No. 3:13-cv-00372-wmc, November 24, 2015, Footnote 60. However, the court in *Stifel* found the tribe was attempting to regulate off reservation conduct on non-tribal land.

12. For example, the Clean Air Act has provisions where the federal government can delegate its authority to tribes. 42 U.S.C. § 7410. Most recently, Congress amended the Violence Against Women Act to allow tribes to adopt laws that criminally punish non-members for domestic abuse crimes committed against members. 42 U.S.C. §§ 13701–14040.

13. *Montana v. United States,* 450 U.S. 544 (1981).

14. Ibid.

15. *McClanahan v. Ariz. State Tax Comm'n,* 411 U.S. 164, 170–71 (1973).

16. *Williams v. Lee,* 358 U.S. 217, 220 (1959). "Essentially, absent govern-
    ing Acts of Congress, the question has always been whether the state
    action infringed on the right of reservation Indians to make their own
    laws and be ruled by them."

17. 18 U.S.C. § 1162, 28 U.S.C. § 1360, and 25 U.S.C. §§ 1321–1326.

18. *Bryan v. Itasca County,* 426 U.S. 373 (1976). Public Law 280 was a
    grant of jurisdiction to the states, but not to state subdivisions such as
    city, town, village, and county governments. *See Santa Rosa Band of
    Indians v. Kings County,* 532 F. 2d 655, 661 (9th Cir. 1975) ("...P.L. 280
    subjected Indian Country only to the civil laws of the state, and not to
    local regulation."). If an activity is generally permitted subject to regu-
    lation, the law is probably civil regulatory. *California v. Cabazon,* 480
    U.S. 202 (1987). If the law violates state public policy, it is probably
    criminal prohibitory. This distinction only matters in PL 280 states since
    neither type of law applies to members in the remaining states.

19. *United States v. Wheeler,* 435 U.S. 313, 318, 322–323 (1978); *Walker v
    Rushing,* 898 F.2d 672 (8th Cir. 1990).

20. For example, nothing requires tribes to compensate local governments
    for services local governments provide to tax exempt trust land. In addi-
    tion, tribes may have more to gain with positive intergovernmental rela-
    tionships. For the Oneida Tribe, some of their intergovernmental agree-
    ments contain provisions where the local government will not object
    when the Tribe applies to have more land taken into trust status. Tribes
    have an interest in making sure the local government is able to pro-
    vide services, and making service agreement payments helps. As long
    as the tribe and local government maintain positive relationships, they
    both benefit from positive intergovernmental relationships. Rebecca M.
    Webster, "Service Agreements: Exploring Payment Formulas for Tribal
    Trust Land on the Oneida Reservation," *American Indian Quarterly* 39,
    no. 4 (2015): 347–363.

BLOOD, IDENTITY, AND THE AINU SOCIETY IN CONTEMPORARY JAPAN

By Yuka Mizutani

[Told by an anonymous Ainu person, H.] When I am told,
"You are mixed blooded," I can answer, "Well, it is difficult
to talk about ancestors by blood." By saying so, I mention
that it is mainstream Japanese people[1] who brought
mainstream Japanese blood to the Ainu people.

(Sekiguchi 2007, 145–146)[2]

Introduction

Ainu people have lived at the northern edge of Japan's current territory and nearby areas, including part of present-day Russia. The Ainu have been underrepresented in the national and international social and political fields. The same trend has existed in academia; as historian David L. Howell expressed, "[T]he idea that the Ainu have a history worth studying is relatively new" (Howell 2014, 102). However, the situation surrounding the Ainu people is changing drastically, since the National Diet of Japan[3] passed a resolution to officially recognize the Ainu as an indigenous people in Japan on June 6, 2008.

Among other important events, discussion of the establishment of Ainu policies reached the national government level in 2008. The Council for Ainu Policy Promotion was set in the Cabinet Office of the Japanese government, whose members mainly consist of Ainu representatives and non-Ainu researchers. The main issues being discussed are the construction of the Symbolic Space for Ethnic Harmony, promotion of Ainu policy, and nationwide Ainu policy making.[4] As a part of the nationwide policy-making process, some issues related to the Ainu blood have been taken up. Having the Ainu blood means certain things within contemporary Ainu society and mainstream Japanese society. This chapter aims to discuss the social or political use, function, and sociocultural meaning of the blood, by examining publicly available data and published narratives by the Ainu people.

The Ainu Blood and Identity in the Present Day

Affiliation with contemporary Ainu society has not been solely determined by blood. The results of a social survey conducted in 2008 (mainly quantitative) and 2009 (mainly qualitative) support this idea. These surveys were done by a group of researchers led by sociologist Toru Onai, in collaboration with the Ainu Association of Hokkaido (hereafter the Ainu Association), which is a major organization in charge of various Ainu issues. Respondents of the questionnaire were Ainu people living in Hokkaido who were between 18 and 85 years old (Onai 2010, 3). A total of 2,903 households and 5,703 individuals replied to the questionnaire (Onai 2010, 4). Information regarding various aspects of the contemporary Ainu life was uncovered by the survey, including some data about the Ainu blood and identity.

Regarding a question about the Ainu blood inherited by the respondents, only 5.7% answered that all of their grandparents had the Ainu blood, while 13% answered that both of their parents had the Ainu blood, 22.3% had a father with the Ainu blood, and 22.6% had a mother with the Ainu blood (Onai 2014, 13). In sum, 63.6% answered they inherited the Ainu blood, and 36.4% were either non-Ainu adoptees or non-Ainu spouses. These 36.4% of respondents without the Ainu blood are also a part of the contemporary Ainu society. Some of them are actively involved in the sustenance of the Ainu culture. Chiori Noto identifies herself as Ainu, and her father is one of the non-Ainu spouses. In an interview, Noto stated the following:

> I chose to live as an Ainu, but my father is mainstream Japanese. However, my father spends so much energy with Ainu wood carving, and he tries so hard to learn about Ainu culture. His attitude makes me wonder what "the Ainu" are and what "the mainstream Japanese" are. (Okada 2008, 210)

Onai (2014, 19) also points out that intermarriage between the Ainu and mainstream Japanese has been increasing. As a result, contemporary Ainu society accommodates people with various amounts of blood quanta and non-Ainu family members. When growing up, it seems the Ainu people today make a personal choice to identify themselves as Ainu or not. In anthropologist Yoshihiko Sekiguchi's book about Ainu people in contemporary Tokyo, an anonymous Ainu interviewee identified as "B" stated that choosing the Ainu identity was up to one's free will, instead of having the Ainu blood or not.

> We are human beings, so there are moments when I feel "I will quit being Ainu." But if we stop, our ancestors will vanish.... If you want to be an Ainu, be Ainu. If not, don't. It depends on us. No one can force us and tell us "You have the Ainu blood, so do this...." You come in, and if you like it, stay. If not, leave.... This way of thinking exists among Ainu people, I think. (Sekiguchi 2007, 52)

If not by blood, what reasons are there to choose an Ainu identity? Interviews with two women – Kaori Arai and Haruka Yazaki – who identify themselves as Ainu provide some ideas.

> [Told by Arai.] I want to identify myself as Ainu. I am Ainu, and I am mainstream Japanese. Although, telling the truth, my Ainu blood is thinner than that of mainstream Japanese.... In my opinion, the definition of Ainu is based on the ties between what is Ainu: a tie between Ainu ancestors, ties between Ainu communities, and a tie between the Ainu culture.... Therefore, having an Ainu blood doesn't instantly mean that they are Ainu. At the same time, not having an Ainu blood shouldn't mean that person is not an Ainu. (Okada 2008, 130–131)

[Told by Yazaki.] The reason I study the Ainu is that I was born into an Ainu family. This is the biggest reason.... However, even if I was not born into an Ainu family, I may have studied the Ainu culture. This is because I live in Hokkaido, and I am interested in issues such as culture and ethnicity anyway. (Okada 2008, 119)

For Arai and Yazaki, it seems the fact that they inherited Ainu blood was certainly a reason to define themselves as Ainu. However, what seemed to have had more importance were their connections with Ainu culture.

While many Ainu people in the present day are aware of their Ainu blood, some people live without knowing about the blood they have inherited, as some parents decide to hide their family history as Ainu in order for their children to have better lives. In an interview from the 2008 social survey, a non-Ainu spouse stated that she was worried about telling her children about the Ainu blood they had inherited (Onodera 2012, 132). I assume most of these people also lack connections with the Ainu communities or the Ainu culture, so their children can grow up among mainstream Japanese people and their culture.

Blood and Identity Regarded in Mainstream Japanese Society: The Case of *hāfu*

In the previous section, I explained some aspects of the Ainu blood and identity. In this section, I would like to focus on how blood and identity are regarded in mainstream Japanese society. Political scientist Masataka Endo (2013, 88) points out the following: When modern Japanese laws were established in the 19th century, what the government regarded as most important was to keep pure blood of the Japanese "race." Time passed, and laws were changed, but this notion seems to have remained as a base of mainstream Japanese society. Eligibility for Japanese nationality is an example. Japanese nationality is given based on blood: Those with a Japanese parent can obtain Japanese nationality, regardless of birthplace. This is contrary to the condition of eligibility for U.S. nationality, which is based on place: Anyone who is born in U.S. territory is eligible for nationality. After examining Japanese laws regarding nationality, Endo concludes his book by pointing out that the Japanese general public has believed that Japan consists of one single race (Endo 2013, 290).

In reality, besides the Ainu people, there are various other ethnicities in Japan. Okinawans (or Ryukyu people) in the southern edge of Japan have their own language (or dialect) and culture. Historically, many Korean, Chinese, and other Asian people migrated to Japan. These are only some examples to show this diversity. Among them, the people who have recently been getting more attention are the *hāfu* ("half"), who have plural ethnic and/ or racial backgrounds with Japanese nationality. Although the conditions surrounding the Ainu and *hāfu* people are different and cannot be compared simply, discussions about them reveal some aspects on the perspective of the mainstream Japanese general public.

Koichi Iwabuchi (2014), a cultural studies scholar, writes that identifying as *hāfu* was already popular in the 1960s and 1970s. Iwabuchi also points out that in the 1990s, the number of mixed-heritage celebrities in various fields, including models, athletes, and journalists, increased dramatically (2014, 11). Today, there are larger numbers of *hāfu* people who are popular, particularly among young people, such as Christel Takigawa (newscaster, Japanese/French),[5] Yu Darvish (baseball player for the Texas Rangers as of 2015, Japanese/Iranian),[6] May J (singer, Japanese/Iranian/ Turkish/Russian/Spanish/British),[7] and Mendy Sekiguchi (dancer in the pop music group EXILE, Japanese/Nigerian).[8]

These people seem to be supported by the general Japanese public, but it was reported that Takigawa had felt inferior due to being *hāfu* and had suffered over her dual identity.[9] In fact, in a TV show in 2009, Takigawa was called *gaijin* ("foreigner") by another newscaster, even though her nationality is Japanese.[10] This incident indicates some Japanese people's reactions that *hāfu*s do not belong to Japanese society. Considering that Takigawa played an important role in Japan becoming host of the Tokyo Olympics in 2020 by addressing a speech in French at a meeting of the International Olympic Committee, it is ironic that she was regarded as a foreigner. Yu Darvish, who currently plays in Major League Baseball, also stated that he had been treated as a foreigner in Japan. In an interview, he explained "I was born as a *hāfu*, and I have been denied by being told, 'You are not Japanese. Something else is in you.'"[11]

In 2015, the winner of Miss Universe Japan, Ariana Miyamoto, who is also *hāfu*, was treated the same. It was the first time that Miss Universe Japan had been *hāfu* Japanese. Miyamoto was born to an African American father and Japanese mother, and she was raised in Japan. Right after she was given the title, she was exposed to criticisms, mainly on SNS sites.[12] It was reported comments were written online, such as, "she has too much black blood in her to be Japanese."[13] It was not the first time Miyamoto had been criticized for her blood. In an interview, Miyamoto said that she had been called *kuronbo* ("black kid"), which is a word used to discriminate against people with dark skin.[14] In short, some Japanese people did not support Miyamoto because she inherited non-Japanese blood and thus does not represent Japanese citizens as a beauty queen.

Back in the 1950s, people born between Japanese and foreigners were severely discriminated against. They were physically segregated into special orphanages, schools, and other facilities, and researchers studied their physical and psychological characteristics (Horiguchi and Imoto 2014, 60–62). The situation has obviously improved since then. However, the stories of Takigawa and Miyamoto show that people who have non-mainstream Japanese blood would not be recognized as members of Japanese society.

The Ainu and Native Americans: Differences in Surrounding Conditions

In this section, I will list the differences between the social and political conditions surrounding the Ainu people and Native Americans in the United States. Although indigenous peoples around the world share the same or similar problems, each group is differently positioned in terms of its relationship to the national government and the mainstream society. The differences are prominent in how some indigenous peoples are situated within various countries. From my perspective, as a mainstream Japanese scholar specializing in Native American issues, there are four major differences between the conditions surrounding the Ainu people and those of Native Americans. Please note that I needed to generalize the conditions of Native Americans in order to show the differences between the Ainu clearly, though I am aware that differences exist among Native American nations and peoples.

The first difference is the form of political unit. Native American people today are organized as tribes or nations, as defined by the U.S. federal government, and tribal governments hold nation-to-nation relationships with the federal government. Meanwhile, Ainu people in Japan lack a political body for autonomy. Yet several organizations are deeply associated with sustaining their culture and society. Among them, the Ainu Association plays an important role. According to the association, it is "an organization made up of Ainu who live in Hokkaido, which aims to 'work to improve the social status of Ainu people and to develop, transmit and preserve Ainu culture in order to establish the dignity of the Ainu people.'"[15] However, this association does not hold a nation-to-nation relationship with the government as occurs in the United States.

The second difference is the manner of counting their respective populations. In the United States, at the tribal level, the population is recorded by the tribal government. In the case of the Ainu, who do not have an autonomous governmental body, the number of members of the Ainu Association provides the only clue to estimating their population. Article 5 of its membership regulation states that the association grants membership to "organizations which are composed of those who have Ainu blood, or non-Ainu individuals who are spouses of individuals with Ainu blood," or "non-Ainu individuals who are adopted into Ainu families (one generation only)," or "individuals who have the Ainu blood, non-Ainu individuals who are spouses of individuals with Ainu blood, or non-Ainu individuals who are adopted to Ainu families (one generation only), and are also over 18 years old and reside in Hokkaido."[16] According to the association's website, there were 2,380 members as of December 2014.[17] However, participation in this association is spontaneous; therefore, the number of members is not equal to the Ainu population. Moreover, Ainu people living outside of Hokkaido are not eligible for membership in the Ainu Association, although the number of the Ainu people in and around Tokyo alone is estimated to be over 5,000 (Watson 2014, 27). When the population of Ainu people outside of Hokkaido is added, the number becomes much larger. Unlike in the United States, questions regarding ethnic identity are not included in the national census of Japan. Therefore, it is impossible to estimate the Ainu population by examining the census data.

The third difference is in the ways of proving one's blood. In the United States, an individual may try to find his or her ancestors on a tribal base roll. However, as mentioned above, there is no Ainu government, and their information – as well as that of all Japanese citizens – is managed by the family register (*koseki*) of the national government. Information on all important life events, such as birth, marriage, and death, is summarized in the family register. The Japanese government started registering some Ainu people in Hokkaido in the early 19th century; then, in 1871, all Ainu people in Hokkaido came to be registered (Endo 2013, 151–152). On the family registers, the Ainu used to be described as "former aboriginal" (*kyū dojin*), which is a discriminatory term, and they were distinguished from the mainstream Japanese (Endo 2013, 153). This system of calling them former aboriginals has been abolished; also, the copy of the current family register does not state whether the person has inherited the Ainu blood or not. It is possible, however, for an individual to obtain copies of old family registers of ancestors by tracking his or her own family register, and then checking if one of the individual's ancestors were regarded as Ainu.

The fourth difference is blood quantum. In the United States, blood quantum may be proved by the Certificate of Degree of Indian Blood (CDIB) issued by the Bureau of Indian Affairs, or membership in a particular tribe. In Japan, although the family register managed by the government may show one's blood, no government-issued documents tell one's blood quantum of being Ainu. Moreover, blood quantum as Ainu is merely asked. As written in an earlier part of this section, blood quantum is not asked about when becoming a member of the Ainu Association. Recently, the Japanese government has been making efforts to start providing social services for Ainu people outside of Hokkaido in order to change the former system, which only allowed Ainu people in Hokkaido to receive services. In March 2014, the Japanese Ministry of Land, Infrastructure, Transport and Tourism issued a guideline to define the recipients of the new social services. It states that an individual who lives outside of Hokkaido and can prove his or her blood as being Ainu by family register or other sources, such as a book, will be a beneficiary of the services. Adoptees can receive services as well, but their children won't be considered as recipients (Japanese Ministry of Land, Infrastructure, Transport and Tourism, 2014). In this new system too, blood quantum of the applicant is not asked about, although having an Ainu blood is necessary.

Blood: A Fluid Boundary

Just as in many other indigenous communities, blood can also function as a boundary to protect Ainu society and culture. In the case of the United States, dealing with non-indigenous people who act as indigenous people, who are often called "wannabes," is often regarded as problematic. Ainu people face the same concern. For example, below is a story told by Arai.

> [W]hat shouldn't happen is that someone pretends to be Ainu. It is not right that a person who doesn't have any Ainu blood or even any relationship with the Ainu community wants to become an Ainu or to tell a lie that s/he is an Ainu, only because it is cool. Ainu people suffer by such acts. (Okada 2008, 131)

It is important that Ainu people themselves limited the range of people who can become part of their culture. It can be determined by having Ainu blood or not, if Ainu people decide to do so. Yet, blood cannot always serve as a boundary. Arai points out that boundaries become fluid online:

> "Wannabe Ainu" are often found on the Internet. On the Internet, it is easy to fake an identity; thus, it is possible to pretend to be an Ainu. It shows a potential risk of the Internet. (Okada 2008, 137)

Opportunities for Ainu people to be involved in cultural activities and networking through cyberspace are increasing. These opportunities can bring benefits. However, in such circumstances, it is almost impossible to set a boundary by blood between Ainu people and those who pretend to be Ainu.

Blood can be used as a negative boundary for segregation. In Japan, prejudice and discrimination toward the Ainu people remain strong. In the social survey conducted in 2008, 5.7% responded that they wanted to hide their identity (Nozaki 2010, 22). I assume that the reason for this response was fear of discrimination by mainstream Japanese. In Japan, discrimination often becomes obvious at the time of marriage, because keeping the blood in mainstream Japanese is highly regarded in Japanese society, as explained in the section about the *hāfu* people. The results of the social survey indicate that 16.8% of the respondents faced difficulty getting married due to being Ainu (Nozaki 2012, 37). In an interview for the social survey, an Ainu woman married to a mainstream Japanese man reported the following story: She got married and her married life went well. However, 20 years later, her father-in-law told her that he didn't say anything because his son chose her, but he hated that his grandchildren would be born with Ainu blood (Onodera 2012, 131). Moreover, the parents of some Ainu people objected to their children marrying other Ainu, and the Ainu blood was the reason. According to a report published from the interviews conducted as a part of the social survey, an Ainu woman was told the following by her parents:

> I was told that marriage between an Ainu man and an Ainu woman was bad for the children born between them…. It was because the Ainu blood gets thicker. They said they made efforts to make it thinner and then asked why I wanted to make it thick again. (Nozaki 2012, 37)

These words were probably told by Ainu people who survived the time when assimilation into mainstream Japanese society was regarded positively.

When blood functions as a boundary between the Ainu and the mainstream Japanese, can it completely separate Ainu people from mainstream Japanese people? The answer seems to be no. Interviews with some contemporary Ainu people indicate that they freely cross the boundary and live both as Ainu and mainstream Japanese. Below are the words of Noto and also an anonymous Ainu woman identified as H, who appears in Sekiguchi's book about Ainu people in Tokyo.

> I am not skillful enough to be able to live sometimes as a mainstream Japanese, and other times as an Ainu…. However, it doesn't mean everyone else needs to be this way. (Okada 2008, 212)

> When I was in middle school, I didn't think about my ethnic identity. At that time, I thought "sometimes I am Ainu." So, I was mainstream Japanese but also Ainu, seriously. Normally, I was mainstream Japanese, but in special occasions, I was Ainu. (Sekiguchi 2007, 142)

In 2001 (revised edition, 2009), a photo album of the daily lives of Ainu people in Tokyo was published, entitled *Ainu tokidoki nihonjin* (*The Ainu, but Sometimes [the Mainstream] Japanese*). It may be symbolizing the interchangeable contemporary Ainu identity. The act of psychologically crossing the boundary between Ainu and mainstream Japanese seems to be regarded positively by Ainu people. Sekiguchi analyzed the interchangeability of the Ainu identity as being a result of Ainu people's resistance toward the dichotomous idea of categorizing the Ainu and mainstream Japanese identities (Sekiguchi 2007, 237). I imagine there are more reasons in addition to what Sekiguchi identifies. Another reason may be that by making the boundary crossable, the Ainu society becomes more accommodating. In an interview, Arai stated the following:

> Self-identifying as an Ainu comes with a huge responsibility. Therefore, no one can say that "you are Ainu, so tell the others so," or "you have to inherit the Ainu culture." (Okada 2008, 133)

For me, it seems the responsibility of living as Ainu comes in two different ways. The first is commitment. It takes time and effort to sustain any culture. Just as in other indigenous communities, in the Ainu communities there are many rituals and meetings to attend, and cultural activities require practice. As a majority of the people are engaged in wage work today, it is simply hard for some to scrape time out to be involved in these events. Additionally, the financial burden is likely a problem for some people. Although organizations such as the Foundation for Research and Promotion of Ainu Culture provide several grants to support Ainu cultural events and activities, the Ainu people often need to cover at least a part of the cost on their own. Many Ainu people are struggling with poverty. According to the Ainu Association, as of 2006, the number of Ainu people under social welfare is about 1.6 times higher than the national average.[18] Considering this situation, I assume some people cannot afford the costs of transportation and ritual items.

The second is action. When a person publicly identifies oneself as Ainu, the others may regard the person's speech and actions as representing the entire Ainu society. Although I am not Ainu, I imagine that such responsibility could be too heavy.

The social survey shows 18.2% of the respondents answered that they would like to live as Ainu actively, while 74.3% stated that they wanted to live without thinking about ethnic identity (Nozaki 2010, 22). I wonder if the 74.3% includes some people who may care greatly about Ainu culture, but who may not be confident enough to take the full responsibility that comes with the Ainu identity. Instead of chasing this population away into mainstream Japanese society, Ainu society may be keeping them close by letting them float on the boundary between the Ainu and mainstream Japanese and be undecided in their ethnic affiliation. This, in fact, allows these 74.3% to join Ainu society when they are ready to do so. In other words, they are a potential population that may "become" Ainu one day.

Conclusion

As explained throughout the chapter, blood – instead of blood quantum – seems to play important roles in terms of blood and Ainu society. This is partially due to the character of the mainstream Japanese society, which regards blood as a crucial factor in affiliation to the mainstream Japanese society. Yet for some Ainu people identifying themselves as Ainu, the feeling of being connected with Ainu culture is more important than the biological possession of the Ainu blood. Also, blood may function as both a positive and negative boundary between the Ainu and mainstream Japanese, yet this boundary is fluid, dynamic and ever-changing. This condition is contributing to keeping the contemporary Ainu identity interchangeable, and it can be a strategy for the Ainu society to keep a potential population in order to sustain the Ainu culture and society.

The drastic changes in the social and political conditions surrounding Ainu people are an ongoing issue, at the time of this writing. It is hard to foresee the final figure of the Ainu policies at the national level, or how Ainu people will react to them. What is probably good news is that eligibility systems for certain services using blood quantum are not being planned by the Japanese government so far, although proving one's Ainu blood is required. However, the requirement to prove one's Ainu blood still makes me worry that some people who are regarded as Ainu within Ainu society would be excluded from the social services provided by the Japanese government. What can be even more problematic is that people who are excluded from these services would start feeling that they do not belong to Ainu society. In other words, a new boundary to separate the Ainu from mainstream Japanese would be drawn by enforcing the new nationwide Ainu policies of the Japanese government. At the same time, the establishment and enhancement of national policies for indigenous issues are indispensable for sustaining indigenous cultures and societies. Although Ainu people do not have a government, organizations working with Ainu people may need to keep monitoring whether the national indigenous policy of Japan is effectively helping the Ainu and not harming them.

In addition to the Ainu, mainstream Japanese society is experiencing some changes in the notion of blood. As written earlier, mainstream Japanese people have associated the mainstream Japanese blood with Japanese nationality and affiliation with the Japanese society. A new trend reflecting this change is calling people with bloods different from mainstream Japanese *daburu* ("double") instead of *hāfu*. Social anthropologists Horiguchi and Imoto explain that use of the word *daburu* started to become popular around 1994 and resulted from an idea to regard having plural cultural heritages positively (Horiguchi and Imoto 2014, 66). In the near future, Japanese society will be able to accommodate more diversity. Then, Ainu people will be able to celebrate their heritages both as Ainu and mainstream Japanese more publicly.

Notes

1. I define "mainstream Japanese" as a person whose ethnic identity is Japanese. In the Ainu studies, they are also referred as *Wajin* (ex. Hudson 2014, 2). Although Japanese nationality is given to the Ainu people, they are not included in this concept. However, as intermarriage between the Ainu people and mainstream Japanese is common nowadays, some people identify both as the Ainu and mainstream Japanese.

2. The script was translated from Japanese to English by the author. Throughout the chapter, translation was done by the author when citing works already published in Japanese.

3. The National Diet is a legislative body of Japan, which consists of the House of Representatives and the House of Councilors.

4. Comprehensive Ainu Policy Office, Cabinet Secretariat, Government of Japan, "Council for Ainu Policy Promotion," accessed October 9, 2015, http://www.kantei.go.jp/jp/singi/ainusuishin/index_e.html.

5. "Takigawa Christel, hāfu no kyōgū he honne, Angela Aki to hansei wo kataru," March 2, 2014, Modelpress, http://mdpr.jp/news/detail/1341834.

6. "Darvish Yu 'naze boku ha iran jin nano?' to nayanda yōshōki," December 31, 2011, *New Post Seven*, http://www.news-postseven.com/archives/20111231_78286.html.

7. "May J. Profile," Rhythm ZONE, accessed October 9, 2015, http://www.may-j.com/profile/.

8. "Sekiguchi Mendy san no profile: hisaro gayoi? Netsuai no uwasa ya seikaku ha?," last modified May 28, 2015, The New Classic, http://newclassic.jp/20265.

9. "Takigawa Christel."

10. "Takikuri wo "gaijin" to sabetsu hatsugen, fuji terebi ana ni hihan shūchū," October 1, 2009, J-Cast News, http://www.j-cast.com/2009/10/01050772.html.

11. "Darvish Yu "naze boku ha iran jin nano?" to nayanda yōshōki."

12. Rozana Saberi, "Being 'Hafu' in Japan: Mixed-Race People Face Ridicule, Rejection," September 9, 2015, Aljazeera America, http://america.aljazeera.com/articles/2015/9/9/hafu-in-japan-mixed-race.html.

13. Audrey Akcasu, "Half-Japanese Beauty Chosen to Represent Japan at Miss Universe 2015," March 15, 2015, Rocket News 24, http://en.rocketnews24.com/2015/03/15/half-japanese-beauty-crowned-miss-universe-japan-2015-topples-racial-hurdles-along-the-way/.

14. Saberi, "Being Hafu."

15. The Ainu Association of Hokkaido, "What Is the Ainu Association of Hokkaido?" accessed October 9, 2015, http://www.ainu-assn.or.jp/english/eabout04.html.

16. The Ainu Association of Hokkaido, "Kōeki shadan hōjin hokkaidō ainu kyōkai teikan," accessed October 9, 2015, http://www.ainu-assn.or.jp/data/pdfupld/pdffile/1401933783__teikan.2014.5.16.pdf.

17. The Ainu Association of Hokkaido, "Watashitachi ni tsuite," accessed October 9, 2015, http://www.ainu-assn.or.jp/about02.html.

18. The Ainu Association of Hokkaido, "Watashitachi ni tsuite."

References

Endo, Masataka. 2013. *Koseki to kokuseki no kingendaishi – minzoku, kettō, nihonjin*. Tokyo: Akashi shoten.

Horiguchi, Sawako and Yuki Imoto. 2014. "Mix race ha dou katararete kitaka: 'half' ni itaru madeno gensetsu wo tadotte." In *<Hāfu> toha dareka: jinshu konkō, media hyōshō, kōshō jissen*, edited by Koichi Iwabuchi, 55–77. Tokyo: Seikyūsha.

Howell, David L. 2014. "Is Ainu History Japanese History?" In *Beyond Ainu Studies: Changing Academic and Public Perspectives*, edited by Mark Hudson, ann-elise lewallen, and Mark Watson, 101–116. Honolulu: University of Hawaii Press.

Iwabuchi, Koichi. 2014. "<Hāfu> ga terashi dasu jinshu konkō no bunka seiji." In *<Hāfu> toha dareka: jinshu konkō, media hyōshō, kōshō jissen*, edited by Koichi Iwabuchi, 11–26. Tokyo: Seikyūsha.

Japanese Ministry of Land, Infrastructure, Transport and Tourism. "Hokkaido no kuikigai ni kyojū suru Ainu no hitobito wo taishō to suru shisaku no taishō to naru mono wo nintei suru gyōmu ni kakaru junsoku ni tsuite." March 11, 2014. Available at http://www.mlit.go.jp/common/001030628.pdf.

Nozaki, Yoshiki. 2010. "Ainu no kettō to aidentiti." In *2008 nen hokkaidō ainu minzoku seikatsu jittai chōsa hōkokusho: gendai ainu no seikatsu to ishiki*, edited by Toru Onai, 19–26. Sapporo: Hokkaido University Center for Ainu & Indigenous Studies.

———. 2012. "Sedai ni yoru ainu no tayō sei." In *2009 nen hokkaidō ainu minzoku seikatsu jittai chōsa hōkokusho: gendai ainu no seikatsu no ayumi to ishiki no henyō*, edited by Toru Onai, 19–38. Sapporo: Hokkaido University Center for Ainu & Indigenous Studies.

Okada, Michiaki. 2008. *Mirai he: wakaki ainu minzoku kara no dengon.* Sapporo: Sapporo TV.

Onai, Toru. 2010. "Mondai ishiki to chōsa no gaiyō." In *2008 nen hokkaidō ainu minzoku seikatsu jittai chōsa hōkokusho: gendai ainu no seikatsu to ishiki*, edited by Toru Onai, 1–6. Sapporo: Hokkaido University Center for Ainu & Indigenous Studies.

———. 2014. "Konketsuka no jissō to sūsei." In *2008 nen hokkaidō ainu minzoku seikatsu jittai chōsa hōkokusho: gendai ainu no seikatsu to ishiki no tayōsei*, edited by Toru Onai, 11–25. Sapporo: Hokkaido University Center for Ainu & Indigenous Studies.

Onodera, Rika. 2012. "Ainu shakai ni okeru wajin no ainusei: wajin zuma to wajin otto." In *2009 nen hokkaidō ainu minzoku seikatsu jittai chōsa hōkokusho: gendai ainu no seikatsu no ayumi to ishiki no henyō*, edited by Toru Onai, 123–142. Sapporo: Hokkaido University Center for Ainu & Indigenous Studies.

Sekiguchi, Yoshihiko. 2007. *Shutoken ni ikiru ainu minzoku: "taiwa" no chihei kara.* Urayasu: Sōfūkan.

Ui, Makiko. 2009. *Ainu tokidoki nihonjin* (rev. ed.). Tokyo: Hyōronsha.

Watson, Mark. 2014. *Japan's Ainu Minority in Tokyo: Diasporic Indigeneity and Urban Politics.* London: Routledge.

*"Being an Indian in the U.S. today is
a political rather than a racial category."*

– Suzan Shown Harjo

Part 5

WHERE TO GO FROM HERE? MOVING FORWARD

FROM TRIBAL MEMBERS TO NATIVE NATION CITIZENS

by Stephen Cornell and Joseph P. Kalt

Introduction: Determining and Empowering the "Self" in Self-Determination

Much has been said and written about the origins and evolution of the blood quantum criteria that are employed to determine membership in hundreds of American Indian tribes in the United States. Looking back, blood quantum as the determinant of tribal membership – or "enrollment" – has its origins in the exclusionary and racist policies of a foreign power that needed to keep "rolls" in order to determine who would have certain civil rights, who it would imprison on reservations, and who would or would not get rations.[1] Today, blood quantum criteria are tearing at the social and political fabric of many tribes as the children and grandchildren of families which form the core of Native communities increasingly find themselves being told that they do not belong to those communities when it comes to membership and its entitlements. Looking forward – and for some tribes, not very far forward – blood quantum constitutes a built-in formula for eventual *de facto* termination of tribes. The reason for this was once put to us by a wise tribal leader in Arizona: "The kids all have cars these days; they drive into Phoenix, meet somebody who's not Indian or not of their tribe, fall in love – and all of a sudden your own grandchildren don't meet the blood quantum requirement."

Those cars aren't going away, and young people are surely not going to quit falling in love. Sooner or later, all tribes with blood quantum as their criterion of membership will have to confront its limiting and, ultimately, terminating implications. While upsetting the status quo can often be troubling and can touch off disruptive political conflicts, dealing with the blood quantum conundrum can usefully turn tribal attention to its limitations and cultural incompatibilities. These incompatibilities arise because blood quantum is only the crudest of guides to the multifaceted dimensions of identity and collective affiliation that give rise to any community's sense of who the "self" in national "self-determination" is.

In our Nation Building courses, we often give the students an exercise that allows them to explore the issue of tribal membership. We present them with what we often see in the real word: Tribal councils dealing with applications for enrollment from various types of individuals – the below–blood quantum grandchild of the tribal vice-chair, the above–blood quantum thirty-year-old woman who has never lived on the reservation but might someday, the not-of-our-blood Native spouse of an already enrolled tribal member, and so on. The backgrounds of students in these exercises typically span a wide array of sovereign nations and communities, indigenous and non-indigenous, from the United States to Qatar, from Norway to Nigeria.

As they try to come to grips with the kinds of enrollment decisions that many tribal councils face, these students, year after year, reproduce among them approximately the same list of questions for the applicants or their supporters to address. We assert that this tells us something about the criteria or attributes that can legitimately "make you part of us" in any culture – even if each culture is looking for different specific answers and emphases. Blood quantum appears in the set of questions, but it is gradually minimized as the would-be council members probe more deeply:

- "Where does the person live?"

- "What's her blood quantum?'

- "Will she be an economic contributor, or an economic drain, on us?"

- "What are her achievements in education? Commercial affairs? Does she show promise of achievement?"

- "What is the social status of her relatives? Are those relatives well-respected in our community?"

- "Who are her associates and friends? Are those associates and friends well-respected in our community?"

- "Does she speak our language?"

- "Does she own property in the community?"

- "Is she really committed to the community? Or does she just want the benefits it can provide her?"

- "Did she grow up here?"

- "Who are her political allies? What are her political views?"

- "Does she understand and share our cultural values?"

- "Does she participate in our ceremonies?"

The spontaneous outpouring of these kinds of questions is revealing. Not unreasonably, assessing whether someone should be considered "one of us" is a multidimensional matter, involving considerations ranging from candidates' ancestry, status, language, and cultural affinities. As an indigenous nation might see it: We want them to really be part of us in the sense of sharing our cultural values. But importantly, particularly if we are going to confer formal membership status as "one of us," we want them to share the responsibilities of supporting and building our community. We want them to contribute to the community's social, economic, and political well-being. And that means we want them to be not merely members; we also want them to accept, bear, and carry out the duties of *citizens* – to pull their weight, and maybe more than their own weight, in the community's shared decisions and endeavors.

If Indian nations are to not just "talk the talk" of nationhood and self-government, they must "walk the walk." In these efforts, Indian nations are like other nations in the world: They can fight mightily to regain inherent rights of self-rule, succeed in those struggles... and then fall flat on their faces if they cannot effectively exercise those rights. But what works when it comes to tribal self-governance that effectively promotes self-determined values via self-designed means? In this regard, research repeatedly finds clear nation-building lessons that Indian Country is teaching itself (not to mention the rest of the world). Case after case finds that **successful tribal self-determination is founded upon formal and informal leaders that imbue a community with the values and attitude of *sovereignty* – the attitude and goal of shedding the remnants of colonialism and charting**

courses of self-determined and self-governed community action. Moreover, it is equally clear that "walking the walk" of a self-governing sovereign means building or rebuilding mechanisms and institutions of collective decision making and government that are operationally effective and culturally legitimate.[2]

If the pillars of Native nation building are the sovereignty attitude, capable tribal government that matches a tribe's own cultural values and norms, and leadership that sheds colonial mindsets and methods, the foundation on which those pillars must rest are tribal people themselves. That foundation is shaky if the people conceive of themselves and act solely as members and not as citizens.

Membership or Citizenship?

Oren Lyons, the renowned international human rights activist and traditional faithkeeper of the Onondaga Nation, part of the centuries-old Iroquois Confederacy, once asked one of us, "Are you a *member* of the United States? Onondaga is not a club. We don't have members. We're a nation. We have citizens."

Lyons, who travels internationally on an Iroquois Confederacy passport, was acknowledging both the continuing sovereignty of the Onondaga Nation and the significance of the government-to-government relationship between that nation and the United States. He also was challenging a tendency on the part of American Indian nations generally, encouraged (and frequently forced) by the United States in its efforts to determine who is and who is not part of an Indian tribe, to refer to their people as tribal *members*. A nation doesn't have members, he said. It has citizens.[3]

But what does it mean to be a citizen? In most western democracies, particularly those that have roots in struggles to throw off autocratic or monarchical rule by the state, the discussion of citizenship centers on the rights that individuals carry in their relationship to the state. Citizenship, in this perspective, is about protections and/or entitlements of various kinds: to the protection of the laws, for example, or to vote or otherwise participate in public life. In the United States, the rights of citizens include those specified in the Bill of Rights of the U.S. Constitution, including trial by jury, freedom of speech, and others.

Rights, however, are only one dimension of citizenship. As William Eskridge points out, "Individual rights, without more, are a thin way to express or normalize the relationship of the individual to the community." He urges "an alternative understanding of citizenship – one that considers obligations as well as rights, and ultimately their interrelationship..."[4]

To be sure, even in western democracies like the United States, there are often non-codified and informal cultural norms that act to promote the responsibilities of citizens: "If you are going to vote, you should be informed"; "If you want to change things, you should step up and volunteer for that position or that civic organization"; "Everybody has to pay their fair share of taxes"; and so on.

At the same time, some nations' criteria of citizens' responsibilities are codified and quite specific. The northern European republic of Estonia escaped from Soviet domination in 1991. Its constitution, established in 1992 and revised in 2003, recognizes not only the rights but the responsibilities of citizens. Among these are the responsibility to "be loyal to the constitutional order," "to raise and care for their children," "to defend the independence of Estonia," "to preserve the... natural environment," and others.[5] In this conception citizenship is not one-dimensional. There are two parties to the relationship, the state and the citizen, and each has responsibilities to the other.

But whether they focus on rights or responsibilities or both, most of these discussions of citizenship are concerned primarily with the relationship of individuals to a politically and legally defined entity, typically the nation-state. Such discussions have roots in western political traditions and the distinctive history of nation-states in the emerging modern world. Do the conceptions underlying those discussions adequately capture indigenous understandings of the relationship between individual and community? Are they adequate to the nation-building efforts that American Indian nations and other indigenous communities are engaged in today?

The drives for self-determination and self-governance are reinvigorating indigenous conceptions of such matters as government, citizenship, rights, and responsibilities. For most indigenous peoples, the political entity known today as the tribe or nation is itself an instrument of the community. It is the community that matters, and the community consists of persons who share identity and interwoven obligations arising from their social and cultural relationships. These relationships commonly include kinship ties, cultural practices and values, history, connections to specific lands, and other elements. The community's political instrument – e.g., the tribal government – is the locus of formalized, tribal self-government and a vehicle that directly engages with the United States or other governmental bodies. But the relationships that matter most are the ones not between citizens and the tribal state but among citizens themselves. These are the ties that give identity, meaning, and life to the community. The political structure of the nation or tribe emerges out of those relationships as a tool for survival and self-defense; a means of organizing aspects of social, political, and economic life; and a vehicle for the promotion of shared interests.

Former Chairman of the San Manuel Band of Mission Indians Deron Marquez writes that, "Tribes have the ability to define 'citizenhood' beyond the modern understanding." He wishes for "an ethno-cultural understanding" of the concept, something rooted not in western political traditions but in tribes' own understandings of how the individual and the community are appropriately related to each other.[6] Regis Pecos, former Governor of Cochiti Pueblo, says that citizenship for his community involves a commitment to care for, preserve, and enact the core values of community life, values with ancient roots that are seen as essential to community survival and the welfare of coming generations and that shape the organization and processes of tribal self-government. To be part of the community is to take on certain expectations of behavior and commitment. This is what citizenship, in his community, is about.[7]

Other examples from indigenous communities around the world are not difficult to come by. When the Inupiat, living largely subsistence lifestyles on the coast of the Arctic Ocean, bring in a whale, the good fortune is shared; the flesh of the whale is distributed to families, elders, and those in need. As one of the authors was told, successful caribou hunters are expected to share their success, in part, with an elder or others who can no longer hunt for themselves. Such behavior is a taken-for-granted aspect of community life; to fail to do so could seriously undermine one's social standing. While no one used the term during these discussions, this could be considered a form of citizenship: meeting shared behavioral expectations and sustaining a quality of relationship on which community welfare, in a very practical sense, depends.

The emphasis in western nations' legal discourse tends to obscure or downplay such forms and conceptions of what it means to be a citizen. Simply by its dominance, this discourse can encourage indigenous peoples to engage in discussions of citizenship that ignore or downplay those conceptions as well. For example, some Māori tribes in Aotearoa New Zealand today control significant assets through a variety of politico-economic structures. In former times, many of these assets were managed by legislatively constructed Trust Boards. Tribal members thus became, in legal terms, "Beneficiaries." The Maori Land Court eventually extended the term to describe owners of collectively held tribal land as "Beneficial Owners." Similar frameworks of reference are found in the context of the Alaska Native Corporations and their "shareholders."

While most such settings are characterized by far more complex and profound internal relationships, such formalizations, if they fall into common use, send an unfortunate message not only to outsiders, but to the members of these groups themselves, giving primacy to the *benefits* that the individual gains through his or her relationship to the tribe or community. They imply that the primary function of the prevailing collective institutions is to generate and distribute benefits of various kinds – particularly financial dividends or social services – regardless of whether those institutions in fact view that as their primary purpose. Many a tribal official in the United States hears a related refrain in the demand that "you owe this to me; I'm an enrolled *member* of this tribe!" This is a one-way street, or at least a street where most of the traffic moves in one direction, and where individuals are conceived by this terminology not as actors but as passive recipients. In Indian Country, this is a holdover from an era in which federal policy was consciously designed to foster dependence on tribal governments by using those governments as the federally directed funnels through which colonial desires were implemented for a century or more.

Sir Tipene O'Regan, a senior figure in Ngai Tahu, the large *iwi*[8] of the South Island of Aotearoa New Zealand, has challenged such notions of the relationship between the individual and the community, arguing that they fail to capture the relationship that most Māori both desire and need to cultivate if *iwi* are to survive as anything other than asset-holding corporations. He asks what the ultimate purpose of tribal survival and growth, including economic growth, should be: "Until we come to terms with the question of what we want to be as a people, there is… no need for any strategic direction beyond making cash and distributing it more or less efficiently and more or less equitably. If that's all the membership of an Indigenous culture amounts to, then why bother?"[9] In the U.S. context, a parallel argument might be: "If all that being a citizen of an Indian nation amounts to is getting a 'per cap' (or health care, or housing) from the tribal government, then why bother being a nation, much less a community? Just be a member-owned corporation or a nonprofit club."

O'Regan suggests another purpose – the intergenerational transmission of identity and heritage – which yields a very different conception of the relationship, one in which beneficiaries also have responsibilities for the maintenance of identity, community, land, and other forms of heritage. Oren

Lyons from Onondaga has similar concerns. He has written that "when the Peacemaker came among our people some thousand years ago" and gave them instructions on how to govern, included was the instruction "to be responsible... to take responsibility... for the future of our children.... He instructed us to make our decisions on behalf of seven generations coming – those faces that are looking up from the earth, each layer waiting its time, coming, coming, coming."[10] This conception sees nations as communities of interwoven actors, built on ceremony, on intimate relationships with the earth, and on principles of interrelationship and obligation embedded in long-standing cultural practice. Citizenship then involves, among other things, the responsibility of participating in community-interested deliberation and decision making – *in governance* – designed to sustain such foundations across the generations.

Strategies for Moving from Membership to Citizenship

There was a time when indigenous communities' ideas of citizenship were undirected outgrowths of daily participation in community life. That life meant participation in ceremonies that cemented individuals to their kin, their community, and the spirit world; interaction with elders that transmitted lessons and norms of civic engagement; and apprenticeships to the various roles through which the collective life and welfare of the community were sustained. The challenge, today, however, is one of building comparable mechanisms of civic participation and education. It is a difficult challenge. Not the least of the hurdles to be overcome is one of language. Language matters to the fabric of a community; it carries lessons and norms of behavior that are repeated over and over – and the contemporary language of "membership" in Indian Country is hard to change. Yet more and more tribal nations are devising innovative strategies for changing not only the language of "member" to that of "citizen" but also transforming the culture and conduct of members into the culture and conduct of citizens.

In some cases, the efforts at making the transformation from member to citizen are symbolic in nature. Recognizing that symbolism can be powerful in fostering change, Mike Mitchell, former Grand Chief at Akwesasne Mohawk in Canada, tells how he urged other chiefs and his council to abandon the terms that Canada used to describe them and their lands, words such as "band," "member," and "reserve." He placed a jar in the middle of the conference table; anyone who used one of the colonial terms had to contribute spare change to the jar. People soon got the message. The Mohawks are a nation. The people are *citizens*.

Research from around the world, across numerous nations and cultures, repeatedly finds that concepts of citizenship take shape as young people begin to make the transition into young adulthood, interacting with their community's governing institutions, volunteering in civic projects, and, perhaps, receiving explicit civics education.[11] Unfortunately, few Native nations have access to educational opportunities that address these tasks. Moreover, most American Indian children are educated in public schools that pay little if any attention to contemporary Indian populations and seldom even acknowledge, much less examine and educate about, Native nations and their governments.

Few educational institutions other than tribally owned and operated colleges provide education in what Frank Ettawageshik, former chair of the Little Traverse Bay Bands of Odawa, calls tribal civics: The study of Native nations, their governments, their needs, and the responsibilities of tribal citizens. Even institutions that recognize and try to meet such challenges face a shortage of relevant curricular materials grounded in the experiences and aspirations of Native nations. As one Pueblo leader in New Mexico described the situation, "All of our high school kids can name the county seats of New Mexico, but they don't know anything about their own tribe's government."

Some tribes are addressing these needs. In the 1990s, the Cherokee Nation of Oklahoma developed a forty-hour, college-level Cherokee Nation History Course that eventually became a mandatory part of every Cherokee Nation employee's (Native and non-Native) training. The course entailed study of a 1,200-page reading packet of treaty texts, court decisions, historical accounts, essays, and other materials that foster cultural and national identity. The focus was not only on what the Cherokee Nation lost through its history, but also on the resilience and innovation that have allowed the Nation to survive and, in many ways, to flourish. The course has helped some employees replace "anger and discouragement over Cherokee history with a sense of pride and accomplishment." As one Cherokee citizen student in the course realized, while history says much was lost, "We reconstituted. We reorganized. We rebuilt. And not just once or twice."[12]

The Akwesasne Mohawk community in New York developed a different strategy but with some similar goals. In 1979 a standoff between the Mohawks of Akwesasne and New York State over certain Mohawk rights led a group of Mohawk parents to take control of their children's education out of the hands of the state and put it in the hands of the community. Concerned with "the lack of cultural teaching and Mohawk language in mainstream schools," they launched the Akwesasne Freedom School, designed "to rebuild the nation and reverse the assimilation process." The school's curriculum, which covers pre-kindergarten to grades seven and eight and the transition toward high school, includes not only Mohawk language and history but Mohawk cosmology. The school operates year-round and incorporates the seasons and related Mohawk traditions, including the teachings of the Longhouse and ceremonial participation, into the curriculum, which also teaches reading, writing, math, and science. Parents continue to play a central role in the school, as do others from the Akwesasne community, with traditional chiefs and clan mothers instructing some of the classes. Evaluators concluded that the school "gives students the tools to excel academically and personally, while creating new generations of committed tribal citizens and future leaders."[13]

The award-winning Leadership Institute at the Santa Fe Indian School "trains tribal citizens to serve their communities while maintaining a strong connection to their traditions."[14] Started in 1999 by the All Indian Pueblo Council, representing the nineteen pueblo nations of New Mexico and Ysleta del Sur Pueblo in Texas, the institute is an effort to educate tribal citizens about the policy challenges facing their nations and to engage those citizens in the effort to develop policy solutions, all within the context of Pueblo cultural traditions and history. The institute holds several issue-specific community events – called Community Institutes – each year. These link up to forty tribal citizens at each event with topic-area experts for in-depth discussions of relevant history, personal stories, community values, and possible policy solutions. The program assumes that all participants can teach and all can learn, and it turns the development of new approaches to policy into a community endeavor. Some institute programs have a particular focus on younger citizens. These include a Summer Policy Academy that, among other things, immerses high school juniors and seniors in discussions of practical policy issues currently facing their tribal governments. One participant described Leadership Institute programs as a way to explore "the sacred and inherent responsibility of sustaining our Indigenous life ways, while drawing upon our western knowledge so that we are successful in generating a better quality of life for our people today and into the future."[15]

The core question for citizenship is the question raised, and quoted earlier, by Sir Tipene O'Regan, the Māori elder: "What do we want to be as a people?" The answer a Native nation or community gives to that question has central implications for what it means to be a citizen in that nation or community. Some of those implications may have to do with the legal or technical criteria of eligibility for citizenship, but the more profound implications have nothing to do with eligibility in the technical sense. They have to do with the kinds of conduct and engagement the nation or community needs if it is to realize that future vision. The kinds of strategies noted above will contribute to building citizens. They will do so not by telling citizens what they are supposed to do or what they are supposed to be. They will do it by developing citizenship through education and experiences that make participating and contributing as citizens part of everyday life and culture.

Looking for Ways to Self-Determine Who Is a Citizen... without Tearing a Community Apart

If fostering a transition from membership to citizenship is one of the challenges of contemporary Native nation building, it begs the question of *who* are a nation's citizens. Answering that question, with ultimately bright-line formal criteria and yes/no designations, can be off-putting. No one wants to be told whether they are part of a community or not, and the ideal might be seen as conditions under which no one needs to be told whether they are part of a community. Instead, they and the rest of the community "just know." But operating according to such an ideal in a world of real people and their diverse interests and perspectives seems unlikely for any self-governing community that has to make decisions over such matters as the allocation of scarce financial resources, access to limited social services, and the selection of empowered officials and representatives.

Because the stakes that accompany access to governmental authority and resources are real, collective decisions regarding citizenship criteria are fraught with potential for intra-community conflict. Certainly the recent experiences of a number of Native nations who have undertaken the challenge of addressing long-standing blood quantum criteria illustrate the prospects for disagreement and disruption. The case is strong that such conflict is a "relic" of original membership criteria being largely imposed and/or regulated by federal authorities: Such a history creates vested interests in the status quo and can make change feel like rebellion or even revolution.[16] The resulting disputes can be nasty.[17]

We can't find or imagine any "magic bullet" that could make address-ing the citizenship qualification standards of a nation – indigenous or not – non-controversial. The best that can be hoped for is that addressing the issue, in the end, strengthens the community and yields an outcome that has enough of the community's support that it can withstand internal and ex-ternal dissension going forward. In trying to maximize the chances of such results, historical experience provides some useful pointers.

Do It Yourself: Deciding citizenship criteria is a preeminent act of sov-ereignty. Accordingly, a nation that "walks the walk" of a sovereign under-takes a matter as central as citizenship criteria for itself because it wants to decide who it is, who makes up the community called the nation. But perhaps even more importantly, tribal nations need to adopt the "do it your-self" guide because it offers the best chance – albeit not a guarantee – of a framework that lasts precisely because it is most likely to be concordant in both the process of adoption and ultimate policy with the cultural values of the community. As Gabriel Galanda and Ryan Dreveskracht write (quoting from giants in the field):

> Tribal sovereignty is "immersed in historic indigenous val-ues" that "bind a community together" [David Wilkins]; it "consist[s] more of continued cultural integrity than of polit-ical powers" and "revolves around the manner in which tra-ditions are developed, sustained, and transformed to confront new conditions" and "involves most of all a strong sense of community discipline" [Vine Deloria, Jr.]. Tribal sovereignty utilizes "peace-making, mediation, restitution and compensa-tion to resolve the inevitable disputes that occasionally ar[i]se," and is founded in "spiritual values [and] kinship systems... that enabled each Native nation, and the individuals, families, and clans constituting those nations, to generally rest assured in their collective and personal identities and not have to won-der about 'who' they are" [David Wilkins].[18]

As the emphasis here on dispute *self*-resolution suggests, turning to an-other sovereign's courts and laws to resolve disputes arising over Native nation citizenship is to invite the injection of that other sovereign's values and culture and to give up a critical aspect of nationhood.

Constitutionalize It: Constitutions are not a conceit of western democ-racies. Whether stated in glorious prose[19] or unwritten and residing in the deep cultural or spiritual precepts of a society,[20] sustained self-governing societies have always set out fundamental rules of the game by which they organize and make collective decisions, provide for community well-being,… and decide who their citizens are.[21] From Poland to Potawatomi, from Umatilla to the United States, communities protect the most fundamental principles of their collective action by constitutionalizing them. This entails using the ceremony that is embedded in constitutions and their hard-to-change provisions to provide some insulation from the inevitably vacillating winds of day-to-day politics.

Take It Out of Politics: Addressing the foundational nation-building question of citizenship criteria is properly a community process, not a political process. It would be naïve, however, to suggest that politics wouldn't enter the deliberations. After all, the existing criteria create both interests in and animosity to the status quo. But steps like putting the matter of citizenship criteria in the hands of a *culturally* legitimate body can dampen the raw politics.[22] What such a body, formal or informal, might legitimately look like will vary from tribe to tribe. It could take the form of a commission with independence from elected office holders, a council of elders, a youth council, a council of clans, a gathering of families, or any number of alternatives.

Engage and Educate: The average citizen quite appropriately lives her or his life without having to pay deep attention to issues of governance. After all, most individuals have work to do, families to care for, and interests that are not centered on matters such as the nation's citizenship standards. Yet if a process for addressing matters such as blood quantum standards is to be a community process, the community must be engaged.

Here, cases like that of the Tigua people of Ysleta Del Sur Pueblo stand out. Upon restoration as a federally recognized tribe in 1987, the U.S. Congress established Tigua's citizenship criterion – 1/8th blood quantum. By 2012, Tigua counted the "True Tigua Population" at 1,717 enrolled members *plus* 1,598 non-enrolled descendants.[23] Sentiment was strong that: "[Blood Quantum] is an internal insult. We don't measure being a Native American or a citizen of this pueblo based only on blood. It's based on who you are and your involvement with the community."[24]

In response, the Tribal Council created an Advisory Board charged with proposing changes to the Nation's enrollment criteria, garnering community input, assessing potentially affected programs and services, assessing budget impacts, and developing a citizenship campaign. In a setting in which the Nation has been engaged for years in a massive and continuous "nation building" civics education program for all ages, more than 1,400 enrolled and non-enrolled Tiguas have been surveyed on everything from their willingness to give up certain tribal benefits to the use of "citizen" v. "member" v. just "Tigua." Smaller focus groups also have been part of the process, and the Nation has worked successfully to pass legislation in Congress to reestablish Tigua's inherent right to self-determine who is Tigua.[25] Extensive use of oral and digital communication has ensured that it is hard to be Tigua and not know that the community is focused on that goal. As of September 2015, the Nation advised that any applicant for enrollment must be "a Lineal or Lateral Descendant of a member who is listed in the Tribal Base Roll of Ysleta del Sur Pueblo and is an enrolled member of the Tribe."[26]

Regardless of terminology and ultimate outcomes, a process like Tigua's, adapted to fit different communities' varying values and contexts, is not only an investment in citizenship. It is an investment in rebuilding Native nations.

Notes

1. Thornton, Russell, "Tribal Membership Requirements and the Demography of 'Old' and 'New' Native Americans" in *Changing Numbers, Changing Needs: American Indian Demography and Public Health*, ed., Sandifur, G, R.R. Rindfuss, and B. Cohen (Washington, DC: The National Academies Press, 1996); Spruhan, Paul, "A Legal History of Blood Quantum in Federal Indian Law to 1935" in *South Dakota Law Review* 51, no. 1, 2006.

2. The Harvard Project on American Indian Economic Development, *The State of the Native Nations: Conditions under U.S. Policies of Self-Determination* (New York: Oxford University Press, 2007).

3. See also Fletcher, Matthew L.M., "Tribal Membership and Indian Nationhood" in *American Indian Law Review*, 37:1, 2012.

4. Eskridge, William N., Jr., "Relationship between Obligations and Rights of Citizens," *Fordham Law Review* 69, no. 5:1721–51, 2001, at 1722, available at http://ir.lawnet.fordham.edu/flr/vol69/iss5/9, accessed September 7, 2015.

5. Constitution of Estonia 1992 (rev. 2003), available at https://www.constituteproject.org/constitution /Estonia_2003, accessed September 28, 2015.

6. Marquez, Deron, "Marquez: On Legal and Social Citizenship," *Indian Country Today*, June 28, 2007, available at Indian Country Today Media Network, http://indiancountrytodaymedianetwork.com/2007 /06/28/ marquez-legal-and-social-citizenship-91050, accessed September 25, 2015.

7. Pecos, Regis, *Honoring Nations Award Ceremony*, National Congress of American Indians Annual Convention, Atlanta, GA, October 29, 2014.

8. A Māori term commonly translated as "tribe."

9. O'Regan, Sir Tipene, "The Economics of Indigenous Survival and the Development of Culturally Relevant Governance," Vincent Lingiari Memorial Address, Charles Darwin University, Darwin, Australia, August 21, 2014, private printing, at 2.

10. Lyons, Oren, "Foreword," *Rebuilding Native Nations* (op. cit.) at vii.

11. Gauri, Varun and M. Lundberg, "Youth and Citizenship," *Research Brief*, World Bank, February 7, 2006, available at http://econ.worldbank.org/external/default/main?theSitePK=469382&contentMDK=21210591&menuPK=476752&pagePK=64165401&piPK=64165026, accessed September 29, 2015.

12. The Harvard Project on American Indian Economic Development, "Cherokee Nation History Course," *Honoring Nations Annual Report, 2003*, at 57–58, available at https://nnidatabase.org/text/cherokee-nation-history-course, accessed September 29, 2015.

13. The Harvard Project on American Indian Economic Development, "Akwesasne Freedom School," *Honoring Nations Annual Report, 2005*, at 13, available at http://hpaied.org/publications/akwesasne-freedom-school, accessed September 29, 2015.

14. The Harvard Project on American Indian Economic Development, "Leadership Institute, Santa Fe Indian School," *Honoring Nations Annual Report, 2010*, at 25, available at https://nnidatabase.org/db/attachments/text/honoring_nations/2010_HN_leadership_institute_santa_fe_indian_school.pdf, accessed September 29, 2015.

15. Ibid. at 28.

16. See Galanda, Gabriel S. and R.D. Dreveskracht, "Curing the Tribal Disenrollment Epidemic: In Search of a Remedy" in *Arizona Law Review*, 57:2, 2015, for a thorough discussion of these consequences.

17. See, for example, Lurie, Jon, "White Earth Constitutional Reform Stalled by Infighting" in *Twin Cities Daily Planet*, April 20, 2015, available at http://www.tcdailyplanet.net/white-earth-constitutional-reform-stalled-infighting/, accessed September 30, 2015.

18. Galanda and Dreveskracht, op. cit., at 444.

19. Such as, e.g., the Haudenosaunee *Great Law of Peace*.

20. Such as at, e.g., Cochiti Pueblo.

21. Cornell, Stephen, "Wolves Have A Constitution: Continuities in Indigenous Self-Government," in *International Indigenous Policy Journal*, 6:1, 2015.

22. Lemont, Eric, "Developing Effective Processes of American Indian Constitutional and Governmental Reform: Lessons from the Cherokee Nation of Oklahoma, Hualapai Nation, Navajo Nation, and Northern Cheyenne Tribe" in *American Indian Law Review*, 26:147, 2002.

23. Ysleta Del Sur Pueblo, *Passing: HR 5811 Tigua Blood Quantum Bill*, available at http://www.ysletadelsurpueblo.org/files/spaw/Tribal_Council_Blood_Quantum_Bill_FINAL_8.pdf.

24. Ibid. quoting (then) Lt. Gov. Carlos Hisa.

25. Ysleta Del Sur Pueblo, *Project Tiwahu: Redefining Tigua Enrollment*, available at file:///C:/Users/jkalt/Downloads/Tiwahu_Key_Findings%20(2).pdf.

26. Ysleta Del Sur Pueblo, *Membership Enrollment Application Process*, at http://www.ysletadelsurpueblo.org/html_pages.sstg?id=14&sub1=117&sub2=82.

WE CHOSE THIS, NOW WHAT? WHAT COMES AFTER BLOOD QUANTUM?

by Gyasi Ross

"The core element that is necessary for us to truly regain our equilibrium and regain our sanity is to regain the good things about our heritage."

– Darrell Kipp

Utilizing blood quantum to determine tribal citizenship is a bad fit. Stupid, in fact.

Citizenship within Native communities is not about blood quantum. Not one bit. In fact, the only time a person logically should be concerned with blood quantum is if/when, God forbid, they need a blood transfusion. At that point, yes, blood quantum is important. But for citizenship? No, "blood quantum"[1] is one of the worst markers of citizenship that there is.[2]

Citizenship is about shared heritage.

Citizenship is about language. It's about knowledge of our homelands. It's about our heritage. But unfortunately, most Native nations do not require any of those things to be considered citizens of their nations *currently*. Citizenship is about *investment, commitment* and *reciprocal* gain – in nations across the world, the citizens give to the nation and the nation gives to the citizen. Every nation in the world requires investment, commitment and reciprocal gain from its citizens – the nation provides such things as social services, protection and education. In return, the citizen pays the nation for those services by displaying a certain level of competence in language, by voting in elections, by paying taxes, by volunteering for military or selective services, etc. There is always a cost to citizenship. Services cost and a nation that does not have the ability to pay its costs and also simultaneously determine who is a citizen is not a nation at all.

Citizenship is never free.

History tells us that pre-European-contact Native communities behaved as nations. There were rules in order for folks to come and go into those communities. Many of us contend that Native communities are still nations, just like the United States, Nigeria and China. If that is true, Native nations also *must* require as a matter of survival and legitimacy, investment, commitment and reciprocal gain from their citizens. Why wouldn't they? No nation can exist if it only *gives* to its citizens and never *receives* from its citizens. No nation can exist, likewise, if it has no ability to determine who is a citizen and who is not – if there are no rules. Therefore, when Native people speak of Native communities as "Nations," it's an acknowledgment: "Not only do we expect *outsiders and non-Natives* to treat our communities as nations, but that *we will likewise* treat our communities as nations." A sacred agreement.

That means investment, commitment and reciprocal gain.

Moving forward, in order for our Native communities to truly reclaim their historical position as nations, the community will need to require the citizenry to have some "skin in the game" – to be invested in the infrastructure and development of the community in exchange for citizenship and services. And until those nations find a way to effectively require those *much more meaningful* things that show heritage and citizenship, blood quantum will unfortunately have to do for several reasons:

1. Blood quantum is an ugly, sloppy yet *necessary* adaption that our ancestors saw wisdom in strictly for the purposes of survival. As John Mohawk brilliantly stated, "Culture is a learned means of survival in an environment." Our beloved ancestors were not stupid – in the rapidly changing environment, they *chose* blood quantum as the best measure of heritage out of *many* other possible options as the means of survival at that time. Today, agree or not, those ancestors who were confront-

ed with the possible extermination of Native people felt that blood quantum was the best survival mechanism to indicate heritage and preserve Native people as a separate people.[3]

2. Put very simply, we've gotta have *something* to indicate citizenship in our Native communities. As mentioned supra, there is a bit of logic that is required in these conversations about Native nationhood.

3. If Native people and communities expect *others* to acknowledge our communities as "nations," then *we* have to acknowledge our communities as nations.

4. Nations invariably have criteria for citizenship that typically require some sacrifice on behalf of the citizenry. No nation can exist simply by giving to its citizens with no expectation of ever getting. Until individual citizens of Native communities decide that we will contribute like every other citizen of every other nation through a language proficiency test, residency, taxes, civil service enrollment, etc., blood will have to do, as imperfect as it is.

Regarding the second reason, some folks will point out, "Well, blood quantum is not traditional." That's true! But enrollment in a Native community is not "traditional" either – our communities have only calculated and quantified enrollment since around the same time as the blood quantum regime has been in effect. Therefore, blood quantum is almost *exactly* as traditional as enrollment. Moreover, per capita payments are *very* untraditional within our communities – the notion of receiving benefit without contributing? Hell no. Never happened historically – individuals had to go hunt/fish/grow their own food. Also, Native communities paying for college is likewise untraditional. Yet all or some of those benefits often come with citizenship in a Native community. As such, our communities are faced with new challenges that are not solved with a magic application of "tradition" – no, the environment changed and so Native people did what Native people have always done – they adapted to those changing environments.

Adaption

One of our dearly departed Amskapipikuni elders, Darrell Robes Kipp, once dropped some knowledge on me. Darrell was a genius and a visionary who founded some of the first Native-language schools in the United States. He was a servant who saw the importance of Natives retaining those things that are most intrinsic to Native people: language, land, service and relationships.

When he talked, I listened. So did a lot of other folks.

He was a prophet, understanding the crucial value of Native people speaking their language and serving their communities. His entire life was dedicated to those things. Sure, he was a product of Harvard University, but that was not what was important to him – those were white men accolades and pedigrees that white men cared about. Darrell's focus was his community, his people and how to leverage those white men accolades into helping his community.

You can clearly see Darrell's powerful and prophetic influence in every single Native community that has an immersion language program at its tribal college or at the state university.

Thank you, Darrell.

Darrell blessed me with many email conversations and some phone conversations and even a few face-to-face conversations. Every single time that we did, I was amazed at the intimacy of his knowledge, the depth of his wisdom; indeed, his wisdom came from tens of thousands of years of survival and adaption. His thoughts, as brilliant as they were, were not *theory* – they were actualized over many, many generations of our people getting things *right* and a relatively few generations of our people getting things wrong.

In times of question, Darrell defaulted to relying upon the spirit of our ancestors, who came up with powerful solutions in difficult circumstances. That is our heritage. In my experience, he wasn't so much focused on the actual specifics of the solution – people evolve, technology changes, we adapt[4] – but seemed to always want to maintain the *spirit* of our ancestors' pragmatic brilliance.

We cannot abandon that spirit or heritage; we are Amskapipikuni and that means something. If we simply abandon who we were for the most expedient solutions, then we are simply Americans, simply brown-skinned white people.

That was unacceptable – there has to be some tangible marker of "heritage." Does that marker have to be blood quantum? God forbid, no; I do not know for a fact, but I doubt Darrell or anyone invested in the well-being of Native communities thinks that blood quantum should be the appropriate marker. Most people recognize how bad the fit is for our communities. But there does have to be some standard, and many of the arguments to get rid of blood quantum do not bring forth an alternative marker of identity in place of blood quantum. Many simply say to get rid of the one marker that is in place without another structure to take its place.

That is not enough. There has to be something.

Bad Fit

"I've really got to use (I've got to use)
My imagination (I've got to use)
To think of good reasons (I've got to use)
To keep on keepin' on (I've got to use)
I've got to make the best of (Best of, best of)
A bad situation"

– Gladys Knight and the Pips,
"I've Got to Use My Imagination"

There is absolutely no question that the adoption of blood quantum was in bad faith, with bad intentions, and a bad fit for Native people. As many people rightfully point out, and we discussed above, there was nothing traditional about adopting blood quantum as the standard for heritage or citizenship for Native people; it was based upon greed, condescension and a belief that Native ways were inherently evil and unproductive, thus the need to turn Natives ostensibly into white people, with white values and white goals.

The goal was an end to Native heritage.

The Dawes Act of 1887 marked the beginning of a new policy toward American Indians. Individual Indians could receive private allotments of land and U.S. citizenship in exchange for their commitment to adopt an agricultural, European American way of life. The U.S. government would hold the land allotments in trust for twenty-five years before the Indian owners would receive the rights to sell or lease them.[5]

Or as Senator Dawes, the brains behind the Dawes Act himself, said:

> It came to be apparent that very soon we should not only have the savage Indian upon our hands, but he would be houseless and homeless also, two hundred and fifty thousand, at least, savage Indians, with no resting or abiding place in the land. A white man, idle and with no home, is a tramp. Two hundred and fifty thousand savage Indian tramps roaming over this land was an appalling consideration with the government, threatening the peace of the nation, the sanctity of the home, the sacredness of human life, with the utter impossibility to control them. This was the exigency out of which sprung the present policy of the nation in the management of the Indian.

No, nothing honorable or traditional about this policy. There was nothing humane about it, nothing that even hinted that Native peoples' interest were ever considered.

Yet, this thing that was intended to *end* Native heritage became a *marker*, a euphemism *for* Native heritage. And although reliance upon blood quantum as a shorthand for heritage was a bad fit, Native leaders evidently thought there had to be *some* measure of heritage to be considered a citizen of that particular nation. The world was changing right before their very eyes – it would never be the same. And most of those changes were unquestionably for the worse at that time. Yet, as Native people always do, as hunter-gatherers who *invariably* must change strategies and adapt to difficult circumstances, those leaders made the best of a very, very bad situation. The push was toward assimilating or extermination of Native people–allotment, "Kill the Indian, Save the Man," the murder of Native food sources. Yet, Native people resisted both assimilation *and* extermination by virtue of creating standards for what it meant to be "Indian."

If there were no standards, we would have disappeared. Therefore, the creation of standards that previously did not exist was for survival purposes, and was done because those leaders believed that Native people had something worth protecting.

Hence, those Native leaders *chose* blood quantum out of the many other identifiers that could have been used to indicate "heritage." That says that those Native leaders *had to* see that there was some value to this extremely rugged measure of heritage, this silly thing called "blood quantum."

How do we know this?

The list goes on and on.

Yet *many* Native nations decided that, instead of any of those other criteria, implementing and maintaining blood quantum requirements was going to be the standard for citizenship in their nation.

That is, there *was* a choice and there still *is* a choice whether to rely upon blood quantum or not. "Despite policymakers' efforts to undermine tribal governments and political leaders, native groups maintained or created formal tribal governments and began regulating their own membership, especially in regard to land allotments, royalties from the sale of resources, distributions of tribal funds, residence, and voting."[6] Indeed, since at least 1905, U.S. courts have consistently upheld tribal rights to determine membership based on their own laws and customs.[7]

We chose this.

And unless we're willing to accept that Native leaders are incompetent en masse, we have to accept that Native nations *chose* blood quantum because they felt it was a fair proxy for historical concepts of heritage.

That's right – Native people were not victims of blood quantum; we chose it. That is fact. Our chosen leaders evidently saw some value in utilizing blood quantum as a sign of heritage and citizenship as opposed to other criteria that we could have easily utilized to determine citizenship. Relying on blood quantum was an act, like *Santa Clara Pueblo v. Martinez*, of Native self-determination, sovereignty and agency. *Santa Clara Pueblo* remains a controversial case because there is, undoubtedly, collateral damage as a result of it; similarly, blood quantum creates some collateral damage as well. There are people who cannot be enrolled as a result of the decision of a Native community to act as a nation by creating hard and fast (and sometimes unattainable) standards for citizenship in that nation.

Hopefully those standards will be moved to something that more closely reflects our communities' standards. Those standards are questions for the community to make; presumably they know what's best for themselves.

To wit, there is an ongoing fiery debate within the United States concerning a path to citizenship for immigrants. That debate has fueled protests and compelled political compromise and presidential vetoes. The point – *it's not an easy discussion.* It's never an easy discussion; when a nation decides who will be *a part* of their citizenship, they necessarily likewise decide who will *not be a part* of their citizenship. That's tough. But when a nation believes that it has a resource worth protecting – citizenship, heritage, *op-*

portunity – the leaders make those tough decisions for survival purposes, to create hard boundaries and standards.

That boundaries and standards sometimes have collateral damage to individuals – that is unfortunate. Yet, the nation must think of the survival and the good of the nation first. Nations, as a matter of historical fact, survive when they are in control of citizenship and have criteria that makes sense to them.

Perhaps...

It's time to move toward a more appropriate regime to determine citizenship. It's definitely time that Native communities move from one euphemism for heritage – blood quantum – to a combination of other criteria: lineal descent, language competency, residency within the nation's borders, taxation. No matter what our communities decide, however, it probably should not be to make citizenship *easier*. Why? Because *nations* protect their citizenry and have criteria that are not intended to be easy to circumvent. *Nations*, as history shows, know that sometimes there is collateral damage when a nation has something worth protecting – that just anyone cannot be a part of it.

Our communities have something worth protecting. Just like our ancestors realized – we're special, our homelands are special, our bloodlines are special, our languages are special. That's not even to mention the very real and very tangible benefits that come with being a member of a federally recognized Indian tribe.

Conclusion

Blood quantum is a bad fit. It's terrible and and dishonest. At the same time, simply opening the floodgates to everyone who would join our communities is also a bad fit and dishonest. That's never been what our communities have done – we've always had standards, expectations and responsibilities in order to be a member of our communities. It's up to us to think hard and to figure out what those more appropriate standards are going to be in the twenty-first, twenty-second and twenty-third centuries. If we take this notion of Native "nationhood" seriously, then we have to contemplate what we want our communities to look like three-, four hundred years from now;

how do ensure that our communities maintain the beautiful things that have always made us a separate culture, like language, spiritual practices and biology? Should biological fractions matter? Are we fine with families who have never touched, seen or experienced our homelands for generations being considered a part of our communities?

All those will be our choices. No matter what we think, however, we should begin to create the realities that we want to see now.

Notes

1. Of course the term "blood quantum" itself is a misnomer. "Blood" is a metaphor, something born from European insecurity. As Melissa Meyer (1999) states, "Measuring Indian 'blood' is a curious phenomenon that merits examination in its own right," as other authors in this volume and elsewhere have done. "It is incorrect to assume that the term 'blood' is and always has been simply a metaphoric reference to genetic composition. Especially before knowledge of genetics, blood seemed the very stuff of life. The weakening effects of the loss of a great deal of blood – producing even death – cannot have been lost on the earliest humans. Among most band level people, blood has been and is regarded as a very powerful element. From the earliest times it has been regarded as the quintessential substance which carries and transmits the special qualities of the stock. Ancient Greeks linked blood to beliefs about human reproduction. Some believed that the mother's blood seeped into the fetus or that the testes separated blood from seed rendering semen a distillation of blood. Herodotus thought that African semen was black, and it took Aristotle to set the record straight. (What lively reading his field notes must be!) These beliefs concerning blood are probably among the oldest surviving ideas from the earliest days of humankind. They are widely distributed among the peoples of the world in much the same form (Meyer, Melissa L. "American Indian Blood Quantum Requirements: Blood Is Thicker Than Family." *In Over the Edge: Remapping the American West*. Eds. Valerie J. Matsumoto and Blake Allmendinger. Berkeley: University of California Press, 1999).

2   "The etymological roots of the term 'blood' extend deep into the Anglo-Saxon tribal psyche. In Old English, 'blot' denotes blood spilled in sacrifice, a ritual intended partially to ensure continuity of the familial

or tribal lineage. In Middle English, the connection with sacrifice is obscured except for Christian associations with the Eucharist. By 1200, 'blood' increasingly connotes lineage, descent, and ancestry in association with royal claims to property and power and presages modern conceptions of 'race.' Associations with intermarriage and discussions of whole- and half-blood appear. By the early eighteenth century, modern physiological meanings take the fore and 'race' begins to displace the connotations of lineage and ancestry formerly attributed to 'blood'" (Meyer, Melissa L. "American Indian Blood Quantum Requirements: Blood Is Thicker Than Family." In *Over the Edge: Remapping the American West*. Eds. Valerie J. Matsumoto and Blake Allmendinger. Berkeley: University of California Press, 1999.)

3   And as imperfect as using blood quantum as a measure of heritage and citizenship is, it has worked toward the goal of helping Native people to survive! How do we know this? Well, whereas this myth of the "vanishing Indian" has been in full effect for over 500 years, the truth is that there are exponentially more Native people on this continent *now* than there were when blood quantum enrollment requirements were implemented! Indeed, around the time of the Dawes Act, which implemented blood quantum enrollment, Native people seemed destined for extinction, with population numbers *nationwide* dwindling down to 250,000 people. In 2015 there were approximately 3 million Native people (National Congress of American Indians, http://www.ncai.org/about-tribes/demographics). Also, it's important to note that there are more people *claiming* Native heritage. It's self-reporting which needs to be treated carefully.

From the evidence, blood quantum requirements have done anything *but* trigger extinction of Native people! In fact, based upon the evidence, it's done the exact opposite.

4   Native people adapt better than anyone else. Darrell utilized an Ivy League education to further traditional knowledge – his life was proof of our adaptive spirits. Darrell often used the example of horses and dogs to explain Native people's willingness to adapt to new technology but maintain an ancient spirit. Horses are a fairly recent animal in North America; they were released after the Pueblo Revolt of 1680. After 1680, Amskapipikuni people became proficient with horses and in fact were considered the "Raiders of the Northern Plains," some of the best horse riders in the world. That came from

embracing the ancestral relationship and spirit that Amskapipikuni people had with dogs and translating that relationship and spirit to the horse. According to Darrell, "People today often think that horses have been with the Indian for ages, but horses were something new to Nitsitapiiks, "Blackfoot people," as they were brought to the continent in the 1700s. The Blackfoot people then called a horse *ponokaomita* by combining *ponoka* "elk" and *imita* "dog," and this word is standard today.

5   Lauren L. Basson, *White Enough to Be American? Race Mixing, Indigenous People, and the Boundaries of State and Nation.* The University of North Carolina Press, 2008.

6   "American Indian Blood Quantum Requirements: Blood Is Thicker Than Family. In *Over the Edge: Remapping the American West.* Eds. Valerie J. Matsumoto and Blake Allmendinger. Berkeley: University of California Press, 1999.)

7   *Waldron v. United States,* 143 Fed. 413 (1905) and the still controversial *Santa Clara Pueblo v. Martinez,* 436 U.S. 49 (1978), for example. Oneida lawyer and scholar Francine Skenadore says, "Much has been written about tribal sovereignty.... In my opinion, tribal sovereignty, a tribe's right to make its own laws and enforce those laws against its own members, transcends the equal rights aspect because a tribe's right to define its membership is important to maintaining cultural identity ... surveys the feminist problem of equal rights that exists in the case and discusses both the Indian feminist perspectives on tribal identity and sovereignty and mainstream feminist perspectives on equal rights.... *Santa Clara Pueblo v. Martinez,* a 1978 United States Supreme Court decision, is a landmark case for tribal sovereignty in federal Indian law.... In contrast to the mainstream feminist perspective, Indian feminists appear to have little problem with the Santa Clara case based upon their understanding of tribal sovereignty.... This distrust in turn dismisses tribal sovereignty and questions the legitimacy of a tribe's membership rule and traditions in light of existing American equality values and laws.... Some of these scholars bring another perspective that I consider to blend both Indian feminist ideals that respect tribal sovereignty with mainstream feminist ideals that strongly value equal rights...." *Wisconsin Women's Law Journal,* 17(347): 2002.

APPLYING INDIGENOUS VALUES TO CONTEMPORARY TRIBAL CITIZENSHIP: CHALLENGE AND OPPORTUNITY

by LaDonna Harris, Kathryn Harris Tijerina, and Laura Harris

Self-governing comes with responsibility and privilege. Key to sovereignty is the right to define for ourselves who we are as a nation. Tribal governments, part of the U.S. federal system of governments, have the opportunity and challenge of defining the requirements of their citizenry. As the inheritors of immense and complex civilizations, we have the chance to decolonize tribal governmental policy and compose a new concept of contemporary tribal citizenship. Tribal nations, Alaskan Native villages, Native Hawaiian communities, and Indian Pueblos can throw off the repressive and dysfunctional U.S. policies of assimilation that were intended to destroy our culture and end our political status. The challenge is to reaffirm our true traditional values. Consciously incorporating Indigenous values into our governing structures provides the opportunity for tribal governments to make value-centered decisions – decisions that can move us beyond the legacy of colonization and ensure that Native nations remain distinct and that we will continue as a people.

As we consider contemporary tribal citizenship, we must remember that Native American identity in the United States is political. Our right to self-governance is not race based. Our continued relative autonomy within U.S. federalism relies on the recognition that we are political entities and that tribal sovereignty comes from the fact that we have always been self-determining nations. Blood quantum is not a political determination and should not be legally used to determine the citizenry of a government.

As other authors have mentioned in this volume, the policy that the degree of Indian blood dictates our right to be a citizen of a tribal government was heavily influenced by the African American slave trade and the racist theory of Eugenics. Many tribes adopted a blood quantum measurement when IRA (Indian Reorganization Act) governments were forced on us during the New Deal era. The supposition of the federal government and so-called Indian experts of the time was that disconnecting from culture, inbreeding, and intermarriage with non-Indians would solve the "Indian Problem." In other words, American Indians – the "vanishing race" – would fade away into the sunset and the associated political rights, land ownership, distinct cultures, and political structures would disappear too. Blood quantum was the colonial imposition of an alien concept that had no relationship to traditional forms of governance or Indigenous cultural values. The laws associated with blood quantum were necessary to a colonial government to enforce racist policy. This genocide-by-policy and institutional racism remain today.

LaDonna:

Not too long after I married Fred Harris, we were working with the University of Oklahoma as we developed Oklahomans for Indian Opportunity (OIO), the first statewide Indian organization in Oklahoma. In 1961 at one of the first meetings, a member of the OU faculty asked Fred and I, "How do you plan to address the 'Indian Problem.'" Fred quickly replied, "I married my Indian Problem." We had to approach implicit bias and outright racism with a bit of humor. Otherwise, our mental health was endangered.

I guess, in a way, I was a bit sheltered as I grew up in rural southwestern Oklahoma. I lived on a farm with my Comanche grandparents because my mother worked for Indian Health and was required to live on campus back then. We lived in a house full of cousins. I was always surrounded by relatives. In fact, I felt like everyone was related to me. I thought everybody lived the way we did until I started school where I was taught that the average American family consisted of a mother, a father, two children, and a dog named Spot.

After Fred and I worked jointly with other activists to integrate Lawton, Oklahoma, and organize OIO, we moved in 1964 to the suburbs of Washington, D.C., in Virginia. I was shocked to learn that because of a popular Eugenics movement, under state law, our marriage was not legal. A White man was prohibited from marrying a woman of color. My eldest daughter, Kathryn, advocated for going to jail in protest. Fortunately, the U.S. Supreme Court overturned the law in the famous case Loving vs. the Commonwealth of Virginia before Kathryn and I had the chance to be symbolically arrested.

Preceding chapters describe how some tribal governments and individual Native Americans continue to hold on to foreign policies and practices, like blood quantum. As we know, oppressed peoples often believe the negative stereotypes imposed on them by others. These derogatory images and characteristics can be internalized, causing negative self-image, low self-esteem, and the self-destructive behaviors that result. Replicating and enforcing the policies of the oppressor is a symptom of internalized oppression. Rather than viewing our current situation as an opportunity to create new systems that better reflect our values and worldviews, sadly, some Indigenous peoples often perpetuate and promote the very systems that oppress us. Yet, we have the power to rise above our oppression both personally and as governments.

Another possible cause for clinging to imposed systems is the fear of change, stemming in part from the physiological fear of abandonment caused by historical trauma. The historic trauma started with the death of most tribal members through the Indian wars and disease, followed by more recent trauma from federal boarding schools and relocation, and ended with personal trauma for some with physical and psychological abuse. These traumas often led to a fear of abandonment, which is defined as, "An irrational belief that one is in imminent danger of being personally rejected, discarded or replaced." Those with a fear of abandonment may live "with an exaggerated sense of dependency on another individual ... often live in a chronic sense of fear that their world is about to collapse through the abandonment of those closest to them."[1] "The new field of epigenetics has demonstrated that our genes are affected by trauma, including sudden loss, warfare, any drastic changes over which the individual or family had no control, and extended grief. The epigenetic effect is passed on to the next generations with real consequences. The epigenetic impacts may include lowered ability to handle stress effectively, cognitive challenges when managing strong emotions, and memory loss. Research into how to reverse the impacts of historical and intergenerational trauma focus on positive changes that build the capacity for resilience."[2] The abandonment fear is overlaid with an emotional attachment to anything that is multigenerational when so much else was lost. Fear was often perpetuated through federal assimilation policy, like Termination, which eradicated many North American tribes. Thus, we hang on to systems that we know, rather than change to something unknown. Historical trauma, epigenetics, fear, and abandonment issues are often passed along to subsequent generations and can negatively impact family systems, which, in turn, affect communities and government structures.

A fear of abandonment in Indian Country sometimes compels us to hold on to the outdated use of blood quantum as a determinant for citizenship. We often hold the misperception that "old" equals "traditional," and therefore is sacred. The phrase, "This is the way we have always done it" is often heard. Part of this misconception is the failure of the U.S. education system to teach Native American history. Because of federal policies such as forced assimilation through boarding schools, compulsory religious conversion, removal, and relocation, we have been dislocated from a knowledge of tribal traditions. As a result, we too often hold on to "old" attitudes and policies even when they become dysfunctional or ineffective. For instance, one tradition among the Comanche was the exercise of a very liberal form of inclusiveness. Having a lot of relatives was considered a form of wealth, going so far as taking captives to enlarge one's family when birthrates were low. The taking of captives makes it difficult to find an actual "full blood" Comanche both today and back in the early 1800's.

Kathryn:

When I was a young woman, it occurred to me that I would need to find a tribally enrolled Comanche to father my chil-

dren in order for them to be full citizens of the Comanche Nation. Never mind that both my maternal grandparents were descendants of Spanish captives. At that time, the Comanche requirement was one-fourth degree of Comanche blood. Further, Comanche, like many tribes of North America, have strong incest taboos with very broad definitions of who you are related to. I can't tell you how many times I would meet a good-looking young Indian man only to be told by an aunt, "No, no, he's your cousin!" By the time I was twenty-four, I was actively looking for a Comanche to marry. By the time I was twenty-six, I concluded that I had missed that wave of the prairie grass. Most Comanche men around my age were either already married, or they were relatives, in prison, or otherwise not a good bet for marriage.

I ended up falling in love with a Chicano from south Texas, which I figured was fitting for a Comanche. When I asked my great-uncle, Robert Coffey, a Baptist minister, to marry us, he asked me if the groom was Numunuh (Comanche). I responded, "No, he's u-taibo (Mexican)." Uncle Robert replied, "Well that's almost as good." Manuel and I chose not to have children, in part because they would not be enrolled Comanche.

More disturbing is the growing trend of disenrollment from a tribe, taking away voting rights, access to social services, and most devastating, stripping a citizen of their cultural identity. Assimilated values of accumulating personal wealth have interacted with blood quantum, bringing about the loss of communal ownership and the concentration of private property. Embracing the value of building individual wealth has led to enrollment policies based on maximizing profit for individuals with less regard for the common good. Using genetic testing for enrollment is also a scary precedent. Further, relying on the determinations of "Indianess" by non-Indian historians weakens our self-determination. Instead of falling prey to the old colonial policy of "divide and conquer," we can recognize that true prosperity comes from providing for the common good of the tribe.

Undisputedly, blood quantum as a litmus test for citizenship is not sustainable. The reality is that by the year 2050, disappearance into the larger American society is inevitable if we continue blood quantum–based policies. If degree of Indian blood continues to be used, Native Americans will no longer exist as a politically autonomous peoples. We cannot continue to foist this responsibility onto future generations. Just as our ancestors made difficult choices to ensure our survival, our generation must thoughtfully and creatively address our future cultural identity. While these decisions will be far from simple, we must face this challenge bravely and with confidence by applying our core cultural values.

To ensure a strong cultural identity for future generations, we must discard genocidal and assimilationist policy. As we contemplate how to move forward, we can reduce reactionary behavior by understanding how we arrived at our current situation through the impact of federal policies, such as the forced attendance of Christian missionary/residential schools, Removal, Reservations, Allotment, Termination, and Relocation. We can proactively apply our Indigenous values and worldviews to overcome these crippling strategies of assimilation. When we apply our values to the rights, responsibilities, and definition of tribal citizenship, we have an opportunity for innovative advancement and can courageously determine who we will be in the future, who will be with us, and how we will get there.

During our work over the years, many people have asked us why Indians want to be different, separate from the larger American society. Tribal peoples in the United States must ask ourselves the same question. If our governments mirror the U.S. government and just replicate Euro-American perspectives, we ultimately will lose our cultural autonomy and will no longer be different. Why should we exist as "mini-Americas" when we have our own worldviews, social norms, and different standards for the treatment of others?

What is the purpose of being an Indian nation or autonomous political entity? Why remain separate and different? We opine that being loyal to and supporting strong tribal governments does not exclude us from being good Americans. In fact, with our values intact and while implementing self-government, we are more active United States citizens and can contribute more to American society. Native Americans have often proven our patriotism. We belong to this land and share many of the same principles expressed in the U.S. Constitution and Declaration of Independence. The active implementation of Indigenous values can strengthen U.S. democracy. We are witness to the breakdown of the American education and criminal justice systems. The European colonist countries are struggling under the weight of immigrants from their former colonies. The health of the Earth is diminishing. The divide between rich and poor continues to grow. In practicing our traditional cultures and weaving our values into our governments, our workplace, and in our family life, we contribute Indigenous worldviews and cultural values to the larger U.S. society.

All Indigenous communities and Native nations have strong attributes and principles, such as bravery and generosity. We know that many pre-contact governments in the Americas were often more equalitarian, more democratic, and more participatory than current U.S. democracy. Traditional systems and values can influence the way we govern ourselves today.

After forty-five years of research and working to advance the rights of Indigenous peoples, Americans for Indian Opportunity (AIO) identified a set of core cultural values that we found to be universal throughout Tribal America: Relationships, Responsibility, Reciprocity, and Redistribution. Affectionately known as the Four R's, the philosophy of these values is articulated and shared in an effort to help us all weave traditional values into a contemporary context. The Four R's are not a definitive list or proscriptive. Nor are the values unique solely to Indigenous cultures. We do not propose the return to an unrealistic, romanticized Native American paradise. However, these values have enabled us to coexist for millennia. These concepts can be applied by all for the good of the whole.

Most influential is **Relationships**, or *kinship*. In the most profound sense, we are all related. Humans are related both to each other and to all things. As Western scientists are now finally learning, we – and all matter – are "the very stuff of stars." Thus humans have a kinship with rocks, plants, animals, and the Earth. The concept of relationships includes the need to value each person, group, and element as an important part of the whole. Valuing and respecting all matter, especially other people, and nurturing our relationships leads to peaceful coexistence and consensus decision-making drawn from diverse perspectives. Many pre-contact Native American groups organized into intertribal confederacies united in complementarity, rather than competing for resources and territory.

The famous social biologist E. O. Wilson, credited with introducing the concept of ecosystems, has long studied the evolution of advanced social behavior. He contends that our social interconnectedness and group bonds have evolved biologically and that advanced cooperative instinct goes beyond the immediate family to include all humans. Wilson and other like-minded scientists believe that the very survival of the planet – and humans as a species – requires us to develop relationships with all life. As Wilson noted, Darwin's theory of natural selection includes the concept of group selection, meaning that the fitness of an individual strengthens the survivability of the group. Thus Wilson declares humans are genetically predisposed to sharing. We are built to belong. Inclusion brings us joy. Exclusion brings suffering.

When applying the value of relationships to citizenship, tribal nations can be inclusive when determining who they are related to. Of course, a tribe cannot practically offer citizenship to all humans. However, when the definition of who can be a citizen does not value inclusiveness, we cheat ourselves of our best and brightest, and we inflict suffering on those who are excluded. Our Comanche Kaqu (grandmother) taught us that everybody has value and something to contribute. Inclusiveness brings to the tribe diversity of skills and more brain power. Maintaining or increasing tribal rolls can lead to increased communal property and shared profit, and can add to our overall collective resiliency.

The next R, **Redistribution**, pertains to *generosity*. Core cultural values guide us to share our resources and help us to maintain balance. Most tribes in North America had complex and sophisticated systems for the redistribution of wealth in order to maintain relatively flat societies, like *potlatches* among the tribes of the Northwest, *giveaways* from the Plains, and Pueblo Feast Day *throws*. The collective and communal traditions of our ancestors teach us that wealth must be shared for the greater good of the whole.

In contemporary society we can articulate the value of redistribution as the sharing of information, knowledge, advocacy services, and other resources. Traditionally, generosity could include the gifting of songs, stories, and dances. Trade was often governed by guidelines of overall goodwill and benevolence instead of the competitive nature of modern capitalism. Native Americans, today, often value intellectual and cultural property more than material ownership. International social justice organizations are now looking toward the strength in networks of colleagues instead of hierarchical institutions with authoritative leaders. Tribal governments can improve family systems and kinship ties in order to build responsive governance and inclusive policy.

Currently, many tribes distribute per capita payments for land sales, natural resource development, or gaming dividends evenly amongst all enrolled tribal citizens after the initial monies are invested in the common good through social welfare programs, infrastructure construction, senior and youth programs, and scholarships. Even distribution practices and reinvestment in social capital can be built upon by tribal governments to expand more communal policies in other areas of governmental services.

People often say that tribal governments should look and act more like businesses. We believe that a business model does not fit a traditionally communal society or a democratic government. The role of a business is to maximize profits. While business and economic development are necessary for jobs and income, the capitalist model can be positively influenced by Indigenous values such as redistribution. At the heart of private business is accumulation of individual wealth. As we know from our own traditions and from our values of relationships and redistribution, communal property, collective processes, and shared responsibility are central to tribal communities.

Reciprocity or *interconnectedness*, is the third R. Our relationships shape our roles in life and are reciprocal, as is the nature of the Universe and all aspects of life. Articulation and an understanding that all things are connected and cyclical are fundamental in knowing how we fit into the Universe, our community, and our family. Reciprocity represents cause and effect as we strive for balance. The concept of Reciprocity is central to finding the proper balance to citizenship, as it is to life.

Like the concept of Karma, negativity begets more negativity. Conversely, generosity, inclusiveness, and proactivity bring positivity, like the old saying, "What goes around, comes around." When we drive our relatives away from our nation, we create a bleak and less rewarding community. When we do not value every person, we cut off the possibility of receiving everybody's contribution. Exclusion makes us more vulnerable and threatens our collective existence.

In the 21st century, we can apply the value of reciprocity to the reintegration of our urban citizens. According to the 2010 census, 78% of all Native Americans in the U.S. live in urban areas. Due in large part to the federal program of Relocation, tribal governments and rural Indian communities are not able to take advantage of the brain power and financial resources of both populations. Engaging in the value of reciprocity could mean structures and systems that include more of our relatives and more ways for them to give back to the tribe. Some tribal governments are already addressing the needs of urban populations through absentee ballots, coming home rituals, official polling sites in major cities, and creating formal connections with their citizens living away from their traditional land base. For instance, the Comanche Nation has established a governmental outreach center in Dallas with plans for more cities, and the Menominee Tribe provides programs for their folks in Chicago.

From stories and traditions we know that there were no orphans in tribal communities. Our own Harris family often provided long-term care for the children of relatives in need. Tribal governments implement the Indian

Child Welfare Act to ensure the placement of foster children with Indian families whenever possible. Tribes can look to this practice and develop methods for defining citizens that reflects the best aspects of communal society. Good government meets the needs of its citizens and provides avenues for civic engagement and participation. Tribal governments have a unique opportunity to develop and reinforce reciprocal systems, laws, and social norms that expect and promote generosity and inclusiveness. When we replace reactionary behavior with a proactive value-based approach, we strengthen our communal societies.

The fourth value is **Responsibility**. Our relationships shape our responsibilities, which are also reciprocal. Responsibility is inherently a principal aspect of *community*. We have a duty to care for our relatives. Each human is accountable for the well-being of their kin. If we call the Earth our mother, then we have an obligation to take care of her. We respect and recognize the impact of our lives on the natural and social environments, and that we have a responsibility to use our "medicine" (inner strength) in strengthening our relationships. We have the responsibility to empower our relationships and relatives, not diminish them.

Responsibility to love and care for our relatives should be a defining concept in delineating citizenship in our nations. Responsibility is also a central aspect of what we expect from our citizens. And reciprocity dictates that responsibility is a central aspect of what we expect from our governments. The Pueblo peoples of the Southwest are a valuable example of shared responsibility. Pueblo tradition obligates Pueblo women to feed anybody and everybody who comes through their doors on Feast Day. Pueblo governments require all citizens to participate in Ditch Day, a day dedicated to cleaning and readying irrigation canals for Spring planting. And every head-of-household takes turns serving the Pueblo in an official governmental capacity.

The idea of returning to our original values and finding more humane and sustainable systems is a global concern. Our Indigenous brothers and sisters to the South have articulated and are sharing a traditional Indigenous worldview – *Vivir Bien*. "Living Well," as described in many cultures throughout the world, including in the Philippines, India, and Bolivia, is the concept of having enough to enjoy a happy life. The opposite is "living better," which denotes the accumulation of wealth and growth of capital. "Living Well" is to live in community with Nature and our other relatives, and to seek balance with all things, valuing complementarity over competition. Similar concepts are expressed in other parts of the world as well. For instance, Archbishop Desmond Tutu explains the southern African concept of Ubuntu: *"I am human because I belong, I participate, I share. A person with Ubuntu is open and available to others…"* Ecuador, Bolivia, and Peru have incorporated aspects of *Vivir Bien* into their national constitutions. These actions are not meant to build a pre-contact utopia, but rather to merge current systems with traditional values and make relevant lessons of our ancestors to enlighten our future.

UNICEF and other anti-poverty organizations have outlined a new concept for education, *Global Life Skills*, aimed at nurturing good citizenship based on the standards of the local community instead of providing education outside the values and needs of the community. *Global Life Skills*, as described by UNICEF, are centered on relationships and local community knowledge. Additionally, international social equity movements are offering the idea of *Economy for Life* as an alternative economic system that embraces the concepts offered by *Vivir Bien* and the Four R's. Indigenous peoples in North America have similar traditions of balance, like *Nizhoni* of the Navajo or *Zaniya* of the Lakota. Tribal governments have many resources and examples of changing outdated systems to better fit our own values. These efforts can help make a better world, protect our Earth, and enable us to live in harmony with our relatives.

We Can Do This!

So how do we move forward in a positive manner with a sustainable definition of citizenship? Each Native nation with its own unique worldview will have to answer these questions for themselves. However, we must realize that when we apply traditional Indigenous values and view our tribes as political entities, blood quantum is not an acceptable format for determining citizenship.

The Comanche Nation recently experienced a critical mass of *Kaqu*—a group of grandmothers whose grandchildren were not eligible for enrollment because their blood degree was less than one-forth. The grandmothers led a difficult campaign that resulted in the Comanche Nation, with a vote of the whole, acting in a reactionary manner to lower its blood requirements for citizenship to one-eighth. Of course, this only puts us in a holding pattern until the next generation of grandmothers raises the same concern.

Laura:

We recently attended the Comanche Nation Fair where I watched in pride while hundreds of dancers entered the arena. I was gratified to observe so many young people, from toddlers to teenagers, in full Comanche dress confidently dance around the circle. As I watched, I realized that it would be my responsibility to teach my granddaughter Comanche tradition. We are expecting the family's first biological grandchild. My stepdaughters have already made me a grandmother five times over. My son, Sam Goodhope, and his wife, Rachelle, are expecting a girl who will be my mother's first great-grandchild. As her Kaqu, *I will put together her first powwow outfit. I will lead my granddaughter in her first gourd dance. I imagine her proudly dancing by my side as her little (probably) blonde braids bounce with the beat of the drum.*

Like my sister, I, too, searched for a Comanche man to father my children so they would be on the rolls. Finding this search to be a nearly impossible mission, I had the good fortune to find an Inuit. My son's blood mix is typical for the modern Native American. On my side, he's Scotts-Irish and Numunuh (Comanche). On his father's side, he's German and Inupiaq, with a touch of Japanese fisherman thrown in. He self-identifies as Comanche and Inupiaq and is proud of his European ancestry as well.

I have always thought of myself as Numunuh, even though I basically grew up in Washington, D.C., and I have mixed blood. I'm particularly proud of my Spanish and Mexican Indian captive genealogy, which means my Comanche ancestors were strong warriors who valued the wealth of extended family. Comanche carry our inheritance with great pride, and, no matter if we are able to tackle the challenges of citizenship in a progressive manner or not, I will proudly teach my granddaughter what it is to be a Numunuh woman and about her rich Comanche heritage – not just the songs and dances, but our values, history of governance styles, and our past economic empire. For my granddaughter, my sisters and I may have to bring on our own critical mass of Kaqu.

Tribal governments might consider direct descent. Another alternative is citizenship based on tribal connections, such as cultural and political engagement, knowledge of history and language, or some other benchmarks of connection. Perhaps voting rates or levels of giving back to the tribe through volunteerism, contributing best thinking, or some other form of service may serve as an alternative to blood quantum. A constitutional convention and in-depth exploratory process must be undertaken by tribal citizens, along with our urban relatives, and in coordination with our tribal governments so that we may apply our rich heritage of creativity and innovation to this issue vital to our survival.

No matter how we move forward in addressing the issue of tribal citizenship, we must do so confidently. Our ancestors made value-based decisions. We must trust our ability to break the stranglehold of colonial policy dictated to us by others who felt they brought "truth" to the "uncivilized" nations of the Americas. The world is currently experiencing a wake-up call in the face of systemic crisis. We must strive to strengthen the connection between our values and modern practice to uphold our communal traditions. We must reject the notion that there is only one "truth" or that we are caught in an either/or situation. We must move away from non-sustainable policy, which has conditioned us to be reactionary. We must grab ahold of this opportunity to be a world model for proactive, inclusive governance.

Ultimately, the antiquated blood quantum measurement, based in racism, will not protect our cultural and political autonomy. In fact, blood quantum is fundamentally harmful to our future existence and to tribal sovereignty. Strong Indian Pueblos, Native Hawaiian communities, Alaskan Native Villages, and Tribal Nations made up of citizens who practice the values of relationships, reciprocity, and redistribution will have a strong sense of responsibility to those Nations. When we return to our own values, there is no end to what we can accomplish together.

References

Abandonment. http://www.goodtherapy.org/therapy-for-abandonment.html.

AIO's Family Systems Project. Albuquerque, NM: Americans for Indian Opportunity, 1989.

Aparicio Parry, Glen. *Origin of Thinking: A Radical Re-Visioning of Time, Humanity, and Nature.* Berkeley, CA: North Atlantic Books, 2015.

Cobb, Daniel and Loretta Fowler. *Beyond Red Power: American Indian Politics and Activism since 1900.* Santa Fe, NM: School of Advanced Research, 2007.

Corntassel, Jeff and Richard C. Witmer. *Forced Federalism: Contemporary Challenges to Indigenous Nationhood. Corntassel.* Norman: University of Oklahoma Press, 2008.

Economy for Life in Our Earth Community. **Social Movements for an Alternative Asia (SMAA), Gerak Lawan, La Via Campesina, and #EndWTO Campaign, 2013,** http://focusweb.org/content/economy-life-our-earth-community.

E.O. Wilson—Of Ants and Men. DVD. Shining Red Productions for PBS, 2014.

Gover, Maggie. *You Don't Have to Be Poor to Be Indian: Readings in Resource Development.* Albuquerque, NM: Americans for Indian Opportunity, 1979.

Gover, Maggie and LaDonna Harris. *Messing with Mother Nature Can Be Hazardous to Your Health.* Albuquerque, NM: Americans for Indian Opportunity, 1975.

Gover, Maggie and LaDonna Harris. *We the Peoples ... In Order to Promote the General Welfare: A Self-Evaluation Process for Indian Tribal Governments.* Albuquerque, NM: Americans for Indian Opportunity, 1981.

Harris, Ladonna and Jacqueline Wasilewski. *This Is What We Want to Share: Core Cultural Values.* Americans for Indian Opportunity, 1985. Albuquerque, NM

The Harvard Project on American Indian Economic Development. *The State of the Native Nations: Conditions under U.S. Policies of Self-Determination.* Cambridge, UK: Oxford University Press, 2008.

King, Martin Luther, Jr. *Where Do We Go from Here: Chaos or Community?* New York: Harper & Row, 1967.

Laouris, Yiannis, Kevin Dye, Marios Michaelides and Alexander Christakis. *Co-Laboratories of Democracy: Best Choices for Designing Sustainable Futures*. Tokyo: Springer Japan, 2014. http://www.academia.edu/6408428/Co-laboratories_of_Democracy_Best_Choices_for_Designing_Sustainable_Futures.

Mann, Charles. *1491*. New York: Vintage Books, 1999.

National Urban Indian Families Coalition. *Making the Invisible Visible*, 2015. http://nuifc.org/wp-content/uploads/2015/08/NUIFC_digital_Bookplain.pdf.

Pekka, Hämäläinen. *Comanche Empire*. New Haven, CT: Yale University Press, 2008.

Sayers, Helen. *Ubuntu: The Spirit of Humanity – I Am Because We Are*. Oman: Oasis Human Resource Development (www.oasisoman.com), 2010.

Solon, Pablo. *Vivir Bien: Notes for the Debate*. Debate. 2014. http://systemicalternatives.org/2014/07/30/1099.

To Govern and to Be Governed: Tribal Governments at the Crossroads. Americans for Indian Opportunity, 1985. Albuquerque, NM

UNICEF's *Global Life Skills*. http://www.unicef.org/lifeskills/.

United Nations Declaration on the Rights of Indigenous Peoples, adopted 2007. http://www.un.org/esa/socdev/unpfii/documents/DRIPS_en.pdf.

Walters, Karina. *Isht Ahalaya: Transcending Historical Trauma with Loving Responsibility*. Video. November 2014, Nga Pae O Te Maramatanga, University of Aukland, NPM Media Center. http://mediacentre.maramatanga.ac.nz/content/isht-ahalaya-transcending-historical-trauma-loving-responsibility.

Weatherford, Jack. *Savages and Civilization: Who Will Survive?* New York: Ballantine Books, 1994.

Notes

1 Out of the Fog, http://outofthefog.website/top-100-trait-blog/2015/11/4/fear-of-abandonment.

2 Ann Filemyr, Vice President of Academic Affairs at Southwestern College, Santa Fe, NM, email to author, April 3, 2016.

CONTRIBUTOR BIOGRAPHIES

Martha Berry

Martha Berry (Cherokee) creates beadwork in the early nineteenth-century Cherokee style, using period-authentic materials. She began studying and creating authentic, traditional Cherokee beadwork in the 1980s. At that time, there were no classes, no how-to kits, and no books on the subject. She taught herself the art form by studying both real historic artifacts and photographs of them. Berry creates bandolier bags, ceremonial sashes, belts, purses, and moccasins. To the extent possible, she uses materials, techniques, styles, and designs period-authentic to the early nineteenth century. She has won many awards in art shows and contests, has lectured in major cities across the United States, and has work in collections all over the United States and in Europe. In August of 2013, the Cherokee Nation designated Berry a Cherokee National Living Treasure for her work in preserving and perpetuating the art of traditional Cherokee beadwork. She is also a 2015 recipient of the Cherokee National Historical Society's SevenStar Award. She now divides her time between research, creating beadwork, and teaching others this exquisite and intricate art form. Berry resides in Texas with her husband, who is a retired journalist and photographer.

Reed Adair Bobroff

Reed Adair Bobroff (Navajo) is a poet, playwright, and performer from Albuquerque, NM. As a poet, he has published work in The Breakbeat Poets anthology, Indian Country Today, and performed with Rise Against, Black Rebel Motorcycle Club, and on HBO. As a playwright, his work has been showcased at the Wordcraft Circle of Native Writers & Storytellers Annual Gathering, the University of New Mexico, and in the Yale Young Native Storytellers Festival. He graduated from Yale University with a B.A. in Theater Studies and is currently researching how creative writing can be used in therapy in indigenous communities.

Robert Chanate

Robert Chanate is Kiowa from Carnegie, Oklahoma, but currently resides in Denver, Colorado. Robert works for the Woodbine Ecology Center and writes occasional columns for various publications. Robert is an adviser for the Native Youth Leadership Alliance and volunteers for other Tribal and Native organizations. He is also a direct action trainer for the Indigenous Peoples Power Project (IP3), and in that role he has been fortunate to travel to numerous Indigenous Homelands in North America and support their work in defending their territories. Robert strives to be a good relative, friend, and ally as he was taught by his family.

Stephen Cornell

Stephen Cornell is professor of sociology and faculty chair of the Native Nations Institute at the University of Arizona and co-founder, with Joseph P. Kalt, of the Harvard Project on American Indian Economic Development. With a PhD from the University of Chicago, he taught at Harvard University and the University of California, San Diego before joining the Arizona faculty in 1998. He has spent much of the last thirty years working with Indigenous nations in North America, Australia, and Aotearoa New Zealand on self-determination, governance, and development issues. For seventeen years he served as director of the Udall Center for Studies in Public Policy at the University of Arizona, where he led the development of the Native Nations Institute.

Terry L. Cross

Terry L. Cross, PhD, MSW, LCSW, and ACSW, is an enrolled member of the Seneca Nation of Indians and the founder of the National Indian Child Welfare Association, an organization he now serves as senior adviser. Mr. Cross is the author and co-author of numerous books, including *Positive Indian Parenting, Cross-Cultural Skills in Indian Child Welfare*, and *Reclaiming Customary Adoption*. He also is the author of *Heritage and Helping*, an eleven-manual curriculum for tribal child welfare staff. He served as a member of the Substance Abuse and Mental Health Services Administration (SAMHSA) National Advisory Council from 2008 to 2012, received the Civic Engagement Award for Excellence in Community Based Research from Portland State University in 2009, was a finalist for the EcoTrust Indigenous Leadership Award in 2010, and received the prestigious Robert F. Kennedy Children's Action Corps Embracing the Legacy award in 2011. Mr. Cross has more than forty-three years of experience in child welfare, including ten years working directly with children and families. He is a visiting professor at Portland State University School of Social Work, and serves on the Oregon Higher Education Coordinating Commission.

Jill Doerfler

Dr. Jill Doerfler (White Earth Anishinaabe) is an associate professor and the department head of American Indian Studies at the University of Minnesota, Duluth. Her primary area of scholarly interest is American Indian – specifically Anishinaabe – identity with a political focus on citizenship. Her research is premised on a strong commitment to bridging scholarly efforts with the practical needs of American Indian peoples, communities, and nations. She has been involved in constitutional reform efforts with the White Earth Nation since 2007. In 2012, she coauthored *The White Earth Nation: Ratification of a Native Democratic Constitution* with world-renowned Anishinaabe scholar Gerald Vizenor, and in 2013, she co-edited *Centering Anishinaabeg Studies: Understanding the World through Stories* with Niigaanwewidam James Sinclair and Heidi Kiiwetinepinesiik Stark. Jill's most recent book, *Those Who Belong: Identity, Family, Blood, and Citizenship among the White Earth Anishinaabeg* (2015), examines staunch Anishinaabe resistance to racialization and the complex issues surrounding tribal citizenship and identity.

Kristen Dorsey

Kristen Dorsey is a metalsmith/jeweler and owner of Kristen Dorsey Designs, LLC, a fine jewelry company based in Los Angeles, California. Dorsey, a citizen of the Chickasaw Nation, looks to her cultural heritage to inform her jewelry designs. Dorsey honed her craft at the School of the Museum of Fine Arts in Boston, Massachusetts, while earning a degree in American studies, concentrating in Native American studies at Tufts University. Her academic and artistic interests converge in her jewelry. The materials and techniques Dorsey uses reflect her research and passion for the history of Native American southeastern adornment. As a result, her work presents unique historical and cultural perspectives. She is also noted for her work in the traditional southeastern technique of creating relief work from flat sheet metal, commonly known by the French name repoussé. According to Dorsey, "[W]orking with these materials and imagery connects me to my ancestors. I firmly believe that culture is never lost, but rather forgotten, and creating art is a way to remember." Her work has been exhibited at museums nationwide including the Heard Museum, the Peabody Essex Museum, the Chickasaw Cultural Center, the Portland Art Museum, the Philbrook Museum, and the National Museum of the American Indian.

Sam English

Sam is an enrolled member of the Turtle Mountain Chippewa Indians from North Dakota. A distinguished contemporary Indian artist, Sam has donated his artistic talents to scores of Indian service organizations for their conferences on domestic violence, alcohol abuse, drug abuse, and wellness. The list continues to grow. He also takes time to talk to groups concerning positive self-esteem and escaping the clutches of alcoholism. Sam believes that art is the foundation of language. He says, "You can use an art experience to launch a thought." He has used his images to inspire spirituality, family, and community. He makes his home in Albuquerque, New Mexico, and has his studio/gallery in Old Town Albuquerque.

Suzan Shown Harjo

Suzan Shown Harjo, Cheyenne and Hodulgee Muscogee, is a Cheyenne citizen of the Cheyenne & Arapaho Tribes and Wind Clan of the Nuyakv Grounds. A writer, curator, and advocate, she has helped Native Peoples recover more than one million acres of land and attain laws in six decades to promote and protect Native nations, sovereignty, children, arts, cultures, lands, waters, languages, religious freedom, repatriation, and sacred places, and to eliminate "Native" sports stereotypes. Morning Star Institute president and Indian Country Today Media Network columnist, she is guest curator and editor of the National Museum of the American Indian (NMAI) exhibition (2014–2018) and book (Smithsonian/NMAI Press 2014), both titled *Nation to Nation: Treaties Between the United States and American Indian Nations*. A founding NMAI trustee, she began work in 1967 that led to NMAI, repatriation laws, and museum reform.

President Obama presented Dr. Harjo with a 2014 Presidential Medal of Free-
dom, the United States' highest civilian honor. The National Women's History
Project selected her as a 2016 National Women's History Month Honoree.
In 2015, NCORE (National Conference on Race and Ethnicity) in American
Higher Education established the annual Suzan Shown Harjo Activist for Sys-
temic Social Justice Award. She was honored with the 2015 Native Leadership
Award by the National Congress of American Indians, for which she served as
executive director during the 1980s. She also served as legislative liaison, Na-
tive American Rights Fund; as special assistant-Indian legislation and liaison,
Carter Administration; and principal author, *President's Report to Congress
on American Indian Religious Freedom* (1979). The first Vine Deloria, Jr.
Distinguished Indigenous Scholar (University of Arizona, 2008), she also was
the first Native woman to receive the Montgomery Fellowship (Dartmouth
College, 1992), the first person awarded unprecedented back-to-back fellowships as a 2004 School of Advanced Research Scholar and Poetry Fellow, and
the first woman awarded an honorary doctorate of humanities (2011) by the
Institute of American Indian Arts.

Debra Harry

Dr. Debra Harry, Kooyooe Dukaddo from Pyramid
Lake, Nevada, is the executive director of the Indigenous Peoples Council on Biocolonialism (IPCB), and
the Emerging Indigenous Leaders Institute (EILI). Dr.
Debra Harry's research analyzes the linkages between
biotechnology, intellectual property, and globalization
in relation to Indigenous Peoples' rights. She currently
serves as adjunct faculty at the University of Nevada, Reno, and also teaches online courses for UNR,
UCLA's Tribal Learning Community and Educational Exchange Program, and
UC Denver's Department of Political Science.

Richard W. Hill

SENIOR PROJECTS COORDINATOR, DEYOHAHÁ:GE:
INDIGENOUS KNOWLEDGE CENTRE
SIX NATIONS POLYTECHNIC
OHSWEKEN, ONTARIO

Rick Hill is a citizen of the Beaver Clan of the Tuscarora Nation of the Haudenosaunee at Grand River.
He holds a master's degree in American Studies, State
University of New York at Buffalo. He is the former
assistant director for Public Programs, National Museum of the American

Indian, Smithsonian Institution; museum director, Institute of American Indian
Arts, Santa Fe, New Mexico; and was assistant professor, Native American
Studies, SUNY Buffalo. He currently teaches and conducts historical research
at Six Nations Polytechnic, Ohsweken, Ontario.

Olivia Hoeft

Olivia Hoeft is an enrolled member of the Oneida
Nation of Wisconsin and grew up on her tribe's reservation in Oneida, Wisconsin. She is turtle clan. Olivia
left for her sophomore year of high school to attend St.
George's School in Newport, Rhode Island, and experienced firsthand the irony of being Native American
in the modern boarding school system. She spent her
junior year of high school in Zaragoza, Spain, where
she lived with a host family and studied with the
School Year Abroad (SYA) program. Olivia graduated from Stanford University in 2015, where she spent a quarter studying in Paris and was involved in
a number of communities on campus. During her senior year, she worked as
a diversity outreach associate for Stanford's Office of Undergraduate Admission and as a liaison for the Native American community on campus. Olivia
was crowned Miss Oneida 2014–2015, through the Oneida Nation Royalty
Program, through which she acted as a public figure in Oneida and neighboring communities during public events. Olivia currently works at Google as a
staffing services associate and resides in Mountain View, California.

Miriam Jorgensen

Miriam Jorgensen is research director of the Native
Nations Institute at the University of Arizona and
research director of the Harvard Project on American
Indian Economic Development. She specializes in
Indigenous governance and economic development,
with a particular focus on the ways communities'
governance arrangements and sociocultural characteristics affect development. Her work – in the United
States, Canada, and Australia – has addressed issues as
wide-ranging as welfare policy, policing and justice systems, natural resources, cultural stewardship, enterprise management, financial education, and
philanthropy. She is a co-author of *Structuring Sovereignty: Constitutions of
Native Nations* (UCLA AIS Press, 2014) and *The State of the Native Nations:
Conditions under U.S. Policies of Self-Determination* (OUP, 2008), editor
and co-author of *Rebuilding Native Nations: Strategies for Governance and
Development* (UA Press, 2007), and a member of the editorial boards of the
International Indigenous Policy Journal and *British Journal of Interdisciplin-*

ary Studies. Jorgensen co-founded the Indigenous governance graduate education program at the University of Arizona and teaches Indigenous community development at the Brown School of Social Work at Washington University in St. Louis. She received her BA in economics from Swarthmore College, an MA in human sciences from the University of Oxford, and an MPP and PhD from Harvard University.

Joseph P. Kalt

FORD FOUNDATION PROFESSOR OF
International Political Economy (Emeritus)
John F. Kennedy School of Government
Harvard University

Joseph P. Kalt is the Ford Foundation Professor (Emeritus) of International Political Economy at the John F. Kennedy School of Government at Harvard University. In 1987, Professor Kalt founded (with Stephen Cornell) the Harvard Project on American Indian Economic Development. He is a principal author of *The State of the Native Nations: Conditions under U.S. Policies of Self-Determination* (with the Harvard Project), co-editor and a primary author of *What Can Tribes Do? Strategies and Institutions in the Economic Development of American Indian Reservations* (with Stephen Cornell), and a principal author of *Rebuilding Native Nations: Strategies for Governance and Development.* In 2005, Professor Kalt received the National Center for American Indian Enterprise Development's First American Leadership Award. In 2010, he and Professor Cornell received the National Congress of American Indians' award for Public Sector Leadership. Professor Kalt is chairman of the board of directors of the White Mountain Apache Tribe's Fort Apache Heritage Foundation, a member of the Navajo Nation Council of Economic Advisers, and a member of the Advisory Board of the Chickasaw Nation's Community Development Enterprise.

Sarah Kastelic

Dr. Sarah Kastelic is executive director of the National Indian Child Welfare Association (NICWA), the leading Indian child welfare advocacy and research organization in the United States. Kastelic is only the second executive director of the thirty-year-old organization, succeeding founding director Terry Cross in this role. Previously, Dr. Kastelic spent four years as NICWA's deputy director, assuming increasing responsibility of operations and management. Prior to joining NICWA,
Dr. Kastelic led the National Congress of American Indians' (NCAI) welfare reform program and was the founding director of NCAI's Policy Research Center. In November 2014, national leadership network Independent Sector awarded

Dr. Kastelic its American Express NGen Leadership Award, calling her "a transformational leader working to further policy research that empowers American Indian and Alaska Native communities." Dr. Kastelic is Alutiiq, an enrolled member of the Native Village of Ouzinkie. After receiving a bachelor's degree from Goucher College, she earned a master's degree and PhD from the George Warren Brown School of Social Work at Washington University in St. Louis.

Adrienne Keene

Adrienne Keene is a citizen of the Cherokee Nation and an assistant professor in the Department of American Studies and Ethnic Studies at Brown University. Her research focuses on American Indian, Alaska Native, and Native Hawaiian students navigating the college application and transition processes, as well as the role of pre-college access programs in student success. Through her blog *Native Appropriations*, she also is deeply interested in representations of Native peoples in the media and pop culture, including issues of cultural appropriation, and how Indigenous peoples use social media for activism and speaking out against misrepresentation.

Doug Kiel

Doug Kiel (Oneida Nation) is an assistant professor in the Department of History and the Alice Kaplan Institute for the Humanities at Northwestern University. He received his PhD in history from the University of Wisconsin–Madison and studies American Indian history and nation rebuilding, federal Indian law and policy, settler colonialism in the Midwest, and race relations. He is working on a book manuscript entitled *Unsettling Territory: Oneida Indian Resurgence and Anti-Sovereignty Backlash*. His recent publications include a special issue of the *Middle West Review* (co-edited with James F. Brooks) entitled "Indigenous Midwests." Before joining Northwestern in 2016, Kiel taught at Williams College, Columbia University, the University of Pennsylvania, and Middlebury College. Kiel has received grants and fellowships from the Ford Foundation, the School for Advanced Research, the Lyndon Baines Johnson Foundation, the American Historical Association, and American Philosophical Society, among others.

Jessica Kolopenuk

Jessica Kolopenuk (Iyiniw) is from Winnipeg, Manitoba, Canada. On her mother's side, she descends from Chief Peguis's people (who are Cree and Anishinabe) from the Red River region north of Winnipeg, Manitoba: the city whose name bears the characteristic of the mighty muddy rivers whose forks have brought peoples together for as long back as they have been peoples. With training in political theory and Indigenous politics, Ms. Kolopenuk is a PhD candidate in the Department of Political Science at the University of Victoria located on Lekwungen and W̱SÁNEĆ territory in British Columbia, Canada. Jessica is interested in understanding the spaces where science and politics intersect, especially when they interfere with Indigenous peoples' relationships to each other, to territory, and to other human and non-human relatives. Her dissertation explores the power generated through science to impose meaning onto the everyday lives of Indigenous people, whether it be through racialized configurations of blood quantum, genetic testing of Native American DNA, or a new wave of large-scale telescope construction that is reordering Indigenous and non-Indigenous relationships to space – earthly and otherwise. Jessica's work is committed to interrogating contemporary global relations of power that are being increasingly driven by flows of technology and discourses of science.

Leslie Logan

Leslie Logan (Seneca) is a freelance writer and public relations consultant. She has contributed writings to *Indian Country Today* and the National Museum of the American Indian's publication, *American Indian*, and was managing editor of the award-winning magazine Native Americas. She resides on the Cattaraugus Territory in Western New York with her two children.

Henrietta Mann, PhD

Dr. Henri Mann, *Tsetsehestaestse* (Cheyenne), was the first individual to occupy the Katz Endowed Chair in Native American Studies at Montana State University, Bozeman, where she is professor emerita. She is the founding president of the Cheyenne and Arapaho Tribal College, and is now president emerita. In 1991, *Rolling Stone* magazine named Dr. Mann as one of the ten leading professors in the nation. In 2008, she received the Lifetime Achievement Award from the National Indian Education Association. The College Board, Native American Student Advocacy Institute (NASAI) presented her with its first Lifetime Achievement Award in 2013, and has since created the Dr. Henrietta Mann Leadership Award to acknowledge and thank leaders for their advocacy in improving lives within Native communities. In 2014, *Money* magazine named her a MONEY Hero Award Winner, one of 50 Unsung Heroes/50 States, conferred for her extraordinary work with the Cheyenne and Arapaho Tribal College in improving the financial well-being of others. In 2016, Dr. Mann and Dr. K. T. Lomawaima became the first two Native American educational scholars ever to be elected to membership in the National Academy of Education.

Yuka Mizutani

Yuka Mizutani is an associate professor at the Center for Global Discovery at Sophia University, Tokyo, Japan. She is a Japanese cultural anthropologist mainly focusing on contemporary North American Indigenous issues. From 2006 to 2009, she conducted her research as visiting research student at the University of California, Berkeley, and she received her PhD in area studies from Sophia University in 2009. Her research interests include political issues of Indigenous people on the U.S–Mexico borderland, the relationship between Indigenous and non-Indigenous people, issues surrounding Indigenous people and museums, interpretation and use of Western concepts and technologies by Indigenous communities, and comparative Indigenous studies. She actively writes and presents both in Japanese and English. Her book about the history of the Yaquis in the US Southwest entitled *Senjumin Pascua Yaqui no Beikoku Hennyu* (*Integration of the Pascua Yaqui into the United States*, Hokkaido University Press, 2012) won a prize from the Japan Consortium for Area Studies in 2012.

Richard Monette

Richard Monette is a member of the Turtle Mountain Band of Chippewa (a peoples) and, at the time of this writing, a citizen of Turtle Mountain (a place). Richard is professor of law at the University of Wisconsin–Madison. He has served as chairman, in-house general counsel, and special judge for Turtle Mountain. Richard has also served short stints as staff attorney for the US Senate Committee on Indian Affairs and as director of the Office of Congressional and Legislative Affairs for Indian Affairs in the US Department of the Interior.

Leonie Pihama

Associate Professor
Iwi: Te Ātiawa, Ngā Māhanga a Tairi, Ngāti Māhanga
Position: Director Te Kotahi Research Institute, University of Waikato

Associate professor Leonie Pihama is a mother of six and a grandmother of three. She is director of Te Kotahi Research Institute at the University of Waikato, and director of Māori and Indigenous Analysis Ltd., a Kaupapa Māori research company. She has worked as an associate professor in education at the University of Auckland and was director of the International Research Institute for Maori and Indigenous Education. Leonie is a leading Kaupapa Māori educator and researcher. She was recipient of both the Hohua Tūtengaehe Post-Doctoral Research Fellowship (Health Research Council) and the inaugural Fulbright-Ngā Pae o te Māramatanga Scholar Award (2011) at the Indigenous Wellness Research Institute, University of Washington. Leonie was principal investigator on the Ngā Pae o te Māramatanga research project Tiakina Te Pā Harakeke: Māori Childrearing within a Context of Whānau Ora. This project has made a significant impact by making available a depth of traditional knowledge to those working in early childhood education and Maori education, as well as Maori providers working in Whānau Ora contexts. Leonie is also a member of the research advisory oversight group for the Te Kura Mai I Tawhiti: He Piki Raukura – Health and Wellbeing through the Lifecourse: Whānau Early Invention project alongside Te Kopae Piripono (Taranaki), which is one of the Early Childhood Centres of Innovation. She has served on the Māori Health Committee for the Health Research Council and on a number of key boards including Māori Television and Te Māngai Pāho. Leonie has extensive expertise connecting her to a wide range of communities and *iwi*, which enables her to relate to people throughout Aotearoa New Zealand. Leonie was recently named recipient of the Inaugural Health Research Council Ngā Pou Senior Research Fellowship. She was also awarded the 2015 New Zealand Association for Research in Education Te Tohu Pae Tāwhiti Award for excellence in Maori educational research.

Gyasi Ross

Gyasi Ross is an author, speaker, and storyteller. Gyasi comes from the Blackfeet Nation and resides on the Port Madison Indian Reservation near Seattle. TV and radio programs and print and online publications regularly seek his input on politics, sports, pop culture, and the intersections thereof with Native life. Ross is the author of *Don't Know Much About Indians (but I wrote a book about us anyways)* (2011) and *How to Say I Love You in Indian* (2014). "I come from a family of storytellers. My family tells long stories, drinking coffee and blowing smoke in your face. It just fit for me to tell stories, and then I started writing them." He is in demand as a speaker on race, social justice, and white privilege as well as issues specifically affecting contemporary Native Americans and guests on MSNBC, ESPN, Democracy Now, and radio shows nationwide. Ross writes for the Huffington Post, Indian Country Today, Deadspin, and Gawker. Ross has also released a spoken word/hip-hop CD titled *Isskootsik (Before Here Was Here)* on Cabin Games Records. You can follow Gyasi Ross on Facebook at http://facebook.com/gyasirossauthor, on Twitter at http://twitter.com/bigindiang-yasi, and on Instagram at http://instagram.com/bigindiangyasi.

Adrian T. Smith

Adrian (Addie) Tobin Smith is a childhood dependency task force administrator for the state of Oregon. Previously, Smith served as staff attorney for government affairs at the National Indian Child Welfare Association based in Portland; in that role, she was responsible for analyzing and responding to national legislative and administrative child welfare and children's mental health policies that affected Native children, families, and communities. Her previous experience includes work as a juvenile probation officer and as a social worker at a child welfare legal clinic. Smith earned both a JD (magna cum laude) and master's of social work from Washington University in St. Louis and a BA from Boston College.

Kim TallBear

Kim TallBear, author of *Native American DNA: Tribal Belonging and the False Promise of Genetic Science (2013),* is associate professor in the faculty of Native Studies at the University of Alberta. She studies the racial politics of "gene talk" in science and popular culture. A former environmental planner, she has become interested in the similarities between Western constructions of nature and sexuality as they are defined and sanctioned historically by those in power (i.e., the church, scientists, and heterosexual men). TallBear is interested in how sex and nature can be understood differently in Indigenous worldviews. She draws on Indigenous, feminist, and queer theory in her teaching and research, both of which focus on undermining the nature/culture split in Western society and its role in colonialism, racism, sexism, homophobia, and environmental degradation. Kim TallBear blogs about these topics and more at www.kimtallbear.com. You can find her on Twitter @KimTallBear. She is a tribal citizen of the Sisseton-Wahpeton Oyate in South Dakota and is also descended from the Cheyenne & Arapaho Tribes of Oklahoma.

Maile Taualii

Maile Taualii received her PhD in Health Services, with an emphasis in Public Health Informatics and Public Health Genetics from the University of Washington, where she also completed her MA in Public Health. One of Taualii's primary research focuses is the utility and validity of health information for racial minorities. Her current research is related to perceptions of bio-banking for research among Native Hawaiian people. As

Assistant Professor of Native Hawaiian and Indigenous Health at the University of Hawaii, she brings cultural, ethical, and community-oriented perspectives to the instruction of public health. In 2016, Taualii was awarded the University of Hawaii Board of Regents Excellence in Teaching Award. Taualii's federal commitments include serving as a member of the National Advisory Committee on Racial, Ethnic, and Other Populations with the U.S. Census Bureau.

Russell Thornton

Russell Thornton is distinguished professor of anthropology at UCLA. Born and raised in Oklahoma, he is an enrolled member of the Cherokee Nation of Oklahoma, and former chair of the Nation's Sequoyah Commission. He is former chair of the Smithsonian Institution's Native American Repatriation Review Committee, a US congressionally mandated committee to monitor repatriation at the Smithsonian. His scholarly interests include American Indian demography and epidemiology, American Indian revitalization movements, American Indian studies, American Indian winter counts, and contemporary American Indian issues, especially repatriation, education, and identity. He has lectured widely in the United States and other countries on various topics related to American Indians. He is the author, editor, or co-editor of six books, including *American Indian Holocaust and Survival: A Population History since 1492* (1987). He has also authored more than 100 papers, many appearing in such major scholarly journals as *American Anthropologist, Current Anthropology, American Journal of Physical Anthropology, American Sociological Review, American Journal of Sociology, American Studies, Ethnohistory*, and *Population Research and Policy Review.*

Kathryn Harris Tijerina

An enrolled citizen of the Comanche Nation, Kathryn Harris Tijerina was born and raised in Comanche country. She earned her BA from Harvard, magna cum laude, and her JD from Stanford Law School. She is a member of the DC Bar. Kathryn was formerly president of the Institute of American Indian Art (a national fine art college), and she has worked on the Indian Policy Review Commission and the US Senate Indian Affairs Committee. She directed the Indian Resource Development Program for the state of New Mexico's universities, and served as the First Leader of the Comanche Nation College Council. In addition, she worked for two chief justices of the New Mexico Supreme Court; was deputy secretary of the New Mexico Natural Resources Department; served as director for Cultural and Recreational Services for Albuquerque, New Mexico; and was the executive director of the Railyard Stewards. Currently, she is the chair of the Native Fund of the Santa Fe Community Foundation, a member of the Santa Fe Indian Center, on the Executive Committee of the LANL Foundation, a member of the Board of Trustees for Southwestern College, and a national adviser for AIO's Ambassador Program. Kathryn is married to Manuel Tijerina.

Marty Two Bulls

Marty G. Two Bulls Sr. is a graphic designer, teacher, artist, silversmith, sculptor, and editorial cartoonist. He has been drawing and writing editorial cartoons for most of his thirty-four-year career. It all started with the desire to make his uncles laugh. As a young child, his uncles would make cartoons of each other, and the simple drawings would make them laugh out loud. Marty was mesmerized by the power of the drawings and subconsciously formed a deep respect for the medium.Marty was first published in his high school newspaper, but he had always thought of it as a hobby, concentrating more on his artistic studies. After college, he became a graphic designer working at various commercial printers until he began working for daily newspapers, where he spent most of his thirty-three-year career. For the last sixteen years, he has been producing a weekly editorial cartoon for the news publication Indian Country Today. An amazing feat for an artist who still considers it a hobby. "I love to draw cartoons," Marty said recently. "To call it work would undervalue the way I feel about it." "After all," he said, "all I ever wanted to do was make my uncles laugh."

Rebecca M. Webster

Rebecca M. Webster is an enrolled member of the Oneida Nation in Wisconsin. She is an assistant professor at the University of Minnesota, Duluth in their American Indian Studies Department. She teaches undergraduate and graduate courses in their Tribal Administration and Governance programs. Prior to joining the American Indian Studies team at Duluth, she served the Oneida Nation as an attorney for thirteen years where she provided legal advice for the Nation's administration on government relations, jurisdiction concerns, and a wide variety of tribal land issues. Her research interests focus on advocating for tribal sovereignty while also exploring ways for tribes to improve cooperative relationships with neighboring governments. She received her BA, MPA, and JD from the University of Wisconsin–Madison and her PhD in public policy and administration from Walden University.

David E. Wilkins

David E. Wilkins is a citizen of the Lumbee Nation and holds the McKnight Presidential Professorship in American Indian Studies at the University of Minnesota. He has adjunct appointments in political science, law, and American studies. He earned his PhD in political science from the University of North Carolina at Chapel Hill in December 1990. He is the author or editor of a number of books, including *Dismembered: Native Disenrollment and the Battle for Basic Human Rights* (with Shelly Hulse Wilkins, 2017), *Hollow Justice: Indigenous Claims Against the U.S.* (2013), *The Navajo Political Experience*, 4th ed. (2013), *The Hank Adams Reader* (2011), *The Legal Universe* (with Vine Deloria, Jr., 2011), and *Documents of Native American Political Development: 1533 to 1933* (2009). His articles have appeared in a range of social science, law, history, and ethnic studies journals.

Shelly Hulse Wilkins

Shelly Hulse Wilkins is a senior legislative analyst with nearly twenty years of state and national experience in tribal-state relations. Much of her work has focused on the challenges faced by Native state legislators as they contend with their duties as both tribal citizens and elected officials. Most recently, she has written on the topic of the disenrollment of tribal citizens, co-authoring a book scheduled to be published by the University of Washington Press in 2017.

About the Editors

Kathleen Ratteree, MS, MPH

Kathleen began working with the Oneida Nation Trust and Enrollment Committee in 2013. She has served as project manager for Sustain Oneida, a subcommittee of Trust and Enrollment. She assists in facilitating constructive community dialogue on tribal enroll-ment criteria. Over the past three years she has written a series of articles for the Oneida tribal newspaper, *The Kalihwisaks,* on identity, cit-izenship, blood quantum, demographics, sovereignty, and trib-al governance. The articles are designed to raise awareness of enrollment issues and population trends, and they encourage community engagement in the membership/citizenship dia-logue. Kathleen holds a master of science in medical anthro-pology, and a master of public health and a certificate of global health from the University of Wisconsin–Madison. During her graduate studies, Kathleen conducted fieldwork on two Lakota reservations in South Dakota: Pine Ridge and Cheyenne River. She worked with Native cancer patients as part of the cultural-ly competent Patient Navigator program at the Rapid City Re-gional Hospital. She also student taught courses in American Indian studies and anthropology at UW–Madison. More recent-ly Kathleen worked for the Menominee Nation as a prevention program evaluation consultant at the Maehnowesekiyah Well-ness Center.

Kathleen lives just outside Green Bay with her husband, two young children, a 100-pound dog, nine hens, one rooster, and various wildlife.

Norbert S. Hill Jr.

Norbert is the area director of education and training for the Oneida Tribe of Indians of Wisconsin. Hill's previous appointment was vice president of the College of Menominee Nation for their Green Bay campus. Hill served as the executive director of the American Indian Graduate Center (AIGC) in New Mexico, a nonprofit organization providing funding for American Indians and Alaska Natives to pursue graduate and professional degrees. Previous positions include executive director of the American Indian Science and Engineering Society, assistant dean of students at the University of Wisconsin–Green Bay, and director of the American Indian Educational Opportunity Program at the University of Colorado, Boulder. He founded *Winds of Change* and *The American Indian Graduate,* magazine publications of AISES and AIGC, respectively. Hill holds two honorary doctorates from Clarkson University (1996) and Cumberland College (1994). Past board appointments include Environmental Defense Fund, chair and board member of the Smithsonian Museum of the American Indian, and the Wisconsin Historical Society. In 1989, Hill was awarded the Lifetime Achievement Award from the National Action Council for Minorities in Engineering.

Hill resides on the Oneida reservation with his wife.

FULCRUM